Here's What the Reviewers Say...

"Wide ranging, thorough, and virtually a complete all-in-one, this book is a fine, useful companion for travels in Belize; it also includes long and wide ranging digressions into Guatemala, Mexico, and even a short section on Copán, the foremost Maya site in Honduras, two countries away." – *Travel Books Worldwide*

"I found your book very informative. The maps were great and the historical backgrounds of each place were just what we needed. Everywhere we went the locals wanted to look at it. They thought that it was good, too!" – *K.C.*

"By far it is the best book ever written about this almost impossible-to-describe country." – *Petra Linneman, Manager, Sittee River Lodge*

"Congratulations on creating an exceptional guidebook to Belize; it has become one of the most popular books in our trip library." – *Tim Boys, Island Expeditions*

"One of the most comprehensive and useful guides to Belize... It takes an ecologically aware approach. Very detailed." – *Lan Sluder, Belize First Magazine*

Other books by Harry S. Pariser
available from Hunter Publishing

Jamaica: A Visitor's Guide, 3rd Ed. 1-55650-703-8 $15.95
Adventure Guide to Barbados, 2n[d]
Adventure Guide to Costa Rica, 3rd
Adventure Guide to Puerto Rico, 3
Adventure Guide to the Virgin Islands
Explore the Dominican Republic, 3

D1397442

Available in bookstores nationwide, or directly from the publisher. To order, send a check for the title(s) desired, plus $3 shipping & handling, to:

Hunter Publishing, Inc., 130 Campus Drive, Edison, NJ 08818

Explore
Belize

4th Edition

Harry S. Pariser

HUNTER

Hunter Publishing, Inc.
130 Campus Drive, Edison, NJ 08818
(732) 225 1900 / (800) 255 0343   Fax (732) 417 1744
hunterpub@emi.net

Visit our Web site at
www.hunterpublishing.com

In Canada:
1220 Nicholson Road, Newmarket, Ontario
Canada L3Y 7V1
(800) 399-6858   Fax (800) 363 2665

ISBN 1-55650-785-2

© 1998 Harry S. Pariser (4th Edition)

Cover photo: *Keel-Billed Toucan,* Kevin Schafer
All other photos by author.

Maps by Joyce Huber, Lissa K. Dailey and Kim André
© 1998 Hunter Publishing

WE LOVE TO GET MAIL

Things change so rapidly that it's impossible to keep up with everything. Like automobiles, travel books require fine tuning if they are to stay in top condition. We need input from readers so that we can continue to provide the best, most current information possible. Please write to let us know about any inaccuracies or new information. Although we try to make our maps as accurate as possible, errors can occur. If you have suggestions for improvement or places that should be included, please let us know.

READER'S RESPONSE FORM

Explore Belize, 4th Edition

I found your book rewarding because:

Your book could be improved by:

The best places I stayed in were (explain why):

I found the best food at:

Some good and bad experiences I had were:

Will you return to Belize?

If so, where do you plan to go? If not, why not?

I purchased this book at:

Please include any other comments on a separate sheet. Mail to Harry S. Pariser, c/o Hunter Publishing, 130 Campus Drive, Edison NJ 08818 USA; fax to (561) 546 7986 or e-mail comments to the author at vudu@jps.net.

ACKNOWLEDGMENTS

Thanks go out to my publisher, Michael Hunter, and his staff, mapmakers Joyce Huber and Kim André, as well as the following individuals for their help and advice: Ellen and Shawn, Fernando Cruz, John and Lea Young, Susan Vesala, Michalle Longsworth, Kevin Gonzalez, Lori Reed, Jacqueline Tipton, Kitty Fox, Fallet Young, Heidi, Johnny Grief, Luke Ramirez, Norris Hall, the Novelo brothers, Tim Boys, Don Penlon, Cynthia Robin, Diana Lozano, Richie Woods, Wade Bevier, Dr. Arlen Chase, Therese Rath, Phyllis Cayetano, Benjamin Nicoholas, Glenn-Crawford, Sue E. Williams, Ben Ruoti, Fernando Cruz, Galvin Nell, Desmond Leslie, Anne Floiss, Abel Novelo, Mrs. James Novelo, Lucen at LZ-Line, Mary Jo Prost, Eugenio Ah, Jeff Medina, Donna M. Koehnen, Halina Gagne, Dorothy Beveridge, Caroline Ramclam, Ms. Joy Vernon, Rosanna Palma, Yvonne and Alfredo Villoria, Chet, Donna Marshall, John and Carolyn Carr, Meb Cutlack, Katie Stevens, Roasanna Palma, Thomas P. Rackowski, Melissa Johnson, Kathy Schaulfler, John & Lea Young, Rosita Arvigo, Bob and Nestora Jones, Michael A. Panton, Manuel Hoare, David Keleher, Donnan B. Runkel, Bart and Suzi Mickler, Ernesto Sacqui, Ellen MacCrae, Susan Scott, Man Man, Dave Henson, Nelson Feinstein, Ralph Young, Carlson Tuttle, Meg White, Jack Chivers, Miguel Herrera, Rosa Castro, Alistair King, Franziska and Nickie Nicholson, Brenda K. Meyers, Matilda Shack and Katarina Shol (Kekchi vocabulary), Catherine Cochran (Turneffe Island Lodge), Todd Vickstrom, Todd Wagner, Margie Scanlon, Peter Tonti (Maya Mountain), David Morris, Victoria Collins, Joan Medhurst, Jennifer Wood, Kelli Carturight, Bill Tunis and staff, Bradley Rinehart, and the Snaddon family. Thanks also go to my mother, who always worries about me, as well as to many others.

ABOUT THE AUTHOR

Harry S. Pariser was born in Pittsburgh and grew up in a small town in southwestern Pennsylvania. After graduating from Boston University with a B.S. in Public Communications in 1975, Harry hitched and camped his way through Europe, traveled down the Nile by steamer, and by train through Sudan. Visiting Uganda, Rwanda, and Tanzania, he traveled by ship from Mombasa to Bombay, and then on through South and Southeast Asia before settling down in Kyoto, Japan. There he studied Japanese and ceramics while supporting himself by teaching English to everyone from tiny tots to Buddhist priests. Using Japan as a base, he traveled to other parts of Asia: trekking to the vicinity of Mt. Everest in Nepal, taking tramp steamers to Indonesian islands like Adonara, Timor, Sulawesi, and Ternate, and visiting rural areas in China. He returned to the United States in 1984 from Kanazawa, Japan, via the Caribbean, where he did research for two travel guides: *Guide to Jamaica* and *Guide to Puerto Rico and the Virgin Islands*, both published in 1986. That same year he returned to Japan, and lived in Kagoshima, a city at the southern tip of Kyushu, across the bay from an active volcano. During that year and part of the next, he taught English and wrote numerous articles for *The Japan Times*.

Harry has written for the *San Jose Mercury News*, *Belize First*, and other journals. His *Adventure Guide to Barbados, 2nd Edition*, won a Silver Award from the Society of American Travel Writers in their 1996 Lowell Thomas Travel Journalism Competition. He currently resides in San Francisco. Besides traveling and writing, his other pursuits include printmaking, painting, cooking, backpacking and hiking, photography, reading, and listening to music – especially jazz, salsa, calypso, and African pop. He may be found on the Web at www.catch22.com/~vudu/ and www.jps.net/vudu, or e-mailed at vudu@jps.net.

GOING METRIC?

To make your travels in Belize a little easier, we have provided the following charts that show metric equivalents for the measurements you are familiar with.

1 kilometer	=	.6124 miles
1 mile	=	1.6093 kilometers
1 foot	=	.304 meters
1 inch	=	2.54 centimeters
1 square mile	=	2.59 square kilometers
1 pound	=	.4536 kilograms
1 ounce	=	28.35 grams
1 imperial gallon	=	4.5459 liters
1 US gallon	=	3.7854 liters
1 quart	=	.94635 liters

INCHES

CENTIMETERS

For Fahrenheit: Multiply Centigrade by 1.8 and add 32.

For Centigrade: Subtract 32 from Fahrenheit and divide by 1.8.

CENTIGRADE		FAHRENHEIT
40°	=	104°
35°	=	95°
30°	=	86°
25°	=	77°
20°	=	64°
15°	=	59°
10°	=	50°

A NOTE ABOUT PRICING

Many prices are listed in Belizean dollars (BZ$). To convert to US dollars, divide by two. Prices quoted are subject to fluctuation and should be used only as a guideline. A 6% hotel tax and 10% service charge may be added to your hotel bill; check with the hotel in question. Credit cards may be subject to as much as a 5% surcharge. Establishments for which no prices are listed are classified as follows: *inexpensive* (under US$30), *moderate* (US$31-$50), *expensive* (over US$50 s or d), and *luxury* (over US$100).

ABBREVIATIONS

AID – Agency for International Development
BZ$ – Belizean dollars (US$1 = BZ$2)
d – double
E – east, eastern
ha – hectare(s)
km – kilometer
m – meter
N – north, northern
ow – one way
pd – per day
pw – per week
PUP – People's United Party
rt – round trip
S – south, southern
s – single
UDP – United Democratic Party
W – west, western

☎ CALLING BELIZE

If calling or faxing Belize, be sure to leave off the zero preceding the prefix. For example, dial 011-501-6-23232 instead of 06-23232.

Contents

Maps

Introduction

Caribbean yet Central American, Belize is a cultural pot-pourri. Its many treasures include the hemisphere's longest coral reef, hundreds of sandy offshore islands, 250 varieties of wild orchids, 500 species of birds, cats and other wildlife, and innumerable Maya ruins – many still unexplored.

Set in an isthmus renowned for population density, Belize, a small nation, also contains a small population (est. 225,000) relative to its size. The greater part of its territory is dominated either by the craggy Maya Mountains or lowland swamps. Both the small population and the nation's physical isolation have made the construction of roads a formidable task, and many parts of the nation remain inaccessible today.

If you're looking for a large resort with a pristine white beach and attendants catering to your every need, then this is not the place for you. Belize is for the adventurous traveler – one willing to trade a measure of discomfort for an abundance of experience.

The Land

THE BIG PICTURE: The Central American isthmus is the only region in the world that is both interoceanic and intercontinental. The region comprises seven nations: Belize, Guatemala, El Salvador, Honduras, Nicaragua, Costa Rica, and Panama. All except Belize are former members of the Spanish Empire and, although some contain large native American populations, they share a similar cultural base, which includes the Spanish language and the Catholic religion. Despite their surface similarities, each has evolved its own national character, making political union unlikely. To the region's north lies Mexico, to its south is the continent of South America, connected to the isthmus at Colombia.

GEOGRAPHY: Situated on the east coast of Central America, Belize is bounded by Mexico to the north and by Guatemala to the west and south. Approximately twice the size of Jamaica, Belize is the second smallest nation (after El Salvador) on the North and South American continent. Including the offshore cayes, its total area is 8,886 sq. miles, the size of Massachusetts. From the Honda River in the north to the River Sarstoon in the south, the nation is 174 miles long and is widest (68 miles) between Belize City and Benque Viejo.

While quartz and granite rocks predominate in the Maya range, the northern plain as well as parts of the south and west are formed from limestone, which has dissolved to form fertile soil. The Maya Mountains to the south fall away precipitously near the coast. Although 70% of the total area is covered by hills, the remainder is coastal plain. The low-lying plain to the north is swampy near the coast but rises to a slight plateau in the west.

RIVERS: Once forming a crucial link in the nation's communication system, rivers are among the most arresting geographical features. The northernmost Río Hondo delineates the border with

Caves and Caving

Belize is riddled with thousands of caves, the vast majority of which remain unexplored, unnamed, and unknown to modern man. The preponderance of karst terrain (named after similar turf in the land once known as Yugoslavia) results in the large number of these caves, limestone sinkholes carved by water dripping over thousands of years.

It is impossible to discuss Belizean caves without mentioning the Maya. Nearly every cave appears to have been explored and utilized by the Maya at some point in time. Sadly, many have been looted, and this is the reason that an official archaeological permit is required to visit most caves today.

The Maya believed that caves marked the dark kingdom of Shibalba, said to harbor the spirits of the deities. Caves served as *the* place to commune with these spirits and to learn the correct time to plant corn, to burn the *milpas* (fields), and to offer sacrifices. Most caves contain pottery shards as well as human remains. Though there it controversy about this, the skeletons and heads found here may be those of sacrificial victims. It is likely that the pots were used for ritual purposes.

Caves are found around San Ignacio (notably Chechem Hah and Barton Creek), in the Cave Branch area (off the Hummingbird Highway), and the White Ridge area near Gales Point, and the Blue Creek Cave in the Toledo District. Although almost totally undeveloped, the Chiquibul area, on the western side of the Maya range in close proximity to the Guatemalan border, is spectacular. The Chiquibul river is one of the largest vanishing rivers in the Americas. The most significant single cave here is Cebada, part of a major system that extends across the border into Guatemala.

You may find a bibliography of writing on Belizean caves in the National Speleological Society Bulletin: *Journal of Cave and Karst Studies*, August 1996 (Vol. 56, No. 2). Also included is an article that reviews the current state of cave exploration and other info. Copies may be obtained from the NSS, Huntsville Alabama (www.caves.org).

Mexico; the New River runs parallel to it 10 miles to the south. Both flow east into Chetumal Bay. Once known as the Old River, the Belize River begins in the southwestern hills, flows to the north, and then turns towards the Caribbean. Navigable for at least 120 miles, it has numerous tributaries. The shorter Sibún River runs to its south and reaches the sea approximately 10 miles south of Belize City. Unlike those in the north, the southern rivers are short and steep, extending from the Maya Mountains to the east or southeast where they empty into the sea. Few can be navigated and their rapids pose a natural obstacle. This difficulty is one of the reasons that the northern part of the country was colonized first.

CAYES: There are a number of types of cayes. Limited to the exposed eastern sides of the atolls, faroes, and the Barrier Platform, **sand cayes** are generally oriented N-S, parallel to the barrier reef axis. Coconut palms, sapodilla, and sea grapes proliferate here. Sand cayes grow and shrink over time and are particularly susceptible to destruction by hurricanes.

Mangrove-sand cayes are both the largest and most numerous. They are chiefly distributed to the west of the Barrier Platform; they tend to be closer to the shore when the barrier is broken. Ones situated closer to shore have greater development of mangroves because of the calmer environment. They generally have a strand of coral sand on their windward sides.

Mangrove cayes are located closest to the mainland and are often clustered. The mangroves are chiefly red mangroves. Belize's mangrove cayes are unusual because they are marine in origin and are linked with the distribution of the coral reef. Of the three, they are the most resilient to hurricane damage.

Climate

As holds true for the rest of Central America, Belize has a delightful climate. Its mild, subtropical weather varies little throughout the year, with most of the changes in temperature due to differences in elevation. Rain, which usually comes in short showers, is most likely to occur from June or July through the end of November; the driest months are February and March, extending up to May.

RAINFALL: This varies greatly from year to year. While Corozal receives an average of 40 inches annually, Punta Gorda may get as much as 160. Monthly averages also vary widely from one year to the next. While it might rain as little as 12 inches in Punta Gorda one month, 36 inches might fall that same month the following year. Obviously, this is problematic for farming.

Northers are frontal storms that arrive during the winter months from Dec. to March. They bring several days of *chubascos* (thunderstorms). Another phenomenon is the *mauger* (pronounced "magah") season, which is a period of dry, calm weather with still winds and a generally oppressive, stagnant atmosphere characterized by dry heat and biting insects. It usually lasts for a week or more during August.

TEMPERATURES: In Belize City these vary between 50° and 95°F and average out at 79°-80°F. While temperatures in the Cayo District may reach 100°F in the shade during April or May, it may be cooler here than in Belize City during the winter months. The worst humid-

	Jan.	Feb.	Mar.	Apr.	May	Jun.	Jul.	Aug.	Sep.	Oct.	Nov.	Dec.
Average Belize City Temperature (°F)												
Low	66	68	69	75	75	73	73	72	72	72	68	68
High	84	84	86	88	88	90	90	90	90	90	82	82

ity is found on the coastal strip between Belize City and Punta Gorda, but coastal breezes tend to cool down the same area.

SEASONS: There is a clearly demarcated dry and wet season throughout the country, but with considerable differences in its length between north and south. While the dry season lasts for four months from Feb. to May in the north, it may last only for the month of March in areas of the extreme south, such as the Toledo District.

HURRICANES: One unfortunate characteristic of Belize's climate is its tendency toward hurricanes. These low-pressure zones are serious business and should not be taken lightly. Where the majority of structures are poorly built, property damage from hurricanes may run into the hundreds of millions of dollars. A hurricane begins as a relatively small tropical storm, known as a cyclone when its winds reach a velocity of 39 mph. At 74 mph it is upgraded to hurricane status, with winds of up to 200 mph and ranging in size from 60-1,000 miles in diameter. A small hurricane releases energy equivalent to the explosions of six atomic bombs per second. A hurricane may be compared to an enormous hovering engine that uses the moist air and water of the tropics as fuel, carried hither and thither by prevailing air currents – generally eastern trade winds that intensify as they move across warm ocean waters. When cooler, drier air infiltrates as it heads north, the hurricane begins to die, cut off from the life-sustaining ocean currents that have nourished it from infancy.

Routes and patterns are unpredictable. As for their frequency: "June – too soon; July – stand by; August – it must; September – remember." So goes the old rhyme. But hurricanes are not confined to July and August. Hurricanes forming in Aug. and Sept. typically last for two weeks, while those that form in June, July, Oct., and Nov. (many of which originate in the Caribbean and the Gulf of Mexico) generally last only seven days. Approximately 70% of all hurricanes (known as Cabo Verde types) originate as embryonic storms coming from the west coast of Africa.

Fortunately though, they are rarer here than in the Caribbean islands and the southern US. Since record-keeping began, a number of hurricanes have wreaked havoc here. Some of the earliest of these were in 1785, 1805, and 1813. The hurricane of 1931 caused considerable damage to Belize City and killed 150. Punta Gorda was devastated in 1945 and Corozal was nearly wiped off the map a decade later. The most serious of a series, 1961's Hurricane Hattie persuaded the government to build Belmopan, a new capital set 50 miles inland. Hurricane Fifi hit the northern cane fields hard in 1978.

Flora & Fauna

One of the things that makes Belize such a spectacular destination is its natural beauty – better preserved here than in other Central American countries. Belize still has 80% of its forests intact, as compared with only 2% in similarly-sized El Salvador. Sixteen tracts, comprising 30% of the total land area, have been designated national reserves in which only selective logging is permitted. Additional land has been placed in national parks.

NATURE WATCHING: Don't be disappointed if you fail to see any animals; the dense underbrush frequently makes viewing difficult. In addition the biomass of the rainforests is 99.9% plants so animals are definitely in the minority. Many of the smaller animals are strictly nocturnal and others are wary of humans. Some animals, however, are highly visible. These include the active monkeys, peccaries, and coatis. Only by attuning yourself to its rhythms, can you truly experience the rainforest's wonders.

opportunities: One alternative to winging it is a tour. See "nature tours" under "practicalities." The best way to see wildlife is to stay in a lodge near the tropical forest or to camp within the forest itself. The latter, while preferable, requires equipment and adequate preparation.

Plant Life

Plants abound in the fertile valleys filled with citrus, bananas, and cacao; there is a marked contrast between these valleys and the outlying mangrove swamps or the pine ridges and tropical forest. Although approximately 90% of the land is forested, trees disguise the acid, infertile soils. While the mixed hardwood forests may contain some 700 species of trees, only 15-20 of them have any marketable value. Some of these are the ziricote, rosewood, mahogany, and cedar as well as secondary trees such as the mayflower and the Santa María, the most important timber tree in the central plateau. The comparatively small area of land

that is suitable for agriculture is in the least accessible region.

> ⓘ **Did You Know?**
> *If you take a hike with a Belizean, you may meet up with a "bastard tree." A bastard tree is not a species, but one of many trees that have a thick layer of razor-sharp thorns wherever you try to find a handhold!*

The Rainforests

Containing the planet's most complex ecosystem, rainforests have a richer animal and plant life than any other type of forest. Unlike other areas in which living organisms face conflicts with a hostile climate, in the rainforest organisms struggle for survival against each other. Since the climate has been stable in this region for some 60 million years, each being – whether plant, animal, insect, or microbe – has been able to develop its specialized niche. Rainforests occur in regions without marked seasonal variation and which commonly receive more than 70 inches of rain annually.

VARIETIES: There is no single "true rainforest," and forest botanists have varying definitions of the term. It can be argued that there are about 30 types including such categories as semi-deciduous forests, tropical evergreen alluvial forests, and evergreen lowland forests – each of which may be subdivided into three or four more categories. **Equatorial evergreen rainforests** comprise two thirds of the total. As one moves away from the equator on either side, the forests develop marked wet and dry seasons. **Cloud forest** is another name for montane rainforest, which is characterized by heavy rainfall and persistent condensation due to the upward deflection of moisture-laden air currents by mountains. Trees here are typically short and gnarled. No cloud forests are found in Belize.

The so-called **elfin woodland** is marked by the presence of extremely stunted moss-covered trees. In Belize, elfin woodland is found only on the upper slopes of the Maya Mountains.

Rainforests without as much rain, **tropical dry forests** once covered Pacific coastal lowlands stretching from Panama to Mexico, comprising an area the size of France. Today, they have shrunk to a mere 2% of that area and only part of this is under protection.

In addition to rainforests, which generally contain Santa María, mahogany, guanacaste, and other woods, Belize has large tracts of pine forest – known as **"pine ridge"** – which are mixed pine, oak, palm, calabash, and other trees. **"Broken ridge"** is pine mixed with many other trees. These generally grow in sandy soil. **"Cohune ridge"** is dominated by cohune palms and the soil is more fertile.

LAYERS: Life in the rainforest is highly stratified in vertical layers. The upper canopy layer contains animals that are mainly herbaceous and, in Belize, have prehensile tails. They rarely descend to earth. Typically more than a hundred feet in height, these canopy trees lack the girth associated with tall trees of the temperate forest, perhaps because there are fewer strong winds to combat and each tree must compete with the others for sunlight. The next lower layer is filled with small trees, lianas, and epiphytes. Some are parasitic, others use trees solely for support purposes. The ground surface layer is littered with branches, twigs, and foliage. Most animals here live on insects and fruit; others are carnivorous. Contrary to popular opinion the ground cover is thick only where sunlight penetrates sufficiently to allow it. The extensive root system of the trees and associated fungi (*mycorrhizae*) form a thick mat that holds thin topsoils in place when it rains. If these are cut, the soil will wash away: the steeper the slope, the faster the rate of runoff. As the sun beats down on the soil, sometimes baking it hard as a sidewalk, the crucial fungal mat and other organic life die off. It may take hundreds of years to replace important nutrients through rainfall, and the forests may never recover.

INTERACTIONS: As the name implies, rainforests receive ample precipitation, which promotes a rich variety of vegetation, to which animals and insects must adapt. Lowland rainforests receive at least 100 inches. Although some rainforests see almost no rain during certain parts of the year, they are generally cloaked in clouds from which they draw moisture. The high level of plant-animal interaction – taking forms such as predation, parasitism, hyperparasitism, symbiosis, and mutualism in Biologyspeak – is believed to be one major factor promoting diversity. The interactions are innumerable and highly complex: strangler figs steal sunlight from canopy trees; wasps may pollinate figs; bats and birds transport seeds and pollinate flowers. When a species of bird, for example, becomes rare or extinct, it may have

Common Misperceptions About Rainforests

■ Rainforests are not "the lungs of the planet." Mature trees produce as much oxygen as they consume. The danger in destroying rainforests lies with the effects on rainfall, flooding, and global warming resulting from increasing amounts of carbon dioxide being released into the atmosphere.

■ The rainforests are not bursting at the seams with colorful plants, wild orchids, and animals. The overwhelming color is green; flowers are few; and the animal you're most likely to encounter is the ant.

■ Rainforests are not a renewable resource. It is impossible to cut trees without destroying plants and affecting the environment.

■ Rainforests are not merely a source of wood. There are other values associated with them that must be considered.

■ Once damaged, rainforest does not simply grow back as it once was. It may take centuries for the complex ecosystem to regenerate. Reforestation cannot restore the environment.

■ Despite its verdant appearance, rainforest soil may not be fertile. Most of the nutrients are contained in the biomass.

■ There is no need to "manage" a rainforest. They've been doing just fine for eons on their own. Everything in the rainforest is recycled, and anything removed has an effect.

■ "Selective" cutting has detrimental consequences because it affects the surrounding soil quality and weakens the forest as the strongest specimens are removed. No way has yet been found to exploit a rainforest so that all species can be preserved.

■ One "endangered" species cannot be effectively protected without safeguarding its ecosystem. Botanical gardens or seed banks cannot save important species. These are too numerous in quantity, seeds have too short a lifespan, and the species depend upon animals for their lifecycle equilibrium.

■ Any reduction in consumption of tropical hardwoods will not preserve rainforests. The only effective method is formal protection of the forests in reserves and parks. The forests are falling at too fast a rate for any other methods to work.

an effect on a tree that depends solely upon it to distribute its seeds. There is no such thing as self-sufficiency in a rainforest; all life depends upon its cohabitants for survival.

BIODIVERSITY: Those who are unfamiliar with the rainforest tend to undervalue it. Tropical deforestation is one of the great tragedies of our time. We are far from cataloging the species inhabiting the rainforests, and when the forests are cut down, these will be lost forever. More than 70% of the plants known to produce compounds with anti-cancerous properties are tropical, and there may be many cures waiting to be found.

One survey of Costa Rican plants found that 15% had potential as anti-cancer agents. Cures for malaria and dysentery have been found in the forests. Louis XIV was cured of amoebic dysentery by ipecac, a South American plant that remains the most effective cure. Cortisone and diosgenin, the active agents in birth control pills, were developed from Guatemalan and Mexican wild yams. These are some of the 3,000 plants that tribal peoples use worldwide as contraceptives. Continued research could yield yet other methods of birth control. Shaman Pharmaceuticals is one company working to develop useful drugs based on rainforest products.

Not all rainforest products are medicinal. Rice, corn, and most spices – including vanilla, the unripe fermented stick-like fruits of the Central American orchid *Vanilla fragrans* – are also medicinal. Other products native people have extracted from the rainforest include latex, resins, starch, sugar, thatch, dyes, and fatty oils. The rainforest also acts as a genetic pool, and when disease strikes a monocrop such as bananas, it's possible to hybridize it with rainforest varieties to see if this produces an immunity to pests or fungus.

GREENERY AND GREENHOUSE: Biodiversity is only one of many reasons to preserve the forest. Rainforests also act as watersheds, and cutting can result in flooding as well as increased aridity. This is because much rain is produced through the transpiration of trees, which helps keep the air saturated with moisture. Although it is commonly believed that rainforests produce most of the earth's oxygen, in fact there is an equilibrium between the amount mature forests consume through the decay of organic matter and the amount they produce via photosynthesis. However, many scientists believe that widespread burning of tropical forests releases large amounts of carbon dioxide. The amount of carbon dioxide in the atmosphere has risen by 15% in the past century (with about half of this occurring since 1958), and forest clearance may account for half of that gain. Since carbon dioxide along with other atmospheric elements traps heat that would otherwise escape into space, this means that temperatures may rise worldwide. Rainfall patterns would change and ocean levels would rise as the polar ice packs melt. In many areas, deforestation has already had an adverse effect on the environment. Although many uncertainties remain about the "greenhouse effect," one certainty is that by the time the effects are apparent, they will be irreversible.

FATE OF THE FORESTS: Just a few thousand years ago, a belt of rainforests, covering some five billion acres (14% of the planet's surface) stretched around the equator. Wherever there was sufficient rainfall and high enough temperatures there was or is rainforest. Over half that total area has now been destroyed, much of it in the past couple of hundred years, with the rate accelerating after the end of WWII. Squatters and logging continue to cause deforestation throughout the region. At current rates, much of the world's remaining forest area will vanish by the end of the century. One reason for the continued destruction of the remaining forests is the need for land resulting from the concentration of arable land in a few hands. For example, in El Salvador fewer than 2,000 families control 40% of the land. Another motivation is the desire to secure control over an area by one group or another. Cattle ranching, logging, mining, and industry are other reasons to cut the forests. Forests do not recover quickly. Depending on how much has been cut, recovery may take centuries or an eternity.

EDUCATING YOURSELF: Don't miss an opportunity to visit the rainforest while you are in Belize. When you return home, one of the best organizations to join is **Rainforest Action Network** (☎ 415-398-4404, fax 398-2732). Write Ste. 700, 450 Sansome, San Francisco, CA 94111. Another is **Earth Island Institute** (☎ 415-788-3666, fax 788-7324), which was founded by longtime environmental activist David Brower. Write Ste. 28, 300 Broadway, San Francisco, CA 94133. A third is the **Rainforest Alliance** (☎ 212-941-1900, fax 941-4986). Write 270 Lafayette St., #512, NY, NY 10012. **Greenpeace** (☎ 202-462-1177) also has a rainforest program. Write 1436 U St. NW, Washington, DC 20009. Other specifically Belize-oriented organizations are listed under *Foundations* in the *Practicalities* section. A number of books about the rainforest can be found in the list at the back of this book.

If you want to inform yourself about the state of North America's National Forests, join the **Native Forest Council** (PO Box 2171, Eugene, OR 97402). A donation of $25 or more gives you a subscription to their informative newspaper, the *Forest Voice*. If you're planning a visit to the Pacific Northwest and would like a guided tour, **Ancient Forest Adventures** offers both resort-based trips and less expensive backpacking trips. Contact Mary Vogel, ☎ 503-385-8633, or write AFA, 16 NW Kansas Ave., Bend, OR 97701-1202.

Trees & Tropical Vegetation

The hallmark of the rainforest is diversity, and trees are no exception to that rule. While temperate forests contain only an average of four species per acre, tropical forests may have from 20 to 86. Rainforest trees often have shallow root systems and they may be physically supported by basal buttressing or silt roots. These root systems are bound together in mutually beneficial relationships with the lowly fungi. If you look carefully, you can spot a link between the white threads of fungi, decomposing a leaf or fruit, with the rootlet of a tree. Fungi are able to recycle 20 times as much potassium and

The Cohune Palm

If there is one tree in Belize that will make an impact on you, surely it will be the cohune palm. The Maya have always believed that where these trees grow the soil is more fertile than anywhere else, and cohune ridge is common near archaeological sites. In fact, virtually anywhere in Belize that you visit and find broadleaf tropical forest, you will find a preponderance of these attractive and shady palms.

The fronds of the cohune *(coroso)* palm have traditionally been used for thatch and the leaf stems for the sides of houses, for table tops and for beds. Its name is thought to derive from its testicle-shaped nuts (*cojone* is testicle in Spanish). Oil is obtained from the nuts and food from the heart of the "cabbage." In order to harvest the oil, the kernels are extracted and added to a pot of water; the oil slowly floats to the top. The oil has been used for cooking, as massage oil, and for making laundry soap. The nuts have even been used for tobacco pipes: men would bore a hole and put a stem on them. During WWI, the nuts were harvested extensively by the British, who used them to make charcoal filters for their gas masks. Shavings from the stem can be used on wounds as a coagulant, and will stave off infection. Although none too palatable, you can also eat the nut: it tastes like an oily coconut kernel.

phosphorus to a tree as it will lose in the rains. The rainforest's high humidity and relatively uniform temperatures allow fungi to flourish. Perhaps in a largely unsuccessful evolutionary attempt by nature to avoid the burden of stranglers and other plants, the trees are generally smooth-barked.

Tree buttresses are triangular when viewed from the side, and in cross-section resemble an irregular two-, five-, or even an occasional 10-armed star. They function much like the guy ropes on a tent: hitting them with the blunt side of a machete will produce a "bong," showing that they are under tension. There are three types of buttresses: plank (resembling giant wedges), flying (of the stilt-root type), and serpentine – often looped or undulating from side to side. These extend some distance from the tree. Many trees exhibit buttresses of more than one type.

A special characteristic of rainforest trees are the **drip-tip leaves**, which are elongated at the end by an inch. This allows them to shed water after a shower more quickly and resume assimilating and transpiring. A further advantage is that the quick passage of water may also act to deter the growth of mosses and lichen. Another feature of tropical trees is **cauliflory**, or flowering from the trunk. Southeast Asian examples of fruit produced in this fashion include jackfruit and durian. The example you are most likely to see in Belize is cacao, the tree from which chocolate is made.

VARIETIES: Perhaps the most common tree you will see on Belizean cayes and along the coast is the **coconut palm.** Unfortunately, it is threatened by a lethal virus

The Tie Tie

One of the most popular handicrafts produced in Belize are the tie tie baskets, made using the basket tie tie (broom vine, bastard tree, *Desmoncus martius*). Bark is stripped off this spiny palm, taking the spines along with it. The inner portion is then used either whole or split lengthwise into quarters or halves, depending upon the intended use. The baskets are made in places such as Gales Point and in Creole villages in the Cayo District.

that yellows the fronds. There is no known cure save the planting of resistant strains. Trees affected are of the "loca" or Jamaica tall variety. Ambergris Caye has been the only place where trees have been treated. Mature trees have already vanished from the Yucatán, and it will be years before the Belizean coast recovers. Locals still seem to deny that there is actually a problem.

Banak is called *sangre palo* in Spanish after the dark red sap that exudes from its bark when wounded. The *yemeri* or **white mahogany** is another variety. **Black poison wood** *(chechem)* is also called Honduras walnut. The name comes from its caustic sap. **Oak** and **Caribbean pine** are found in the higher elevations of the Mountain Pine Ridge area of the Cayo District. Its milk will blister your skin. The **white poison wood** is much less toxic. **Sapodilla** – which provides chicle, the white resinous latex used to manufacture chewing gum – and **mahogany** dominate the deciduous forests of the north.

Another famous tree is the **ceiba**, which the Maya have believed is a "tree of life" because it separates heaven and earth and has a long life. It's noted for its eye-catching "plank" root buttresses. The silky fibers surrounding the seed in its

fruit have given it the English name of silk cotton tree.

The bark of the **craboo** tree is used as a cure for dysentery; a dessert and a rum can be made from its berry-like fruit. The **gumbo limbo,** popularly known in Spanish as the *Indio desnudo* ("naked Indian") and in English as the "tourist tree," utilizes chloroplasts under its orange bark in order to continue synthesizing during the months of Nov. to May, when it is leafless. Known locally as the "tubroose," the Guanacaste or **ear fruit** receives its English name from the unique shape of its fruits. These trees require an enclosed, non-competitive tropical forest in order to thrive. The **cashew**, the center of a festival held in Crooked Tree, is called the "Devil's fruit" because it's said that the Devil made it and forgot to put the fruit inside. It is commonly used to make a type of wine.

EPIPHYTES AND BROMELIADS: Taken from the Greek words meaning "upon plants," epiphytes provide the luxuriant verdancy commonly associated with rainforests. Although they may be found in temperate and drier tropical forests as well, the combination of rain and warmth unique to the rainforest help them flourish here. Treetop life has many advantages.

Major Archaeological Sites, Reserves, National Parks & Natural Wonders

MEXICO

MEXICO

⑮ ● Chetumal
⑭
Corozal Town
⑯
⑰

COROZAL DISTRICT

⑬

⑫ ●
Orange Walk Town

⑩

⑨
Crooked Tree

⑪
Bomba

ORANGE WALK DISTRICT

⑱

Belize

⑧

① Ambergris Caye

② San Pedro
Caye Caulker
③
Caye Chapel

Caribbean Sea

Turneffe Islands ④

Belize City

Lighthouse Reef ⑤

BELIZE DISTRICT

⑲ ⑳

San Ignacio
⑳
⑰
Belmopan
㉓
㉑ ㉒
㉕
Mountain Pine Ridge
㉔

STANN CREEK DISTRICT
㉙

Dangriga
⑦

Glovers Reef
⑥

㉖
CAYO DISTRICT

㉗

㉘

㉚

TOLEDO DISTRICT
㉛

㉜

㉝

㉞ Punta Gorda

㉟

Gulf of Honduras

GUATEMALA

NOT TO SCALE

N

The Cayes
1. Bacalar Chico Marine Park
2. Hol Chan Reserve
3. Proposed Siwa-ban Reserve and Caye Caulker Reef Reserve
4. Great Blue Hole
5. Half Moon Caye National Monument
6. Glovers Reef Reserve
7. South Water Caye/ Tobacco Caye Reserve; Laughingbird Caye National Park

The North
8. The Bermudian Landing Community Baboon Sanctuary
9. Crooked Tree Wildlife Sanctuary/Chau Hix ruins
10. Lamanai Archaeological Reserve
11. Altun Ha ruins
12. Cuello ruins
13. Nohmul ruins
14. Santa Rita ruins
15. Four Miles Lagoon
16. Cerros ruins
17. Shipstern Wildlife Reserve
18. Rio Bravo Conservation Area/ La Milpa ruins

The West
19. Guanacaste Park
20. Belize Zoo/Monkey Bay Wildlife Sanctuary
21. Blue Hole/St. Herman's Cave
22. Five Blues Lake National Park
23. Tapir Mountain Reserve
24. Mountain Pine Ridge Forest Reserve/ Slate Creek Preserve
25. Hidden Valley Falls
26. Caracol ruins/Chiquibul Forest Reserve
27. Xunantunich ruins
28. To Melchor, Tikal, Flores (Guatemala)

The South
29. Cockscomb Jaguar Reserve
30. Bladen Branch Nature Reserve
31. Nim Li Punit ruins
32. Lubaantun ruins
33. Uxbenka ruins
34. Pusilhá ruins
35. Monkey River

Birds and bats arrive to pollinate and deposit nutrient-rich dung, and their seeds are likely to be dispersed by the wind. But water may be harder to come by and evaporation is a problem, so many bromeliads have evolved tanks that hold up to two gallons of water.

Don't make the mistake of thinking that these plants are parasitic. Although they are unwelcome guests, most do not feed on their hosts. Generally, they arrive in the form of tiny dustlike seeds that establish themselves on moss or lichen. Minute epiphytes residing on leaf surfaces, epiphylls (algae, liverworts, lichens, and mosses) are generally found on lower plants. Named after Swedish botanist Olaf Bromel, **bromeliads** are ground-dwelling epiphytes, the most famous of which is the pineapple.

HELICONIAS: Famous worldwide as an ornamental, the heliconia (*platanillo*), lends an infusion of bizarre color and shape to the tropical landscape. The name of these medium to large erect herbs comes from Helicon, a mountain in southern Greece that was believed to have been the home of the muses. They are a member of the order known as the *Zingiberales*, and there are thought to be around 200-250 species. Relatives within this category include the banana, bird-of-paradise, ginger, and prayer plants.

The family name *Zingiberales* comes from the Sanskrit word *sringavera*, which means "horn-shaped" in reference to the rhizomes. Each erect shoot has a stem and leaves that are frequently (although not always) topped by an inflorescence with yellow or red bracts. Each inflorescence may produce up to 50 hermaphroditic flowers. Leaves are composed of stalk and blade and resemble banana leaves. Flowers produce a blue-colored fruit with three seeds.

In Belize you're most likely to find heliconias near rivers and along roads; they thrive in light gaps. Most are found in the tropical lowlands or in middle-elevation or cloud forest habitats. Lured by the bright colored flowers and bracts, hummingbirds, arrive to pollinate the blooms. The birds spread pollen as they fly from flower to flower in search of nectar.

ORCHIDS: Belize's extraordinary natural wealth includes some 250 varieties of orchids. Not all are epiphytic and the ones that are generally possess thicker leaves and keep their stomata – tiny pores on their leaves that absorb carbon dioxide – shut during the day, utilizing a metabolic process to store carbon dioxide for the next day's use. Nearly all orchids are pollinated by insects or hummingbirds, and many may only be pollinated by a single specific one. Aside from their aesthetic value, orchids are of little economic importance. They were once thought to have medicinal properties, but this has proven largely false and not a single species is currently used in modern medicine. Their only valuable product is vanilla, an extract obtained from the cured unripened pods of various species belonging to the genus *Vanilla*. Orchids were named by Dioscorides, a Greek physician who, noting the similarity of its tubers to male genitals, named the species *orches* (testicles).

VINES AND COMPANY: Woody vines (lianas and bush ropes) and

Mangroves

Mangrove (*mangle* in Spanish) forests are found along the coasts and on the cayes. These water-rooted trees serve as a marine habitat by sheltering sponges, corals, oysters, and other members of the marine community around their roots –organisms that in turn attract a variety of other sealife. Some species live out their lives in the shelter of the mangroves, and many fish use them as a shelter or feeding ground; lobsters use the mangrove environs as a nursery for their young. Above the water level, they shelter seabirds and are important nesting sites. Their organic detritus, exported to the reef by the tides, is consumed by its inhabitants, providing the base of an extensive food web.

Mangroves also dampen high waves and winds generated by tropical storms. By trapping silt in their roots and catching leaves and other debris that decompose to form soil, the red mangroves act as land builders. Eventually, the red mangroves kill themselves off, building up enough soil for the black and white mangroves to take over.

The red mangroves, meanwhile, have sent out progeny in the form of floating seedlings – bottom-heavy youngsters that grow on the tree until reaching six inches to a foot in length. If they drop in shallow water, the seeds touch bottom and implant themselves. In deeper water they stay afloat and, crossing a shoal, drag until they lodge.

Named after their light-colored bark, the white mangroves are highly salt tolerant. If growing in a swampy area, they produce pneumatophores, root system extensions. These grow vertically to a height that allows them to stay above the water during flooding or tides so they can carry on gaseous exchange.

Producing a useful wood, the black mangrove also puts out pneumatophores. Smaller than the others, the buttonwood is not a true mangrove but is found on the coasts where no other varieties occur.

Belize is the only nation that maintains 90% of its coastal mangroves. Although these remaining mangroves are theoretically protected by law in Belize, they are endangered by the activities of marauding developers. Vast tracts are being removed in the areas under development along the Northern and Western Highways near Belize City. Caye Caulker's hopes for a large preserve have been dashed by developers who have built on most of the proposed area (and destroyed much of the remaining mangrove expanse with it). Hopefully, the burgeoning "eco-tourism" industry will not continue to result in further mangrove destruction. The tourism industry *has* been directly responsible for mangrove destruction as a number of projects can attest – including extensive cutting near Caye Caulker's airport as well as a hideous channel cut on Placencia Caye just off the village of the same name.

herbaceous climbers help give the rainforest its tropical quality. Using trees as trellises, vines crawl up from the ground to reach the light. Scramblers grow in gaps in the rainforest. Over 90% of **liana** species are found in the tropics where they commonly grow as long as 230 ft.

are found in the tropics where they commonly grow as long as 230 ft. and as wide as six in. or more. Lianas twist themselves around the tree and extend tendrils or hooks to secure themselves. Like vines, they drop their shaded understory leaves as they reach maturity. In order to guard against damage from kinking as trees sway, lianas have evolved bends, coils, and twists. In addition to closing the canopy, thus stabilizing the microclimate, lianas also offer protection to animals such as the Central American sloths. The sloths sleep in a mass of lianas, and tie in to a tensile network of vines that will alert them to the presence of an arboreal predator. The longest lianas are rattans – one of the rainforest's harvestable products – and may grow to more than 500 ft.

STRANGLER FIGS: Beginning life as epiphytes, some species of *Ficus* and *Clusia* send down woody, clasping roots that wind themselves around the trunk as they extend into the earth. As the roots grow in size, they meld into a trunk that surrounds the tree. These "strangler figs" kill the tree, not through strangulation but by robbing it of canopy space. They can grow in the ruins of buildings as well. Strangler figs are often the only trees left in an otherwise cleared tract of forest. There is little incentive to use their poor quality wood, and their spreading branches provide shade. The holes, cracks, twists, and turns in its trunk host geckos, anoles, ants, stingless bees, scorpions, and other life – each inhabiting its ecological niche. Bats, birds, and other fruit eaters flock around the trees, attracting ornithologists in the process. Even peccaries and other ground dwellers

arrive to share in the bounty that falls to the ground. These creatures all help distribute its seeds when they defecate.

OTHERS: A free-floating aquatic perennial, the water hyacinth *(jacinto de agua)* has spread during this century from its South American homeland to become one of the most troublesome and widespread aquatic weeds.

Animal Life

As with the plants, the Animal Kingdom is also wonderfully diverse. Many of the indigenous species are in danger of extinction, largely from loss of their traditional habitats through deforestation. Sea turtles, though, are threatened by often-illegal overhunting and a viral disease. The panoply of wild Belizean species includes manatees, ocelots, deer, coatis, coyotes, jaguars, margays, peccaries, tapirs, and howler and spider monkeys. Unlike their temperate counterparts, they are relatively difficult to spot. You need to have a keen eye, to keep still, and – best of all – to have a local friend or guide along.

📖 **Suggested Reading**
A fascinating book to peruse before your arrival is Costa Rican Natural History, *edited by the eminent biologist and conservationist Daniel Janzen. While it includes many species not found in Belize, it is an invaluable reference nevertheless. Another superb book is* Neotropical Rainforest Mammals: A Field Guide, *by Louise H. Emmons.*

Mammals

PRIMATES: New World monkeys differ from their Old World monkey and ape cousins in many respects. Their noses have wide-apart, sideward-pointing nostrils as opposed to close-set, downward-pointing ones; they are primarily arboreal; and they show a greater geographical variation in color patterns.

ⓘ *Did You Know?*

Why do howlers howl? Once heard, the sound of the howler monkey is never forgotten and is what has made it a must-see among visitors. There are numerous local explanations as to why howlers roar, such as when it is going to rain, or when other animals are feeding. Actually, they react to loud noises and to rain, and roar more frequently at midday. The cacophonous howling begins with a series of low-pitched grunts by the male, which accelerate into long, deep roars; the females then join the fun with higher-pitched sounds. The howler's vocalization is produced by a special bone in its throat that functions as an amplifier.

Actually sounding more like a "growler" than a howler, the sounds of the **black howler monkey** ("baboon," *saraguate*) reverberate up to several miles away. Another unique characteristic of the howler is its prehensile tail, which has a dermatoglyph, or fingerprint. Living in groups of up to 20 led by a senior male, howlers dine on flowers, fruits, and tender leaves. Howlers are entirely black, except for a pale-colored fringed mantle on their sides. Their robust shoulders contrast with comparatively diminutive hindquarters. If you should see a colony, don't stand underneath it: a favorite pastime is to urinate on *Homo sapiens*! Another species, the gold mantled howler, is thought to exist here but has not been documented.

Moving rapidly through the trees, the **black-handed spider monkey** ("monkey," *mono araña*) has a very complex language and lives in bands of about 20, which frequently subdivide into smaller groupings.

RACCOON FAMILY: Omnivorous, solitary, nocturnal, crafty, and clean, the **raccoon** *(mapache)* will dine on anything from frogs and fish to fruit and vegetables. Its nimble cousin, the mischievous and sociable white-nosed **coati** ("quash" or *pizote*), hunts at dawn and dusk – resting in treetops or in hollow trunks the rest of the time. The term coati-mundi refers only to solitary coatis, adult males over two years old.

Mainly nocturnal, the gregarious **kinkajou** ("nightwalker," *mico de noche, micoleon*) dines on small animals, birds, eggs, and honey. It has short woolly fur, large soulful eyes, small ears, and a long prehensile tail. They use their tail as an anchor while they move from tree to tree. During the day, the kinkajou naps in a tree hollow.

Smaller and lacking a prehensile tail, the **olingo** or pale-faced kinkajou, is a close relative. Actively agile, they journey high in the rainforest canopy. A third related species is the **cacomistle**, a nocturnal and solitary tawny-brown creature that barks and has a tail longer than its head and body.

WEASEL FAMILY: The long-tailed weasel (comadreja) has attractive, short, thick, and soft fur. Its slim frame allows it to slither into the burrows of mice. It also dines on rabbits, birds, and reptiles. You are unlikely to catch more than a glimpse of one, as it is a nervous, nocturnal, and solitary creature.

The grison ("bush dog," huron, grisón) resembles a large weasel with extremely short legs and tail and with a long neck and back. Perhaps the nation's least popular mammal, the striped hog-nosed skunk ("polecat," zorro hediondo) is probably better left unseen and unsmelled. Although it is not a true rainforest creature, it is sometimes found there.

An excellent swimmer, the southern river otter ("waterdog," nutria, perro de agua) eats fish, shrimp, and turtles. On land, this graceful creature waddles awkwardly. In danger of extinction, they have been protected by law in Belize since 1974. Resembling a lanky mink with a long-haired tail, the tayra or bush dog (tolumuco) feeds on grubs, bird nests, fruit, eggs, and chicken or goat meat; it resides in an underground burrow.

CAT FAMILY: The principal predator in rainforests worldwide, cats have a physique that suits their killer lifestyle. Their teeth are designed for killing and meat eating, while their excellent sight and hearing, strong shoulders, and sharp claws come in handy when going after game. Some are territorial, most are solitary, and all prey on anything that comes their way – from large insects to small mammals. The best time to see them is after nightfall when they take to trails and their bright eyeshine makes them visible. Should you come across a den with kittens, leave them alone. They have not been abandoned: the mother has gone off to search for food.

The graceful, nocturnal and diurnal "king of the tropical rainforest," the jaguar ("tiger," tigre) is this hemisphere's largest cat; it may reach six feet long and three feet high at shoulder level. It will dine on peccaries, deer, monkeys, sloths, and even fish. The only large, spotted cats in the Americas, jaguars are easily identifiable. You might hear them roar at night – a series of hoarse, deep grunts. Although an encounter is extremely

Belizean Animal Names

Alligator – crocodile	Honeybear – kinkajou
Ant Bear, Antsbear – anteater	Mountain cow – Baird's tapir
Antelop – deer	Nightwalker – kinkajou
Baboon – howler monkey	Polecat – skunk
Bamboo chicken – iguana	Quash – coati
Bush dog – tayra	Red tiger – puma
Dilly – armadillo	Tiger – jaguar
Fillymingo – jabiru stork	Tommygoff – fer-de-lance
Georgie Bull – northern jacana	Warrie, warree – peccary
Gibnut – agouti	Wowla – boa constrictor
Hilari – jaguarundi	

unlikely, it is fraught with danger. If you should see a jaguar, walk toward it, shout and clap your hands. If you run, it may pursue you, which could have unfortunate consequences!

Sometimes called a cougar or mountain lion, the **puma** ("red tiger") ranks second in terms of size. Slightly smaller than a jaguar, it has an unspotted tan or dark brown hide, a leaner, more low-slung frame, and a longer, thicker tail. It is the only large, uniformly colored cat. Although pumas may tag along behind humans out of curiosity, few attacks on *Homo Sapiens* have ever been documented.

Resembling a miniaturized jaguar, the **ocelot** *(manigordo)* feeds on anything from rabbits to insects. Unlike a jaguar, it has stripes and not spots on its neck. It captures game on the ground and may be encountered walking on man-made trails at night. The **tiger cat** *(tigrillo)*, a smaller, similar version of the ocelot, has a combination of spots and stripes. Ranging from 33.5 to 51 in., it may weigh up to 22 lbs. The **margay** *(mandu, tigrillito, maimselle)*, more solitary and nocturnal than the ocelot, is the size of a large house cat. Weighing from 6 to 11 lbs., it has a somewhat bushy tail that is well over half the extended length of its head and black-spotted body. It may easily be confused with an ocelot.

With unspotted blackish-brown or chestnut-to-red fur, the **jaguarundi** ("hilari," *onca*) has a small flattened head, long sleek body, short legs – all of which make it appear to be a cross between a cat and a weasel.

MARSUPIALS: The four species of opossum found here are the com-

mon, common grey four-eyed, woolly, and regular. Arboreal, the possum is a nocturnal omnivore. The woolly mouse and slatey slender mouse opossums *(zorra, zorricí)* are also found.

Five-toed, **opossums** *(zorro)* have short legs, long tails, large and delicate ears, and their first hindfoot toe functions as an opposable "thumb" that is used to clutch thin branches for climbing. Born only eight days after fertilization, opossum infants follow a trail of their mother's saliva from the cloaca to her pouch, where they secure themselves to their mother's nipples for the next 60 days. These malodorous creatures – which feed on small animals and fruits – enjoy rolling in fresh dung. When handled, they are aggressive, defecating and squirting vile-smelling urine with a twist of their tail.

EDENTATAS: Indigenous to the Americas, the name of this order – which includes anteaters, sloths, and armadillos – refers to the few teeth found in the latter two and their complete absence in the anteaters. They represent the last remnant of an order that evolved during the period when South America was an isolated island continent. Sloths and anteaters are both arboreal, soft furred creatures.

The nocturnal **silky anteater** ("antsbear," "pigmy silky," *tapacara*) has a prehensile tail and a long retractile tongue. It breaks open ant and termite nests to feed. The best way to find one is to gaze into clumps of lianas up to 33 ft. above the jungle floor for something resembling a golden tennis ball, which is in reality a sleeping anteater. Another species is the **banded or lesser anteater** *(taman-*

The Manatees

Popularly known as the "sea cow," the manatee *(manatí)* is found along Belize's Caribbean coast in spots ranging from Gales Point to Placencia. They move along the ocean floor (at a maximum pace of six mph) searching for food, surfacing every four or five minutes to breathe. Surprisingly, as the manatee's nearest living relative is the elephant, the creature was thought to be the model for the legend of the mermaid – perhaps because of the mother's habit of sheltering her offspring with her flipper as the infant feeds. Weighing between 400 and 1,300 lbs., the pudgy creature is covered with finely wrinkled grey or brown skin decorated with barnacles and algae; it may reach 12 ft. in length. Although to you they might appear ugly with their small eyes, thick lips, bristly muzzles, and wrinkled necks, they are affectionate with one another, kissing and sometimes swimming flipper-to-flipper.

Manatees dwell in lagoons and brackish water, and may eat as much as 100 lbs. of aquatic vegetables per day. Strictly vegetarian, their only enemy is man, who has hunted them for their hide, oil, and meat. Once ranging from South America up to North Carolina, their numbers have dwindled dramatically. Their tough hides were once used for machine belting and high pressure hoses. Belizeans have widely and incorrectly believed that manatee flesh holds special properties and comes in a variety of flavors. Although community education may be the key to stopping hunting, propeller blades of motor boats continue to slaughter manatees accidentally, and the careless use of herbicides is also a threat. To its credit, the government has established a special protection zone in an area near Gales Point. Manatee watching is a highlight for many visitors to Belize.

---

dua, *oso jaceta, oso hormiguero),* distinguished by the black V-shaped mark across its back, resembling a vest worn backwards. The **northern tamandua** *(oso mielero)* is black-vested and nocturnal. During the day, you will see them accompanied by a dense halo of flies and mosquitoes, which they brush away with a forepaw. The **giant anteater** *(oso caballo)* is a large shaggy creature that ambles about on its knuckles.

Mainly nocturnal insect-eaters, **armadillos** ("dillys") are protected by banded and bony plates separated by soft skin – which permits the creature to bend. Resembling trotting windup toys, armadillos may run right into you. Their burrows can be recognized by the smooth, dome-shaped roof. Each litter conceived in the burrow is a set of four identical quadruplets hatched from a single egg.

The **nine-banded long-nosed armadillo** *(cusuco)* dines on beetles, ants, termites, fungi, berries, slugs, centipedes, millipedes, and other such exotic cuisine. Chiefly nocturnal, it is the most commonly seen variety. The rare **northern naked-tail armadillo** *(armado de zopilote)* walks about on the tips of its foreclaws. It is slow-moving, and you might see no more than its naked tail disappearing under a log.

PERISODACTYLES: This group, which includes horses and the African and Asian rhinoceros, is characterized by two unmatched or unequal hoof-covered toes. One of the Americas' most corpulent mammals and the rainforest's largest terrestrial mammal, the **baird's tapir** (*"mountain cow," danto, danta*) weighs as much as 550 lbs. and may grow six feet long and up to three feet high. Dining on seeds, leaves, twigs, and fruit, a tapir devotes 90% of its waking time to foraging for food because the microorganisms that live in its stomach and that digest its plant material through fermentation are not very efficient. Its excellent hearing and sense of smell compensate for this ungainly creature's poor eyesight. Solitary, nocturnal, and marsh-dwelling, it bolts when frightened – flattening everything in its wake! Despite the fact that they are the mammalian equivalent of an all-terrain vehicle, tapirs are shy creatures and difficult to see. However, hunters can easily locate them through dogs and calls, and their meat is considered a delicacy.

PECCARIES AND DEER: These are the two families of *Artiocactyla* (even-toed hoofed animals) found in the rainforest. Resembling a gigantic pig, the **collared peccary** ("wari," saino or *javelina* after its spear-like tusks) lives in a group of two to 15, whose members recognize each other by their pungent, musky body odor resembling chicken soup or cheese. They may be identified by a faint but nevertheless distinct collar of pale yellow hairs running from their lower cheek down to the top of their shoulders. Peccaries are most often found at salt licks or mud wallows. Another species is the **white-lipped peccary** ("wari," *cariblanco*). Generally black in the rainforest environs, it may also be brownish or red. There's always at least a sprinkling of white hair on its jaws and body and some are even snow white. Feeding in large herds on fruits, palm nuts, or similar fodder, white-lipped peccaries cover a large area daily, leaving the ground churned and pocked in their wake. The noise coming from large groups (tooth clacking, screaming, bellowing) has given them a greatly exaggerated reputation for aggressiveness. They generally retreat in the face of humans, although one might rumble past without seeing you.

Male deer have antlers that are shed and regrown annually. The **white-tailed deer** ("deer," *venado, venado cola blanco*) are identical but smaller than the white-tailed deer found in the US. Not rainforest animals, they are generally found out in the open. Another variety is the **red brocket deer** ("antelop," *cabra de monte*). Its tapered shape is ideal for pushing through rainforest. Diurnal and solitary, it feeds on fallen fruits, flowers, and other vegetation.

RODENTS: The trademark of rodents is their sharp and versatile front incisors. Supported by several different complex systems of jaw and muscle structures, the incisors may be used to slice, dig, pry, and cut. Some can even fell trees and kill animals. These differences allow them to be separated into three groups: squirrel-like (*Sciuoromorpha*), cavy-like (*Caviomorpha*), and mouse-like (*Myomorpha*). By far the most diverse order of mammals, rodents number some 1,750 species worldwide – nearly equal to the 2,300 other species of mammals.

Omnivorous, **squirrels** found in the rainforest may feed on palm nuts as well as fruits, insects, fungi, and even leaves, bark, and flowers. The red-tailed squirrel (*ardilla roja, ardilla chisa*) is widespread in some parts and may commonly be observed scurrying up a tree. Other species include the variegated squirrel, Deppe's squirrel, Richmond's squirrel, the Central American dwarf squirrel, and the Montane squirrel.

Long-legged creatures with feet like hooves, bristly hair, and strong jaws, the cavy-like rodents all have four toes on their front feet. Residing near rivers and active during the day, the edgy brown-colored Central American **agouti** ("gibnut," *guatusa*) eats tender shoots, fruits, and seeds. Diurnal and largely solitary, they are frequently seen in protected areas, especially in late afternoon. Newborn young stay apart in their own burrow; mama calls them out for nursing and care. Its cousin, the nocturnal and largely solitary **paca** ("gibnut," *tepezcuintle*), lives in a burrow. It is larger and twice as heavy, with a pig-like body and horizontal rows of cream-colored spots along its flanks.

A clumsy vegetarian covered with short, strong, and rigid quills, the skinny prehensile-tailed **porcupine** (*puercoespín*) forages at night for fruits and seeds. Its barb-tipped spines detach readily, and work their way into in the flesh of an attacker. Rothschild's porcupine is entirely spiny and mostly black. The spines of the Mexican hairy porcupine are largely covered with dark fur. Another common rodent is the **gopher** (*taltusa*).

RABBITS: Dwelling in thickets and forests, cottontail **rabbits** (*conejos*) eat grass and tree bark; they may have up to five litters per year. The only other species found is the Brazilian, which is smaller, reddish, and has a small tail.

BATS: Bats are the most important animals – by sheer number of species – in most Western Hemisphere rainforests. The only flying animals, bats have wings made of amazingly elastic skin that contracts rather than folds when their wings are closed. Emitting largely ultrasonic high-frequency sounds through their nose or mouth, bats plot their route by calibrating distances to solid objects based on returning echoes. Contrary to popular belief, they will not become tangled in your hair nor will they bite, except in self-defense. In addition to consuming large quantities of insects, bats benefit the environment through pollination of many important plants and through seed dispersal. Some feed on nectar, others on frogs, others on fish, and still others on sleeping birds and lizards.

Hiding out in cave harems guarded by a single male, the **short-tailed fruit bat** (*murciélago*) flies out at night. It resides in the rainforest understory and is an important seed disperser.

The infamous **vampire bat** (*vampiro*) also lives in Belize. Stealthily landing on a horse or cow, it makes an incision, a process that may take up to 20 minutes, and – exuding an anticoagulant – proceeds to lap up the blood. The vampire may run and hop with agility on all fours, using its thickened thumb as a foot. Its feces contain a fungus that causes histoplasmosis, a debilitating disease.

The **fishing** or **bulldog bat** (*murciélago pescador*) skims the water as it flies and feeds on insects and fish, which it grasps with its enormous feet. Nectar-feeding or long-tongued bats are important pollinators, often attracted by plants with large flowers and musky odors that open at night.

Reptiles & Amphibians

TURTLES: Belize has a wide variety of turtles, and you are certain to see at least one sliding into the water along a river. The **hickatee**, a river turtle, spends its entire life in the water and may weigh up to 50 lbs. Because it is becoming rarer and rarer, restrictions have been placed on its capture and a closed season has been instituted May 1-31. (Green and leatherback turtles may not be captured between April 1 and Oct. 31.)

The large-finned, herbivorous **green turtle** (*tortuga blanca* or *tortuga verde*) is of medium-size, with a total length of about three ft. and weighing around 400 lbs. It lays eggs every two to three years, storming the beaches in massive groups termed *barricadas*. It is readily identifiable by its short rounded head.

One of the smallest sea turtles, at 35 in. or less in length, the **hawksbill** (*tortuga carey*) has a spindle-shaped shell and weighs around 220 lbs. Because of its tortoise shell – a brown translucent layer of corneous gelatin that covers it and peels off the shell when processed – it has been pursued and slaughtered throughout the world. It feeds largely on sponges and seaweed. Worldwide demand for its shell, which sells for a fortune in Japan, appears to have condemned it to extinction. Sales of its meat or any product taken from it are illegal in Belize.

The short-finned **loggerhead turtle** ("lagra," *tortuga cabezona*) has a large bird-jawed head, twice the size of the green turtle's, and rarely reaches more than four feet in length. It dines on sea urchins, jellyfish, starfish, and crabs, but is threatened with extinction from coastal development, egg gathering, and hunting by raccoons.

The **leatherback,** which is black with very narrow fins, gets its name from the leathery hide that covers its back in lieu of a shell. Reaching up to six ft. in length and weighing as much as 1,500 lbs., the leatherback's chief predator has always been the poacher.

FROGS AND TOADS: The glands of the **marine toad** (*Bufo marinus*) contain toxins. Don't try to pick one up: it will urinate on you! The predominantly nocturnal marine toad exercises control over its parotid gland and directs its poison in a fine spray, one that can prove fatal to dogs and cats that pick it up in their mouths. If you carry it around, it will be likely to defend itself by urinating. An equal-opportunity eater, it will consume anything from wasps to dog and cat food set out for pets. The **gaudy leaf frog** (*rana calzonudo*) is Central America's most colorful, with a bright, leaf-green dorsum, creamy-white throat and belly, orange hands and feet, dark blue side markings, and blood-red irises.

LIZARDS: The **basilisk** ("cock malakka") is sometimes called the "Jesus Christ lizard" because, while fleeing predators or pursuing prey, it may dart across the surface of a stream, balancing with its tail. It resembles a miniature sailfin dinosaur. You'll undoubtedly see one of these lowland dwellers scurrying across your path. There are also a wide variety of **anoles**, small sit-and-wait predators that North Americans mistakenly call chameleons.

The territorial, primarily vegetarian **iguana** ("bamboo chicken") has a drab red coloration and black bars along its back. The iguana population is decreasing because of the Belizean practice of eating pregnant females. There's also the prevalent misconception that iguana eggs serve as an aphrodisiac. In order to escape predators, it will jump into the water and can stay below for as much as a half-hour without surfacing. The **scaly iguana** ("wishy-nilly") is distinguishable from its cousin by a large scale on the side of the head slightly below and behind the rear angle of the lower jaw, as well as by its green coloration and longer tail.

Other lizards include the **skink** and the **spiny lizard**. The two species of crocodilians (termed "alligators" locally) are the **Morelet's crocodile**, which reaches only eight feet in length, and the larger **American crocodile**, both of which reside in many lowland swamps and slow-moving streams.

SNAKES: Of the 54 species, only nine are poisonous. Most infamous is the **yellow-jawed tommy goff** (tomigoff, fer-de-lance, *terciopelo*) – colored olive green to dark brown, with yellow, V-shaped markings along the sides. It may also be grey or brownish, with a lateral pattern of darker, black-edged triangles running down its back. Reaching lengths of 6½ ft. or more, this lowland-dwelling snake dines on mammals, especially opossums, with an occasional bird thrown in for variety. Hatching in litters of around 75, the young have yellow-tipped prehensile tails. The adult is both extremely poisonous and aggressive, chasing its victim and striking repeatedly. It will attack with little provocation.

Biting only if provoked, the small **coral snake** *(coralillo)* comes in three varieties. The most common is the Atlantic coral snake, found throughout the country; it can be identified by its stripes – alternating bands of red and black, with the black often trimmed with yellow and the red scales individually tipped with black, creating a speckled effect.

Undoubtedly the most unusual snake is the **"two snakes in one."** Combining the markings of the poisonous coral snake and a non-poisonous variety, it has a black head and then a few inches of coral snake markings: red, cream, and black. Its body then enlarges and the coloring changes to olive brown; the underside markings change from the smooth pink of the coral snake to the brown snake's yellowish cream. It is thought that it sticks only its head out of a hole in order to confuse predators.

Climber par excellence, the large, non-venomous **wowla** (boa constrictor) devours everything from lizards to dogs. After striking its prey, the *wowla* coils around it. It then locates the head and swallows the prey whole. Other varieties of Belizean snakes include the **coachwhip** or Central American whipsnake, the **spotted rat snake**, the Belize or **black water snake** *(cativeo)*, the **speckled racer**, the **Cohune Ridge tommy goff** (also spelled tomigoff) and the **grey and green vine snakes**.

Birds

Belize is one of the world's bird-watching paradises. There are over 500 species of birds – a population that includes warblers, thrushes, mockingbirds, wrens, humming-birds, banana birds, cowbirds, blackbirds, grackles, vireos, tana-gers, finches, woodpeckers, night-hawks, anis, cuckoos, trogons, macaws, parrots, vireos, toucans, vultures, hawks, swifts, swallows, flycatchers, pigeons, doves, wild turkeys, kingfishers, acorn and other woodpeckers, cormorants, herons, and sooty terns.

📖 **Suggested Reading**

Birdwatchers will want to pick up a copy of Carol Miller's 100 Birds of Belize *(Gallon Jug, Belize: American Bird Conservancy, 1995), which is for sale inside the country. This is a delightful and informative illustrated guide. Other useful books include* Peterson's Field Guide to the Birds of Mexico *and* The Birds of Costa Rica *by F. Gary Stiles and Alexander Skutch, which also apply to this area. These are both authoritative guides.*

WHERE TO FIND BIRDS: One of the reasons birdwatchers flock to Belize is the number and variety of its species. Even if you aren't a die-hard, be sure to bring binoculars. Everyone has a favorite spot. It may be around your hotel or at a nature preserve or lodge. The parks and reserves are sure bets. If you're on your own, check to see where the birding groups stay. Good places in the country include Pooks Hill Lodge, Crooked Tree, Cockscomb Preserve, and Chaan Chich/Rio Bravo.

SEA BIRDS: Distinctive for its huge bill, slow flight, and clumsy diving, the **brown pelican** *(Pelecanus occidentalus)* is a prominent inhabitant of the coast and cayes. The nearly jet-black **frigate bird** *(Frigata magnificens, Rabihorcado magno)* swoops ominously over-head, occasionally veering down to the water to make a capture. The female is identifiable by her white breast. The mating male causes her to swill (become sexually aroused) by puffing up his red throat pouch. Dubbed Man-O-War, the bird may frequently be seen around Man 'O War Cay.

The six varieties of **terns** include the sooty tern and the royal tern. The **laughing gull** *(Larus atricilla)* has a black head, a white body and tail, and grey wings. Known locally as the Laughing Bird, it is perhaps the only bird in the world to have had a national park (Laughing Bird National Park) named after it. Others include the **brown booby**, which nests on Man 'O War Cay, and the rare **red-footed booby** *(Sula sula)*, which nests on Half Moon Cay. The booby's name is said to have come from the Spanish word *bobo*, which means "dunce" – an apt description as, unlike other species, they make no attempt to defend their eggs or young from frigate birds or other intruders.

BIRDS WITH CHARACTER: Sporting gaudy pink plumage, the **roseate spoonbill** *(ajaia ajaia)* features a strangely shaped beak that is broader at its tip than at its stem. Its Spanish name of *chocolatera* comes from the wooden spoon used in cacao processing. The bill's function is to scoop up unwitting marine life.

A favorite local bird is the **pauraque** (*Nyctidromus albicollis*, "who-you"), to which many legends have attached themselves. It is maintained that if someone picks up a "who-you" egg, they cannot put it down without breaking it, and that the eggs can never be consumed in a fire. If someone has a ticklish emotional relationship, it's said that they've picked up a "who-you" egg.

The enormous **king vulture** (*Sarcoramphus*, "King John Crow," *rey de zopilote, carroñera rey, oc*) has creamy white and black on its wings and a head with splotches of red, orange, yellow, purple, and black accompanied by a bright orange caruncle; its bulging white eyes are ringed in red. The **black vulture** (*Coragyps atratus, carroñero común, ch'om*) is locally known as "John Crow" and has a dark naked head with white patches on the tips of its wings.

The **northern jacana** (*jacana spinosa*, "Georgie Bull") hops gracefully from lily pad to lily pad in search of prey; it's colored cinnamon-red with a bright yellow forehead shield on its black head and yellow-green patches on its wings. It is one of the few bird species to practice polyandry: the male bird builds the nest and cares for it while the female defends the territory of the two to four males who have fertilized her eggs.

Largest and most powerful of the eagles of Central America, the **harpy eagle** may approach speeds of 50 mph. The **blue-crowned motmot** (*Momotus momota*) numbers among the most beautiful of the birds. Because it sometimes appears to move like a band conductor beating time, it has been called the "time bird." Belizeans call it the "good cook." First arriving in the New World from Africa around 1877, the **cattle egret** or common white heron *(Bubulcus ibis, garcilla bueyara)* follows cattle and dines on the insects sent scurrying as the beasts meander.

Seldom seen, the **chestnut-bellied heron** *(agamia agami)* is quite solitary; the Belizeans call it "blue jacket." The **boat-billed heron** (cochlearis cochlearis, garza cucharón) stands out because of its distinctive bill, which brings to mind Tom Tomorrow's *Sparky the Wonder Penguin*. The Belizeans know it as "cooper."

Thriving in deforested territory, the sedentary **roadside hawk** *(Buteo magnirostris, aguililla caminera, ch'uy)* preys on lizards, snakes, rodents, and large insects. The **black-collared hawk** (*Busarellus nigricollis, gavilán conchero*) is known by Belizeans as the "chestnut hawk" or "fishing hawk." It may be sighted in lagoons. The **ornate hawk-eagle** (*Sprizaetus ornatus*, "currasow hawk," *aguila elegante*) is one of the planet's most magnificent eagles, one that lives in primary tropical forest. Dark colored antbirds or **ovenbirds** *(hormigueros)* are best seen on solitary excursions; they follow army ant columns and eat insects frightened by them.

Related to the oriole and the grackle, the omnivorous **Montezuma oropendola** *(Psarocolius montezuma*, "yellowtail")* is mostly black with yellow outer tail feathers. The female constructs her sagging sac-like nests on the ends of tree branches.

One of the most splendid birds is the elegant and graceful **vermilion flycatcher** *(Pyrocephalus rubinus, cardenalito)*. The male is colored bright red and has a catchy aerial mating dance.

The distinctive **Ocellated Turkey** *(Agriocharis ocellata)* is colorful to the point of surrealism, and is in danger of extinction. It is seen near the Tikal and Caracol ruins.

TROGONS: Sedate, arboreal and spectacularly-plumed, the trogons (from the Greek for "gnawer") are widely distributed in the warmer areas of both the Old and New Worlds. Of the 40 species of trogons found in the Americas, Belize has five: red, slatey-tailed, collared (yellow), vidaceous, and citreoline. The most spectacular trogon of all, the resplendent quetzal, is *not* found in Belize (despite the fact that it is prominently featured in a famous guidebook about Belize!). Male trogons have glittering green, blue, or violet upper plumage and chests with posterior underparts of contrasting red, orange, or yellow. Females are duller with brown gray or slatey coloring, where males are green, but with underparts nearly as bright as the males.

THE SCARLET MACAW: The scarlet macaw *(Ara Macao, loras)* is one of the nation's most beautiful birds, and may well be one of the most stunning birds you will ever see! If you are extremely fortunate, you might see this spectacular parrot flying overhead and sounding raucously. However, it now survives only in very remote areas. Its bright red orange plumage has touches of yellow and blue, and does not vary with age or between sexes. Scarlet macaws mate for life, which is one reason they are in danger of extinction. Another is their black-market value – up to US$500 per bird. Less than 30 were thought to have survived in Belize. But in 1997 a whole flock was shot down over a settlement near the remote village of Red Bank in Toledo! So, while there may be more than once was thought, they are still in great danger.

You are more likely to see the macaw's relatives: Belize's seven varieties of **parrots** (white-fronted, red-lored, blue-crowned, yellow-

The Toucan: National Bird of Belize

The **keel-billed toucan** *(Ramphastos sulfuratus,* "bill bird"), the largest in Central America, is the national bird. It is most commonly seen on conservation posters but may be seen in the forest with a bit of effort.

One of the forest's largest fruit eaters, its trademarks are its piercing call and colorful, six-colored bill and body. Thought to frighten off enemies, its bill has the feel of laminated balsa wood with the serrated edges of a stainless steel paring knife. With a partially lemon-yellow face and chest, its eyes are ringed by greenish skin; the area below its tail is cadmium red, and its legs and feet are iridescent blue! Generally feeding on the fruit of large trees, it rips off a chunk with its beak, flips it into the air, and catches it in its bill. The two other species found in Belize are the **collared aracari** and the **emerald toucanet**.

lored, yellow-headed, brown-hooded, and white crowned), as well as the Aztec parakeet.

THE GREAT CURASSOW: An unforgettable resident of the forest, the 36-inch **great curassow** (*pavón grande, granadera*) can be seen on the forest floor. As large as hen turkeys, but more elegant, the curassows dress by sex: the males sport a black suit with a green glossy bib and white lower markings, plus a caruncle – a large, bright-yellow knob over their beaks. Females can be either brown or reddish brown, but the head and neck are striated black and white. They lack the male's caruncle. Dining off the forest floor, the couple builds a nest about 30 feet up in a tree. This bird spends its days scratching the ground in search of fallen fruit and small animals. If frightened, it generally runs away, emitting high-pitched yips like a small dog.

STORKS: The Americas' largest flying bird, the **Jabiru stork** (*Jabiru mycteria, fillymingo, turk, el rey de ellos*) stands up to five feet high and has a wingspan extending from nine to 12 feet. It is characterized by its all-white plumage, a black head, large and slightly upturned black bill, and a neck bordered at its base by a bright red band. Feeding in wetlands, solitary pairs arrive in Jan. and build their nesting platforms – some up to 10 feet across! The young are brownish-grey in color. Bordering on extinction, they are generally sighted around swamps and ponds where they feed on reptiles, fish, snails, frogs, and small mammals. They may be seen in Crooked Tree and occasionally near Hopkins.

Sometimes called "John Crow Culu" by Belizeans, the **wood stork** (*Mycteria americana, ciguená Americana*) may be seen in coastal swamps and lagoons. Although white, it differs from other waders in that it has a greyish-black head and neck as well as a distinctive downturned bill. Sadly, it is a favored menu item on Belizean BBQ menus and is losing habitat.

OTHERS: There are at least 21 varieties of hummingbirds, five types of swifts, and nine types of swallows. Of the 49 types of flycatchers, one of the most spectacular is the vermilion flycatcher. Other indigenous species of note include the Muscovy duck, an assortment of woodpeckers, the rufous-necked woodrail, the turkey vulture and its relatives, the red-caped manakin, the green kingfisher, the boat-billed heron, the bananaquit, the groove-billed ani ("cowboy"), the five species of tinamou, the homely brown jay, the chestnut-collared swift, the rufous-tailed jacamar, the ruddy quail dove, the laughing falcon, the mangrove swallow, the ochre-bellied flycatcher, the white-fronted nunbird, the tropical screech owl, the spotted barbtail, the great-tailed grackle, western and spotted sandpipers, the variable seedeater, ruddy-tailed and common-tody flycatchers, the barred antshrike, the tropical kingbird, the wrenthrush, and the rufous-colored sparrow.

Insects

Insect life is both varied and abundant. Lest you be tempted to view insects as uninteresting, remember that they have been around for at least 400 million years, while butterflies are believed to have evolved around 200 million years ago during the Triassic. Whether it suits you or not, insects will definitely play a part in your visit to Belize.

BUTTERFLIES: All told there are some 700 species found in Belize. The nation's most beautiful butterfly, the **morpho** is common in forests from sea level on up. It has almost completely iridescent blue upper wings. The three species of **owl butterflies** have two glaring eyes on the underside of their wings. These may serve as mimicry to suggest a vertebrate or large, distasteful tree frog, or as target spots for predators, which allow the butterfly to escape relatively unscathed. Other species of note include the heliconids, many beautiful skippers, several swallowtails, and the sulfur butterfly. Butterfly lovers should be certain to visit the butterfly farm at Shipstern near Sarteneja, the small one at Chaa Creek Cottages near San Ignacio, as well as the one at Fallen Stones Butterfly Ranch in the Toledo District.

lifestyle: As they have no jaws, butterflies must take all nutrients in liquid form. They feed on water with mineral salts found in the earth, juice from decaying fruit, juices from carrion, honeydew secretions from aphids, and other such delicacies. While you may find them warming up in the sun or drinking water at mud banks, they rest on the undersides of leaves to protect themselves during rainstorms.

MEMORABLE VIEWING: The pencil-thin **helicopter damselfly** (gallito azul) beats each of its four wings independently, resembling a slow-motion windmill. Its wing movement renders it invisible to spiders, upon whom it launches a

single attack burst, snipping and capturing the succulent abdomen as the rest falls.

The **ant lion** (hormiga león) is actually the larval form of a beautiful fly similar to a damselfly. It spends its childhood digging a pit, heaping up loosened particles on its head and tossing them clear. Then, burying itself (only the jaws project), it awaits its prey. Any captured game has its contents sucked out and the empty skin is tossed from the pit. After having stored up enough food to support its next incarnation, the ant lion enters a cocoon, to re-emerge as a sexually mature adult.

A pretty good handful, the male **rhinoceros beetle** (cornizuelo) sports a long upward-curved horn, but the females are hornless; they are endangered by habitat destruction. The **frangipani sphinx** (oruga, falso coral) appears to mimic the coral snake, both with its bright yellow coloring and red orange head and in the way it thrashes back and forth when touched like the coral. It also bites viciously!

With a color that harmonizes perfectly with the large branches and logs on which they rest, the **machaca** (peanut-head fulgaria, lantern fly) is one of Latin America's best-known insects. Its enormous hind-wing eye spots and lizard-shaped head are probably designed to confuse predators. If pestered it will release a fetid skunk-like spray or drum its head against a tree trunk. A popular Latin American folk saying maintains that if a young girl is stung by a machaca, she must have sex with her boyfriend within 24 hours or die. Other intriguing bugs include the tarantula and the paper wasp, the local version of the praying mantis.

ANTS: One resident of the rainforest you'll undoubtedly encounter is the ant. If you sit down, you may well have some unpleasant bites to contend with. Shake a bush and ants will scurry out. In many tracts, they may outweigh all of the vertebrates present. Species range from the acacia and cecropia ants to the memorable leafcutter ants (see *The Wee Wee Ants*, below).

Joined in a symbiotic relationship with the acacia tree, the **acacia ant** *(hormiga de cornizuelo)* wards off herbivores while the tree supplies the ants with nectar, protein and protection in return. The ants produce an alarm pheromone that can be smelled for some six ft. downwind. You can easily recognize these trees by their hollow swollen horns, resembling those of cattle.

Another example of mutualism is found between the *Azteca* or **cecropia ants** and their namesake. The cecropia tree attracts the ants, which it provides with specialized food: budlike leaf tips that the ants harvest and use to nourish their larvae. These are raised inside the tree's hollowed-out thorns. In return, the ants defend the tree. Their tough jaws, which secrete caustic chemicals, can bite an unwary intruder.

Semi-nomadic **army ants** may travel in packs of up to 20 million members, sweeping in a continually foraging 20-foot-wide front. They bring back bits of twigs, lichen, leaves and other insects to feed their queen; their detritus nourishes the roots of nearby plants. Their colonies regularly pass from stationary to nomadic phases every couple of weeks. A number of species – from birds to flies to millipedes – use the presence of army ants to help them find food.

TERMITES: Resembling gigantic wasps nests and found on trees, dark brown or black termite nests are a frequent feature of the forested landscape. Made of "carton," wood chewed up by workers and cemented with fecal "glue," the nest has a single reproductive king and queen commanding hordes of up to 100,000 attending workers and soldiers. Termites digest raw cellulose, a substance low in nutritional value, with the aid of protozoan symbiots dwelling in their guts. The **assassin bug** *(reduvio)* camouflages itself with bits and pieces of termite nest and preys at the entrance. In death as in life, termites contribute to the rainforest ecosystem. Their defecated roughage is a feast for fungi, which also feed on their carcasses.

LOATHED BY HUMANS: Small gnats that favor the tender skin of the ears and neck, **no-see-ums** *(purrujas,* biting midges, sand fleas, sand flies) are almost invisible and are most active on warm days and windless evenings. Only the females bite humans. Their bites also last for days; sulfur powder will discourage them. They can be a problem out on the keys and on the coast. A breeze will keep them away, and they live and procreate only in mangrove swamp areas; they aren't found on sand-and-palm cayes.

In the forest, you'll also find an abundance of **ticks** *(garrapatas).* With 20 body segments, the forest-floor **millipede** *(milpies)* is readily identifiable both by its movements and its dull whitish-yellow color. Its ability to curl up in a spiral and violently expel a solution of hydrogen cyanide and benzaldehyde as far as 12 inches discourages predators. A relative, the **scorpion** *(alacrán, escorpión)* stings only in self-defense; scorpions are active at night, when they prey on insects and spiders.

flies: Biting flies can be a problem in season, and the most loathsome insect of all is the **botfly** *(Dermatobia hominis)*, whose larvae (known locally as "beefworms") mature inside flesh. An egg-laden female botfly captures a night-flying female mosquito and glues her eggs on to the mosquito before releasing it. When the mosquito bites, the host's body heat triggers an egg to hatch, fall off, and burrow in. Secreting an antibiotic into its burrow to stave off competing bacteria and fungi, the larva secures itself with two anal hooks; its spiracle pokes out of the tiny hole, and a small mound forms that will grow to the size of a goose egg before the mature larva falls out. Should you be unfortunate enough to fall prey to a larva – an extremely unlikely occurrence for the average visitor – you have three cures available. One is to use the acrid white sap of the *matatorsalo* (bot killer), which kills the larva but leaves the corpse intact. Another is to apply a piece of soft, raw meat to the top of the airhole. As the maggot must breathe, it burrows upward into the meat. At the Massachusetts General Hospital, physicians apply slices of raw, fatty bacon. A third cure is to apply a generous helping

The Wee Wee Ants (Leafcutters)

Commonly seen marching along a forest trail holding aloft pieces of leaves and flowers, **wee wee ants** (leaf cutting ants, farmer ants, *zompopas*) cut leaves into shreds and carry them off to their nests, where they then clear the leaves of unwanted fungal spores, chew the plant material, and mix it with a combination of saliva and excrement to cultivate a spongy, bread-like fungus *(Rhozites gongylophora)* on which they dine. This particular species of fungus no longer produces sexual spores and relies solely upon the ants for propagation.

Ranking among the largest and most complex societies in the world, each colony may have a million members, and each member has a role to play. The smallest tend to eggs and larvae, larger ones forage, and the still larger soldiers defend the nest. Watch them as they meet, stroke antennae, and exchange chemical cues. If you draw a thick line across their formation, they'll lose their scented track and become momentarily bewildered until the line is re-established. Thumping around the base of a nest with a machete will draw them out.

A young queen, fertilized by males during swarming, begins a new colony by digging a tunnel and creating a royal chamber. Spitting out fungus from her own colony, she fertilizes it with fecal material. Laying eggs, she feeds the larvae on malformed eggs while fasting. In 40-60 days, the new workers emerge and begin work. All told, there are more than 200 species of leaf cutting ants.

of Elmer's glue or cement to the hole; cover this with a circular patch of adhesive tape; seal this tape with a final application of glue. Squeeze out the dead larva the next morning. The only other alternative is to leave it to grow to maturity, giving you an opportunity to experience the transmogrification of part of yourself into another creature. It only hurts when the maggot squirms and if you swim, presumably because you are cutting off its air supply. Whatever you do, don't try to pull it out because it will burst. Part of its body will remain inside and will infect the area.

Nearly invisible, **chiggers** (coloradillas) thrive in locations ranging from lowland cattle pastures to rainforests. Chiggers insert the tip of their well-developed mouthparts into your skin, and love to squeeze into protected places such as bra and belt lines and the genital area, where they bite and gleefully deposit a histamine that makes the surrounding area itch like hell for up to 10 days! Fortunately, they are common only in the far north.

A biting fly, the hardy but hunch-backed black or **botlass fly**, is small and incredibly annoying! It silently zooms in on you and will feast on your hands and whatever else it can land on. Another annoying fly is the **doctor fly**, which is known for its itchy histamic injections. The injected area will swell up, especially if you are allergic. These flies are rife in the south and proliferate when the mango trees fruit in April and May. They are perhaps the nation's most noxious insect.

other nuisances: The mosquito (zancudo) needs no introduction, nor does the giant cockroach (cucaracha). Finally, although they should not be a problem for visitors, Africanized "killer" bees are proving a menace; since their arrival in 1983, they have attacked more than 500 people, resulting in nine deaths.

Sealife

ECHINODERMATA: Combining the Greek words for *echinos* (hedgehog) and *derma* (skin), this large division of the animal kingdom includes sea urchins, sea cucumbers, and starfish. All share the ability to propel themselves with the help of tube "feet" or spines. Known by the scientific name *Astrospecten*, **starfish** (estrella de mar) are five-footed carnivorous inhabitants that use their modified "tube-feet" to burrow into the sea. Sluggish **sea cucumbers** ingest large quantities of sand, extract the organic matter, and excrete the rest. Crustaceans and fish reside in the larger specimens.

Avoid trampling on that armed knight of the underwater sand dunes, the **sea urchin**. Consisting of a semi-circular calcareous (calcium carbonate) shell, the sea urchin is protected by its brown, jointed barbs. It uses its mouth, situated and protected on its underside, to graze by scraping algae from rocks. Surprisingly to those uninitiated in its lore, sea urchins are considered a gastronomic delicacy in many countries. The ancient Greeks believed they held aphrodisiac and other properties beneficial to health. They are prized by the French and fetch four times the price of oysters in Paris. The Spanish consume them raw, boiled, in *gratinés*, or in soups. In Barbados they are termed "sea eggs," and the Japanese eat their guts raw as sushi. Although a disease in recent years has devastated the sea urchin population, they are making a comeback.

contact: If a sea urchin spine breaks off inside your finger or toe, don't try to remove it: it's impossible! You might try the cure people use in New Guinea. Use a blunt object to mash up the spine inside your skin so that it will be absorbed naturally. Then dip your finger in urine; the ammonia helps to trigger the process of disintegration. It's better to apply triple-antibiotic salve. Avoiding contact is best of all. Sea urchins hide underneath corals, and wounds are often contracted when you lose your footing and scrape against one.

SPONGES: Found in the ocean depths, reddish or brown sponges are among the simplest forms of multicellular life and have been around for more than a half-billion years. They pump large amounts of water between their internal filters and extract plankton. There are numerous sizes, shapes, and colors, but they all can be recognized by their large, distinctive excurrent openings. Unlike other animals, they exhibit no reaction when disturbed.

CNIDARIANS: The members of this phylum – hydroids, anemones, corals, and jellyfish – are distinguished by their simple structure: a cup-shaped body terminating in a combination mouth-anus, which, in turn, is encircled by tentacles. While hydroids and corals (covered later in this section) are colonial, jellyfish and anemones are individual. This phylum's name comes from another identifying characteristic: nematocysts, stinging capsules primarily used for defense and capturing prey.

Growing in skeletal colonies resembling ferns or feathers, **hydroids** ("water form" in Greek) spend their youth as solitary medusas before settling down in old age. Some will sting, and the most famous hydroid is undoubtedly the floating Portuguese man-of-war; its stinging tentacles can be extended or retracted; worldwide, there have been reports of trailing tentacles reaching 50 feet! It belongs to the family of *siphonophores*, free-floating hydroid colonies that control their depth by means of a gas-filled float.

The true **jellyfish** are identifiable by their domes, which vary in shape. Nematocysts reside in both the feeding tube and in their tentacles. Also known as sea wasps, **box jellies** can be identified by their cuboidal dome, from each corner of which a single tentacle extends. Many of them can sting painfully; keep well away. If you should get stung by any of the above, get out of the water and peel off any tentacles. Avoid rubbing the injured area. Wash it with alcohol and apply meat tenderizer for five to 10 minutes. The jellyfish season is Aug. to Oct. **Sea anemones,** polyps that lack a skeleton and use their tentacles to stun prey and force them to their mouth, are solitary bottom-dwellers. They often protect shrimp and crabs who, immune to their sting, reside right by them. Their tentacles may retract for protection when disturbed. One type of anemone lives in tubes buried in the murky muck or sand. Their tentacles only come out to play at night.

CRUSTACEANS: A class of arthropods – the largest phylum, with more than two million species – crustaceans are distinguished by their jointed legs and complex skeleton. The decapods (named after their five pairs of legs) are the largest order of crustaceans. These include shrimp, crabs, and lobster. The **ghost crab** *(Ocypode)* abounds on the beaches, tunneling down beneath the sand and emerging to feed at night. Although it can survive for 48 hrs. without contacting water, it must return to the sea to moisten its gill chambers as well as to lay its eggs, which hatch into planktonic larvae. The **hermit crab** carries a discarded mollusc shell in order to protect its vulnerable abdomen. As it grows, it must find a larger home, and you may see two struggling over the same shell.

OTHER UNDERWATER HAZARDS AND CURES: Not a true coral, **fire coral** mimics its appearance; it may appear in many forms and has the ability to encrust nearly anything and take its host's form. Generally colored mustard yellow to brown, it often has white finger-like tips. Its bite is quite painful. As with coral wounds, you should wash the affected area with soap and fresh water and apply a triple-antibiotic salve.

Found on rocky or coral bottoms, **spotted scorpionfish** are well camouflaged so it's easy to step on them. Although the Caribbean species is non-lethal, their bite can be quite painful.

Another cleverly camouflaged denizen of the deep, the **stingray** will whip its tail if stepped on – driving the serrated venomous spine into the offender. If this happens, see a doctor. Fuzzy creatures with painful-when-touched defense mechanisms, **bristle worms** have glass-like bristles that may break off in the skin and be very painful. Apply tape to the skin and attempt to pull the bristles out; reduce the pain with rubbing alcohol. With a tendency to bite at things thrust at them, **moray eels** have a tight grip and can be difficult to dislodge. Once again, preventing bites is best. Always exercise caution before reaching into a crevice!

The Coral Reef Ecosystem

One of the least appreciated of the world's wonders is the coral reef. This is in part because little has been known about it until recent decades. One of the greatest opportunities the tropics offer is to explore this wondrous environment, one which in many ways goes beyond the limits of any wild fantasy conjured up in a science fiction novel. It is a delicate environment – the only geological feature fashioned by living creatures. Reefs throughout the world – which took millions of years to form – have already suffered adverse effects from human beings.

Corals produce the calcium carbonate (limestone) responsible for the buildup of most offlying cays and islets as well as most of the sand on the beaches. Bearing the brunt of waves, they also conserve the shoreline. Although reefs began forming millenia ago, they are in a constant state of flux. Seemingly solid, they actually depend upon a delicate ecological balance to survive. Deforestation, dredging, temperature change, an increase or decrease in salinity, silt, or sewage discharge may kill them. Because temperature ranges must remain between 68° and 95°F, they are only found in the tropics and – because they require light to grow – only in shallow water. They are also intolerant of fresh water, so reefs can not survive where rivers empty into the sea.

THE CORAL POLYP: While corals are actually animals, botanists view them as being mostly plant, and geologists dub them "honorary" rocks. Acting more like plants than animals, corals survive through photosynthesis: the algae inside the coral polyps do the work while the polyps themselves secrete calcium carbonate and stick together for protection from waves and boring sponges.

Bearing a close structural resemblance to its relative the anemone, a polyp feeds at night by using the ring or rings of tentacles surrounding its mouth to capture prey (such as plankton) with nematocysts, small stinging darts. The coral polyps appear able to survive in such packed surroundings through their symbiotic relationship with the algae present in their tissues: Coral polyps exhale carbon dioxide and the algae consume it, producing needed oxygen. Although only half of the world's coral species possess such a symbiotic relationship with these single-celled captive species of dinoflagellates *(Gymnodinium microdriaticum)*, these species – termed hermatypic corals – are the ones that build the reef. The nutritional benefits gained from their relationship with the algae enable them to grow a larger skeleton and to do so more rapidly than would otherwise be possible. Polyps have the ability to regulate the density of these cells in their tissues and can expel some of them in a spew of

mucus should they multiply too quickly. Looking at coral, the brownish colored algal cells show through transparent tissues. When you see a coral garden through your mask, you are actually viewing a field of captive single-celled algae.

An added and vital but invisible component of the reef ecosystem is bacteria, micro-organisms that decompose and recycle all matter on which everything from worms to coral polyps feed. Inhabitants of the reef range from crabs to barnacles, sea squirts to multicolored tropical fish. Remarkably, the polyps themselves are consumed by only a small percentage of the reef's inhabitants. They often contain high levels of toxic substances and are also thought to sting fish and other animals that attempt to consume them. Corals also retract their polyps during daylight hours when the fish can see them. Reefs originate as the polyps develop – the calcium secretions form a base as they grow. One polyp can have a 1,000-year lifespan.

CORAL TYPES: Corals may be divided into three groups. The hard or **stony corals** (such as staghorn, brain, star, or rose) secrete a limey skeleton.

The **horny corals** (for example, sea plumes, sea whips, sea fans, and gorgonians) have a supporting skeleton-like structure known as a gorgonian (after the head of Medusa). The shapes of these corals result from the fashion in which the polyps and their connecting tissues excrete calcium carbonate; there are over a thousand different patterns – one specific to each species. Each also has its own method of budding. Found in the Caribbean, giant elk-horn corals may contain over a million polyps and live for several hundred years or longer.

The last category consists of the **soft corals**. While these too are colonies of polyps, their skeletons are composed of soft organic material, and their polyps always have eight tentacles instead of the six or multiples of six found in the stony corals. Unlike the hard corals, soft corals disintegrate after death and do not add to the reef's stony structure. Instead of depositing limestone crystals, they excrete a jelly-like matrix that is imbued with spicules (diminutive spikes) of stony material; this substance gives these corals their flexibility. Sea fans and sea whips exhibit similar patterns.

There are also false corals. One such type is the precious **black coral**. Prized by jewelers because its branches may be cleaned and polished to high gloss ebony-black, it resembles bushes of fine grey-black twigs. (Do not buy this jewelry because—although licensed in Belize—it contributes to reef destruction).

COMPETITION: To the snorkeler, the reef appears to be a peaceful haven. The reality is that, because the reef is a comparatively benign environment, the fiercest competition has developed here. Although the corals appear static to the onlooker, they are continually competing with each other for space. Some have developed sweeper tentacles that have an especially high concentration of stinging cells. Reaching out to a competing coral, they stick and execute it. Other species dispatch digestive filaments that eat the prey.

Soft corals appear to leach out toxic chemicals called terpenes to kill nearby organisms. Because predation is such a problem, two-thirds of reef species are toxic. Others hide in stony outcrops or have formed protective relationships with other organisms. The classic case is the banded clown fish. They live among sea anemones, whose stingers protect them. Cleaner fish protect themselves from larger fish by setting up stations at which they pick parasites off their carnivorous customers. Mimicking the coloration and shape of the feeder fish, the sabre-toothed blenny is a false cleaner fish that takes a chunk out of the larger fish and runs off!

CORAL LOVE AFFAIRS: Not prone to celibacy or sexual prudery, coral polyps reproduce sexually and asexually through budding, and a polyp joins together with thousands and even millions of its neighbors to form a coral. (In a few cases, only one polyp forms a single coral.) During sexual reproduction polyps release millions of their spermatozoa into the water. Many species are dimorphic – with both male and female coral. Some species have internal, others external fertilization. Still others have both male and female polyps. As larvae develop, their "mother" expels them and they float off to found a new coral colony.

EXPLORING REEFS: Coral reefs are extremely fragile environments. Much damage has been done to reefs worldwide through the carelessness of humans. Despite their size, reefs grow very slowly, and it can take decades or even hundreds of years to repair the effects of a few moments. Do nothing to provoke moray eels, which may retaliate when threatened. Watch out for fire corals – recognizable by the white tips on their branches – which can inflict stings. In general, "look but don't touch" is the maxim to follow.

UNDERWATER FLORA: Most of the plants you see underwater are algae, primitive plants that can survive only underwater because they do not have the mechanisms to keep from drying out. Lacking roots, algae draw their minerals and water directly from the sea. Calcareous red algae, are very im-

portant for reef formation. Resembling rounded stones, they are 95% rock and only 5% living tissue. Plants returned to live in the sea, sea grasses are found in relatively shallow water in sandy and muddy bays and flats; they have roots and small flowers. One species, dubbed "turtle grass," provides feed for turtles. In addition, sea grasses help to stabilize the sea floor, maintain water clarity by trapping fine sediments from upland soil erosion, stave off beach erosion, and provide living space for numerous fish, crustaceans, and shellfish.

The Belize Barrier Reef

The Belize Barrier Reef is the hemisphere's second largest coral reef. Unique in the Western Hemisphere, it is only one of two found in the entire Caribbean. (The other extends six mi. N of Providencia Island.) Stretching for 180 mi., Belize's barrier reef is both the longest and largest in the Western Hemisphere. It forms a nearly continuous bulwark from the Sapodilla Cayes in the Bay of Honduras up to the Isla Mujeres inside the Mexican border. It nearly merges with Ambergris Caye at Rocky Point but then veers off and parallels the Mexican coast to near Tulum where it fragments and finally terminates near Cozumel Island.

Its individual segments are called **ribbon reefs**. Much of its topography is spur and groove – coral ridges interspersed with deep trenches culminating in flat sand bottoms. The spur walls often have tunnels and overhangs. The diverse environments of this topography allow a diversity of marine life to coexist in relative proximity. In addition to some 230 fish species, there are also stingrays, eels, and innumerable other creatures.

The Belize barrier reef system is one of five new sites the United Nations has added to its list of natural places of "outstanding universal value." In 1997, neighboring giant Mexico suggested renaming the reef "The Great Maya Reef," a move that aroused Belizean nationalist ire.

The barrier reef is complemented by two different types of reefs:

Fringing reefs host relatively few coral species, mainly those that can tolerate turgid water and varying salinity. They are found only between Placencia and Punta Ycacos.

Patch reefs are found in the central lagoons of atolls and faroes as well as on the Barrier Platform. Scarce in the Northern Shelf Lagoon, they proliferate in the Southern Shelf Lagoon, in particular to the S of Dangriga where, along with faroes, they are one of the two principal reef types.

History

When one visits modern Belize, it is difficult to imagine that it formed part of the Maya Empire for centuries longer than it has been colonized. While the Maya of today's Belize are not their direct descendants – having immigrated from Mexico and Guatemala – they still share some characteristics, such as tending their *milpas* in the traditional style.

In contrast with other indigenous groups, which have scattered over Mexico and Central America, the Maya remain centered in Belize, the western parts of Guatemala and Honduras, and in Mexico's Yucatán and the states of Chiapas and Tabasco – an area that also encompasses all of their civilization's ruins.

Of the three main areas of Maya civilization, Belize, Guatemala, and parts of Honduras enclose the area where the great ceremonial centers flourished. Their ruins have been covered by dense jungle since around 850 AD and it's amazing that, using only stone axes and wheel-less technology, they were able to tame the flourishing foliage and raise their remarkable cities.

After the Maya came under the influence of Teotihuacán, a city-state in central Mexico from about 400 AD, indigenous Maya architecture bloomed only in the lowlands. Around 800 AD, just as the culture – with the development of pottery figurines, jade carvings, and invention of the Maya calendar – was at its peak, things began to fall apart for unknown reasons. Note: For more information about the Maya and their world read the "Mundo Maya" appendix.

COLUMBUS AND COMPANY: On his fourth voyage in 1502 Columbus "discovered" the Bay of Honduras, a name derived from *Hondo*, the Spanish word for deep. A few years later Pinzón and Desolís reached the Gulf of Honduras. Sailing west to the Río Dulce, they then proceeded north along the Belize coast. Some other explorers followed suit, but interest in the area waned after the mid-16th century. A few missionaries ventured in thereafter. One of them had his clothes stolen by a band of Englishmen in 1677, the first recorded mention of an English presence.

ENTER THE ENGLISH: As there are few written records, much of Belize's early years remain shrouded in mystery. The first recorded settlement was by the Providence Company, a settlement that landed in May 1631, and was terminated after the Spanish attacked in May 1641, capturing 400 of the colonists and sending the remainder fleeing elsewhere. Most of the legends about the early years mention one Peter Wallis or Willis, a Scottish buccaneer. Although there is no way to corroborate that Wallace ever so much as set foot in Belize, some accounts maintain that Belize derives from a corruption of his name. Other explanations are that the name derives from one of three Mayan words: either *belakin* (land towards the sea), *balitza* (land of the Itzá), or *beliz* (muddy waters). The third term appears to be the most appropriate and, thus, the likeliest explanation.

ENTER THE LOGCUTTERS: The timber industry began in the Yucatán during the second half of the 17th C. Up until that time the

Spanish had monopolized the logwood trade in the Gulf of Campeche. Used in making dye manufacture, it was vital for dying woolen goods in the colors of grey, black, purple, and dark red. As the English buccaneers encountered more and more resistance on the sea, they learned about the value of logwood and began harvesting timber in the Yucatán, eking out a meager existence while fending off sand flies and mosquitoes. At first the English presence didn't bother the Spanish, but they had begun to attack by the 1680s. The first mention of Belize in print was in the accounts of a John Fingas in 1705, who described the area as "the river of Bullys where the English for the most part now load their logwood."

On four occasions (in 1717, 1730, 1754, and 1779) Spanish attacks on the settlers forced loggers to leave, but they always returned. Concluded at the end of the Seven Years War in 1763, the Treaty of Paris gave the British the right to cut logwood but legitimized the Spanish claim to the territory. The Versailles Treaty (1783) and the Convention of London (1786) reinforced the rights of the "Baymen" while giving control of the area to Spain. The last attempt by the Spanish to expel the English took place off of St. George's Cay in 1798. While the Spaniards were forced out of Central America in the 1820s, the British failed to declare Belize a colony until 1862. The time gap spurred Guatemala to make claims on the territory, a conflict that has endured right up to the present. Because they could not control the indigenous Maya for labor and because they regarded their slash-and-burn techniques as a threat to the timber reserve, the British forced out the indigenous Maya and brought in slaves as supplemental labor.

SLAVERY: Although slaves were used in Belize for harvesting timber rather than for producing plantation crops as elsewhere in the Americas, they were equally ill treated. The first mention of slavery in Belize comes in a Spanish missionary's 1724 account of a visit. A century later, some 1,500 Africans formed the body of a 2,300-person slave population. They had grown to a majority of the population by mid-18th century, and by the early 1800s they comprised approximately 75% of the population, with the rest consisting of whites (10%) and "free people of colour" (14%). Shortly prior to emancipation in 1838, the number of slaves had diminished to half the population, with the remainder being white (10%), along with freed blacks and mulattoes.

Despite their minority status, the whites continually dominated both the economy and government. While logwood grew in clumps near the coast and could be cut with minimal labor, the growth of demand for mahogany necessitated more finances, land, and slaves. After 1770 approximately 80% of all slaves age 10 and over were woodcutters. The huntsmen found the trees, the axemen cut them, and cattlemen cared for the beasts of burden that pulled the logs to the river. Rafts brought the logs downriver. Other slaves served as domestic servants and in occupations such as blacksmiths, nurses, sailors, and bakers. Conditions were horrid and many revolted, committed suicide, or escaped to establish maroon colonies within Belize. Re-volts took place in 1765, 1768, 1773, and in 1820.

Free blacks and colored could not hold military commissions nor could they become jurors or magistrates. In order for them to vote in elections, they would have to own more property, and have lived in the area longer, than whites. In an effort to distinguish themselves from the slave population, the free colored shamelessly embraced the status quo, affirming their European-ness and their loyalty. During an era when their peers in other West Indian outposts were being granted equal rights, the Colonial Office threatened to shut down the Public Meeting, the Baymen's legislative assembly, unless it kept in line. The "colored Subjects of Free Condition" were granted civil rights only on July 5, 1831. Slavery was abolished in 1833, but the Abolition Act required slaves to labor on for five years in a system of "apprenticeship" for free, and it compensated slave owners for their losses.

At the time of legal emancipation in 1838, Belize had become a stratified, hierarchical society with gross institutionalized inequalities. The Crown had freely distributed land in the past to the white owners, but no lands were granted African-Americans after emancipation for fear that they might no longer be willing to labor for cheap wages.

THE SETTLER OLIGARCHY: At the end of the 18th century there was no official Crown control of the colony, but the "principal inhabitants" had passed the location laws in 1787, a series of resolutions granting themselves land to be classified as freehold private property. The economic shift during this era from logwood to mahogany also resulted in the concentration of land and power in the hands of an elite few. In the same year that the location laws were instituted, 12 individuals held 85% of the approximately 2,300 sq. miles made available under the 1786 treaty. In 1790 the 20 largest estates owned about half of the total slave population, and the ruling elite determined the price of logwood and mahogany, taxation rates, and the import trade – of great importance, as locals were forbidden from cultivating provisions locally. Their economic monopoly allowed them to dominate both the Public Meeting and the Magistracy. Political power was used to keep both other settlers and ex-slaves under their control.

Belize came to have the same boom-bust price cycles common to other plantation economies but with an added twist: the boom of 1835-47 led to a severe depression because all of the easily accessible trees had been cut, including young growth. Costs rose as loggers had to move farther into the interior, and mahogany exports plummeted from 14 million feet in 1846 to 5.5 million feet in 1859 down to 2.75 million feet in 1870 – a low for the century. Registered in 1859, the British Honduras Company became the colony's leading landowner, changing its name to Belize Estate and Produce Company in 1875. Based in Belize City, it owned roughly half of Belize's land and has remained a driving force in the economy ever since. Its supremacy eclipsed that of the settler elite and by 1881 the white settlers, predominantly male, had dropped to 1%.

All of this came in the face of increasing governmental control over the country. Although Belize was not yet officially a colony, the superintendent took over the appointment of magistrates in 1832. During this period the territory's status, ignored in official accords and treaties, remained vague. After the British were pressed by the US government to abandon the area, a formal constitution was introduced, along with a figurehead legislative assembly, while the colonial office pulled the strings. In 1862, British Honduras was formally declared a colony, and the legislature was replaced by an appointed Legislative Council in 1871. Meanwhile, Maya – fleeing to the area during the War of the Races period – had mounted rebellions against the British. The Maya were defeated in a battle at Orange Walk in 1872, and they were subsequently herded into reservations. The 1900s heralded a change of perception among black Belizeans. The Ex-Servicemen's Riots in 1919, with veterans protesting the society's racism, marked the beginning of a growing political consciousness.

THE GREAT DEPRESSION: In the early 1930s, the contracts for chicle collection and for mahogany dwindled, causing massive unemployment. The hurricane of 1931 demolished Belize City, but the British response was late and inadequate. By 1933, the total value of imports and exports had dropped to a quarter of the 1929 level. In what proved to be the initiation of a broad social movement, a group calling itself the Unemployment Brigade marched through Belize City on Feb. 14, 1934 and presented its demands to the government. Others among the poor

turned to the Governor who, in his beneficence, responded by offering work breaking stones at 10¢ per day and ordering a ration of poorly cooked rice served at the prison gates daily.

Those demanding the dispensation of cash found a new leader in barber Antonio Soberanís Gomez (1897-1975). Putting the Unemployment Brigade's leaders in their place at a meeting on Mar. 16, 1934, Soberanís took over the movement. Biweekly meetings of his Laborers and Unemployed Association (LUA) attacked the establishment. All of this led to a riot in Belize City and a strike in Stann Creek by the year's end. After Soberanís was jailed under a new sedition act in Nov. 1935, factional infighting weakened the movement, and its power had diminished by the time of his release in Feb. 1936. The demonstrations had pressed the Governor to create relief work – over 200 miles of road were built – and to urge the institution of a semi-representative system of government.

The April 1935 constitution, while bringing back elections, included restrictions ensuring that working class Belizeans could not qualify. LUA and the Citizens' Political Party endorsed black lawyer Arthur Balderamos and Creole chicle millionaire R. S. Turton, who led the opposition to the big business interests in the newly elected 1936 council.

THE 1940s-50s: The culmination of years of agitation, major labor reforms were passed during the 1940s as the newly-legalized labor unions grew in power. In 1947, George Cadle Price won election to the Belize City Council. Educated by Jesuits in the US, Price had served as Turton's personal secretary. Coming from a middle class background, Price widened his political base by appealing to both the labor and nationalist political factions. Price triumphed in the 1947 election, running on a platform opposing immigration and import controls, and rode into office on the massive sentiment generated against the proposed inclusion of British Honduras in the West Indian Federation. The devaluation of the British Honduras dollar on the last day of 1949 – coming after repeated denials by the British that they would devalue – sparked the organization of the People's United Party, which coalesced its internal structure in 1950-54.

The new party's success was largely due to the support extended by the General Worker's Union (GWU), whose organization formed the core of the new party. The imprisonment of two of the party's chief members (charged with sedition after they had refused to hang a portrait of the King) and the resignation of another left George Cadle Price in the saddle, and he comfortably secured a victory in the 1952 Belize City Council elections.

Universal suffrage was achieved only in 1954 when the constitution created a Legislative Assembly with nine elected members, three appointed members, and three unofficial appointed members. For nearly a year and a half prior to the election, the government had supported the National Party (NP), an openly fanatical Anglophilic party backed by the Anglicans and Methodists as well as the upper classes. It charged the PUP with being pro-Guatemala, racist, practicing religious prejudice (i.e., being pro-Catholic), and with being communist. On election day a vote for the PUP had become a mandate for self-government and, with 12,274 people or nearly 70% of the electorate voting, the PUP secured 66.3% of the vote and eight of nine elective seats in the new Legislative Assembly. It continued to triumph in elections right through 1984. During these years it was a populist party, one whose strategies and policies were determined by an elite at the top rather than by the membership. In succeeding years, the party was plagued by factionalism and a tendency for the aging leadership to become increasingly removed from its constituency. Issues were often obscured by political deification and mudslinging.

After the GWU split off from the PUP in 1956, it created the National Independence Party (NIP); the PUP created the Christian Democratic Union, a new trade union. However, Price and the PUP triumphed in the 1957 elections, securing all nine elected seats. But later events served to shake the PUP. After Price met with the Guatemalan minister for discussions during constitutional talks in London at the end of that year, the British secretary of state denounced Price and broke off talks. Price was removed from the Executive Council because his actions were allegedly in conflict with his oath of loyalty to the Crown. Accusing Price in a radio broadcast of attempting to sell the colony to Guatemala, the governor brought in a British frigate from Jamaica. Price's partner Nicholas Pollard defected and formed the Christian Democratic Party (CDP); the two other opposition parties united under the

National Independence Party (NIP). However, the colonial administration's tactics backfired: the PUP won 29 of 33 seats up for grabs in seven districts in Nov. 1958, and Price became mayor of Belize.

The PUP continued its sweep through the next three consecutive national elections, winning all 18 seats in 1961, 16 in 1965, and 17 in 1969.

The CDP was dissolved in 1961, and the NIP became a mere shadow of an opposition. The NIP split apart in 1969 when Dean Lindo left to form the People's Development Movement (PDM). Price called an election, and – although the parties hastily realigned – both were trounced. With the introduction of the ministerial system, Price became first minister in 1961 and premier in 1964.

THE NEW GENERATION: As the 60s wore on an increasingly radicalized, impatient generation began to emerge. Like the PUP of two decades before, they were unfairly labeled as racists and communists. Inspired by the example of the Black Power movement in the US, leaders like US-educated Evan Hyde and British-trained lawyers Said Musa and Assad Shoman organized meetings and demonstrations, and began breakfast programs for poor children as well as public education seminars on cultural and economic imperialism. Even though Hyde's United Black Association for Development (UBAD) and Musa's Political Action Committee (PAC) collaborated for a brief period in 1969, they soon parted ways as Musa and Shoman joined the radical wing of the PUP while Hyde began publishing

Amandala and associated himself with the opposition parties.

In the 1970s, the National Independence Party, the People's Development Movement, and the Liberal Party joined forces in the United Democratic Party (UDP). In the Oct. 1974 general election, the PUP won 51% of the vote with the opposition's coalition receiving 38%, giving them six out of the 18 seats. Although the PUP won 52% of the vote in the 1979 election, it continued to lose support, especially among the young voters. After the UDP won a landslide victory in the Belize City Council elections of Dec. 1983, Prime Minister Rogers resigned, leaving Price with no clear successor within the PUP. A balance-of-payments crisis coupled with a deficit-ridden budget triggered the PUP's first electoral setback. Held in Dec. 1984, the election gave the UDP 53.3% of the vote. Humiliatingly, Price himself was defeated by the party's youngest candidate.

Expelled from the PUP in 1985, rightists Louis Sylvestre and Fred Hunter formed the now-moribund Belize Popular Party (PPB) that same year. Two months after the party's formation, Briceno was convicted in North Carolina of drug smuggling and sentenced to a federal penitentiary. During the elections, the party, under leader Manuel Esquivel, had presented a platform espousing the need for foreign investment and private sector solutions for problems. One of the administration's more controversial policies was the sale of Belizean passports to foreign investors (mostly Hong Kong Chinese) in exchange for US$25,000 interest-free loans with a 10-year maturity. Campaigning on the slogan "Be-

Important Dates In Belizean History

1763: Signing of the Treaty of Paris permits the British to cut wood and export logwood while affirming Spanish sovereignty over the region.

1779: British settlers are attacked by Spaniards for the fourth time since 1717.

1783: Treaty of Versailles provides similar (although more limited) terms as the earlier treaty.

1786: Convention of London affirms rights of Baymen to cut wood but not to establish fortifications, plantations or government lands in Belize. First British Superintendent arrives.

1798: Spanish defeated by British in Battle of St. George's Caye.

1821: The Central American region declares independence from Spain.

1831: Civil rights granted to "Coloured Subjects of Free Condition."

1834: Slaves, who comprise less than half of the population, are emancipated.

1839: Central American federation falls apart. Guatemala asserts claim over Belize.

1840: British Government asserts that the Laws of England are in force in Belize. Formation of Executive Council, which will assist superintendent.

1854: Formal constitution adopted that includes provision for Legislative assembly.

1855: Regularization of legal system.

1859: Although Guatemala recognizes British sovereignty, it claims it signed treaty because both parties agreed to build a road from Guatemala City to the Caribbean coast.

1862: Colony of British Honduras officially established.

1871: British Honduras becomes a Crown colony under the Governor of Jamaica.

1884: British Honduras reestablished as separate colony.

1894: Riot by mahogany workers protesting conditions.

1919: Ex-Servicemen's Riot.

1931: Hurricane hits, causing extensive damage.

1934: Labourers and Unemployed Association (LUA) formed. Demonstrations and boycotts staged.

1936: New constitution includes election but bulk of electorate still disenfranchised by property, income and literacy qualifications. Although Britain offers £50,000 toward building road, Guatemala demands £400,000.

1939: Establishment of the British Honduras Workers and Tradesman Union, forerunner of the General Workers' Union (1943).

1941: Mass meetings demand adult suffrage and right to elect government.

1945: Guatemala lists "Belice" as the 45th department in its new constitution.

1950: People's United Party (PUP) formed. Women permitted to vote at 21 instead of 30.

1954: New constitution provides for universal adult suffrage as well as elected majority in legislative council.

1955: Although a semi-ministerial government is introduced, governor retains reserve powers. PUP sweeps elections, beginning a 30-year trend.

1968: National Independence Party (NIP) formed, and PUP faces its first opposition.

1963: Breaking off negotiations, Guatemala threatens war.

1964: Belize granted control of local government and Governor General appoints George Price as Premier.

1972: Breaking off negotiations again, Guatemala mobilizes troops at border. Britain responds by sending several thousand troops along with naval fleet.

1973: Name changed to Belize and Belmopan declared as capital.

1980: UN passes unanimous resolution demanding secure independence of Belize prior to 1981 session. Guatemala abstains.

1981: Promulgation of new constitution. Negotiations with Guatemala bring on riot and state of emergency in the country. Belize becomes fully independent member of Commonwealth; Price becomes first Prime Minister. Belize joins UN and Non-Aligned Nations. US begins training Belize Defense Force.

1984: After a landslide victory, the UDP's Esquivel becomes Prime Minister. VOA transmitter installed in Punta Gorda.

1989: Price becomes Prime Minister again by narrow margin.

1991: Newly inaugurated Guatemalan President Serrano pronounces the end to his nation's claim on Belize.

1993: Esquivel again becomes Prime Minister.

1994: British troops depart Belize. Guatemalan government re-asserts its claim on Belize.

---

lizeans first" – a reference to the contention that the UDP had opened the door to foreign speculators while Belizeans were not benefitting from new investment projects – in the Aug. 1989 snap election, the PUP regained power by a small 5% margin in the 28-seat House of Representatives, and George Price once again assumed the role of Prime Minister.

THE 1990s: In the 1993 election, Manuel Esquivel and the UDP again resumed control, taking 16 of 29 seats. Although the PUP actually garnered more votes than the UDP, the UDP won one seat in Belize District by a single vote and two others by a mere eight votes. The Esquivel government has proved generally unpopular. It introduced a program of "economic citizenship" which sold passports in return for investment in Belize. It was similar to a program introduced by previous administrations.

Attention regarding the controversial logging concessions granted Malaysians in government reserves in the Toledo District came to international attention in 1996. Maya in the area have vigorously protested the concessions, which benefit only a few of them.

In Feb. 1997, Belize became one of nine countries not "certified" by the US as a "full cooperating ally" in the "war" against drugs. Belize shared this notoriety with the nations of Colombia, Afghanistan, Burma, Nigeria, Lebanon, Pakistan, and Syria. Owing to "national security reasons," the non-certification for Belize was waived as it was for Lebanon and Pakistan. San Pedro police had uncovered some 250 lbs. of cocaine February 9 in the Basil Jones/Rocky Point area north of San Pedro Town; a subsequent 40 lbs. was found two days later in the Bacalar Chico area adjoining Mexico.

Also in 1997 George Price retired and Said Musa became the new PUP head. A British-trained criminal lawyer and a former foreign minister and education minister, Musa is likely to become the next prime minister in the 1998 elections. In June, the ruling party announced that all Belizeans would be "re-registered," meaning that all those residing outside of Belize would be effectively disenfranchised! The decision sparked a number of protests.

Government

With one of the strongest democratic traditions in the Central American region, Belize remains among the most politically stable nations in the hemisphere. Although independent only since 1981, the nation's history of self-government dates back to 1964. From that year up until independence, the British controlled only foreign affairs, defense, and international security. Belize is a constitutional monarchy and a member of the Commonwealth of Nations. The nation's foreign policy has been shaped through its close ties with Britain and, more recently, the United States.

POLITICAL STRUCTURE: Drafted a few months before independence

in 1981 and ratified by the National Assembly, the **Belizean Constitution** defines governmental structure, identifies certain rights and freedoms for the individual, and defines specific, additional rights for citizens. **Elections** are held at intervals of five years or less; there is universal suffrage, and the voting age is 18. Represented by the **Governor General**, the Queen of England is the (mostly ceremonial) head of state. Appointed on Independence Day, the current Governor General is Dr. Minita Gordon.

Called the **National Assembly**, the bicameral legislature is divided into a Senate and a House of Representatives. The **Senate** is a body comprised of eight members appointed by the Governor General, and is intended to reflect the elected political status in the lower chamber. Five members are recommended by the Prime Minister, two by the leader of the opposition, and one is selected by the Belize Advisory Council – a body put together by both the party in power and the opposition, which advises the Governor General on such issues as the pardon of a convicted person. The Senate's chief function is to consider and pass laws sent to it by the House. It may either refuse to ratify legislation or send it back to the House supplemented by recommended amendments.

The 28 members of the **House** (10 of whom are from Belize City) are elected for a term not to exceed five years. Selected either from the ranks of the House or from outside, the speaker – whose job is to serve as an impartial chairperson – is elected. The Governor General has the authority to dissolve the National Assembly, either on the recommendation of the Prime

Minister or after a no confidence resolution has been passed by the House. Normally the leader of the party commanding a parliamentary majority, the Prime Minister selects the members of the cabinet who together form the executive branch. A government may be brought down by a no confidence vote in the House; this has yet to happen in Belize.

The main problem with this system is that cabinet members are drawn solely from the National Assembly, which means that the executive and legislative branches are closely linked and that many able candidates for cabinet posts cannot be chosen. On the local level, there are six administrative districts (Belize, Cayo, Corozal, Orange Walk, Stann Creek, and Toledo), which are governed by locally elected seven-member town boards (with the exception of Belize City, which has a nine-member city council).

POLITICAL PARTIES: Belizean politics has always been a question of personalities and the degree of stress placed on issues. While the PUP is anti-communist, it has strong social-democratic elements and shows mixed feelings about US regional influence. Although the UDP is generally more conservative and pro-US than the PUP, it also recognized the Nicaraguan government and the People's Republic of China. The UDP espouses privatization and free market principles, while the PUP supports a mixed economy. Since the mid-1950s, the PUP has been largely dominated by George Cadle Price, a middle class Catholic Creole of ascetic character. The party has become increasingly centrist in recent years. In 1997, Said Musa

was selected as the new party leader (and most likely the next prime minister). Founded in 1973, the ruling UDP combined three national parties: the National Independence Party (NIP), People's Development Movement (PDM), and the Liberal Party (LP). However, only the NIP could have been considered to be a true party before the merger. Coming from the Liberal Party, which had its origins in the Chamber of Commerce, Manuel Esquivel has led the UDP since 1984.

Economy

In order to understand the Belizean economy a number of factors must be taken into account. First of all, the nation's very small size and relatively small population have hampered industrial development. Incessant regional instability coupled with socio-cultural and political differences, have served as obstacles to development of a truly unified regional economic block. Secondly, Belize has always been a plantation economy with agricultural exports commanding chief importance. Finally, the same lack of industrial development that has hampered the economy in other ways has also made it necessary to import a large number of items from the "developed" world (the US in particular), running up an enormous trade deficit in the process. Another factor to consider is the government's role as employer: about 5,000 work in the public sector.

SIZE AND SURVIVAL: The Lilliputian size of its economy makes Belize more susceptible than most to the vagaries of international commerce. Rising fuel costs and shrinking sugar prices have, in recent years, played havoc. Low sugar prices caused the near-bankrupt government to apply for an emergency IMF loan in the 1980s. On the other hand the economy's small size means that even relatively modest amounts of foreign aid, tourism income, or remittances from abroad can balance the books. Belize currently has a substantial trade deficit (BZ$129.4 million in 1989). If informal trade with Mexico were factored in, the trade deficit would be quite a bit higher.

PERSONAL INCOME: Income distribution is more equitable than in surrounding countries. GNP per capita hovers around US$2,000 pp, and for paid employees, who make up two-thirds of the labor force, it runs about US $6,000. Although there is no general minimum wage, those wage rates that are set range between US$1.25 and $2.50 ph. Shops must pay 63¢ per hour to their employees, while liquor stores are required to pay 75¢. Domestic servants in institutions are paid 63¢ per hour. While a skilled laborer may be paid US$2.50 per hour, a secretary earns US$700 a month. Employers with more than one employee between 14 and 65 must contribute to the Social Security system. Women are generally paid a quarter to a third less, even though they may be performing the exact same task. Unemployment (estimated at 15%) and underemployment (estimated at 35%) help keep wages low. Unions are nonexistent.

CLIMATE AND THE ECONOMY: Climatic factors have played an important role throughout the nation's economic history. The seasonality of rainfall affected the logging industry, which depended on a dry season for felling and a wet one for floating the logs downriver to the sea for transport. The longer dry season in the north enabled mahogany cutters to work more months every year, and caused them to resist Spanish attempts to drive them further south. Its dependence upon the climate has made and continues to make the timber industry a high-risk investment. Many roads also become impassable during the rainy season, while variations in rainfall affect agricultural production.

TRADE WITH THE US: US recognition of British control over Belize prevented the covert and overt interventions that have characterized US relations with the rest of Central America. As trade and transport links improved, the market shifted from Britain to the US, to the point where by 1920 70% of all trade was with the US. In May 1976, the Belizean dollar was tied to its US counterpart at a two-to-one ratio. At present, over half of exports go to the US, which, in turn, supplies more than a third of imports.

LIGHT INDUSTRY: Despite the passage of a series of Development Incentive Laws, manufacturing remains a minor economic sector, representing only 20% of the national income. The bulk of production is in agro-industry, which includes such activities as citrus extraction, feed manufacture, and flour milling. One of the largest manufacturing areas is the garment industry but, as the cloth and other materials utilized are all imported, the revenue it brings in is rather low, and both productivity and wages are uncompetitive with other Central American countries. High electricity rates are another problem: Belize hopes to develop hydro power or attract assembly plants to Santa Elena on the Mexican border where cheaper Mexican power can be utilized. Other small manufacturing concerns produce cigarettes, beer, soft drinks, matches, batteries, footwear, mattresses, furniture, and fertilizers. A newcomer on the manufacturing scene is Heritage Diskettes, a firm that commits a percentage of its profits to rainforest preservation. Plans to build a plant were announced in 1994.

MINING: The nation's first commercial mining operation, a dolomite extraction and processing plant, opened in Toledo in 1992. Dolomite is a carbonate sedimentary rock rich in magnesium and calcium; it's used as fertilizer by agro-industries throughout Central America and the Caribbean. Eventually, it's expected to generate BZ$4 million annually. The emphasis is on sustainable development: the environment is protected and there is little environmental impact caused by the mining. In 1993, Belize Natural Resources discovered an area off the coast potentially containing millions of barrels of oil. What impact this discovery will have on the economy and ecology of the country remains to be seen.

TOURISM: Ranking second to sugar production as a source of foreign exchange, tourism is becoming an increasingly integral part of the economy. Among Belize's attributes are its proximity to the Yucatán and the Tikal ruins in Guatemala, the widespread convertibility of the US dollar, use of the English language, and abundant flora and fauna, complemented by the largest barrier reef in the Americas just offshore. Recently, the nation has been focusing on "eco-tourism," and Belize is the only country where the Minister of Tourism is also the Minister of the Environment. (Sadly, this has sometimes meant that the environment comes in second after tourism.)

Although much has been made of the benefits of tourism, particularly "eco-tourism," it commands more than its share of problems. The much-maligned backpacker or low-budget traveler stays in local accommodation and eats what is available in local restaurants, thus funneling money directly to the local economy. Package and upscale tourism is often paid for abroad and much of the money can and does stay there. Tourism necessitates expensive imports, as little is made locally in Belize. Wages in the hotel industry are low, sometimes exploitive. Some hotels hire illegal immigrants from Honduras and Guatemala in order to cut costs. Regrettably, it can also attract both undesirable visitors and residents who have condescending attitudes towards locals. Another problem is the price of land, which has skyrocketed beyond the range of the average Belizean. In other words, the average Belizean may see few of the benefits from tourism.

Agriculture

In contrast with British and other nations' former colonies in the Americas, Belize has no tradition of large agricultural plantations operated with slave labor. Instead of harvesting cane or gathering cotton, Belizean slaves cut down logwood for shipment to Europe. After demand diminished for logwood, they cut mahogany and other hardwoods. Chicle, a gum extracted from the sapodilla tree used to make chewing gum, was another major export until it was superseded by the development of synthetics. Approximately 70% of the nation's trade comes from agriculture. Sugar accounted for 33% of export income in 1988; textiles came next with 22%, then citrus at 16%, bananas at 11%, seafood at 8%, lumber 3%, and vegetables at 3%. Out of 5.7 million acres, more than 2.2 million could be used for agriculture; the government has been attempting agricultural development and diversification during the past few decades.

PROBLEMS: Despite the immense agricultural potential, numerous serious obstacles stand in the way. The inconsistent rainfall creates problems. Although corn is usually planted between May and June and Nov. and Dec., the lowlands may flood in a really wet year or corn may wither on the hills during a hot one. Another impediment to agriculture is the ferocity of the insect population, which has done in many a foreign immigrant agricultural project. Still another reason for the neglect of agriculture in Belize stems from efforts by the post-abolition colonial power structure to control the former slaves by limiting access to land, a policy continued today.

The Land Tax Ordinance passed in 1967 was a progressive piece of legislation. Unfortunately, the Belize Estate and Produce Company refused to pay the tax until it succeeded in exempting 1.23 million acres or 95% of its land. Despite attempts such as the Alien Landholding Ordinance, passed in 1973, most of the land remains undeveloped and in the hands of foreigners.

SUGARCANE: The nation's modern sugar industry began with the 1937 opening of a small factory at Pembroke Hall (now Libertad) in Corozal. It was supplied by foreign-owned estates. Purchased by the British corporation of Tate and Lyle in 1967, the firm enlarged the plant and opened another at Tower Hill near Orange Walk Town. With production of some 100,000 tons annually, more than 60,000 acres are now under cultivation. The bulk of that amount is controlled by small farmers who grow on less than six acres. The price of sugar has undergone sharp fluctuations and, as Belizeans have put it at times, "sugar is no longer sweet." In 1985 Tate and Lyle closed the Libertad plant and essentially handed over another plant to its employees, retaining only a 10% stake. Once comprising up to 60% of total export income, sugar exports today represent only about a third. Farmers receive approximately BZ$50 per ton of cane, of which BZ$20 is profit.

CITRUS: Second only to sugar as an export earner, the citrus industry produces orange and grapefruit concentrates in the Stann Creek District. Citrus exports, mostly comprising frozen orange juice concentrate shipped to the US, tripled in value between 1980 and 1990, when over 40,000 acres were under cultivation. Like agro-industries elsewhere, citrus production depends upon the brutal exploitation of migrant laborers, many of whom are undocumented workers from El Salvador and Guatemala. The better jobs are reserved for the Creoles and Garifuna.

One of the most controversial projects in the nation's brief history has involved citrus production. In Oct. 1985, the government facilitated the sale of 686,168 acres to US private investors for a bargain basement price: US$6 million for land valued at US$150-200 million. Sold by Belizean businessman Barry M. Bowen, the property constituted one-eighth of the nation's land area, a tract described as "the largest single piece of potentially arable land in the whole of Central America." Of the property, 50,000 acres were sold to Minute Maid, 50,000 acres to Houston tycoons Walter Mischer and Paul Howell, and 50,000 acres were retained by Bowen. The remaining acreage was divided on a 30:30:40 basis between the three.

It was both the largest single overseas investment in Belizean history and the largest single investment by a US company in a nation covered by the Caribbean Basin Initiative. Plans were for Coca Cola's juice subsidiary Minute Maid to establish a 5,000-acre nursery, which was to expand to 25,000 acres within seven years, quadrupling citrus exports in the short run. In addition to the government's violation of a 1973 ordinance outlawing the sale of more than 10 acres of rural land, it also agreed to grant Coca Cola a 15-year tax holiday and to construct roads and bridges in the area. After coming under attack both from environmentalists and from the Florida citrus lobby, Coca Cola reconsidered and now retains just 50,000 acres. In 1993 exports dropped to 2.8 million boxes, a decrease of about 22%.

citrus pests: Currently, the industry is gearing up for an invasion of the Tristeza virus, transmitted by the brown citrus aphid. Once infected, a tree's growth is stunted: its leaves will shrink and yellow, the peel of its fruits thickens, juice content diminishes, and honeycomb-like holes appear on its inside bark. Ultimately, the tree will die. Of the nation's 47,000 acres, 90% consist of sour oranges, which are quite susceptible to the virus, and the highest impact is expected in the Stann Creek District; growers in the Cayo and Toledo Districts have already planted virus-tolerant trees. Originating in Asia, the virus arrived in South Africa and South America in the early part of this century. The plague has been moving up from South America since the 1980s (where it decimated more than six million acres in Venezuela). Belize and Honduras are expected to be hit hard soon. Although the virus has been in Belize since 1983, it has not had much impact because the brown citrus aphid, which spreads the virus, has not yet arrived. Reportedly, it is at the southern border of Honduras and is expected to move north.

Another pest, the citrus leaf miner, has already appeared. Its larva sucks the sap from tree cells, stunting tree growth and fruit production. A native of Asia, the moth lays its eggs on the underside of leaves. It was first spotted in Dade County, FL last year and quickly spread across the US. It appeared in Belize in 1994 and is thought to have been introduced by someone who smuggled in a citrus or budwood tree.

BANANAS: Commencing in the late 19th century, production was ruined by Panama disease in the first part of the century. With British assistance during the 1960s, production began again, only to suffer severe hurricane damage in 1975 and 1978. Exports expanded through the 1980s. Before the construction of the port at Big Creek, shipments had to be channeled through Puerto Cortéz, Honduras, an expensive arrangement. With the new port, which handles the ships of the United Brands British subsidiary, Fyffes, things should go more smoothly. Producing only 11 tons per acre, Belize is less competitive than Costa Rica and Honduras, which produce 14 tons per acre. Production rose to 76.6 million pounds in 1993.

OTHER CROPS: These include rice, corn, red kidney beans, poultry, beef, and honey. One of the world's largest mango farms is located near Big Creek. Hershey's Belizean subsidiary operates a research farm. Grown organically, cacao produced by the Toledo Cocoa Growers Association (TCGA) is being sold to Green & Black's Whole Earth Foods in Britain. It is processed in France and marketed in Britain under the Maya Gold label. Its "Fairtrade" label indicates that a fair price has been paid for the product. The TCGA has contracted with the company to supply 15,000 tons during 1994-95.

nontraditionals: With Reagan's Caribbean Basin Initiative (CBI) having served to open up the US market for nontraditional agricultural exports, AID has funded crop diversification projects in Belize, mostly to little effect. The program is seen by small farmers as a failure because it does not guarantee markets. Although Belize imports 25% of its food, opposition from AID resulted in the temporary dissolution of a marketing board, which guaranteed prices to farmers. While farmers producing nontraditionals for export receive credit and technical assistance, there is little aid offered for small farmers producing food for local consumption.

BELIZE BREEZE: Belize's most notable export is illegal: the ubiquitous and highly potent form of *cannabis sativa*. The US Drug Enforcement Agency (DEA) has alleged that Belize is the fourth largest marijuana supplier to the US (behind Colombia, Mexico, and Jamaica). With acreage under production quadrupling since 1982, estimates put the sale of ganja (marijuana) to the US at 1,100 metric tons, with a staggering retail value of US$300 million in 1986. That is more than the nation's GNP for that year and dwarfs the $36 million-a-year molasses and sugar industry! The US began funding an attack on the marijuana fields in recent years, however, and exports have decreased. Threatened with the potential loss of some US$26 million in bilateral aid, the government began spraying fields with paraquat, a US-banned herbicide. Although the spraying destroyed 90% of the marijuana crop, it also led to a slip in the PUP's popularity. After complaints from farmers, they were reimbursed for crops accidentally sprayed, and paraquat was replaced with another pesticide, supposedly harmless glyphophosphate (marketed as "Roundup").

Sending over 300 police and soldiers into the marijuana fields in 1986, the government claimed to have destroyed more than 34 million plants in some 2,400 fields. Production in Belize has been sharply reduced but production in Guatemala has grown. At the same time, cocaine use has risen, and the country has become an important trans-shipment point. Society members at every level – from "base boys" to the police and politicians – are involved in this nasty but lucrative business. The people at the top of the pyramid have seldom been apprehended.

This changed in 1994 when three officers were charged in Jan. with theft of 10 kg of coke, which had disappeared from the Eastern Division, and with the arrests of three prominent Belizeans at Dangriga in March for alleged cocaine smuggling. (However, they were later released!)

A second incident that drew fire from abroad was the 1996 arrest and release of the son-in-law of the Minister of Home Affairs. Elito Urbina was arrested for maintaining an illegal airstrip where an aircraft tracked by the US Drug Enforcement Agency was found to be carrying 386 kilos (849 lbs.) of cocaine. A 1997 State Department report (prepared by the Bureau for International Narcotics and Law Enforcement Affairs) noted that "No convictions were obtained in this case, however, owing to mismanaged investigations and the destruction of files in a mysterious police car fire."

One problem in fighting drug abuse has been that the propagandists have failed to draw the important distinction between relatively harmless marijuana and potentially-deadly cocaine, while neglecting legal and well-advertised alcohol and tobacco – drugs posing serious health threats. The government has also not provided sufficient resources to stave off the smugglers. For example, the constable in Placencia has no boat!

FORESTRY: Cutting down trees was once the chief "industry" in Belize, until overcutting resulted in the depletion of reserves, to the point where a mahogany tree is a rare find today. While in 1950 forest products accounted for 85% of the value of total domestic exports, they shrunk to only 1.8% in 1981, and since then have been practically nil. However, in November, 1997, Wall Street Financial Corporation (WFS) announced that its subsidiary, Mayan Plantations Hardwoods Company, Ltd., had accepted a purchase order to sell 1.2 million board feet of lumber to a major US lumber and furniture company. WSF also stated that Mayan Plantations will retain the services of the Rainforest Alliance to ensure that the 32,000-acre estates's timber range is being managed in an ecologically sound, sustainable manner through the Alliance's Smartwood Certification Program.

WSF is developing the first ever mixed-use resort destination in Belize on the southern portion of its estate, which stretches more than 20 miles along the Caribbean seafront. Plans call for both hotel and residential development, as well as the nation's first golf course. In the

Toledo district, other logging by a Malaysian firm is of old-growth forest, and remains the subject of controversy.

FISHING: The fishing industry accounts for only a small part of agricultural production. There are now five fishing cooperatives, and fishermen are legally obliged to sell a proportion of their catch at controlled prices to the local market. Fish products have risen as a percentage of total export earnings largely as a result of a concentration on higher-priced lobsters and shrimp. One major investor in the shrimp farming industry is US-owned Maya Maricure Ltd. However, overfishing and out-of-season poaching has resulted in lowered catches, and conch and lobster are very likely to be either scarce or extinct in the future.

The People

Belizean culture is truly polyglot. Given the small area, nowhere in the Americas will you find a more unusual blend. It is the only place where Maya have met English, African-American, and Garifuna (Black Carib) cultures. These social and ethnic groups differ greatly but have been united by the colonizer's monopoly on power. There is relatively little racial tension, and the nation lacks the class structure found in other former British colonies such as Jamaica.

SOCIAL STRATIFICATION: Determinants of class in early Belizean society were skin color and language. Rising to important positions and coming to own slaves themselves, Free Creoles looked down upon their darker brothers, causing resentment in turn. In the 19th century, a series of intricate divisions classed the "white" elite at the top, with soldiers, skilled craftsmen, house servants, and field laborers following in order.

SOCIAL CHARACTERISTICS: The contemptuous attitude towards physical labor, long considered to be demeaning, is one of the remaining legacies of colonialism. Consequently, unemployed woodcutters have refused to become farmers. Although both are equally back-breaking, a woodcutter contracts out his labor whereas a farmhand works for wages – a small but distinct difference. Other characteristic attitudes that may stem from the days of slavery include the exceeding politeness shown to employers and visitors and an unwillingness to say "no," substituting the word "maybe" or "possibly" instead. Instructions also tend to be carried out literally, allowing little space for flexibility.

POPULATION: The least populated independent nation on the American mainland, Belize has some 235,000 people. There are about 50,000 registered aliens in the country with an additional 10,000 or more estimated illegals. Although its overall population density is only 17 persons per sq. mile, the specific figure may range from seven (Toledo District) to 32 (Belize District). From about 1930, more than half have resided in the seven largest towns. In order of decreasing size these are: Belize City, Orange Walk Town, Corozal Town, Dangriga, San Ignacio, Benque Viejo, Punta Gorda, and San Pedro. Despite a net emigration from Belize in this century, its population more than doubled between 1945 and 1985. Accounting for the increase are a longer life expectancy, coupled with a dramatically declining infant mortality rate (from 190/thousand in the 1930s to 20/thousand in the 1980s. Approximately 46% of all Belizeans are aged 14 or younger, and the birth rate is 39 per thousand. Among women aged 15-19, the birth rate is 137 per thousand, contrasting with 99 for Costa Rica, 100 for Jamaica, and 104 for the Dominican Republic. A survey conducted by the World Health Organization and the Pan American Health Organization ranked illegal abortions (no legal abortions are permitted) as the leading cause of death for women nationwide.

A growing problem in Belize is the breakdown of the traditional family, which has been brought about through emigration, poverty, and the emergence of single-family households. Emigration has frequently left children in the hands of elderly relatives who were incapable of properly supervising them. There are now large numbers of rootless teenagers who lack skills and education; a gang culture is growing, as is child abuse and neglect.

THE MAYA: The nation's only indigenous group, the Maya reentered the country during the British colonial era. Today, there are three groups (Yucateco, Mopanero, and Kekchí), each speaking a distinct dialect. Although granted land in the Toledo District, they were not confined there and have also settled in the districts of Orange Walk and Corozal; in Cayo District **Mopan Maya** live in Succoths near Benque Viejo and Yucatecans reside in San Antonio. While the largely deculturated **Yucatec Maya** emigrated during the 1850s from the Yucatán in order to escape the Caste Wars, the Mopan arrived from the town of San Luis in Guatemala's Petén to settle in southern Belize in 1886.

Residing in the villages of San Miguel, San Antonio, and Crique Sarco near Punta Gorda, the **Kekchí** are the least acculturated of the three. They fled from the Veracruz area of Guatemala in the 1870s and 1880s in order to avoid exploitation by German coffee growers. Their largest settlement is in San Pedro, Colombia. Today, because they continue to live in relatively remote areas, they remain less assimilated than other ethnic groups.

In addition to raising cattle and pigs, the Maya still practice shifting cultivations on one- to 10-acre plots of land, growing small crops of maize, black beans, and tobacco. Those who are not farmers are generally chicle tappers. Modernization and the outside influences that come with it threaten the traditional Maya lifestyle; another threat comes from the activities of evangelical Christians. Some groups have gone so far as to prohibit converts from participating in *fajina*, the communal tradition of cleaning and maintaining the village.

THE CREOLES: Introduced as slaves sent in to help with the timber harvest, the first African-Americans quickly outnumbered their former owners. They were joined in 1817 by 500 men from the all-black 5th West India Regiment who were given land grants and temporary visas along with transport to Belize. Their families arrived the next year. During the 1830s, captured slave ship inmates were permitted to settle. The high frequency of racial intermarriage created the Creoles who now dominate the civil service. Two-thirds of all Creoles reside in Belize District, which is for the most part a Creole settlement.

MESTIZOS: These are Maya with some Spanish blood. They arrived after the War of the Races, which broke out in the Yucatán during 1848. By 1859 an estimated 12-15,000 refugees had arrived. After the conflict's conclusion in 1874, more than 8,000 of the refugees chose to remain. Settling largely upon the River Hondo along the nation's northern border, they worked as logcutters and farmers. Their most important contribution was the introduction of sugarcane, which came to form the basis for a thriving industry. Today found largely in the Corozal and Orange Walk districts, their presence has resulted in a large number of bilingual Belizeans.

THE GARINAGU (GARIFUNA PEOPLE): This ethnic group (also known as the Black Caribs) has been living in Central America since 1797. Its presence and origin are quirks of history. In 1675 a sailing vessel with a cargo of slaves ran aground off the minuscule island of Becquia near St. Vincent in the Caribbean's easternmost rim. At this time the island was inhabited by the Calinago, whom the Spanish called Carib, meaning "cannibal." Intermarriage with the indigenous Caribs gave birth to this unique group. Later, they spread to St. Vincent, an island already populated by runaways from Barbados. Under the leadership of Chattoyer in 1795, they rebelled and were deported to the islands of Roatan and Bonacca in the Bay of Honduras, where they still live today. Some migrated to the mainland, and they first came to Belize in the early 1800s as smugglers, carrying contraband British goods into Honduras. Some eventually stayed on to labor in the mahogany harvest.

In 1832, after participating in an unsuccessful governmental overthrow in Spanish Honduras, large numbers settled permanently in Punta Gorda and later in Dangriga (Stann Creek Town), Hopkins, Seine Bight, and Barranco. They were treated by the British as squatters and were ordered in 1857 to obtain leases from the Crown or face losing their land along with any property. The Crown's land ordinance of 1872 set up Garifuna reservations as well as Maya ones. Prevented from owning their own land, they were valued for their labor.

The Garinagu rarely intermarry with outsiders, even with those residing in the same town. They harbor a hodgepodge of Carib, African, and Spanish ideas and values. The Garinagu are difficult for the outsider to identify by appearance alone, but can be recognized by their Hispanic surnames. Traditionally, they have been fishermen but are more and more turning to farming – an occupation they once deemed only appropriate for women. While their tongue is basically Carib, their music and dance are largely African. Their *wanaraqua* – a group of costumed dancers and drummers who appears during the Christmas season – is the equivalent of the John Canoe spectaculars found elsewhere

Web Pages about the Garifuna

www.vir.com/~derekp/gardap.html
www.concentric.net/~Brnd z/
www.garifuna.com
www-scf.usc.edu/~sidneyme/

in the Caribbean. They also retain other customs such as the *dugu*, a week-long healing ritual, during which a female shaman goes into a trance and talks to the dead (see *Religion*).

Despite the fact that the Garinagu have become more integrated through the years, the urbanized Creole still finds it difficult to accept them. The Garinagu, in turn, have often clashed with the African-Americans, whom they regard as having "diluted" their racial purity. Today, however, they are leaving their self-enforced isolation and many have entered the mainstream. Many are now schoolteachers.

THE EAST INDIANS: In 1857, the Sepoys – a group of British-trained and -equipped Indian soldiers – mutinied in New Delhi, massacring thousands of British residents before the rebellion could be put down. About 1,000 of the unfortunates who had come to their assistance were sent to British Honduras to labor in the Corozal District's sugarcane fields. Today, their highly acculturated descendants reside in areas such as Calcutta in Corozal District. Although they are culturally distinguished from their Creole neighbors only by a few traditional foods, there are a number of more recent immigrants (mostly shopkeepers) who contrast more markedly.

THE CHINESE: In the early 1860s, the mahogany reserves in British Honduras were running low, and simultaneously demand was dropping because of the introduction of iron and steel in the shipbuilding industry. The need to diversify the nation's economic base led to the establishment of an immigration fund in 1864. Through the fund, a group of Chinese laborers was brought over in 1865. Although they initially met with a hearty and curious welcome, the newcomers encountered resentment in the *mestizo*-settled areas where they were first sent. The *mestizo* could not understand why Chinese had been brought in rather than encouraging immigration from neighboring countries. The Chinese were moved from the Corozal to the Toledo District the following year, and no others followed. By 1868, of the 474 who arrived, only 211 remained. Although their descendants still live mostly in Belize City and in Punta Gorda, the majority of today's Chinese population stems from immigration that has occurred since the 1920s. Taiwanese started arriving here a few years ago. For many, Belize is a stepping stone to Canada: they arrive, work hard, save some money, and move on.

EUROPEANS AND NORTH AMERICANS: Caucasians are referred to as *backras*, a term deriving from their "raw backs." Most of the white folks in Belize these days come from Europe or North America. Strangely enough, the first US immigrants to arrive were Confederates fleeing a defeated South. Given land grants in the Toledo District, they started large sugar plantations near Punta Gorda. Among them were former army officers, ministers, and doctors. All had been lured by the New Orleans Immigration Company. In the face of sugar price drops and the 1868 cholera epidemic, many returned home. Those remaining introduced the banana industry. Their children were sent back to the South to be educated, where they frequently stayed on, and the community gradually disintegrated. In 1879 around 450 Italians arrived from Guatemala and were granted land near Gales Point Manatee.

Until recently, Belize has had one of the world's highest per capita quotas of Peace Corps volunteers. Although they are a significant source of foreign exchange, they have in the past been accused of taking scarce jobs, involving themselves in areas felt to be best reserved for nationals, and of being improperly used by the Belizean government as a source of free labor. However, they have been invaluable on the local level and have helped with obtaining funding for needed projects such as nature reserves. There are also a large number of Lebanese expatriates ("Syrians") who, in the best Phoenician tradition, now number among the nation's most prosperous businessmen. The best known of these are the Zabaneh.

The most recent wave of Caucasian immigrants has come in recent years. A wide variety of Europeans have settled here. And, more recently, a number of North Americans have been attracted as well. The pioneer quality of Belizean life is a big attraction. It is not unusual these days to see a US-born woman in the Toledo District down on her knees scrubbing clothes in the Columbia River. Retirement communities are planned in such unlikely areas as Sittee River. And still others are pursuing a dream and building a little lodge of their own.

THE MENNONITES: Members of this conservative religious sect have had a memorable impact on Belize. Named for Dutch priest Menno Simons, the Mennonites were one of the Anabaptist sects to emerge during the Radical Reformation of 16th-century Northern Europe. Their refusal to serve in the army made them unpopular with governments, who forced them to move on. From Frisia in the Netherlands they moved to Switzerland to Prussia (E Germany) and then to Canada in 1863. Over the decades their numbers were supplemented by others fleeing the aftermath of upheavals in the Soviet Union. They became disaffected with prairie life after the Canadian government imposed a heavy tax burden because they refused to send their children to public school. Invited to come to Mexico, thousands emigrated to the Chihuahua and Durango states during the 1920s.

They found themselves cramped after a few decades, and 3,000 relocated to Belize in 1959. Purchasing a 100,000-acre stretch along the River Hondo, they built a road from the Blue Creek settlement to Orange Walk. Additional settlements were later founded at Spanish

Lookout and at Shipyard. Isolating themselves from the local community, they market farm products, including eggs and vegetables.

The Mennonites have become split into two camps: modernist or progressive and traditionalists. Progressives believe that the church should participate in the world, and they may use all manner of vehicles, power tools, machinery, and electricity. Traditionalists, on the other hand, believe that contact with modern ways contaminates their faith's purity. As traditionalists do not believe in engines, all work and transport are accomplished with horses.

Even though they have not traditionally sought converts, progressives have spread the faith among the Garifuna and Maya communities, and today there are 28 different types of Mennonites. In 1973, many of the stricter Mennonites – finding the jungle too tough for hand cultivation – departed for Bolivia, where they found more suitable land as well as freedom from price controls. Today, the Mennonites are a common sight in many of the nation's towns. Many Belizeans consume Mennonite-produced vegetables (as well as milk and cheese), and furniture made by them can be seen in many homes. Some resorts even use cabins (priced at an affordable BZ$10,000) that have been constructed by the Mennonites and then trucked in!

EDUCATION: The Church of England founded the nation's first public school, and the vast majority of the nation's schools are operated by churches (largely Catholics, Anglicans, and Methodists). The government subsidizes church salaries and the Catholic Church runs some 60% of the schools. Despite the fact that primary education is free, only some 80% of children are enrolled in school and only about 55% complete the first eight years. Even fewer Belizeans graduate from high school and only a tiny elite continue on to college. The government administers the Belize School of Agriculture, the School of Nursing, and the Belize College of Arts, Sciences, and Technology, as well as the Belize Technical College Sixth Form. St. John's Sixth Form is privately operated.

Religion

Any visitor to Belize will soon discern the importance of religion. Churches abound, even in small villages, and the country practically grinds to a halt during the Christmas and Easter seasons. While the majority are Catholics, evangelicals are playing an increasingly prominent role, and there are a small number of Jews, Muslims, and Ba'hais.

CATHOLICISM: Although today the majority of the population are Catholics, the religion was slow to take hold initially. Mullins River was the first and only Catholic community. With the influx of *mestizos* during the War of the Races, the church grew a thousand-fold. Two Jesuit priests, arriving in 1851, built the first Catholic Church at Corozal Town, followed by another in Orange Walk. Arriving in Jan. 1883, six Sisters of Mercy established the first convent as well as a girls' school. The Jesuits established St. John's College, a high school, in 1887. Belize became a Catholic bishopric in

1956. Many Maya have also become Catholics, but the majority are little more than nominal members. The religion is now a national institution that cuts across ethnic lines. Although he never left the airport grounds, the 1983 visit by Pope John Paul II was a national event, and he was received by heads of the Anglican and Methodist Churches as well as by his own bishops.

PROTESTANTS: The first Church of England (Anglican) was established in Feb. 1777, and Central America's first Anglican Church, St. John's Cathedral, was constructed with government funding. It served for state as well as secular functions, but only the white elite attended, and it remained the white folks' religion until the late 1820s. The Baptists and the Methodists ("Methodizzies" as the locals contemptuously termed them) arrived and helped the ex-slaves make the transition from slavery to freedom through instruction in English and other means. The first Baptist church was established in 1822, followed by a Wesleyan Methodist church in 1825. The first Seventh Day Adventists arrived in 1891, and they built their first church in 1932.

Other sects include a Scottish Presbyterian congregation, the Salvation Army, and the Nazarenes. Today, the most influential sects with the strongest memberships are these evangelical fundamentalists, one of the most important post-independence phenomena. Unlike Catholicism, which has made its peace with local customs and beliefs, evangelicals have declared war on indigenous beliefs, even on such practices as the In-

dian custom of sacrificing pigs before planting. Religion has served to reinforce existing class divisions: while East Indian Muslims are hated by evangelicals, evangelicals in turn are looked down upon by other Christians. Among the Maya, the large variety of denominations and sects has tended to undermine community unity.

DUGU: This is the religion of the Garifuna people, a system of beliefs that has the same name as its major ceremony. Not only does *dugu* coexist with Catholicism, Catholic masses are held on the first Friday of the month in Dangriga's temple. *Dugu* revolves around the shaman *(buye)*. *Buyes* do not choose their position; they are chosen. The Garinagu believe that the dead are always with us. A *dugu* may be held owing to an illness in a family or simply because it is time. The many phases of the ritual include food offerings, dance, and prayer. It all culminates in the *awisahdi*, a farewell ritual. An expensive and complex affair, the preparation for a *dugu* may take up to 15 months.

RASTAFARIANISM: You may see these colorful Belizeans sporting dreadlocks in the towns and on the cayes. Originating in Jamaica during the 1930s, the Rasta creed has been diffused worldwide with the popularity of reggae music. Most simply explained, Rastas believe blacks to be the reincarnation of the ancient Israelites and the late Haile Selassie to be their king. Rastafarians have traditionally avoided meat or chicken, leather goods, and tobacco. In Belize many followers have been dubbed "Rastaphonians." The main thing that they have in common with real Rastas are the now-fashionable dreadlocks and a penchant for smoking marijuana. For more information on Rastafarianism, see *Jamaica, A Visitor's Guide* (Hunter Publishing, 1996), by Harry S. Pariser, or Leonard Barrett's *The Rastafarians* (Beacon Press, 1977).

OBEAH: In contrast with other areas of the Caribbean, *obeah* never put down strong roots in Belize. Today, few Belizeans are active practitioners. Over the centuries many deaths have been blamed upon *obeah-men* who are said to have used a black doll made from a stocking stuffed with dark chicken feathers and held together with black thread and pins. It is then buried under the victim's doorstep. *Obeah-men* are also believed to be able to affect crops, love affairs, and business enterprises.

COMMON SUPERSTITIONS: Although educated Belizeans may deride *obeah*, many still fear a certain species of black butterfly commonly believed to bring either bad luck or an early death. Others wear *obeah* charms and cross their shoes in front of the bed in order to deter evil spirits during sleep. Mayan-derived superstitions are also prevalent; many of them are a mix of Mayan, European, and African beliefs. Portents of a family member's coming death include dreams of breaking a water jug, of floating on air, of a black bull attempting to enter one's house, and of having a tooth pulled. Dreaming of red tomatoes foretells the death of an infant. Placing gourds filled with food in the doorway is believed to ward off sickness brought by dwarves. One may not give away burning wooden embers lest one's turkeys

die. Eggs laid on Friday, considered to be an unlucky day, will not hatch. Saturday and Monday are lucky days. In the past, Maya would buy lottery tickets on Saturday and get married only on Mondays. There are stories of ceramic statues, spirited away from their ceremonial resting places, magically returning under their own power. Weather omens are also common. If cornhusks are thin, the winter will be mild; if swallows fly low overhead, it will rain.

SPIRITS AND CREATURES: Perhaps because nature is so alive here, the air seems lush with spirits. The *Greasy Man* and the *Ashi de Pompi* both live in forsaken dwellings (the *Ashi* in burned houses) and stir at night, taking pleasure in scaring the bejesus out of locals.

The most infamous mythological creatures are the *Duendes* (Spanish for "dwarves"). According to reported sightings, *Duendes* are up to four feet tall with flat, yellowish faces, long arms and heavy shoulders, their bodies covered with thick, short brown hair. They are reported to carry away dogs on occasion, leaving deep, pointed-heel footprints behind. Maya bas reliefs depict pairs of nude dwarves sporting what appear to be either banana fronds or sombreros on their heads. If you should encounter one of these creatures on a jungle trail, be sure to give him the traditional greeting: with your thumb concealed in your palm, salute him with the backside of your hand. The reason for this is simple: *Duendes* are four-fingered and are reportedly jealous of anyone possessing five! While they are capable of vile and despicable acts, they are also said to perform miracles. If they take possession of you, you will go insane, but you will acquire instant proficiency in your chosen musical instrument.

A far more dreadful creature is the *Sisimito* or *Sisemite*, a gigantic and powerful hairy beast said to tear men to pieces and carry off their wives. They allegedly have been known to kidnap small children in the hopes of learning how to talk, and they make piles of twigs in an effort to start a fire, an art unknown to them. If they come across the embers of a campfire, it is said that they will sit transfixed until the embers grow cold and then they eat them. While a man who looks into their eyes is said to die within a month, a woman doing so will live a longer life as a result. A *Sisimito* has no thumbs and his feet point backward. Should one see you, just jump behind a bush. Puzzled as to where you've gone, he'll glance around, see his own footprints, and then take off in that direction.

Another creature is the *Ixtabay*. She is always spied sitting in a tree combing her hair. Descending to walk above the surface of the ground, she hypnotizes onlookers, who follow her into the bush and go insane. Those who survive the encounter and make it home die a few days later.

Festivals & Events

On each of the official holidays, most government and professional offices, some banks, and many stores are closed. During Easter and Christmas weeks, the entire country almost completely shuts down.

BARON BLISS DAY: On March 9th, the death of this somewhat eccentric British baron with a Portuguese title is commemorated by a formal ceremony at his tomb followed by fishing and sailing regattas. Arriving to fish off the coast in 1926, Henry Edward Ernest Victor Bliss fell ill from food poisoning and died before ever stepping ashore. Certainly the most famous eccentric Englishman in the history of Central America, Baron Bliss gave all of his money to a country on which he never set foot! His sole acquaintance with Belize was through the locals who visited him aboard his yacht! Also known as "the "Fourth Baron Bliss of the former Kingdom of Portugal," Bliss was born in England's Buckingham County.

Falling in love with the country through the friendly people that he encountered aboard his yacht, Bliss left the bulk of his estate to the colony – a sum that came to BZ$1.6 million (in today's money) after estate taxes. He stipulated that an annual regatta be held in his name, that the bequest be used only on capital projects and that all buildings costing £500 or more must bear his name. Money could not be spent on recurrent expenditures (such as salaries and utilities), and no churches or schools (save vocational or agricultural training) could be built. The money was used to found the Bliss Trust (which has been used to build the Bliss Institute), roads and markets, cricket fields, improve water supplies, and purchase the land on which to build Belmopan. The latest project was the Punta Gorda Multi-purpose Center.

The Trust currently has around BZ$4 million, the majority of which is invested in UK Treasury notes and fixed deposits in Belizean banks.

COMMONWEALTH DAY: Celebrated nationwide and held on the Queen's birthday (May 24), this day features horse and cycle races.

NATIONAL DAY: Commemorating the Battle of St. George's Caye (on Sept. 10, 1798) in which the British defeated a Spanish armada, this holiday is spread over an entire week and includes religious services and carnival celebrations. A parade takes place in Belize City on the 10th. This identification by the upper class Creoles with a British victory seems a curious phenomenon to the outsider. A recent addition to the holiday is the **Belizean Carnival,** which has elections for Kings and Queens of the costumed band.

NATIONAL INDEPENDENCE DAY: This nationwide celebration commemorates the nation's independence on Sept. 21, 1981. Activities include a variety of food, music, and cultural activities.

GARIFUNA SETTLEMENT DAY: On Nov. 19, the Garinagu celebrate their legendary arrival from Roatan. Drumming, dancing, and feasting enliven Dangriga. Even if you think you already know what partying is, after participating in this event you'll realize you hadn't a clue!

SPECIAL EVENTS: The **International Billfish Tournament** is held in Feb. San Pedro holds its **carnival** in Feb.

An **agricultural show** is held in Chan Pine Ridge (near Orange Walk) each March. The **Burrell Boom Cycle and Horse Races** take place on Easter Mon; races start from Belize City. The **Easter Fair** takes place in San Ignacio. The **Holy Saturday Cross Country Classic** runs from Belize City to San Ignacio and back. The **Holy Saturday Regatta** is held in Caye Caulker.

The **Cashew Festival** takes place in Crooked Tree Village each May. The **Cayo Expo** is in San Ignacio in May, and Caye Caulker holds a Coconut Festival that same month. The **Toledo Festival of the Arts** is a week-long festival in May in which schoolchildren and cultural groups play a major role.

In June, the **Agriculture and Trade Show** is held at the National Agricultural Showgrounds; it features rodeos, handicrafts, games, and regional gastronomic specialties. The **Dia de San Pedro** is a three-day festival that honors San Pedro's patron saint.

The **Benque Viejo del Carmen fiesta**, held in celebration of the village's patron saint, is held in July. **Fiestarama**, an agricultural trade show, is held in Orange Walk that same month.

The **International Sea and Air Festival** is held each Aug. in San Pedro.

A billfish tournament, the **Belikin Spectacular**, is held each Oct. That same month the **Hike and Bike for the Rainforest** is a one-day event in Cayo whose proceeds benefit the Tapir Mountain Reserve.

OTHERS: Many of the Maya still follow their traditional beliefs and customs, including corn planting and harvesting festivals. In the Mopan Maya village of San José Succotz near San Ignacio, the big fiestas are St. Joseph (March 19) and the Holy Cross (May 3), when the local dances – "Hog Head,"

Official Holidays

Holidays are now movable. For example, if Baron Bliss Day falls on a Wed, it will be celebrated on the preceding Mon.

```
Jan. 1 . . . . . . . . . . . . . . . . . New Year's Day
Mar. 9 . . . . . . . . . . . . . . . . Baron Bliss Day
April . . . . . . . . . . . . Easter (three days or more)
May 1 . . . . . . . . . . . . . . . . . . . . Labor Day
May 24 . . . . . . . . . . . . . Commonwealth Day
Sept. 10 . . . . . . . . . . . . . . . . National Day
Sept. 21 . . . . . . . . . . . . . . Independence Day
Oct. 12 . . . . . . . . . . . . . . . . . Columbus Day
Nov. 19 . . . . . . . . . . Garifuna Settlement Day
Dec. 25 . . . . . . . . . . . . . . . . . . Christmas
Dec. 26 . . . . . . . . . . . . . . . . . Boxing Day
```

Mañanitas, Quinceaños, and *El Baile de los Mestizos* – are all performed to the accompaniment of marimbas.

In the Toledo District, San Antonio has revived its deer dance, which takes place in Aug. In some localities (such as San Antonio), an effigy of Judas is tied to a tree and then shot by firing squad as part of the Easter celebrations.

At Christmas, the traditional Cortez dance held in the village of San Miguel in Toledo District tells the story of the Spanish arrival; the masks and costumes originate in Guatemala.

See these local customs and celebrations while you can: intolerant, hard-sell evangelical Christianity may well render them extinct in the coming decades.

Food & Drink

While Belize may not have one of world's most innovative cuisines, it is hearty and appetizing. There are a variety of restaurants large and small. International cuisine is scarce outside of the resort areas, but Chinese food (or an imitation thereof) can generally be found just about everywhere. In small settlements, such as Burrell Boom or Hopkins, a local family will often cook for visitors. Ask around.

TYPICAL FARE: The staple dish is **rice and beans** cooked with coconut milk. The less-tasty **stewed beans** (whole or refried) and rice – with the rice and beans served separately rather than blended – is also popular. Both are generally served with meat, chicken, or fish on the side along with some semblance of a salad.

Eggs are available everywhere; a fried egg is a "drop egg."

Traditionally cooked in pots above an open fire, game meat – consisting of either gibnut (paca), armadillo, or brocket deer – is largely a thing of the past. Most of today's Belizeans thrive on chicken, beef and imported ham. But game is still served up to tourists, including the Queen of England, who dined to her delight on gibnut (the "royal rat") during her visit. Steak and fried chicken, served with rice or French fries, are also common menu items.

Tortillas (thin wheat or corn pancakes) are an important side dish. *Tamalitos*, steamed ground corn cakes wrapped in corn stalks, are found in Indian areas. Vegetables are seldom served in most local restaurants. About as much as you get is a bit of coleslaw or a piece of tomato. One reason is their extremely high price: green bell peppers, for example, can sell for BZ$3.50/lb. The reason for the high price is that many are imported from Mexico. Another factor is that there is no local custom of eating vegetables. You'll find this to be true throughout Central America.

SEAFOOD: Chinese restaurants around the world often feature seafood, but in Belize this is not usually the case. Fish is generally more expensive than chicken. Specialties include the local spiny lobster, red snapper, conch fritters, and shrimp. Avoid turtle steak at all costs and shun restaurants serving it. Don't eat conch or lobster when the seasons are closed: Feb. 15 to July 14 (lobster) and July 1 to Sept. 30 (conch).

FOREIGN FOOD: Although often serving bland food, Chinese restaurants are found throughout the land. The quality varies from gourmet to grease galore, but the bulk of them feature the same menu: egg foo yung, chop suey, rice and beans, and steak and sandwiches. You may want to ask them to leave out the monosodium glutamate, MSG, a Japanese flavoring derived from soy that, along with cornstarch, ruins the quality and flavor of traditional Chinese cuisine. As one recent Chinese emigrant puts it, "there are no good condiments here. If you want good Chinese cooking, you have to go to Hong Kong or China." Other nationalities have opened restaurants in both Belize City and in San Ignacio. Many Mexican and Guatemalan snacks are served as well.

SNACKS: *Tamales* are ground corn and chicken wrapped in plantain leaves; they are traditionally served at Christmas. *Empanadas* are corn turnovers filled with cheese, beans, or meat and potatoes. *Plátanos* (plantains) are large banana-like grains that must be fried or baked. They are often sliced and fried like potato chips. A *gacho* is a flour tortilla stuffed with cheese and beans and with tomato sauce on top. A *great dog* is a hot dog sausage with coleslaw in a tortilla. A *salbute* is a fried corn pancake topped with shredded baked chicken, tomato, and cabbage. A *full house* is a baked *burrito* with chicken, cheese, and beans. *Panades* are deep-fried cornmeal patties stuffed with fish. *Chirmale* is a beef, pork, or chicken stew with eggs and corn. *Relleno* is almost the same but with chicken or pork.

TAXES AND TIPS: There are no taxes on food. When dining at small restaurants, locals almost never leave a tip; you can do as you like. At larger, more formal establishments, a 10% tip is customary.

ALCOHOL: Drinking is a very popular activity, second to or possibly surpassing churchgoing, and many males would rather drink than eat. One reason for this is the excellent locally brewed beer and rum sold in stores, restaurants, and bars. Some stores will let you drink on the premises, others not. The sign on the storefront indicates their status. Prices in local bars and small stores are virtually identical. Selling for BZ$2.25 a 10 oz. bottle and up, Belikin is the nation's sole beer. Its stranglehold on distribution drove competitor Crown out of business. Belikin also has a larger-sized (and more expensive) premium brand, and markets a superb stout, which some may prefer to the beer. Imported brews are twice the price because of the tax.

Caribbean-style brewed rum comes in two varieties: dark and light. The nation's rum is popular – so much so that Belize is the only rum-producing nation that does not export because its entire output is consumed locally! *Rum-popo* is made by mixing rum with condensed milk and sometimes egg. Another popular concoction is a mix of the local Tropical Brandy with regular milk in a 50-50 ratio.

SOFT DRINKS: Colored sugared water is enormously popular in Belize; imbibers will find a choice selection practically everywhere. Brands include Sprite, Fanta, Pepsi, 7 Up, Coke, and Club Soda. Milk is available in supermarkets. Known in Jamaica as Irish Moss, a local specialty drink is *Seaweed*, made by blending agar, milk, sugar, and alcohol. It's most commonly found in Belize City.

TOBACCO: Nicotine junkies can choose their poison from several local brands, including the popular Independence, which produces just the opposite condition. If you wish to cut down or quit, Belize is an excellent place, as single cigarettes are sold for 10¢ each or "three for a shilling."

DINING OUT: If you're only into fine dining, it's better not to leave Belize City or San Pedro unless you're traveling to a resort. However, if you pass up local eateries, you'll also miss some of the best food and hospitality the nation has to offer. The so-called "jungle lodges" generally have good food. You'll get more vegetables and varied cuisine, but you'll also pay substantially more than the average for the privilege – about what you'd pay in the US or even more.

BUDGET DINING: You'll find no lack of places to eat: there are a number of local restaurants in every town and most are in this book. Ask locals for recommendations. Expect to spend BZ$6-12 per meal. It's always best to ask the price of food before ordering. Australian butter and Dutch cheese are imported staples available at affordable prices.

TIPS FOR VEGETARIANS: This is most definitely a carnivorous society so the more you are able to bend or compromise your principles, the easier time you'll have. If you're a vegan (non-dairy-product user), unless you're cooking all of your own food you will find it even more difficult. But the local fruits may be your salvation. The local rice and beans combination is a good staple, but it can get monotonous after a while, and (as noted above) Belizeans don't eat many vegetables, owing to their scarcity and their high cost. Also try Chinese restaurants, which do use more vegetables. If you eat fish, you should be aware that locals eat it fried and that it may have been fried in lard or in the same oil as chicken or pork. Cheese sandwiches will serve you well in a pinch. If you eat a lot of nuts, plan on bringing your own because those available locally are expensive. The same goes for dried fruits such as raisins. More well-heeled visitors will have fewer problems, as the more expensive lodges will cater to vegetarians and have the ability to cook tasty and wholesome food. **note:** Places serving vegetarian food are listed frequently in the text.

☞ *Traveler's Tip*
Restaurant Pricing: Unless otherwise noted, restaurants in Belize are low-budget (i.e., under $10 for a basic meal with a drink). Restaurants in tourist accommodations tend to be pricier, and gourmet restaurants are noted as such in the text.

Sports & Recreation

While Belize is best known for diving and snorkeling, the range of sports is increasing as the nation expands and tourism increases. Spectator sports are coming of age in Belize with the 1995 opening of the new National Stadium in Belize City.

BEACHES AND SWIMMING: Truth be told, if you're expecting fantastic beaches, forget it! The barrier reef apparently tends to interfere with beach formation, and some beaches (as on San Pedro) have suffered erosion, partially caused by dredging of sand for construction. In many places the water is too shallow for swimming: on Caye Caulker, for example, you have to go to The Cut, a river-like divide that cut off the northern part of the island during the last hurricane. The best beach, hands down, is on the Placencia Peninsula, but even this is only a narrow strip of sand.

SAILING: With a nearly 200-mile stretch of reef-sheltered coastline, Belize is a sailor's paradise, and its potential remains so untapped that you are unlikely to see more than a few other sailboats during your stay. Based on Moho Caye, **Sail Belize** has charters with rates from US$1,000 pw on up. For information contact a travel agent or call 02-45798 in Belize City.

SCUBA AND SNORKELING: With the hemisphere's longest coral reef lying just off the nation's coast, Belize is a great place to do either. The drop-offs from the atolls are spectacular, and the variety of dive sites is seemingly endless. Although equipment is available, serious snorkelers and divers will want to bring their own snorkeling and diving equipment; you can leave it at your hotel in Belize City while you travel around the interior. Resorts generally supply weights and tanks, but you may need to bring the rest. Check with the specific resort if you have questions. Don't forget to bring your NAUI or PADI card; certification is also available.

> ## ⓘ *Did You Know?*
> *You can snorkel and swim for longer periods with confidence if you wear a T-shirt while in the water. Make sure that your mask fits before snorkeling. To do this, put the mask on your face, suck your breath in, and inhale through your nose. While you continue to inhale, the mask should stay on. Try another shape if this does not work. Moustaches, a strand of hair, or suntan lotion may spoil your fit. Moustache wearers should use a bit of Vaseline or lip balm to improve the seal. The strap is to prevent the mask from falling off, not to tighten the seal; it should be set up high for comfort. Before submerging, spit into your mask, coat the lens with your finger, and then rinse; this should have an anti-fogging effect. Avoid exhaling through your nose: this may cause fog as well as release moisture. Snorkel only on the outer side of the reef wall on low-wind or calm days, bring your own equipment or at least a mask you feel comfortable with (especially if you require a prescription mask). If you're using a kayak, it's a good idea to tie a line to it and tow it around when snorkeling.*

dive spots: Found outside the reef at 50- to 100-foot depths, immense canyons have been formed by large coral ridges rising upward from a downward-sloping sandy bottom. Filled with caves and tunnels, these canyons swarm with life, including snapper, grouper, nurse sharks, and – on occasion – hammerhead and blacktip sharks. Barracuda, schools of spotted eagle rays, manta rays, and schools of amber jack can also be found in the reef's vicinity. The nation's most spectacular dive location is The Great Blue Hole in Lighthouse Reef. An almost perfect circle 1000 feet in diameter, its interior walls plummet 412 feet – an almost straight descent for the first 125 feet. At the bottom is a majestic underwater cathedral containing columns, archways, and alcoves. It is a huge cave with 12- to 15-foot stalactites hanging from the ceiling. Another wonderful area is the Hol Chan Marine Reserve. There are other spectacular dives in the same area, off Glover's Reef, and in the Turneffe Islands Atoll.

diving: This is a paradise for divers. Visibility in the Caribbean ranges from 50 to 100 feet. Since the water temperature is around 80°F, a wet suit is needed only for protection against coral outcrops. As the reef is only a few feet deep and about a half-mile offshore, dives are easy and economical on the tanks. Expect to pay around $35 and up for a single tank dive or $45 and up for a two-tank dive. Most hotels will require certification for participation in dives or to rent equipment.

Hotels such as San Pedro's Coral Beach Hotel and Dive Club offer instruction for beginners, and the shallow, still waters surrounding the cayes are an ideal place to practice. Shops with equipment rental and tours are also located on Moho Caye, Caye Caulker, Caye Chapel, St. George's Caye, and on Glover's Reef. There's a decompression chamber on San Pedro, which is funded by a tax on tank refills.

WIND SURFING: Rentals are available from most resorts, but the sport remains relatively underdeveloped here. The Sun Breeze Hotel on San Pedro, Ambergris Caye rents Mistral boards.

ANGLING AND DEEP-SEA FISH-ING: There's a wide and wonderful variety of fish. Sailfish and marlin visit the exterior of the Barrier Reef in spring and fall. Trolling and bottom fishing along the reef can reap grouper, mackerel, amberjack, crevalle, barracuda, and snapper. While barracuda, permit, jack, bonefish, snapper, bonito, wahoo, and tuna may be caught all year, January is best for grouper, February for snook, March for tarpon, snook, marlin, and sailfish. April is a good month for tarpon, snook, marlin, and sailfish; May for tarpon, snook, marlin, and sailfish; June for tarpon and sailfish; July for tarpon; November for tarpon and snook; and December for snook and grouper.

Angler Adventures (☎ 203-434-9624, fax 203-434-8605, 800-628-1447; Box 872, Old Lyme, CT 06371) offers all-inclusive packages and represents a number of fishing lodges. Information on the major lodges is also included in the travel section. These include the Belize River Lodge, El Pescador, the Blue Marlin Lodge, and the Ranguana Lodge.

CAVING: This sport remains undeveloped and – except for the established sites – can be dangerous. There are a number of caves you can visit, including Chechem Hah and the Rio Frio caves in the Cayo District, St. Hernan's Cave near the Blue Hole, and the caves near Punta Gorda.

The Chiquibul is the most extensive cave system, but it is difficult to reach. The Caves River Branch

trip – in which you float into a cave and hike around – is probably the most unusual of its kind in the world. **Slickrock Adventures, Inc.** (☎ 800-390-5715; Box 1400, Moab, UT 84532; e-mail slickrock@slickrock.com; www.slickrock.com) also arranges trips in the Caves Branch system.

TUBING: This relatively new sport involves floating downriver in a giant inner tube. Trips can be arranged at Cayo District resorts, at Ian Anderson's Adventurous Belize at Caves Branch, and at the Cockscomb Jaguar Preserve.

KAYAKING: Reef-Link Kayaking (☎ 515-279-6699; ask for Sonna Newton) operates from Ranguana Caye off of Placencia. Write c/o S. Newton, 3806 Cottage Grove, Des Moines, IA 50311. They publish the informative *Belize by Kayak*, the only kayaking guide available.

Slickrock Adventures, Inc. (see *Caving* above for contact information) offers trips, including one to Glover's Reef. **Monkey River Expeditions** (☎ 206-660-7777, fax 206-938-0978; 1731 44th Av. SW, Ste. 100, Seattle, WA 98116; e-mail mre@halycon.com) has kayak trips to the reef around Placencia and up the Monkey River for about US$1,300; custom trips are also available.

One of the best known kayaking companies is **Island Expeditions** (☎ 800-667-1630, 604-325-7952; fax 604-325-7952; 368-916 W Broadway, Vancouver, BC, Canada V5Z1K7; e-mail island@whistler.net; www.islandexpeditions. Com). They offer kayaking trips around Glovers Reef (where they have a base camp on Southwest Caye) and to other islands, plus rainforest expeditions, mountain biking, as well as trips to Tikal. Prices run from US$569-$1,449.

Ecosummer Expeditions has trips down the Crooked Tree Lagoon and out on the cayes including Lighthouse Reef. They combine kayaking with horseback riding, tubing, and interpretive hiking. In the US, ☎ 800-688-8605 or 206-332-1000, e-mail trips@ecosummer.com, or write 936 Peace Portal Dr., Blaine, WA 98231. In Canada, ☎ 604-669-7741, fax 604-669-3244, or write 1516 Duranleau St., Vancouver, BC. V6H 3S4.

Laughing Bird Adventures (☎ 800-238-4467; Box 131, Olga, WA 98279) offers five- to 11-day trips from December through April in Belize (departing from Kitty's Place in Placencia) and in northern Honduras. Prices start from US$499. In addition to these operations, numerous lodges rent kayaks; these are generally noted in the text. Alternatives: You can 1) bring your own kayak on top of your car or truck; 2) bring a foldable kayak that can be transported by air; 3) or rent a kayak. Foldable kayaks are easier to transport, but solid boats are easier to get in and out of for snorkeling. and they are safer. When planning a kayak trip, remember to allow plenty of time. Safety is more important than distance covered.

WHITEWATER RAFTING: Slickrock Adventures, Inc. (☎ 800-390-5715; Box 1400, Moab, UT 84532; e-mail slickrock@slickrock.com; www.slickrock.com) offers whitewater rafting along the Macal River, for either a day trip or as part of their "Adventure Week."

HORSEBACK RIDING: Trips into the Mountain Pine Ridge are available with Banana Bank, Chaa Creek, du Plooys, Windy Hill Cottages, and Mountain Equestrian Trails – all of which are near San Ignacio.

Practicalities

WHO SHOULD COME: Belize is not the destination for everyone. If the least little sandfly bite or mosquito sting takes you aback, then Belize isn't the place for you, unless you confine yourself to San Pedro's most luxurious resorts. Much of mainland Belize is truly for the adventurous. But you'll find that the rewards more than repay you for any discomfort you may endure.

ⓘ *Did You Know?*

Mexico's Cancún (a smaller area than Belize) contains six times as many hotel rooms than in all of Belize! Although Cancún receives two million tourists annually, Belize receives less than one-tenth that number. While Cancún has high-rises galore, Belize's largest hotel has 118 rooms; most have 10 or less. Also, Belize does not have a single fast food restaurant or chain – a major plus, in this author's opinion.

WHEN TO COME: This depends upon your motives for coming. The best time is definitely off-season, when rates for hotels plummet and there are few visitors to be found in the more popular spots. The rain is heaviest June through January, with the worst months October and November. It can rain during the dry season as well, but squalls generally come and go. If weather is your concern, February through May are probably your best bets. If camping and hiking are important, the dry season would definitely be preferable. If you go to the more inaccessible or untouristed towns, parks, and reserves, crowds shouldn't be a problem no matter what the season! The time **not** to arrive is at Christmas and Easter, when Belizeans themselves go on holiday. Don't count on finding a hotel room in Placencia during Holy Week, for example.

☞ *Traveler's Tip*

If you can, visit Belize off-season. Not only will you save 30-40% on most accommodations, it will be less crowded. You will have to deal with rain, but it is more likely to be in the form of brief showers than all-day torrents.

PLANNING EXPENSES: Expect to spend from US$25 pp, pd at a *minimum* for food and very spartan accommodations. Generally, you'll find yourself spending at least US$30 total and, depending upon your needs, probably more. If you're renting a car and staying in deluxe accommodations you can easily end up spending hundreds of dollars per day. Differences in price from top to bottom reflect facilities and comfort, so the more you can do without the cheaper you can travel. When staying in hotels, be sure to find out the total price including tax and service charge (which can boost the final price by 16% or more). The best way to cut down on expenses is to stay in one (relatively inexpensive) location for a time. Expect prices to be about the same as they are in the US, but much higher for imported items;

Canadians will find Belize to be somewhat cheaper than their homeland. Finally, if a price is not posted, be sure to ask, so as to avoid later misunderstandings.

Arrival

BY AIR: The best way to get a deal on airfares is by shopping around. A good travel agent should seek out the lowest fare; if not, find another agent, or try doing it yourself. If there are no representative offices in your area, check the phone book. Most airlines have toll-free numbers. In these days of airline deregulation, fares change quickly so it's best to check the prices well before departure – and then again before you buy the ticket. The more flexible you can be about when you wish to depart and return, the easier it will be to find a bargain. Whether dealing with a travel agent or directly with the airlines, make sure that you let them know clearly what it is you want. Don't forget to check both the direct fare and the separate fares to the gateway city and then on to Belize City; there can be a price difference. Allow a minimum of two hours connecting time when scheduling.

American Airlines flies daily from Dallas and out of its Miami hub. It is one of the most convenient airlines, with connecting flights to and from virtually every major city. **Continental** flies nonstop from Houston. **TACA** flies from eight gateway cities: San Francisco, LA, Chicago, Washington, DC, Miami, Houston, and New Orleans. The latter three flights are nonstop. ☎ 800-535-8780.

from Canada: American and Continental fly and make connections in Miami. TACA also has connecting flights. ☎ 800-263-4063 in Quebec; 800-263-4309 in Ontario; and 800-387-6209 in the other provinces. Charter flights from Calgary to Cancún run about C$500; it's a two-day bus ride from there to Belize City.

from the Caribbean: Jamaica Express (a subsidiary of Air Jamaica) flies to Belize City from Montego Bay, Kingston, and Grand Cayman.

from Cancún, Mexico: Mexican Airlines (☎ 800-531-7921) now offers flights from Cancún to Belize City via its Air Caribe subsidiary. A cheaper (but more troublesome) way to get to Belize is to take a charter flight into Cancún and then head by bus into Belize via Chetumal.

☞ *Traveler's Tip*
The *Belize Transfer Service* (☎ 415-327-0456, fax 415-326-3557) has all manner of transfers, including bus, limo, and air, for travel from Cancún to Chetumal to Belize City.

---

from Guatemala: Aerovias flies from Guatemala City and Flores (near Tikal), and both of the following fly from Flores: **Tropic Air,** ☎ 026-2012 or 800-422-3435; www.belize.net; e-mail tropic@btl.net and **Maya Island Air** (☎ 02-31348/31362/31403; e-mail mayair@btl.net.

from Honduras: West Caribbean Airways flies from La Ceiba and Roatan.

from Europe: You must fly to Miami or another gateway city and make connections. This generally requires an overnight in the States. Check with your travel agent for details.

BY BUS: Unless you have a damned hard ass and a hell of a lot of patience, or plan on taking a month or so to complete your trip, this isn't really a viable alternative. It will cost you well under US$100 for the total fare from Texas or San Diego. From Guatemala City, you can take a bus to the border town of Melchor de Mencos. You can travel from Mérida to the border "duty free" town of Chetumal, Mexico. If you're changing buses in Mexico City, you need to take a taxi (around US$7) to TAPO, the bus terminal for the south.

BY CAR: It takes at least four days from Brownsville, TX to reach Chetumal, Mexico and a minimum of five days from CA. When you arrive at the border. you'll have to surrender your Mexican Tourist Card and/or car papers. If you are asked to pay an "exit tax" here, it's an attempt to rip you off, so decline to pay. If you've taken out Mexican auto insurance (for a rental car) have your policy officially stamped so that you'll be able to obtain a rebate for the days spent in Belize when you return the car. Be sure to get a temporary import permit from the customs official as well as mandatory auto insurance. The latter can be purchased at the restaurant across from the border station.

One travel agent that can help you with travel to Mexico in your own car is **Sanborn's** (☎ 800-222-0158) in McAllen, TX. If you are intent upon driving, you may wish to purchase *Drive the Interamerican Highway to Mexico and Central America*, which was published in 1992. To order send US$12.50 (plus $2.50 handling and shipping)

Tropic Air Phone Numbers

San Pedro Airport . . . . . . 026-2012, fax 026-2338
Belize Municipal Airport 02-45671
Goldson International Airport 025-2302
Caye Caulker Airport 022-2040
Corozal Airport 04-22725
Placencia Airport. 06-23184
Punta Gorda Airport. 07-22197

to Interlink 209, PO Box 526770, Miami, FL 33152.

BY SEA: You can travel by sea from Guatemala; a ferry arrives in Punta Gorda twice a week from Puerto Barrios and others leave on demand. For cruises, see page 77.

ARRIVING FROM MEXICO: From Chetumal you take a bus for Belize City. There's a stop at Mexican immigration and customs, and the bus then proceeds to the Belize side, where it waits for you to pass through both sides. You will be asked to show sufficient means of support for your stay in Belize. Imports of liquor and cigarettes are forbidden. Change money to Belizean dollars on the Belize side, where you may be able to negotiate a better-than-usual exchange rate if you have US dollars in cash.

ARRIVING FROM GUATEMALA: Ferries leave Puerto Barrios, Guatemala, for Punta Gorda on Monday and Wednesday, with a return run on Tuesday and Friday. You can also fly to Belize City from Flores or Guatemala City (see above), and buses run regularly between Flores and Melchor on the border.

Internal Transport

Belize is an easy country to travel in. Buses are reasonably plentiful, and charters are always available if you're willing to pay the fee. The best **map** is the *Traveller's Reference Map of Belize*, published by ITMB Publishing of Vancouver; fax 604-687-5925 or write 736A Granville St., Vancouver, BC V6Z 1G3 Canada. Essential if you're going off the beaten track, it should be available through your local bookstore. The tourist bureau in Belize City generally has copies on hand for sale, as does the gift shop in the Belize Biltmore.

BY AIR: Tropic Air (☎ 02-45671, 026-2012, 800-422-3435; www.belize.net; e-mail tropic@btl.net) flies from Belize City's municipal airstrip, less than a mile from the city center, to San Pedro on Ambergris Caye, Placencia, Dangriga, Corozal, and Punta Gorda. More expensive flights leave from the international airport as well.

Maya Island Air (☎ 02-31348/31362/31403; e-mail mayair@btl.net) flies to and from San Pedro, Caye Caulker, Caye Chapel, Belize International, Belize City, Dangriga, Big Creek, Placencia, Corozal, Flores (for Tikal) and Punta Gorda.

While it can be slightly more expensive, Tropic is the oldest and best established airline. Service is impeccable, and you will find yourself alone on a small plane if you are the only passenger on a scheduled flight. They use DHC6 Twin Otters, 208B Grand Caravans, and 207A Stationairs. Tropic was founded in 1979 by John Grief, Jr. and it has been onward and upward since then. Prices are around BZ$47 to San Pedro from Belize Municipal, BZ$138 to Punta Gorda from Belize Municipal, and BZ$560 for a Tikal day tour from San Pedro.

BY BUS: Buses run almost everywhere, though service can be scant – especially on Sunday. It's best along the roads leading to the borders with Mexico and Guatemala. In the case of Mexico (Chetumal), buses actually cross the border. Travel times anywhere within the country are reasonable; the longest run (approximately eight hrs.) is between Belize City and Punta Gorda. Because of the bad roads, travel with the smaller local bus companies can be trying. Since there may be only one bus on a route, a breakdown can take the entire route out of service. Buses are supplemented by trucks in some rural areas. Although the buses are relatively peaceful and uncrowded by Latin American standards, the driver may jack up the volume of his radio. Other passengers may compete, so that reggae may be in the front, rock in the back, and heavy metal in the center.

Keep a close watch on your things while in transit. Baggage can be a problem. Although some buses may have storage below, many do not – including the local buses.

Overhead racks inside won't hold large backpacks or suitcases; it's preferable to carry as little as possible. If you're planning to travel on weekends or during three-day holidays, it's advisable to obtain tickets in advance when possible.

BUS ROUTES: Buses run approximately every hour from Belize City to the nearer outlying towns and to Chetumal, Mexico. Bus companies are *Batty* (☎ 02-72025/74924/77146; 54 East Collet Canal, Belize City) and *Novelo* (☎ 02-71161; West Collet Canal, Belize City). To Dangriga, south of Belize City, there are only four daily runs with *Z-Line* (☎ 02-702201/73937; Magazine Rd., Belize City), and there are generally only two runs per day to Punta Gorda with the same line. Ritchie's and James are two other services operating on these routes. There is only limited Sunday service.

The quality of the vehicles ranges from the large buses used on the northern routes – including the luxury buses serving to Chetumal – to the geriatric Bluebirds found frequently in the countryside. Travel is faster on the better roads. But, on the rougher rural roads, fares and travel times escalate. You'll need to have patience! One problem is that buses to more remote areas may leave only once or a few times per day. Your hotel, and a bar or restaurant near the bus stop are all good sources of information on departures. If you're on a tight schedule or have an early departure, you would do well to double-check bus times. Schedules tend to shift over time.

BOATS AND FERRIES: There are regular runs out to Caye Caulker and Ambergris Caye, and ferries operate between these two islands. There are also regular runs between Dangriga and Tobacco Cay during tourist season. Boats to other islands must be chartered – at rates ranging from BZ$100 to BZ$200 and up. Once out on the cayes, you may wish to charter a boat to go fishing, snorkeling, or diving. Coastal runs are from Punta Gorda to Livingston and Puerto Barrios in Guatemala.

Canoes and kayaks may be rented in San Ignacio by the hour, day, or week. Other places to rent them include Placencia, Hopkins, Caye Caulker and Ambergris Caye, and in Punta Gorda.

CRUISES: A number of cruise ships now call at Belize and **American Canadian Caribbean Lines** operates from Belize City to various cayes, including Ambergris, Goff Caye, South Water Caye, and Tobacco Caye, before continuing on to Livingston and other locations in Guatemala. Prices run from US$1,300 on up. For information and reservations, ☎ 800-556-7450 in the US and Canada, fax 401-247-0955, or write Box 368, Warren, RI 02885. In RI only, ☎ 401-247-0955 collect.

Sailing aboard the Ukrainian cruise ship m/v *Gruziya*, **OdessAmerica** offers seven-day "Mayan" cruises from Tampa to Playa del Carmen, Cozumel, Belize City, and Puerto Cortes with side trips to Copán and other sites. Prices range from US$1,300. ☎ 800-221-3254 or write 170 Old Country Rd., Mineola, NY 11501.

Special Expeditions takes 80 passengers for a 13-day trip on its *Polaris* down the Caribbean Coast of Central America from Belize City as far south as Tortuguero National Park in Costa Rica and then continuing through the Panama Canal. Other stops include Lighthouse Reef, Nicaragua's Corn Islands, and Copán. Rates run from US$5,000, not including airfare. For more information, ☎ 800-762-0003, 212-765-7740, fax 212-265-3770, or write 720 Fifth Av., NY, NY 10019.

☞ *Temptress Adventures*
Temptress Adventures (☎ 800-336-8423) offers a seven-night voyage off Belize and Guatemala, which includes a stop in Belize City, a visit to the Barrier Reef, a lunch in Livingston, a visit to the jungles or Maya ruins near Puerto Barrios, snorkeling off Placencia, a visit to the Monkey River and West Snake Caye, a trip to Laughing Bird Caye, and visits to the Baboon Sanctuary, the Belize Zoo, and Lamanai – all for under US$2,000.

HITCHHIKING: Owing to the lack of cars, hitchhiking is slow but very possible and a good way to pass the time while waiting for buses in the boonies. In some places, where there are no buses, it may save you a taxi fare. In the rural areas, Belizeans with cars are generally conscious of the transport situation and, although there may not be many vehicles, a high percentage of those that do pass will stop for you. If you get a ride with a truck that functions as a bus, you'll be expected to pay.

BY TAXI: Reasonably priced from BZ$4 for a short trip, cabs are meterless, with prices fixed by the lo-

Road Distances in Miles
From Belize City

Belmopan	52
Benque Viejo	81
Corozal	96
Dangriga	107
Dangriga (via New Road)	77
Guatemala border	82
Mango Creek	107
Maskall Village	39
Mexican border	103
Mountain Pine Ridge	80
Orange Walk	65
Placencia	150
Punta Gorda	202
San Ignacio	72
Xunantunich	81

cal government. Be sure to agree on the price before getting into a cab. They are easily identified by their green plates. It will cost about US$100 to rent one for a day. Especially if you have a group of people, taxis can be a reasonable alternative to renting a car, but you should negotiate.

RENTING A CAR: Although renting a car may be a viable option, you should know exactly what you're getting into. You can use a valid US or international driver's license here for up to a year. A permit is necessary to drive a motorbike of up to 90cc. Cars may also be rented at the airport. Prices are very high – as much as US$130 per day including insurance! Per-mile charges are added, and gas is around US$2.60/gal. You can skirt these charges by renting a vehicle in Mexico and driving it across (see "by car" in the "getting there" section earlier). However, parts may not be available in the event of an accident or breakdown, and the car may have to be repatriated by tow truck. Don't rent a four-wheel-drive vehicle unless you really need it to get where you're going. Consider renting a car for only a day or two, and then staying in one place or using alternative means of transportation the rest of the time. As you should do everywhere, read the contract thoroughly – especially the fine print. Ask about unlimited mileage, free gas, late return penalties, and drop-off fees. Check the car over for dents and scratches and make sure that the agent notes any damage so you won't be charged later. You can reserve a car by sending a fax.

DRIVING: Of the 1,417 miles of roads, only 273 are paved - the rest are gravel and earth. While the Northern and Western Highways are paved two-lane roads, most of the others turn to muck after a rain. The worst roads are the ones that were once paved but no longer are.

Although it is being improved, the Hummingbird Hwy. to Dangriga is one such case. The road from Dangriga south to Punta Gorda is unpaved, although it too is slated for eventual improvement. Drivers might want to pick up a copy of Emory King's *Driver's Guide to Beautiful Belize*.

Road hazards at night include pedestrians, holes, and livestock. Four-wheel-drive vehicles, minibuses, or pickup trucks are *de rigueur* on some of these roads. As unleaded gas is unavailable, you may have to disconnect your catalytic converter. Good provisions for safe transport include spare tires, extra gasoline, a supply of water, plugs, points, electrical tape, and belts. Be sure to fill up at the main towns before heading out to the sticks where there may be no service stations. Most stations run from dawn to dusk but ones with longer hours have opened in recent years. Bring a rag to wipe the inside windows in the rain.

⚡ **Warning!**
Traffic accidents are now one of the leading causes of death in Belize. Most accidents occur in and around Belize City. Keep in mind that front-seat passengers must fasten seat belts or face a fine of BZ$25!

---

insurance: If you're bringing your own vehicle in, insurance is dispensed at a booth just across the border (closed on Sundays). Third party liability insurance is mandatory; charges run around BZ$2 pd. However, this coverage is not comprehensive, so you'll be liable for **any** damage to the vehicle. A driver's license and registration are necessary for entry. Gas is around BZ$8 per gallon.

RENTAL AGENCIES: These are listed under Belize City and other towns, where applicable. Keep in mind that it is difficult to rent a car outside of Belize City and the International Airport. Golf carts are for rent on Caye Caulker and on Ambergris Caye, although they are largely unnecessary there.

BY BICYCLE: The major highways are easy cycling, and places like Altun Ha can be reached with a mountain bike. Although there's little traffic, backroads are preferable. Rocky roads can be challenging, however. Keep in mind that repairs and spare parts are generally found only in Belize City. There's no problem with cycling in the north, but you'll definitely want a mountain bike if headed south. It's usually possible to put your bike on top of a bus.

Tour de Caña (Box 7292, Philadelphia, PA 19101, ☎ 215-222-1253) offers bicycle tours, as does **The Touring Exchange** (☎ 206-385-0667; Box 265, Pt. Townsend, WA 98368).

rentals: These are becoming increasingly common. Mountain bikes can now be rented in San Ignacio and hotels such as the Victoria Resort in San Pedro include rentals in the room rates.

Tours

One option for visitors without a great deal of time, or with an urge to savor different, hard-to-do-on-your-own experiences, is a tour or excursion. Most of these include hotel pickup, meals, and drop-off in their pricing. The cost is typically about US$60/day. The advantage of tours is that you avoid crowded buses, cover a lot of territory, and your driver may be very informative. The disadvantages can include the added expense, isolation from locals, and the loss of flexibility. However, tours do provide an easy way to visit many of the national parks, reserves, and wildlife refuges. In addition to tour operators listed in the text, some hotels offer their own tours for guests.

NATURE AND ADVENTURE TOURS: It's in to be green these days among tour operators. So many people have jumped into the business of "eco-tourism" so fast that many can not deliver on their promises. You have to choose carefully. Local operators are listed in the text under each town or locality. Due to the high cost of gas and imported vehicles, bad roads, and the nation's relatively high standard of living, tours are an expensive way to see Belize. If you have more time than money, you can cut costs by making your own arrangements. In the case of Maya ruins, there's generally a caretaker on-site who will take you around. The Baboon Sanctuary has guides available, as does Crooked Tree.

On the other hand, if you have little time to spare and want things to go like clockwork, many tour companies do an excellent job, and you can learn a great deal through a guide's expertise.

> ⚡ **Warning!**
> Controversial government regulations now require that visitors to Belize use a registered guide.

PACKAGE TOURS: As they say, all that glitters is not gold. This cliché may be old, but it remains pertinent when it comes to package tours. If you want to have everything taken care of, then package tours are the way to go. However, they have at least two distinct disadvantages: most decisions have already been made for you, which takes much of the thrill out of traveling; and you are more likely to be put up in a large, characterless hotel (where the tour operators can get quantity discounts), rather than in a small inn (where you can get quality treatment). So think twice before you sign up. Also read the fine print and see what's **really** included and what's not. Don't be taken in by useless freebies that gloss over the lack of paid meals, for example.

ENVIRONMENTAL AND ADVENTURE TOURS: If you're pressed for time, and convenience is more important than money, you may want to sign up for one of these.

Billed as "An Opportunity for Positive Action," **Programme for Belize** (☎ 02-75616, fax 02-75635; Box 749, Belize City) offers six- to eight-day tours to the Rio Bravo Research Station. These are combined with visits to Placencia, Ambergris, Cayo, and sites in northern Belize; you can select the tour best suited for you or collect your own group and order a custom tour. Profits are reinvested in the development of the Rio Bravo Conservation and Management Area.

Based in Belize, **The Divide Ltd**. (☎/fax 501-92-3452; General Delivery, Central Farm PO, Cayo; e-mail met@pobox.com) is a "Rainforest Resource Company" offering very special tours to the rainforests in the Chiquibul and Slate Creek

Preserve areas. Trekking and rafting expeditions run from US$400 (three days, four nights).

Some of the best nature expeditions are operated by **International Expeditions**, with all-inclusive tours departing from Miami. ☎ 800-633-4734 or write 1776 Independence Court, Birmingham, AL 35216.

Another good company is **Magnum Belize** (☎ 800-447-2931, fax 218-847-0334; PO Box 1560, Detroit Lakes, MN 56502; e-mail magnum@tekstar.com; www.magnumbelize.com), which operates Captain Morgan's on Ambergris and represents some of Belize's most popular up-market lodges and hotels. Be sure to ask for a copy of their *Magnum Report,* an informative tabloid.

Operating out of the town of Petaluma, CA, personable Sue Hall (☎ 800-783-4400; SUEHALL1@aol.com) offers customized tours and itineraries at her **Adventures in Travel**. She represents International Archaeological Tours in San Ignacio.

Tread Lightly (☎ 800-643-0060, 860-868-1710; e-mail treadlit@aol.com, patread@aol.com) offers three different packages for Belize. They operate in numerous other destinations as well, and support eco-tourism.

Field Guides (☎ 512-327-4953, fax 512-9231; Box 160723, Austin, TX 78716-0723) offers trips to Belize visiting Caye Caulker, Chan Chich, and other areas. Cosponsored by the Siwa-ban Foundation based on Caye Caulker, the **American Littoral Society** (Highlands, NJ 07732, ☎ 908-291-0055) conducts an annual eight-day tour; five days are spent on Caye Caulker.

Travel Belize Ltd. (☎ 800-626-DIVE; 303-494-7797; 637-B South Broadway, Boulder, CO 80303) is a highly competent organization. They offer a variety of trips, including sea kayaking, mountain biking, rafting, and other packaged adventures.

Representing a number of fishing lodges, **Angler Adventures** (☎ 203-434-9624, fax 203-434-8605, 800-628-1447; Box 872, Old Lyme, CT 06371) offers all-inclusive packages. Specializing in adventure travel in Belize, **Island Expeditions** (☎ 604-325-7952, fax 604-325-7952; 368-916 W Broadway, Vancouver, BC, Canada V5Z 1K7) offers kayaking trips around Glovers Reef and the Blue Hole, rainforest expeditions (including trips to La Milpa and Río Bravo), and trips to Tikal.

Steppingstone Environmental Education Tours (☎ 800-874-8784, 910-843 9101, fax 910-843-9102; P.O. Box 767, Red Springs, NC 28377) offers an "Archaeo-Astronomy" tour, to visit the cayes and Maya sites near San Ignacio, as well as conducting orchid and other tours. In addition to kayaking and tours incorporating kayaking, **Eco-summer Expeditions** operates a 22-day traverse across the Maya Mountains, a 15-day trek in their foothills, and a special tour for artists and photographers. In the US, ☎ 800-688-8605 or 206-332-1000 or write 936 Peace Portal Dr., Blaine, WA 98231. In Canada, ☎ 604-669-7741, fax 604-669-3244, or write 1516 Duranleau St., Vancouver, BC. V6H 3S4.

FITS Equestrian offers a horseback tour of Belize through Mountain Equestrian Trails; it also includes a stay in San Pedro. ☎ 800-666-FITS or 805-688-9494, fax 805-688-2943, or write 685 La-teen Rd., Solvang, CA 93463.

Laughing Heart Adventures (☎ 800-541-1256, 916-629-3516; Box 699, Willow Creek, CA 95573) operates trips that include canoeing in the Cayo area, as well as hiking.

Rothschild Travel Consultants (☎ 800-359-0747, 212-662-4858, fax 212-749-6172; 900 West End Av., Ste. 1B, NY, NY 10025) represents a number of dive operators and resorts as well as San Ignacio lodges such as duPlooy's.

Wildland Adventures (☎ 800-345-4453, 206-365-0686; fax 206-363-6615; e-mail WildAdve@aol.com) offers trips that include optional add-on excursions to Spanish Bay Resort, Tikal, and, locales in Honduras.

BZ Travel Services (☎ 800-382-7776; Box 1723, Dickinson, TX 77539; www.compassnet.com/bztravel; e-mail bztravel@compassnet.com) is affiliated with Bottom Time Divers on Ambergris and Belize Diving Services on Caye Caulker; they offer all manner and range of services connected with Belize, including dive packages.

Sea and Explore (☎ 800-345-9786, 504-366-9985, fax 504-366-9988; 1809 Carol Sue Ave., Gretna, LA 70056) offers a wide variety of tours and packages for both the cayes and the mainland. The represent many prominent hotels and lodges.

Other companies include **Great Trips** (☎ 800-552-3419, 612-890-4405, 218-847-4441; 1616 W 139th St., Burnsville, MN 55337); **Ocean Connection** (☎ 800-365-6232, 713-996-7800; 211 E Parkwood, Ste. 108, Friendswood, TX 77546); **Belize Resorts** (☎ 800-333-3459, 305-595-3459; 10127 Sunset Drive, Miami, FL 33137);

International Zoological Expeditions (☎ 800-548-5843; 508-655-1461; 210 Washington St., Sherborn, MA 01770); **Massachusetts Audubon Society** (☎ 617-259-9500; 5 S Great Rd., Lincoln, MA 01773); **Mayan Adventure Tours** (☎ 206-523-5309; PO Box 15204, Wedgewood Station, Seattle, WA 98115); **Triton Tours** (☎ 800-426-0226, 504-464-7964; 1111 Veterans Blvd., Ste. 5, Kenner, LA 70062); and **Tropical Travel** (☎ 800-451-8017; 720 Worthshire, Houston, TX 77008).

in Canada: For Canadians, there are a number of operators. **Eco Summer Canada Expeditions** (☎ 604-669-7741; 1516 Duranleau St., Vancouver, BC V6H 3S4); **South American Tours** (☎ 416-234-9176; 4800 Dundas St. W, Ste. 206, Toronto, Ontario M9A 1B1); and **Winter Escapes** (☎ 204-636-2968; PO Box 429, Erikson MB R0J OPO).

In the **UK** contact **Journey Latin America** (☎ 01-747-3108; 16 Devonshire Rd., Chishire, London W4 2HD). There are also about 40 other tour companies. For a complete list check the information available from the Belize Tourist Board.

GENERAL WHOLESALERS: The only travel wholesaler specializing solely in Belize, **Belize Tradewinds** (☎ 800-451-7776, fax 414-258-5336; e-mail bze@msn.com) owns and operates Tradewinds Paradise Villas right by the town of San Pedro on Ambergris Caye. They can book you all over Belize but are particularly expert where San Pedro is concerned. An off-season "7 Night/8 Day Island Dive Special" runs a mere $455 per person with accommodations in a two-bedroom condo for six; airfare, taxes, RT inter-island flights, and land transfers are included in the cost. If there are just the two of you, you pay $679 pp for a week in a one-bedroom condo. Other packages, diving, and tours are offered; call for a brochure. Their mailing address is 8715 West North Avenue, Wauwatosa, WI 53266.

DIVING AND FISHING BOAT TOURS: Various companies offer boat-based diving tours; fishing can be arranged as well. Trips are offered aboard the *Lucretia B* (write Boulder Scuba Tours, 1737 15th St., Boulder, CO 80302; ☎ 800-826-9834); the 40-ft. *Princess* (write Caribbean Charter Services, Box 752, Belize City; ☎ 02-45841); and the 75-ft. *Isla Mia* (write Rte. 3, Box 214A, Corpus Christi, TX 78415.

The 160-ft. yacht *Aquanaut Explorer* is a combination small cruise ship and dive boat; it holds up to 40 people and has a Jacuzzi and casino. Contact See and Sea, 50 Francisco St., San Francisco, CA 94133, ☎ 800-DIV-XPRT, 415-434-3400, or, in Belize City, 02-45217.

The *Manta IV* is based on San Pedro; ☎ 800-468-0123 or write Box 450987, Sunrise, FL 33345. For information on the *Great Reef,* ☎ 800-255-8503, 512-854-0247, or write Rt. 3, PO Box 214A, Corpus Christi, TX 78415. For information on the *Ocean Spirit,* ☎ 800-338-3483 or 504-586-8686. For the *Reef Roamer II,* ☎ 800-433-7262, 504-385-2416, or (in Belize) 02-62151, fax 2180; write Out Island Divers, San Pedro, Ambergris. For the luxurious 120-ft. *Wave Dancer,* ☎ 800-932-6237 or write Peter Hughes Diving, 1390 S Dixie Hwy., Coral Gables, FL

33146. Based in Belize, Hugh Parkey's **Belize Dive Connection** (☎ 02-34526, fax 02-78808, 888-223-5403; Box 1818, Belize City; e-mail fortst@btl.net) is a well-established source.

Others are **La Strega** (write La Strega, 4572 Telephone Rd., Ste. 913, Ventura, CA 93003; ☎ 800-433-DIVE, 805-654-8100 in CA) or the *Aggressor,* a 100-ft. luxury yacht (write Aggressor Fleet Ltd., P.O. Drawer K, Morgan City, LA 70381, ☎ 800-348-2648, 504-385-2416, fax 504-384-0817, telex 784041; e-mail divbot@aol.com).

EDUCATIONAL TRIPS: The **School for Field Studies** (☎ 508-927-7777, fax 508-927-5127; 16 Broadway, Beverly, MA 0195-2096) offers a "Tropical River Ecology" course, which is based at Possum Point on the Sittee River. The month-long course also includes a week's stay at the jaguar sanctuary. Other courses may be available in the future.

The **Blue Creek Project** (www. qvision.com/MRP), sponsored by Texas-based St. Mary's University, is excavating the Blue Creek ruin, a mi. S of the Mexican border near the junction of the Azul, Bravo, and Hondo rivers. Work has been going on (usually from May to July) since 1992. Volunteers pay around $1,350 for a two-week session; additional sessions are discounted. Work is rough, and you must be Mennonite-tolerant (because that is who lives in the area). For more information, ☎ 210-431-2280, fax 210-436-3500, e-mail guderjan@netxpress.com, or write Maya Research Program, Box 15376, San Antonio, TX 78212-8576.

The **Divide Ltd.** (☎/fax 501-92-3452; General Delivery, Central

Farm PO, Cayo) has rainforest workshops, co-sponsored by International Expeditions (☎ 800-633-4734), which are held at a tent camp in the Slate Creek Preserve. The program includes studies of conservation, biodiversity, life zones, symbiotic relationships, and other topics. Activities include horseback riding, trekking, and night walks. The price is US$665 for five nights and six days.

Maya Mountain Lodge (☎ 09-22164, fax 09-22029; PO Box 46, San Ignacio) runs a number of educational summer workshops for elementary, junior high, and high school teachers and other interested parties. These include courses in rainforest ecology and Maya culture. The **Institute for Central American Development Studies,** based in Costa Rica, discusses issues such as agriculture, social justice, and refugees. They offer internships in Belize. Write Institute for Central American Development Studies, Dept. 826, PO Box 025216, Miami, FL 33102-5216.

Accommodations

Belize has hundreds of hotels – everything from luxury resorts to simple inns. While prices are low compared to the Caribbean or the States, they're high for Central America – two to five times what you'll pay in Guatemala. Rooms with a private bath will run you a minimum of BZ$15 and are generally priced much higher. Budget travelers will want to avoid San Pedro and Belmopan. As the towns are small, it's easy to walk from hotel to hotel to check out the rooms. A 6% sales tax is added to your bill, and many tourist-oriented hotels

and resorts add a 10% service charge as well.

making reservations: Advance reservations should be made for the Christmas season. During the rest of the year, reservations are a good idea, but you generally can have your pick of rooms. Couples should state whether they prefer twin or double beds. Rooms with a shared bath down the hall are the least expensive. Remember that most tourist-oriented hotels give a 20-30% discount during the low season. If communicating with lodges or hotels directly, you may be able to get a discount even in the high season. The major resorts and hotels have three or four sets of rates: winter, summer, shoulder, and (sometimes) Christmas.

> ☞ *Traveler's Tip*
> *Make sure to read rate sheets carefully; look for extra charges (such as tax and service and surcharge for use of a credit card). It will be too late to complain when you check out!*

pricing: For the reader's convenience, prices (generally inclusive of 5% tax and 10% service where applicable) are often listed in US dollars. They are subject to fluctuation and should be used only as a guideline. Wherever you go, there are likely to be one or more newer places not listed in this guide. Local hotels charge double the single price, sometimes slightly less, for a couple. Establishments for which no price is listed are classified as follows: *inexpensive* (under US $30), *moderate* (US$31-50), *expensive* (over US$50 s or d), and luxury (over US$100 s or d). It's a good idea to get the current rates from the hotel before you arrive.

reservations: While reservations may not be necessary for the large hotels except during the winter season, it would be prudent to reserve and send a deposit to the smaller establishments that do accept reservations so you can be certain of your booking. The least expensive hotels often do not take reservations.

checking in: Be sure to read what you're signing. Once that 10% service charge – surprise, surprise – has been tacked on to your bill, you'll have to pay it. Each hotel has its own policy on cancellations, service charges, and tipping, so don't make the mistake of thinking one and all are the same.

ON A BUDGET: Low budget travel in Belize is more expensive than elsewhere in Central America. Among the difficulties you might encounter are blaring TVs, clucking chickens, mosquitoes, spiders, and cockroaches. Some of the rooms are dimly lit. In spite of this, the smaller hotels offer a genuine Belizean experience, one that often brings you closer to the local people and their lives. Your neighbors will be ordinary, hardworking folks, and not wealthy tourists on holiday. If you try it, you'll find that you can survive quite well without a/c – a fan, or sometimes no fan, will suffice. And, once you adjust, everything else just falls into place.

SELECTING A RAINFOREST LODGE: As tourism in Belize has grown, so have the number of private reserves and so-called "jungle lodges." It is becoming increasingly difficult to catalog the accommodations available, let alone evaluate

them all. Practically everyone wants to jump on the "ecotourism" bandwagon, some without really understanding what's involved. The lodges are generally not for those who are finicky about their accommodation. If there *is* a generator, it will probably not run all night, and you won't be near a shopping mall or a boutique. At best there will be a small store in the lodge or in the village nearby.

CAMPING: Although camping is not officially encouraged, you will be able to pitch a tent or sling a hammock in the coastal villages such as Placencia or Hopkins. Camping in San Pedro may be more difficult. In the San Ignacio environs, there is one campground (Cosmos), and a few lodges welcome tents. At Mountain Pine Forest Reserve camping is permitted only at the entrance and at Augustine. In the north, camping should be possible near the ruins of Altun Ha and Lamanai, at the Burrell Boom Baboon Sanctuary, and at the Crooked Tree Wildlife Reserve. Camping facilities in the south are limited to Placencia, but a tent will allow you to explore the more remote villages and ruins. Avoid staying in pastures, which may have ticks and chiggers. For kayakers, camping is often the only option, and a tent will be invaluable. If you decide to camp, be sure that your things will be safe. Finally, be aware that you need permission to camp on any public land, including forest reserves. This must be obtained from the Ministry of Natural Resources (☎ 08-22037/72232).

Entertainment

If you're expecting a flashy and glamorous nightlife, you're going to

Tips for Selecting a Rainforest Lodge

■ Although prices vary, lodges are generally not for people on a tight budget. Costs run around $100 pp, pd for room and board, not including transportation, a guide, horses, or other extras. If you can't afford this, you're better off hiking in a less frequented park or reserve.

■ If you're staying in a cottage with a thatched roof, expect some insects in your room. There is no way to prevent this without zapping the entire jungle with pesticides, in which case the ecosystem you've come so far to experience would collapse. Think of it as part of the charm and consider that you are integrating yourself with your environment. After all, you have zillions of microorganisms continually squirming over you already, so what difference will a few larger ones make? Otherwise, arachnophobes and the like should stay only in well-screened conventional rooms, though even these may not be bug-proof.

■ Before you reserve, ask questions pertinent to what you expect. Is there electricity? Hot water? What kind of food is served? Do you serve Belizean dishes? Are meals served buffet style, at a main table, or are guests waited on individually? Is there a choice of entrées? Do you serve wild game? Do you have a bar or is a BYOB policy in effect? Do you have caged animals? How close is the lodge to the main road? What is the fastest way and/or least expensive way to get there? How much does the transport cost? Do you have trips on horseback? Night hikes? Do your prices include taxes and service charges? Do you have a biologist/naturalist on the premises? What is his or her nationality and professional background? Are guided hikes included in the price or are they extra? What other tours and excursions are available? Do you have interpretive trails? What type of forest is near your lodge? How's the birding?

■ Talk to friends who have recently returned or to travelers you meet while in the country. But make sure that you take stock of their differences in experience and outlook. A lodge that may appear "wild" to Sunday strollers may seem a bit too civilized for an avid backpacker. In any event, **do** write us and let us know your recommendations.

■ These are just a few of the questions you might ask. You may come up with others. You'll find some answers in this book, but be aware that details may change. Allow plenty of time for correspondence with the lodges. Some do not have direct telephones. (E-mail is rapidly becoming the best way to communicate). Whenever possible, avoid travel agencies and deal with the lodges directly. This may save 15-20%, and you'll get the lowdown from the horse's mouth.

be disappointed. Belize lacks both the population and the income levels to support much in the way of clubs and concerts. Still, you'll be able to find plenty of bars, and even a place as small as San Ignacio has two discos with live bands. Occasionally you'll see posters for a *jumpup*, a Belizean dance. But much of the time you'll have to make your own entertainment.

MUSIC AND DANCE: Belize does have one fine steel band: **The All Stars,** an 11-member "music for the sake of music" group that appears infrequently. Contact them at ☎ 02-77348 (daytime) or 02-30866 (evenings), or write The All Stars Band, c/o 71 Pickstock St., Belize City. The best band to see if you have the chance is the **Gil Harry Band.** They specialize in Punta (Garifuna-influenced rock) and calypso.

concerts: The **National Arts Council** holds occasional concerts at the renovated Bliss Cultural Center. Other concerts are held at Bird's Isle and at the stadium.

recording artists: Many are based in Los Angeles and featured on Fresh Breeze Records (☎ 213-234-9159; 4309 S. Vermont Ave., LA, CA 90037). The label's most famous artist is **Andy Palacio,** whose most recent offering, a cassette single release, is *Samudi Guñou* (FBC 91599). **Bella Caríb** is an outstanding singer-songwriter whose best-known song so far is *Bald Head Man,* about the advantages of dating a "shinehead man." It was one of the most popular Belizean songs of 1991. Dubbed the "Queen of Punta," Bella was born in Belize but raised in LA. One of her albums, *Tropical Motions* (1992), includes the touching

Coming Home Belize, a song about her return to the land of her birth. Another artist is **Pupa Curly,** a Belizean dance hall-style reggae vocalist who combines Punta with rapid-fire vocals. In addition to the cassette single *Habinaha Whama* (FBR 91596), Pupa is also featured on the dance hall-style reggae compilation, *Belizean Girls.*

dance and theater: Founded in 1990, the **Belize Dance Company** is the nation's first modern dance company. Pieces are choreographed to the music of Olatunji, Black Uhuru, and Kitaro, among other local stars. There's also the fledgling **Belize Theatre Company.** It promises to re-introduce theater to a new generation of Belizeans.

Visas, Services & Health

VISAS: American and Canadian citizens may enter with a passport and stay for 30 days. All visitors should note that they will be expected to show sufficient funds (around $30/day) and a return or onward ticket. **for other nationalities:** Citizens of the following nations do not require visas for stays of up to 30 days: Great Britain, Belgium, Spain, Denmark, Netherlands, Finland, France, Italy, Norway, Luxembourg. Liechtenstein, Iceland, Sweden, Switzerland, Mexico. All others should check with a British embassy or consulate regarding visa requirements.

EXTENDING YOUR VISA: Go to the Immigration Office (☎ 02-77273) in Belize City (115 Barrack Rd.) or to a police station in one of the major towns. An extension now

Important Belizean Phone Numbers

American Airlines . . . . ☎ 02-32522
Batty Bus . . . . ☎ 02-72025/74924/77146
Belize Audubon Society . . . . ☎ 02-34987
Belize Tourist Board (Belize City) . . . . . ☎ 02-77213
Continental . . . . ☎ 02-78309
Emergency . . . . ☎ 911
Maya Island Air . . . . . . ☎ 02-31348/31362/31403
Novelo's Bus . . . . ☎ 02-77372
Police . . . . ☎ 2022
Post Office (Belize City) 02-72201
Programme for Belize . . . . ☎ 02-75616
TACA . . . . ☎ 02-77185
Tropic Air . . . . ☎ 026-2012
Venus Bus . . . . ☎ 02-73354
Z-Line . . . . ☎ 02-702201/73937

costs BZ$25. Unfortunately, going to Guatemala or Mexico does not automatically guarantee that you will get another 30 days. Immigration officials have been known to give you only a few more days, in which event you'll have to travel to an office for an extension. Hopefully, this shortsighted policy will be eliminated.

SERVICES AND INFORMATION: Tourist information centers run by the Belize Tourist Board are at the airport and in Belize City (☎ 02-77213, 75812, fax 02-77490) at 83 North Front St. The latter is open weekdays from 8 to noon and 1 to 5. Generally, they only give you what you ask for. Be sure to ask for the handy informative brochure that lists hotels. For exploring the towns and ruins, they sell a good fold-out map around BZ$8. They may also have the excellent ITMB map of Belize.

The Belize Information Service publishes *Belize Today*, a free and very informative monthly magazine. To subscribe, write PO Box 60, Belmopan, Cayo District.

LAUNDRY: Laundry services are generally available only in San Ignacio, San Pedro, and Belize City, but your hotel can usually arrange to do laundry or hook you up with a launderer. Otherwise be prepared to do it yourself.

TELEPHONE SERVICE: Belize has a very reliable phone system – one of the best in the region – but there are very few pay phones. While collect overseas calls can be made from your hotel, you may have to go to the local telephone office if you wish to pay. (An alternative is the phone card: see below).

COMMUNITY TELEPHONE: If you're going to be traveling in the outback, be sure to utilize the community telephone (see chart below). The operators can tell you

Community Telephone Numbers

Aguacate 07-22973
Arenal 09-32032
Barranco 07-22138
Bermudian Landing 021-2001
Biscayne 021-2025
Blackman Eddie 081-2019
Buena Vista 031-2003
Bomba 03-23738
Bullet Tree Falls 092-2181
Caledonia 041-2013
Calla Creek 092-3520
Carmelita 03-22639
Chan Pine Ridge 03-22593
Chunox 04-22164
Copper Bank 04-22950
Cotton Tree 021-2021
Crique Sarco 07-22674
Cristo Rey 092-3521
Crooked Tree . . . . 021-2084 or 02-44101
Double Head Cabbage 021-2004
Douglas 03-22076
Flowers Bank 021-2005
Freetown Sibun 021-2006
Gales Point 021-2031
Gardenia 021-2083
Georgetown 06-22026
Gracie Rock 021-2008
Hopkins . . . . 05-22033 or 05-22803
Indian Church 03-23369
Isabella Bank 021-2027
Jalacte 07-22610
La Democracia 081-2001
Laguna 07-22970
Lemonal 021-2010
Los Tambos 081-2033
Lucky Strike 021-2017
Maskal 03-22041
Maya Center 05-22666
Maya Mopan 06-22390
Middlesex 05-23033
Monkey River 06-22014
More Tomorrow 081-2006
Nazareth Convent 07-22094
New Mullins River 05-22143
Nuevo San Juan (Ora) 031-2020
Nuevo San Juan (Ind) 061-2002
Otoxha 07-22308

Pomona. 05-23330
Pueblo Viejo 07-22974
Punta Negra 06-22095
Rancho Delores. 081-2016
Red Bank 06-22233
Rockstone Pond 02-45839
San Antonio (Ora) 03-22101
San Antonio (Toledo). 07-22144
San Antonio (Cayo). 092-3266
San Felipe 03-22047
San Jose (Toledo) 07-22972
San Lazaro 07-22972
San Pedro Columbia 07-22303
San Roman (Ora) 03-22127
San Victor 03-22040
Santa Cruz 03-22541
Santa Elena. 04-37007
Santa Familia. 092-3545
Santa Martha. 031-2007
Silk Grass 05-22083
Sittee River . . . . 05-22083 or 05-22888
St. Margaret 081-2005
St. Matthews . . . . 081-2012 or 081-2035
St. Pauls Bank 021-2014
Tower Hill 03-22142
Trinidad 03-22092
Valley. 05-23032
Valley of Peace 08-22072
Willows Bank. 021-2013

---

about local transport as well as who has a room for rent.

Belize Telecommunications Services, the main office (1 Church St., Belize City) is open from 8 AM to 9 PM daily. It costs BZ$3.20/min. to call the US (prefix 001) and BZ$6/min. to call Europe. Guatemalan calls must be prefaced with 00502. Branches in the major towns of each district are open 8-12, 1-4 and 8-12 on Saturday.

Pay phones can be hard to find. In addition to the classic version, you will find tabletop versions in some restaurants and stores. The BTL offers the following sensible advice: "Since you never know when you are going to need a pay phone, please don't vandalize them."

phone card: A wonderful new introduction is the phone card, which frees you from going insane in search of small change! They are available at any BTL office in denominations of BZ$10-50, and also make an attractive souvenir. If you expect to be traveling around, a BZ$10 card would be a good investment.

The number for local information is 110. To call Central America, dial 114; for other international

Information Online

Web sites dealing with Belize are growing by leaps and bounds. Here are a few of the major ones:

- **www.catch22.com/~vudu** and **www.jps.net/vudu** – By the author of this book.

- **www.ambergriscaye.com** – The place to go for information about Ambergris Caye.

- **www.belize.com** – Commercial site designed by lawyer and San Pedro condo-owner Susan Garcia. Many good hotel listings as well as info on the logging in the Toledo District.

- **www.belizeanweb.com** – The Belizean CyberWeb site includes a number of old photos.

- **www.belizetimes.com** – The *Belize Times*.

- **www.belizeaudubon.org** – Belize Audubon Society.

- **www.belizeit.com** – "You Better Belize It," a potpourri of information.

- **www.belizenet.com** – Commercial site designed by photographer Tony Rath. Many good hotel listings.

- **www.belizeweb.com** – BelizeWeb, sponsored by Belize Telecommunications, Ltd. (BTL), has photos, hotel and travel information, business news and more.

- **www.turq.com/belize.html** – The official Belize Tourist Board site.

- **www.xibalba.com/belizeca/** – An excellent site, maintained by Shawn Brisbin, featuring maps, photos, publications and other interesting information.

- **www.webspawner.com/users/evasonline/home.htm** – Eva's Online in San Ignacio. Good info on small hotels, inexpensive tours.

calls, dial 115. AT&T USADirect can be reached by dialing 555. Finally, where there is no pay phone available, there is generally a pay-by-time phone. Ask around.

calling from abroad: Direct dial service is available from both the US and Canada. To call, dial 011-501, drop the zero from the local prefix (for example the "0" from the "02" area code for Belize City).

Belizean Area Codes

	In Belize	From the US, dial
August Pine Ridge	03	011-501-3
Belize City	02	011-501-2
Belmopan	08	011-501-8
Benique Viejo	093	011-501-93
Blue Creek	03	011-501-3
Burrell Boom	028	011-501-3
Caye Caulker	022	011-501-2
Corozal	04	011-501-4
Dangriga	05	011-501-5
Guinea Grass	03	011-501-3
Hattieville/Tropical Park	025	011-201-3
Independence	06	011-501-6
Ladyville	025	011-501-25
Orange Walk	03	011-501-3
Placencia	06	011-501-6
Progresso	03	011-501-3
Punta Gorda	07	011-501-7
San Estevan	03	011-501-3
San Ignacio	092	011-501-92
San Joaquin	04	011-501-4
San Pedro	026	011-501-26
Sandhill	025	011-501-25
Sarteneja	04	011-501-4
Spanish Lookout	08	011-501-8
Yo Creek	03	011-501-92

☞ *Traveler's Tip*

If you have to call your spouse or significant other, you can use a BTL phone card to call after 10 PM any night at the rate of BZ$2/min. Just use any phone that accepts the card.

POSTAL SERVICE: Window service at the General Post Office, near the Swing Bridge in Belize City, runs from 8-noon and 1-5 weekdays and on Saturday. Other offices are located nationwide and are generally open weekdays from 8-noon and 1-5. Although there can be exceptions, mail generally takes about five days to the US, Canada, or Europe. Sea mail runs four to six weeks to North America. To ensure prompt delivery, mail from your hotel desk or a main post office and avoid enclosing anything other than a letter. If you send or receive a package you must pick it up at the Special Package Office on Church St. You can have mail sent to you at your hotel or to Poste Restante, The Main Post Office, Belize City or any other town. If you have American Express traveler's checks or an Amex card, you can have mail sent c/o Belize Global Travel, 41 Albert St., Belize City.

FAXES: Faxes are growing in popularity; many hotels here now have them. Any BTL office will send and receive faxes for you; they will call you to let you know a fax has been received if your number is indicated at the top of the fax.

BROADCASTING AND MEDIA: Founded in 1952 as Radio Belize, Radio One (834, 910, 930, 940 AM and 91.1 FM, 3.28 SW) transmits a wide variety of music in both English and Spanish, as well as limited programming in Garifuna and Mayan. It keeps all Belizeans informed of developments, and it even transmits personal emergency messages. Calling itself the "Caribbean beat in the heart of Central America," it joined the Commonwealth-Caribbean-Canada (CCC) broadcasting group in 1967. Another government-sponsored station is Friends (88.9 FM). Privately-owned Radio KREM is run by Evan X. Hyde (editor of *Amandala*) and plays a lot of dance hall-style reggae. It also has "Aunt Grace" Coleman's family values and advice talk show on Thursday evenings. LOVE FM (95.1, 98.1 FM), which premiered on the airwaves at the end of 1992, plays music in "adult contemporary" format.

Television entered Belize with the introduction of dish antennas. Although there is no local broadcasting, two channels (7 and 9) rebroadcast a mishmash of US programming, together with local features (such as the government-produced "Belize All Over"); program schedules are found in the paper. Many places also have cable TV, and the world of Belizeans has opened up to the wonders of CNN, HBO, Chicago television, and the worst and most moronic dreck of American programs. Unfortunately, save for the Discovery Channel, no educational programs are broadcast, and the long-term effect of such low quality broadcasting can only be negative. One exception is "Lauren Da Mawnin," a Creole language show that is made by Belizeans for Belizeans. All issues save politics are covered; it's aired weekdays from 7:30 AM.

Despite a broad range of newspapers, there is a dearth of quality. Name calling and accusations dominate the papers, and coverage of international issues ranges from scant to nonexistent. (Most are now online: see box on next page). Of the four weekly newspapers, the largest is the *Belize Times*, the unofficial party paper of the People's United Party. An independent business-oriented weekly, *The Reporter* is supported by the conservative UDP, as is the official *The People's Pulse*. The most politically independent newspaper and the best written is *Amandala*. The *San Pedro Sun* (sanprdrosun@btl.net) is the newspaper of Ambergris Caye; send US$40 to subscribe (26 issues) to Box 35, San Pedro, Ambergris. The folks behind this paper also put out *The Belize Sun*, a quarterly paper that is largely filler but does have some useful information. Other papers include the weekly official *Government Gazette*. The Government Information Service also publishes *Belize Today* monthly.

A newcomer on the scene, *Belize First* is published five times per year by Lan Sluder. It contains current

News Online

A surprising number of Belizean newspapers are online. This a great way to get up-to-the minute information as well as a feel for the country before your arrival.

- **www.belizemall.com/amandala/** – Amandala On-Line

- **www.belizenet.com/reporter.html** – The Reporter

- **www.ambergriscaye.com/sanpedrosun/** – The San Pedro Sun. Informative, fun to read, and less biased than the mainland newspapers.

---

information on hotels, restaurants, history, real estate, and other topics. Subscription rates are US$19.50. Write Equator Travel Publications, 280 Beaverdam Rd., Chandler, NC 28715 or e-mail 74763.2254@compuserve.com.

Serious and leftist, the periodical *Spearhead* is published by SPEAR. Issued three times a year by the Belizean Studies Association at St. John's College, *Belizean Studies* publishes local research and writing. The US Embassy publishes the bi-monthly newsletter *Commercial Opportunities*. Cubola Publications is the local book publisher, and is by far the nation's most professional publishing operation.

HEALTH: The water is safe to drink here; Belize is one of the most sanitary of the Central American nations. Take basic precautions, such as washing both your hands and pocketknife before peeling fruit. When visiting Guatemala or using water from an uncertain source, water purification tablets should be used. While public water is generally chlorinated, water supplied via "catchments" (cisterns that catch roof runoff) may not be.

No immunizations are required, but you might want to catch up on your polio and tetanus injections. Also, a typhoid booster and an injection of immunoglobulin to stave off hepatitis are recommended for extensive mainland travel; ordinary visitors probably won't find these necessary. Malaria persists in the Punta Gorda district in the south, and if you are planning to spend an extended period of time in the area, it would be wise to take a malaria preventative such as Aralen. Start taking it two weeks before departure (two tablets per week).

Health care is practically free to all comers, but equipment is antiquated. It's at its best in Belize City and very limited in rural areas. A new hospital, Belize City General on Princess Margaret Drive, opened in Belize City in 1995, and a new Dangriga Hospital is planned. There are plenty of pharmacies around should you require medicine, but most medications are imported (largely from Europe and the US) and are expensive.

snakebite: In the extremely unlikely event you should be bitten by a snake, don't panic! Stay still and try to take note of its characteristics (size, color, pattern, and head shape). Nonpoisonous snake bites show two rows of teeth marks, but fang marks are lacking. Suck venom from the wound or push it out with your fingers and apply a loose tourniquet. Walk back to the field station.

protection against insects: Although scarce at higher altitudes, mosquitoes are prevalent in the lowlands. A mosquito net is a handy appurtenance, as are the mosquito coils (spirals), which keep the numbers down when you relax or sleep. Small shops will sell you one or two if that's all you need, but make sure you get a stand. Avoid inhaling the smoke. Try antihistamine cream, Euthrax, or Caladryl to help soothe bites. You have to watch for ticks when you undress because they may not be evident otherwise. If you pull one straight off, you risk leaving its pincers in your flesh. Hold a lighted match or cigarette to the bite and squeeze the area to extract it. Gasoline, kerosene, or alcohol will encourage the tick to come out. Repellents are ineffective against sand gnats; use antibiotic ointment and, as is the case with all bites, avoid scratching or risk infection. In summary, prevention is the best cure: take the precautions listed here, and wear adequate clothing.

Money & Shopping

MONEY: The monetary unit is the Belizean dollar, but transactions may be conducted in either currency, so be sure you know which one you're dealing in. The current exchange rate is US$1 = BZ$2, but you'll receive a slightly lower rate at the bank and an even lower rate at hotels. US cash is easily exchangeable at a two-for-one rate in shops, restaurants, and hotels in San Pedro, Ambergris Caye. To a lesser ex-

tent this is true all over. Don't change more than you have to because you lose on the rate when you change it back at the airport. Paper money is issued in notes of 1, 2, 5, 10, 20, 50 and 100 dollars; coins are 1, 5, 10, 25, and 50¢. Although 25¢ is sometimes referred to as a "shilling," coins are commonly referred to by their US names of nickel, dime, and quarter.

monetary history: The first settlers used any currency available, provoking endless squabbles over exchange rates. British colonial money from Jamaica predominated during the 18th century. The 19th century saw an increase in local trade and a subsequent increase in Spanish American *pesos* and *reales*, while the California Gold Rush popularized American gold dollars. In 1887 the Guatemalan silver *peso* was declared legal tender, but the US dollar supplanted it in 1894. Founded by a group of local financiers, the Bank of British Honduras issued private "dollar" notes. The Currency Commission was created in 1937, and the British Honduras dollar was devalued on Dec. 31, 1949 following the lead of the British Pound. Since independence, the currency has been tied to the US dollar, and no devaluation is expected.

changing money: Although you are technically supposed to exchange all notes at the bank, US dollar notes are almost universally accepted at a two-to-one rate; many shops will change money for you and some will change traveler's checks. Most banks charge a service fee of 2% for traveler's checks. Currency other than US dollars, Canadian dollars, or pounds sterling can be exchanged only with difficulty. It would be wise to bring only US currency – including a generous supply of cash. Most banks are open Monday through Thursday from 9 to 1 and Friday from 9 to 1 and 3 to 6. Although they will exchange traveler's checks, hotels generally will not accept personal checks except as a deposit for rooms. You can exchange your US$ upon departure at the airport (you'll lose 2-3%). You can also do so with moneychangers at the border.

CREDIT CARDS: Although there are a large number of establishments (mostly high-priced) accepting credit cards, don't make them your chief source of cash. *Frequently, a 3-5% surcharge is added to your bill.* At the American Express office you may be able to write a personal check to purchase traveler's checks in dollars if you have one of their credit cards. **note:** Be sure you investigate *all* of the charges before going this route.

SHOPPING: Opening hours vary, but stores are generally open 8-4 from Mon. through Fri., with some stores closing from 12 to 1 in the afternoon. Most close down Wednesday and Saturday afternoons and are closed on Sundays. Some reopen from 7 to 9. Aside from the rather mundane local handicrafts, there isn't much to buy that can't be found cheaper (or at the same price) somewhere else. Many of the handicrafts are imported and then sold at inflated prices. As is the case with all luxury items, there's an import tax on photographic equipment and accessories, so bring your own. T-shirts (Belikin beer design, for example) make good souvenirs.

You can bring back a bottle of local rum (a pricey BZ$18) or some of the less expensive items imported from Mexico or China. Hunks of useless Belizean chicle are also being marketed. They might be used for a paperweight or to manufacture your own private line of chewing gum.

> ☞ *Traveler's Tip*
> The "duty free" shopping at the airport is something of a misnomer. You'll find that local rum, cashew wine, etc., sells for more here than in town. What is cheaper is imported alcohol. The best buy is undoubtedly Virgin Islands rum, which sells for US$3.50 a liter.

A blend of habanero peppers, carrots, onions, and vinegar, Marie Sharp Hot Sauce (regular and extra hot) is now exported. Marie Sharp's Fine Foods (a company formerly known as Melinda's) also manufactures green mango chutney, exotic steak sauce, green habanero pepper sauce, and jams (60% fruit, cane sugar, molasses, lime juice), with guava, papaya, banana, mango, pineapple, orange, and mixed fruit.

Dr. Rosita Arvigo, of Ix Chel Farm fame, has marketed a line of "rainforest remedies" that consist of various tinctures. With attractively-packaged and expensive products, Rainforest Rescue pledges 6% of its gross proceeds to the Belize Audubon Society. Souvenirs you *won't* want to bring out are things fashioned from tortoise shell or black coral (although the latter is legally harvested). Avoid buying bootleg tapes. While it is tempting to do so, the quality isn't always good. It also deprives Belizean artists of a royalty, and the originals can be purchased rather inexpensively at the Chamber of

Commerce-run handicraft center on Fort St.

market shopping: The towns all have their own markets, with the largest in Belize City. San Ignacio has a lively market on Sat. mornings, and Melchor, across the border from Benque Viejo in Guatemala, has a fine market daily with relatively good buys. Another place to visit for shopping is the town of Chetumal, which lies just across the border in Mexico. Supermarkets are uniformly expensive, but they are good places to find unusual souvenirs – hot sauce, papaya wine, matches, or what have you.

☞ *Traveler's Tip*

Belize is hardly a shopper's paradise, and reasonably priced pickings are truly slim. So if you've been having mall withdrawal symptoms, the border towns of Melchor and Chetumal offer plenty of shopping and may be visited to obtain a quick fix! Take a day trip to Melchor (across the border in Guatemala to the west) by bus from San Ignacio, or to Chetumal (a large city in Mexico to the north), easily accessible from the northern Belizean town of Corozal.

---

stores: There are a few places you won't want to miss. The National Handicraft Center is on Fort St. in Belize City; it has an excellent selection of crafts, books, and tapes. Cottage Industries, 26 Albert St., sells crafts (mostly reed) made by Belizean women. Galeria Hicaco on Caye Caulker features a good selection of arts and crafts. The Garcia sisters in San Antonio near San Ignacio feature slate carvings in their museum shop, as does the

Magana shop down the road and the crafts center next to the entrance to the Cockscomb Jaguar Reserve access road at Maya Center.

BARGAINING: Although most of the stores have fixed prices, you can bargain in some market stalls and with moneychangers at the borders.

AMERICAN CUSTOMS: Returning American citizens, under existing customs regulations, can lug back with them up to US$400 worth of duty-free goods, provided the stay abroad exceeds 48 hours and that no part of the allowance has been used during the past 30 days. Items sent by post may be included in this tally, thus allowing shoppers to ship, or have shipped, goods like glass and china. Over that amount, purchases are duties at a flat 10% on the next $1,000. Above $1,400, duty applied will vary. Joint declarations are permissible for members of a family traveling together. Thus, a couple traveling with two children will be allowed up to $3,200 in duty-free goods. Undeclared gifts (one per day of up to $50 in value) may be sent to as many friends and relatives as you like. One fifth of liquor may be brought back as well as one carton of cigarettes. Plants in soil may not be brought to the US.

CANADIAN CUSTOMS: Canadian citizens may make an oral declaration four times per year to claim C$100 worth of exemptions, which may include 200 cigarettes, 50 cigars, two pounds of tobacco, 40 fl. oz. of alcohol, and 24 12-oz. cans/bottles of beer. In order to claim this exemption, Canadians must have been out of the country for at least 48 hours. A Canadian who's been away for at least seven days may make a written declaration once a year and claim C$300 worth of exemptions. After a trip of 48 hours or longer, Canadians receive a special duty rate of 20% on the value of goods up to C$300 in excess of the C$100 or C$300 exemption they claim. This excess cannot be applied to liquor or cigarettes. Goods claimed under the C$300 exemption may follow, but merchandise claimed under all other exemptions must be accompanied.

BRITISH CUSTOMS: Each person over the age of 17 may bring in one liter of alcohol or two of champagne, port, sherry or vermouth plus two liters of table wine; 200 cigarettes, 50 cigars, or 250 grams of tobacco; 250 cc of toilet water; 50 gms (two fluid ounces) of perfume; and up to £28 of other goods.

GERMAN CUSTOMS: Residents may bring back 200 cigarettes, 50 cigars, 100 cigarillos, or 250 grams of tobacco; two liters of alcoholic beverages not exceeding 44 proof or one liter of alcohol over 44 proof; two liters of wine; and up to DM300 of other items.

Life, Language & Study

WORKING IN BELIZE: Pretty much the only way to work here is to start your own business. Permits are difficult to obtain. You must apply for a one-year work permit, for which a fee is charged.

📖 *Suggested Reading*
There are two books about retiring in Belize: the Belize Retirement Guide, *by Bill and Claire Grey, and* Free and Easy in Belize, *by Lan Sluder. Both may be obtained from Equator Publications (fax 704-67-2717; e-mail 74763.2254@compuserve.com).*

RETIREMENT: The newsletter *International Living* recently selected

Getting Married in Belize

- Check with your hotel management for advice. They may help with arrangements.

- A variety of presiding ceremonial officials are available — ranging from Baha'i to Catholic.

- Bring proof of citizenship, and a certified/original copy of your divorce certificate if you have been married before. Widowers must produce a death certificate for their deceased spouse.

- You must be physically present in Belize for a minimum of three days prior to application.

- You must apply a minimum of one day before the ceremony. (For a Sunday ceremony, apply on Fri.) Contact the Belize Tourist Board for details.

- License cost is BZ$200. A blood test is not required.

Belize as a top retirement spot. In the boonies, the cost of living is low if you live like the locals. In order to expedite granting of a permit, you must present evidence of a fixed monthly income of US$750 for singles and US$1,000 for couples, or you must show savings of US$27,000 for singles or US$36,000 for couples. This sum must be deposited in a Belize bank. A provisional permit will be issued while the application is being processed. A number of other documents are required. For information write the Director, Immigration & Nationality Dept., Belmopan, Belize, ☎ 08-22423/22611, fax 08-22662.

GETTING MARRIED: It's possible to get married here, but are you sure you want to? Are you sure you like all of his or her friends? Have you settled the argument about whether the window is to be open or closed at night? If your mate snores, have you reconciled yourself to a lifetime of earplugs? Have you considered the Belizean alternative of "common law" marriage? Provided you haven't changed your mind after reading this, the chart above gives some details.

Call Me Belizean

Mister Visitor, don't call me
NATIVE
in my land;
Mister Foreigner, don't call me
LOCAL
in my Country;
Mister Tourist, don't call me
CITIZEN
in my home;

Mister Come Ya, don't call me
ANY FUNNY NAMES
yá da mi birth-place – Belize;
All you Mister Outsiders in Belize
Just don't call me names –
But instead, I appreciate you to
Call me Belizean – Love that!
or
Call me Balícina – Aba isieni!
or
Call me Beliceño – Con Amor!
"Cause me da fu yá – Belize!"

– Luke Ramirez

LANGUAGE: Over half of all Belizeans speak English as their native language, and just under a third speak Spanish. Other native tongues include Garifuna, Maya (divided into Yucateco, Mopanero, and Kekchí dialects), and low German. About a third of all Belizeans are bilingual and a smaller percentage are trilingual. As English is both the language of school instruction and the official language, approximately 80% can speak English, and you should have no trouble communicating.

Today's language combines King James English, West African words, and other foreign expressions in a blend delivered in a lilting singsong that shows both Scottish and Irish influences. Antiquated words still in common use include "frocks" for dresses and "coaches" for automobiles. A meal is referred to as "tea." The Creole tongue is largely a result of combining African constructions and words with standard English. Because Belize also has a large Spanish-speaking population, the more Spanish you speak the better!

Conduct

Keep in mind that Latin and other conservative cultural mores prevail here. Men and women alike tend to dress conservatively. If you want to be accepted and respected, dress respectably: skirts or slacks are appropriate attire for women in towns and villages. Women should wear shorts only in the resort areas. Bathing attire is unsuitable on main streets, as is any revealing female clothing. But, unlike other Central American nations, Belize does accept skimpy bathing suits on beaches. Business dress for men is a short-sleeved cotton or poplin shirt, or a *guayabera*. Formal wear often consists of bush jackets or long-sleeved embroidered *guayaberas*, rather than coat and tie.

hustlers: Ever-present in Belize City are the calls of "Hey white boy/white chick! What's happening?" Sometimes these are Belizeans being genuinely friendly; at other times they want to a) sell you a piece of coral; b) change money; c) bum money; d) offer you a deal on a boat trip; e) offer you sex; or f) sell you crack, cocaine, or marijuana. Don't let yourself be taken advantage of.

TIPPING: If a service charge is added to your restaurant bill, it's not necessary to leave a tip. Nor is it necessary in small, family-run restaurants. But in other eateries a 10-15% tip is expected. A doorman or porter should be tipped BZ$1-2. Taxi drivers do not require a tip unless they handle your baggage.

THEFT: Particularly in Belize City and in Orange Walk (the capital of the drug trade), this can be a problem. Nevertheless, you should be fine if you take adequate precautions. The very best prevention is being aware that you might be a victim. By all means avoid the slum areas of Belize City, don't flash money or possessions around and, in general, keep a low profile – avoid looking affluent. Keep track of your possessions; things like expensive sunglasses are very popular. Don't leave anything unattended on the beach. Avoid carrying anything in your back pockets. Women should carry purses that can be secured under their upper arm. Never, never leave anything in an unoccupied

Belizean Proverbs

Barefoot-tea better than empty belly. A meal without meat and/or cheese is better than nothing at all.

Blood falla vein. "Blood follows vein." Relatives look out for each other; traits are inherited.

Blow your nose same place where you ketch you cold. Ask your friends for help in times of trouble – especially if they were the ones who got you there.

Di olda di violin, di sweeta di music. Older (more experienced) sexual partners are superior.

Falla-foot jumbie, you jump eena water. "If you follow a ghost, you jump in the water." Follow others blindly and you'll get into trouble.

Fishaman neva say e fish 'tink. "The fisherman never says his catch stinks." People don't like to criticize themselves.

Fos laugh no de laugh; las laugh de laugh. "The first laugh is not the laugh; the last laugh is the laugh." He who laughs last laughs best.

If crab no waak, e no get fat; if e waak too much, e lose e claw. New experiences, though necessary, can carry risks.

If you kyaa(n't) ketch Harry, ketch e shirt. "If you can't catch Harry, catch his shirt." Take what you can get.

If you play with puppy o, e lick you most. Familiarity breeds contempt.

No change-i blaack daag for monkey. "Don't exchange a black dog for a monkey." Things that may look similar can be quite different in reality.

Small axe fall big tree. Size is not always the most important factor.

Too much rat no dig good hole. Too many cooks spoil the broth.

Wen cockroach mek dance, e no invite fowl. Hang out with unsavory characters and you're looking for trouble.

Wen puss no de, rat take place. Mice play when the cat's away. Lack of authority brings anarchy.

Wen stone throw eena hag-pen, did hag weh squeal da di hag weh get hit. "When a stone is thrown in the pig pen, the hog that squeals is the one that got hit." The guilty party is often the one that denies it the loudest.

vehicle, not even in a trunk. Remember that locals who form sexual liaisons with foreigners often do so with pecuniary gain in mind. And, if you give one of them access to your hotel room, it can be a bit sticky when you have to go to the police and make a charge! It's useful to photocopy your passport and keep it separate, along with the numbers of your traveler's checks and any credit cards. A useful precaution is to secure unnecessary valuables in the hotel safe; a more effective precaution is to leave them at home.

With an estimated 20-30 planeloads landing each month, Belize is a major transhipment point for cocaine from Colombia, and the drug has permeated Belizean society. Problem areas include Caye Caulker, Ambergris Caye, Orange Walk, Dangriga, and Belize City. It should not affect you as long as you don't associate with the wrong people.

Belize Dos and Don'ts

■ Don't condescend to locals. Do treat the local people with the same respect you would like to receive yourself. Allow them the courtesy of answering at their own pace. Don't make promises you can't or don't intend to keep. Don't make local children into beggars by acting like Santa Claus and dispensing gifts and money. Never pay for photos. In general, refrain from giving out money: it creates a cycle of dependency and creates more problems than it solves.

■ Don't waste time lounging in your hotel. Do get around and explore. But don't try to do too much. Belize is not a place for rushing around. There's always the next visit.

■ Don't dump your garbage at sea or litter in town. Do protect the environment and set a good example for others.

WOMEN TRAVELING ALONE: A large number of women come to Belize alone or in groups, and the attitudes of some of them (particularly in Caye Caulker) have led local males to assume that they are part of a woman's adventure in paradise. You should have no problems with men if you simply say "thanks, but no thanks." Part of the problem here is the influence of Western movies and television programs. Traveling will be a relatively hassle-free experience as long as you exude a certain amount of confidence.

TRAVELING WITH CHILDREN: Belize is as safe as anywhere for children. They are generally only charged half-fare to international destinations. Just take care that they are not overexposed to sun and get sufficient liquids. Remember to bring whatever special equipment you'll need. Disposable diapers and baby food are available but expensive. Be sure to inquire at your hotel as to extra charges for children and if they'll even be wanted. Finally,

keep an eye on the kids while they're in the water. There are no lifeguards. Also, make sure that they apply sun protection.

ENVIRONMENTAL CONDUCT: Dispose of plastics properly. Remember that six pack rings, plastic bags, and fishing lines can cause injury or prove fatal to sea turtles, fish, and birds. Unable to regurgitate anything they swallow, turtles and other sea creatures may mistake plastic bags for jellyfish or choke on fishing lines. Birds may starve to death after becoming entangled in lines, nets, and plastic rings. Remember that the parks and reserves were created to preserve the environment so refrain from carrying off plants, rocks, animals, or other materials. Although production is licensed by the government, buying black coral jewelry supports reef destruction.

If you're camping when kayaking on a small island, don't go to the bathroom on the island itself; instead, wade in the water to go. Ecology also revolves around food.

Avoid eating lobster and conch out of season (Mar. 15 through July 14 for lobster; July 1 through Sept. 30 for conch), and try to avoid eating undersized lobster not of reproductive age.

> ⚡ **Warning!**
> *The following activities are banned by law – removal and export of coral; unlicensed hunting; picking of orchids in forest reserves; removal of archaeological artifacts; spear fishing; overnight camping in any public place, including forest reserves unless you have Forestry Dept. permission.* **drugs:** *With the exception of alcohol, coffee, and tobacco, all drugs – from marijuana to cocaine – are treated as narcotics. No matter how many locals you see smoking in public, you may not receive the same tolerance from police, who positively revel in catching tourists. You can expect hundreds of dollars in fines and a few days in jail. If driving around the country, you may notice the occasional "Customs" checkpoint manned by police. They're looking for drugs, and there are no civil liberties in this regard; there's no such thing as illegal search and seizure on the part of the police!*

UNDERSEA CONDUCT: Respect the natural environment. Take nothing and remember that corals are easily broken. Much damage has already been done to the reef by snorkelers either standing on coral or hanging onto outcroppings, and white patches of dead coral are clearly visible at locations such as Hol Chan Marine Reserve. Stony corals grow at the rate of less than half an inch per year, it can take decades to repair the desecration caused by a few minutes of carelessness. It's wise to keep well away just for your own protection: many corals will retaliate with stings and the sharp ridges can cause cuts that are slow to heal. In order to control your movement, make sure that you are properly weighted prior to your dive. Swim calmly and fluidly through the water and avoid dragging your console and/or octopus (secondary breathing device) behind you. While diving or snorkeling, resist the temptation to touch fish. Many fish (such as the porcupine) secrete a mucous coating that protects them from bacterial infection. Touching them removes the coating and may result in infection and death for the fish. Also avoid feeding fish, which can disrupt the natural ecosystem. Spearfishing with scuba gear is illegal in Belize, and trigger-controlled spear guns are prohibited. If you're diving, be sure you have a realistic appraisal of your own abilities and pay attention to decompression and other factors. In short, look, listen, enjoy, but leave only bubbles.

BOATING CONDUCT: In addition to the behavior patterns detailed above, always exercise caution while anchoring a boat. Improperly anchoring in seagrass beds can destroy wide swathes of the grass, which takes a long time to recover. If there's no buoy available, the best place to anchor is a sandy spot where you create relatively little environmental impact. Tying your boat to mangroves can kill the trees, so it is acceptable to do so *only* during a storm.

In order to help eliminate unnecessary discharge of oil, maintain the engine and keep the bilge clean. If you notice oil in your bilge, use oil-absorbent pads to soak it up. Be careful not to overfill the boat when fueling. Emulsions from petrochemical products stick to fish gills and suffocate them. Deposits in sediment impede the development of marine life. Detergents affect plankton and other organisms, which throws off the food chain.

When you approach seagrass beds, slow down because your propellor could strike a sea turtle. Avoid maneuvering your boat too close to coral reefs. Striking the reef can damage both your boat and the reef. Avoid stirring up sand in shallow coral areas. The sand can be deposited in the coral and cause polyps to suffocate and die. If your boat has a sewage holding tank, empty it only at properly equipped marinas. Avoid using harsh chemicals such as ammonia and bleach while cleaning your boat; they pollute the water and kill marine life. Use environmentally safe cleaning products whenever possible. Boat owners should avoid paint containing lead, copper (which can make molluscs poisonous), mercury (highly toxic to fish and algae), or TBT. Finally, remember that a diver-down flag should be displayed while diving or snorkeling.

ARCHAEOLOGICAL THEFT: In spite of the fact that Belize has had laws on its books prohibiting the export of antiquities since 1929, smuggling has been a continual problem. Removing objects from their archaeological context severely diminishes their worth to an archaeologist because their relevance has a direct relation to their location. Throughout the world, much knowledge has been lost to us forever because of the activities of looters. Looting diminishes our cultural heritage. Never support such activities by purchasing artifacts, and never move anything you might see at an archaeological site.

Sadly, for the most part, those who plan and carry out these thefts are "respectable" US citizens who operate behind the scenes. Their positions in international business provide a veil behind which they can hide their illegal activities. It is also common to combine antiquity smuggling with drug smuggling. The actual looters are often poor farmers who are taken advantage of by middlemen. The middlemen sell the pieces in turn to North Americans for up to 10 times the initial purchase price. These buyers might then resell the object for as much as 100 times what they paid. The US, Switzerland, Japan, and Australia are the nations with the biggest trade in illegal artifacts. There are no laws in these countries prohibiting this trade.

In Belize, an "antiquity" is a man-made object 150 years old or more. An "ancient monument" is any structure over a century old. Historic and colonial remains also qualify as artifacts. Individuals may possess antiquities as long as they are not taken out of the country and are registered with the Dept. of Archaeology. Antiquities may only be exported with a permit issued by the Minister of the Dept. of Archaeology.

More Practicalities

WHAT TO TAKE: Bring as little as possible, i.e., bring what you need. It's easy just to wash clothes in the

WHAT TO TAKE

CLOTHING

socks and shoes
underwear
sandals or thongs
T-shirts, shirts (or blouses)
skirts/pants, shorts
swimsuit
hat
light jacket/sweater

TOILETRIES

soap & shampoo
towel, washcloth
toothpaste/toothbrush
comb/brush
prescription medicines
Chapstick
other essential toiletries
insect repellent
suntan lotion/sunscreen
shaving kit
toilet paper
nail clippers
hand lotion
small mirror

OTHER ITEMS

passport and driver's license
traveler's checks
money belt
address book
notebook
Spanish-English dictionary
pens/pencils

books/maps
watch
camera/film
flashlight/batteries
snorkeling equipment
extra glasses
umbrella/poncho
laundry bag
laundry soap/detergent
matches/lighter
frisbee/sports equipment

HIKING & CAMPING

internal frame pack
daypack/shoulder bag
foam sleeping bag
ripstop tape
tent/tent pegs
canteen
first-aid kit
binoculars
compass
hiking shorts/pants
candles/candle lantern
pocket knife
nylon cord
utensils
camping stove
can opener
food containers
spices, condiments
scrubbing pads
pots, pans
plastic wrap or
   aluminum foil

sink and thus save lugging around a week's laundry. Remember, simple is best. Set your priorities according to your needs. With a light pack or bag, you can breeze through from one region to another easily. Confining yourself to carry-on luggage also saves waiting at the airport. And, if a second bag of luggage gets lost, you at least have the essentials until it turns up. If you do pack a lot of clothes, you could leave things at your hotel and pick them up later. When packing, it's preferable to take dark, loose clothing. If you're going to wear shorts, make them long and loose. Be sure to bring plenty of reading material, especially if you're planning a vacation on the cayes.

protectives: Avon's Skin-So-Soft bath oil, when diluted 50% with water, has a reputation as an excellent sand flea repellent. Recent scientific tests, however, have failed to show any repellent effect in the laboratory. Sunscreen should have an 8-15 protection level or greater and should be purchased in the US. If you're going kayaking or intend to spend a lot of time in the sun and have sensitive skin, zinc oxide cream serves as an effective sunblock. When snorkeling, consider wearing a T-shirt to avoid ending up with a raw back. A flashlight is essential; you might want to bring two, a larger one and one to fit in your handbag or daypack. Feminine hygiene items are rarely found outside of Belize City; bring a good supply. Likewise, all prescription medicines, creams, ointments, and the like should be brought with you.

other items: Books are twice US prices so you'll also probably want to stock up before arrival. It's a good idea to have toilet paper with you, as the least expensive hotels and the park restrooms may not supply it. Film is very expensive, so be sure to bring a supply. Plastic trash bags and an assortment of different-sized baggies will also come in handy. If planning extensive forest trekking during the wet season, high-topped rubber boots are an essential investment. You can bring them with you or purchase after arrival, although if you have unusually large feet it's a good idea to bring your own. Definitely bring windsurfing sandals, if that's your sport.

budget travel: If you're a budget traveler, you'll want to bring along earplugs, some rope for a clothesline, towel and washcloth, toilet paper, cup, small mirror, a universal plug for the sink, and a cotton sheet. But don't overpack; large backpacks will not fit on the overhead racks above the bus seats.

hikers and backpackers: If nature is your focus, you'll want to bring a rain parka, walking shoes or hiking boots, a day pack, canteen, hat, binoculars, and insect repellent, as well as a bird book or two. Loose cotton trousers are recommended; jeans take a long time to dry.

anglers: Necessities include long-sleeved shirts and pants, a wide-brimmed hat, and effective sun protection. For the southeast, rain gear is necessary, even during the dry season. Although lodges can generally arrange rentals, it's better to bring your own equipment. Bring a 20-lb. or stronger line for saltwater fishing.

MEASUREMENTS: The British system of weights and measure is used, but gasoline is sold by the American gallon. Belize operates

National Parks and Nature Reserves in Belize

Name	Date Est.	Acreage
Half Moon Caye Natural Monument	Mar. 1982	10,000
Crooked Tree Wildlife Sanctuary	Nov. 1984	16,000
Society Hall Nature Reserve	Nov. 1986	6,000
Cockscomb Basin Wildlife Sanctuary	Feb. 1986	102,000
Blue Hole National Park	Dec. 1986	600
Hol Chan Marine Reserve	May 1987	3,000
Guanacaste National Park	Apr. 1990	50
Bladen Bank Nature Reserve	June 1990	97,000
Five Blues Lake National Park	Apr. 1991	885
Laughing Bird Caye National Park	Nov. 1991	—
Chiquibul National Park	Nov. 1991	200,000
Budon Canal Nature Reserve	June 1992	6,000
Rio Blanco National Park	Dec. 1992	100
Aguas Turbias National Park	Dec. 1992	8,950
Paynes Creek Nature Reserve	Dec. 1992	27,000
Temash/Sarstoon Nature Reserve	Dec. 1992	41,000
Monkey Bay Nature Reserve	Dec. 1992	2,250
Glovers Reef Marine Reserve	May 1993	—

on Central Standard Time. Electric current is 110 volts AC, but some hotels in the boonies may use 12 volt electricity supplied by generators. While some villages are without electricity, other villages (and resorts that have their own generators) have electricity only part of the day. **conversions:** A meter is equal to three feet and three inches. A kilometer equals .62 miles (about 5/9 of a mile), a square km is equal to about 3/8 of a square mile.

PHOTOGRAPHY: Film is expensive here so you might want to bring your own. Kodachrome KR 36, ASA 64, is the best all around slide film. For prints, 100 or 200 ASA is preferred, while 1000 ASA is just the thing underwater. For underwater shots use a polarizing filter to cut down on glare; a flash should be used in deep water. Avoid photographs on land between 10 and 2 when there are harsh shadows. Photograph landscapes while keeping the sun to your rear. Set your camera a stop or a stop and a half down when photographing beaches in order to prevent overexposure from glare. A sunshade is a useful addition. Keep your camera and film out of the heat, and use silica gel packets to stave off mildew.

If you're intending to photograph animals in their natural environments, it's a good idea to bring two camera bodies (loaded with ASA 64 and ASA 1000 film), along with 300mm zoom and regular lenses. Animal photography is an antsy proposition owing to distances and dense vegetation. You can't hesitate or the animal may be gone! The most exotic animal you are likely to see is a howler monkey or perhaps an agouti or two. If this makes you wonder how the shots of cats and so forth that you see were taken, well, most of them were shot in the Belize Zoo. If you would like similar shots, they are yours for a price!

Replace your batteries before a trip or bring a spare set. Finally, remember not to subject your exposed film of ASA 400 or greater to the X-ray machines at the airport: hand-carry them through. Because local developing is very expensive and of generally poor quality, it's better to take your film home for developing.

VISITING THE NATIONAL PARKS AND RESERVES: Many consider these treasures to be the nation's greatest attraction for visitors. However, they're difficult to get to if you don't have your own transportation, and, in many cases, you'll need your own food as well. One alternative to visiting on your own may be to visit the parks with a tour; see individual listings for information.

SEEING WILDLIFE: Because their survival mechanisms are geared to differing needs and circumstances, Belize's wildlife differs dramatically from that found on East Africa's open plains. While the latter depend upon strength, speed, and size, animals in Belize depend upon camouflage for survival. As a result, they are smaller and more difficult to see. If you're visiting the reserve on your own, with a group, or on a group tour, it is essential to maintain quiet. The quieter you are, the more you will see. Early morning and late afternoon are the best times for viewing wildlife. The best

way to see wildlife, if you are really serious about it, is to camp. During the dry season, the animals come down to drink at water holes during the early morning and late afternoon.

ⓘ Did You Know?

The current names of Maya sites are not what they were when the Maya lived there. No one can be certain what the original names were.

VISITING RUINS: Belize does not boast the most impressive Maya ruins. That honor belongs to Honduras, Guatemala, and Mexico. However, the nation's ruins are frequently located in a lush natural setting, and the ruins have been left comparatively undisturbed. You might imagine how archaeologists felt when they came upon the ruins for the first time. Some ruins require an entrance fee. Most have on-site caretakers who will show you around. Remember not to rush!

FOUNDATIONS: If you would like to help conservation in Belize, a number of organizations welcome donations.

The nation's foremost environmental association, the **Belize Audubon Society** (☎ 02-77369/78239, fax 02-78562; Box 1001, Belize City; e-mail base@ btl.net; www.belizeaudu- bon.org) supervises many of the nation's parks and reserves. One of its principal activities is environmental education. Foreign associate membership is US$25 per year and includes a subscription to their newsletter. **The Programme for**

Belize (☎ 02-75616/7, 168 N Front St., Belize City) is devoted to purchasing land for environmental preservation.

Memberships in **The Belize Zoo** are US$25 on up. Write The Belize Zoo, PO Box 474, Belize City, Belize. Tax deductible donations may be sent to Belize Zoo, c/o World Wildlife Fund-US, 12150 24th St. NW, Washington, DC 20037.

Another worthy organization is the **Belize Center for Environmental Studies**. Tax deductible contributions can be sent to Belize Center, c/o "Project Lighthawk," PO Box 8163, Santa Fe, NM 87504.

The **Siwa-ban Preserve** protects flora and fauna on the north end of Caye Caulker. To make a donation, contact Ellen MacCrae at Galerie Hicaco on Caye Caulker, or send a tax deductible donation to The Siwa-ban Foundation, 143 Anderson, San Francisco, CA 94110.

Established in 1993, The **Cubola New Art Foundation** promotes and develops Belizean artists in the fields of video, creative writing, crafts, performance arts, product design, music, and visual arts. For more information contact, Cubola Publishing (☎ 093-2083) at 35 Elizabeth St., Benque Viejo.

Another worthy endeavor is the **Belize Agroforestry Research Center,** a project of the Tropical Conservation Foundation. Send contributions to The Tropical Conservation Foundation, 14 N Court St., Athens, OH 45701; $25 or more brings a subscription to the newsletter. For more information, write 209 Seneca Rd., Great Falls, VA 22066, ☎ 703-450-4160, fax 703-450-4170. **La Ruta Maya Foundation** is dedicated to helping protect the environmental and cultural assets of the ancient Maya homelands. One of its projects is making replicas of Maya stelae, including ones of Caracol. They also are offering scholarships to Central Americans, promoting parks, and working on sustainable tourism in Flores, Guatemala. For more information, write 209 Seneca Rd., Great Falls VA 22066 (☎ 703-450-4160, fax 703-450-4170).

Earthwatch, ☎ 800-776-0188.is an organization that allows you to visit the country and participate in valuable research at the same time. Volunteers contribute financially and receive an unusual experience at the same time.

The **Environmental Conservation Tourism Association** (e-mail ECTAinfo@aol.com; 129 New Jersey Ave. NW, Washington, DC 20001) provides a forum for members to work together towards promoting sustainable tourism worldwide. Membership is $25.

A very unusual organization working to change the face of world tourism is the **Ecotourism Society.** It publishes guidelines for nature tour operators, a newsletter, and several other publications. Membership is $15 students, $35 ecotourists, $50 professional, and on up. Write Box 755, North Bennington, VT 05257.

In Britain, **Tourism Concern** is an organization devoted to uniting British people who are concerned with the effects of tourism. It advocates tourism that puts long-term social and environmental health of affected areas in front of short-term pecuniary gain. For more information, write Tourism Concern, Froebel College, Roehampton Lane, London SW15 5PU, UK, ☎ 081-878-9053.

Introduction

Belize City

Although it resembles the capital cities of former Anglo-African colonies and those of the West Indies, "Belize," as the city is popularly called, lacks their hustle and bustle. But, with around 25% of the country's total population, it's the chief commercial center and by far the busiest place you'll find. The city (pop. 47,000) overruns both sides of Haulover Creek – the name applied to the last four miles of the Belize River, a stretch along which cattle being transported to market were forced to cross.

Belize City still has the feel of the colonial seaport era. Never intended to be a permanent settlement, the town is located on a swamp without a good harbor. Most of it is pretty run down, with the majority of the houses set on piles above swampy ground. Now largely covered with landfill, its canal network once gave it the title of the "Venice of the Caribbean," and legend has it that the city is built on its former chief imports and exports: gin bottles and mahogany logs.

Belize City's location, set on a peninsular stretch of coast a few inches below sea level amidst a mangrove swamp, has proven to be a singularly unfortunate choice. Its environs have served as a breeding ground for disease. The high water table has deterred the installation of an underground water supply and sewage system, and most homes depend upon rainfall for their water supply through "catchment" – cisterns that collect water rolling down galvanized iron roofs. The septic tanks are treated with chemicals and then spew their contents through open trenches that eventually empty into the ocean. This sewage provides sustenance for the hordes of hungry, government-protected catfish or "shittifish" – the catty colloquialism by which they are known – as well as the gar that live at the river's mouth. Back in town, you may experience the occasional passing nocturnal pesticide-spraying truck, with its noxious fumes intended to counter the mosquito population; shield yourself as best you can.

However, there are a few charming aspects. Along the city's streets, dilapidated houses are flanked by flowering pink, orange, and purple bougainvillea and red poinciana trees, and you can see the sun-bleached white sails of schooners tied up along the banks of Haulover Creek. The names of this odoriferous town's 13 sections – such as Port Loyola, Mesopotamia, and the Barracks – literally reek of history, and the rather imaginative English phrases found on buildings provide endless entertainment for pedestrians. Although the town has high humidity, the northeast trade winds mitigate the steamy summer weather.

History

Belize City's roots lie with logwood. By the late 17th century, logwood was being cut in the area, and the town had its origins as a logging camp – a place where the Baymen (the white loggers) could return during the rains. Their houses once lined the sea front, while the houses of their slaves

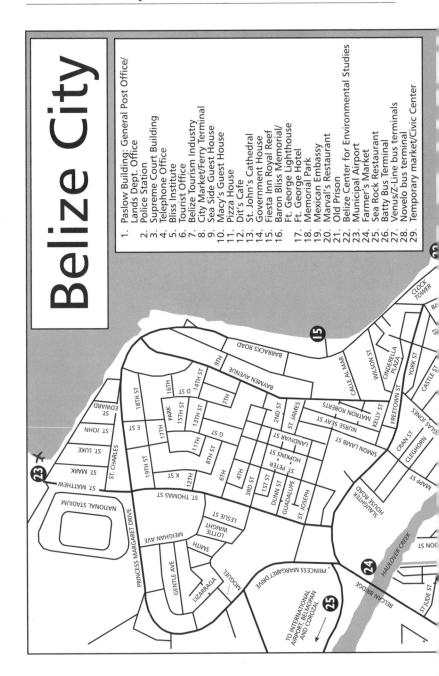

Belize City

1. Paslow Building: General Post Office/
   Lands Dept. Office
2. Police Station
3. Supreme Court Building
4. Telephone Office
5. Bliss Institute
6. Tourist Office
7. Belize Tourism Industry
8. City Market/Ferry Terminal
9. Sea Side Guest House
10. Macy's Guest House
11. Pizza House
12. Dit's Cafe
13. St. John's Cathedral
14. Government House
15. Fiesta Inn Royal Reef
16. Baron Bliss Memorial/
    Ft. George Lighthouse
17. Ft. George Hotel
18. Memorial Park
19. Mexican Embassy
20. Marval's Restaurant
21. Old Prison
22. Belize Center for Environmental Studies
23. Municipal Airport
24. Farmer's Market
25. Sea Rock Restaurant
26. Batty Bus Terminal
27. Venus/Z-Line bus terminals
28. Novelo bus terminal
29. Temporary market/Civic Center

Belize City

were grouped by ethnic origin and located on the south side of Haulover Creek. The locus of settlement moved here from St. George's Caye after a 1798 Spanish attack, and Belize City became the major export center for logwood and mahogany on the Bay of Honduras.

British expatriates arrived in increasing numbers during the 19th century and, as the "Scot's clique" took over the town, colonial-style wooden buildings proliferated along the shore. Arriving Anglican missionaries made the settlement a base for propagation, and the Anglican Cathedral was built in 1812 to serve a diocese that stretched all the way to Panama. Fires devastated the city in 1804, 1806, and 1856, during the same era that epidemics of yellow fever, cholera, and smallpox decimated the populace.

Belize City became the capital of the new colony of British Honduras in 1862. In 1919 returning soldiers rioted in town, protesting continuing racism and their status as second-class citizens. On Sept. 10, 1931, as the town was preoccupied with celebrating the anniversary of the Battle of St. George's Cay, a hurricane struck – flooding the town, destroying houses, and killing 1-2,000 – about 10% of the population. The subsequent neglect and squalor, coupled with an inadequate and tardy response from Britain, gave momentum to the independence movement. The decades following witnessed numerous rallies and marches.

In 1961, the city was devastated by Hurricane Hattie's 160-mph winds. They created a 14-foot tidal wave, killing 275 Belizeans and leaving 3,000 homeless. Damage was estimated at US$50 million. Despite the relocation of the capital to Belmopan after the hurricane, Belize City has continued to thrive.

Transport

Arriving By Air

The new terminal of Phillip Goldson International Airport, located at Ladyville just off the Northern Highway, is the size of just two departure gates in an average US airport. As you stand in line for customs, a drug-sniffing German shepherd is brought by. Customs officials here can be surly, and some delight in going through everything in your bag. Be sure to visit the small tourist information stand. Unfortunately, the only alternative from the airport is to share a taxi (BZ$30) or to walk out to the main highway (two miles) and flag down a bus or truck. Domestic flights arrive and depart from the Municipal Airport, a BZ$5 taxi ride from town or a 40-minute walk.

> ⚡ **Warning!**
> *Taxi drivers at Belize International are notorious for rapacity. Don't let them scam you! Prices are set at BZ$30 per cab. Don't buy the line that it is illegal to share a cab with a friend you met at the airport! Solve this by arranging in advance to have one person get the cab. Be sure that you specify "Belizean dollars" for the fare.*

Orientation & Getting Around

The main streets are Regent (Front) and Albert (Back). The Haulover Creek divides the city into north and south halves. While the north area is more exclusive, the south is the commercial zone where offices, banks, and supermarkets are located. The foreshore area commands high prestige. The slum areas west of Regent and Albert Streets are dangerous at night. Most of the town is small enough to get around in on foot, but be sure to look where you're going as there are open sewers in the sidewalks. Buses are supposed to run each way once an hour; a ride is great for getting oriented – if you can find one of them that is!

To the north are the exclusive areas: the fine houses of Kings Park, the more expensive hotels, and most of the embassies and consulates. The commercial district to the south features some expensive properties lining the foreshore – former residences of the elite. In the northern part of town, the recently constructed Bel-China Bascule Bridge links Northside from Douglas Jones St. to the Southside from Vernon St.

Car Rentals

Renting a car is quite an expensive proposition here, so be sure to check around. **Jabiru** (☎ 02-44680, fax 02-34136) rents 4x4 Suzukis for around BZ$130 pd. **National** (☎ 02-31586) is at 126 Freetown Rd. **Crystal Auto Rental** (☎ 02-30921; Mile 1½ Northern Highway) is popular, as is **Budget** (☎ 02-32435/33986, fax 02-30237, 800-527-0700 in the US and Canada). Both are at the airport, as is **Pancho's** (☎ 02-45554; 5747 Lizarraga Ave.). **Jabiru Tour Belize** (☎ 02-71271, fax 02-71421; cellular 0149478; e-mail tourbelize@btl. net) rents 4x4s with unlimited mileage. Other agencies include

Avis at the Ft. George Hotel (☎ 02-78637); **Lionel Gordon** (☎ 02-72184; 113 Amara Ave.); **Lewis** (☎ 02-74461; 23 Cemetery Rd.); **Maya World Safaris** (☎ 02-31584; West Landivar); **JR's** (☎ 02-75098, fax 02-71565; e-mail bzetropic @btl.net) and **Sutherland** (☎ 02-73582; 127 Neal Pen Rd.) For the most current list, check the yellow pages.

You can rent a car at the international airport, a convenient location for pickup and/or dropoff. Also, when renting, make sure that there is "road service" – i.e., someone will be sent out if the car breaks down.

Vicinity of Belize City

The city can be used as a base for exploring many nearby areas, including Altun Ha, Bermudian Landing, the Zoo, and the Baboon Sanctuary. (For information on tours see above.) Other cayes can be visited for day trips or for longer stays (see the next chapter). Located 16 miles from Belize City on the road to Cayo and housing 2-3,000, **Hattieville** was originally a temporary shelter for hurricane victims. While today most of the buildings are ramshackle, they appear permanent enough. The highest of all the limestone outcrops. **Gracie Rock** near the Sibún River still has the ruins of the set for the movie, *Mosquito Coast.*

From Belize City

Belize City is the transportation hub, and you'll likely pass through here one or more times if you're traveling around the nation by bus. Terminals of the four main bus lines are located in Mesopotamia, a slum area around the Collet Canal and Magazine Rd. The oldest and largest company is Batty, which serves the north and west. If departure times are critical, be sure to check with the bus companies prior to departure. Otherwise, you can just to show up and wait.

to the north: The main bus route runs from Belize City to Orange Walk (two hrs.); to Corozal (one hr.); to Chetumal (one hr.). Batty buses (☎ 02-72025/74924/77146) depart hourly from 4 to 11, leaving from 54 E. Collet Canal. Their buses to Chetumal depart at 4, 5 and 6 (premier); 6:10, 7, 8, 9 (premier), 10, 10:30, and at 11:15. Both the express and the regular bus are the same price.

From Magazine Rd., Venus (☎ 02-3354/7390) buses leave hourly at 11:45, 1, 1:30, 2, 2:30, 3, 3:30, 4, 4:30, 5, 5:30, 6, and 7. Buses to Sarteneja leave on North Front St. at the gas station, near the boats for Caye Caulker; one generally leaves at around noon. For information about buses to other destinations, see the specific destination involved.

The taxi fare for one passenger between any two points in Belize City is BZ$4. If you plan on making several stops, inform the driver and negotiate a price beforehand. The main taxi stand – which has some of the wildest gas guzzlers you'll ever see – is on Albert St. by Central Park. If you need to phone for a taxi, call Caribbean (☎ 02-72888), Imperial (02-72334), or Baldemar Varella (☎ 02-73600).

heading south: James buses leave for Punta Gorda from the Pound Yard Bridge in front of the Esso Service Station on Mon., Wed., and Fri. at 7 AM and on Sat. and Sun. at 9. The late departures allow passengers arriving from Guatemala to

make connections. All stop in Belmopan, Dangriga, and Mango Creek. Z-Line buses (☎ 02-702201/73937) depart for Punta Gorda from Magazine Rd. daily at 10, 12, 2, and 4; an additional bus departs Mon. at 6 PM. Ritchies also has a bus to Placencia.

heading west: Expect to spend around 1½ hrs. for the trip to Belmopan, 2½ hrs. to San Ignacio, and a bit over three hours to Melchor, inside the Guatemalan border. From 54 E. Collet Canal, **Batty** buses leave Mon. through Sat. for Melchor at 5, 5:30, 6, 6:30 (express), 7 (premier), 7:45, 8, 9:45, and 10, as well as on Sun. at 6:30, 7:30, 8:30, 9:30, and 10:30 AM.

From 19 W. Collet Canal, **Novelo's** (☎ 02-71160/71161) buses depart from 11-9; departures on Sundays are limited.

by boat: Boats (BZ$15, going; BZ$12 return) leave for Caye Caulker (at 9, 11, 1, 3, and 5:30) from the **Belize Maritime Museum and Terminal** near the Swing Bridge. The *Andrea* (BZ$30) for San Pedro on Ambergris Caye departs at 9 AM from the same location. Note: fares for children under five are free and 5-10 year-olds ride for half-price.

departing by air: It's a BZ$30 taxi ride to the **International Airport** or you can take the shuttle. If you're leaving the country, be sure to save the BZ$30 you'll need to pay the departure tax. If you want to change money back, you'll need to fill out a form; expect to lose a few percentage points. In the departure lounge – which functions both for international and domestic flights – you'll find the duty-free shops, as well as a cafeteria.

If going to the **Municipal Airport**, you can take a cab or face a long, hot walk. Planes leave for all over the country (Corozal, San Pedro/Ambergris, Caye Caulker, Dangriga, Placencia, and Punta Gorda) from both terminals. For individual listings, see "getting here" under the specific destination.

from Belize International: You may fly to San Salvador with Taca and connect to all of Central America. Both Island and Tropic fly to Flores, and Tropic has a connecting arrangement to Guatemala City.

☞ *Traveler's Tip*

If you travel to Cancún, you can fly to Cuba with Playa del Carmen, Centro Bilingue. Contact them at ☎ 52-987-30701/30588; e-mail escape@pya.com.mx. Packages start at around US$550 RT from Belize City; this is pp for two nights in Havana. You will need to make arrangements well in advance of your arrival.

Sights

The Swing Bridge connects the city's two main sections; it opens twice a day at approximately 5:30 AM and 6 PM to allow large vessels to pass through. In use since 1923, it was built in Liverpool, England and is the only manually operated swing bridge still operating anywhere. During the operation, four men holding long poles turn a capstan that winches the bridge around until it's pointing toward the harbor mouth.

At the foot of the Swing Bridge, the **Belize Maritime Museum and Terminal** has a small museum, open from 8-5 daily. Admission for tourists is BZ$6; for Belizeans, BZ$3.

Originally built in 1820 on the site of another market and demolished in 1989, the current version of the **market** dates from 1991. It offers such culinary raw materials as brightly colored fish, live iguanas, and pitiful, upturned turtles, thrashing about helplessly. Offshore, the catfish eagerly feast on whatever scraps and remains are tossed their way. Just past the market, the Mona Lisa Hotel was used as a set in the 1985 film version of Paul Theroux's novel, *The Mosquito Coast*. The Swing Bridge area was also used in filming *The Dogs of War*. To the north of the Swing Bridge, the **Paslow Building** –an enormous, somewhat dilapidated wooden structure – houses the post office on the first floor and other government offices on the upper stories.

Running south from the Swing Bridge past the rotating Coca-Cola clock, Albert (Back) St. hosts the main shopping area. With its wrought-iron columns and red Georgian brick facade, the **Old Court House** complex, actually a group of former colonial administration and court buildings, was finished in 1926, replacing an earlier building that burnt down in 1918. Gov. Hart Bennett was helping extinguish the fire when the burning flagpole was cut down and fell on him. He later died of his injuries. A plaque commemorates the fire. Each of its four clock faces stopped working at a different time. The Court House faces small **Redemption Park**, which has a decorative but nonfunctional fountain as its centerpiece. Formerly called Central Park, it was renamed on Dec. 31, 1991 when a bust was unveiled honoring labor

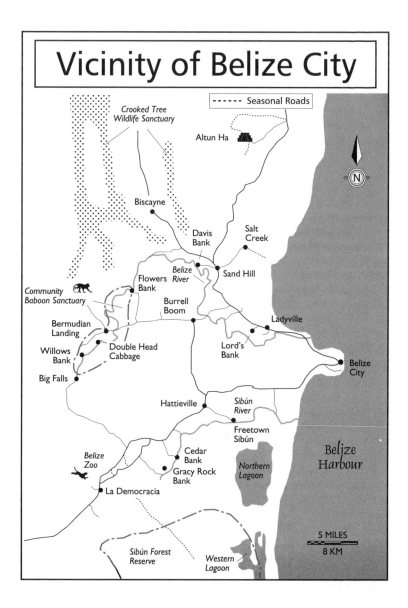

Vicinity of Belize City

----- Seasonal Roads

Crooked Tree
Wildlife Sanctuary

Altun Ha

N

Biscayne

Davis
Bank

Salt
Creek

Belize
River

Flowers
Bank

Sand Hill

Community
Baboon Sanctuary

Burrell
Boom

Ladyville

Bermudian
Landing

Willows
Bank

Double Head
Cabbage

Lord's
Bank

Big Falls

Belize
City

Hattieville

Sibún
River

Freetown
Sibún

Belize
Zoo

Cedar
Bank

Northern
Lagoon

Belize
Harbour

Gracy Rock
Bank

La Democracia

Sibún Forest
Reserve

Western
Lagoon

5 MILES
8 KM

leader Antonio Soberanís (see *History* in the *Introduction*.

Set a block or two behind the Court House on the waterfront, the **Bliss Institute** (open Mon. to Fri. 8:30-noon, 2-8; Sat 8:30-noon) resembles an aircraft control tower. It houses the National Arts Council, which sponsors exhibitions, plays, and concerts. A sadly neglected group of stelae and altars from Caracol can be seen to the left of the entranceway. The National Library is now on Princess Margaret

Drive. Homesick Brits can find British newspapers there.

Both Central America's oldest Anglican (Episcopalian) cathedral and one of the nation's oldest buildings, **St. John's Cathedral**, at the south end of Albert St., resembles a large English parish church. Construction commenced in 1812 using bricks brought over as ballast in ships. This is the only Anglican cathedral in the world outside England in which kings were crowned. Four Kings of the Mosquito Coast were crowned in the Cathedral between 1815 and 1845, each claiming title to the British protectorate that stretched along the eastern coasts of Honduras and Nicaragua. In order to cement their links with England, they also had their children baptized here. Inside, a plaque commemorates yellow fever victims. Named after the magistrate who owned the land, the **Yarborough Cemetery** to the west of the Cathedral ran out of plots at the end of the 19th century. The cemetery was first used from 1781 to bury notables. Only later were the stiffs of ordinary folk welcomed, exhausting the space by 1870. At the southern end of Albert St. across the Yarborough Bridge, the Belize City Vaults, entombing 24 souls, now enclose a children's playground. After the closure of the Yarborough Cemetery, this vault method of burial was introduced by Gustav Von Olhaffen, a German officer who was the last corpse to be interred in the cemetery.

Set between the cathedral and the seafront at the southern end of Regent St. and also bordering on the Southern Foreshore, **Government House**, constructed between 1812 and 1814, was the Governor's official residence during the colonial era. Designed by British architect Christopher Wren, this elegant clapboard structure hosts official occasions and houses visiting royalty. The Prime Minister's office is also located in Government House. It now houses the **Archaeological Reserve Museum**. The museum, which opened in 1996 and is more about history than archaeology. Various antiques from the colonial era are on display as well as photographs and historical records. It's open 8:30-4:30 from Mon. to Fri., and admission is charged.

Complete with a concert area, **Bird's Isle**, right at the tail end of a strip of land, is attached to the mainland by a narrow wooden walkway. Many homes on Regent St. have a brick first floor and a second level of timber and shingle. Slaves were chained inside the brick sections when not at work. One example is Mrs. Thompson's House at the corner of Regent and Prince opposite the plumbing supply store. The home at the corner of Dean and Regent Streets dates from 1857.

FORT GEORGE AREA: This area received its name in 1803 after the small fort of the same name erected on a little swampy island. Losing importance after the West India Regiment moved on, the environs mutated into a fishing village, with a small bridge connecting it to the mainland. Privately leased in the 1920s, a strait separated it from town, and Key Hole Alley led to the bridge. The strait was filled in by the US-based Jefferson Construction Co. during 1922-24 at a cost of BZ$300 million. The island was fenced in by a concrete wall and, in tribute to the

WWI dead, Memorial Park was built on the mound at the tip of the strip.

To the east, following along the shore, are the Custom House and adjacent wharves, the lighthouse, and the concrete tomb of Baron Bliss. Traversing the shoreline you come to the Ft. George Hotel and the neighboring Memorial Park, commemorating the WWI dead. Several of the well-preserved colonial mansions here are occupied by embassies and hotels. At the corner of Gabourel Lane and Hudson Street is a colonial building that still houses a portion of the American Embassy. Originally built in New England, the house was taken apart and transported as ship's ballast to Belize, where it was reconstructed.

Built in 1857, the former **Belize City Prison** is on Gabourel Lane and Gaol Lane. Overcrowded and without running water, it has been replaced by a new facility along the Boom/Hattieville Rd. The Central Bank of Belize plans to restore it and open it as a museum. Up on Eve St., two traditional structures house the former **Belize City Hospital** and the current Belize Center for Environmental Studies/Association for Belizean Archaeology.

Practicalities

THEFT AND CONDUCT: Although Belize City is becoming increasingly dangerous, you can be reasonably safe if you take adequate precautions. Walking alone at night may be asking for trouble. The most dangerous areas are the environs of Mesopotamia and King's Park, as well as the streets running over the South Side Canal near the bus station. Take a cab if arriving at night. Another dangerous area lies to the west of Regent and Albert Streets.

Hyde's Lane is a crack center, as is the alley between the Majestic Theatre and the Chon San II.

The best way to avoid being hassled by hustlers is to shake your head and wag your finger if approached – although even this often doesn't work. In any case, don't let yourself be intimidated, because that's their game plan. The Belizeans you *want* to meet will not be ones who approach you in this fashion. Then there's the woman who comes around to hotels with a sob story: don't believe her. Avoid dealing with untrustworthy streetside moneychangers. Park your car in carparks at night for safety. Attractive women are simply inviting harassment if they wear too short skirts or revealing clothing. Don't make eye contact or answer taunts, such as, "Where is your husband?" Never wear expensive jewelry around town. Don't carry much money on your person, and try to keep on the main streets. The most recent crime wave is by thugs on bicycles, who grab gold chains, wallets, or cameras. Victims are Belizeans and tourists alike.

Accommodations

LUXURY: Towering over the city, ultramodern **Radisson Ft. George Hotel** at 2 Marine Parade offers 70 rooms, a pool, and a roof deck with superb views. Paintings by Dangriga artist Benjamin Nicholas adorn the hotel. It has purchased the Holiday Inn Villa Belize across the street, which has been incorporated into the hotel. Call 02-77400, fax 02-73820 or ☎ 800-552-3419, and 612-890-4405. In the US, ☎ 800-44-UTELL. E-mail rdfgh@btl.net.

The 25-room **Chateau Caribbean** (☎ 02-30800/32988, fax 02-30900; Box 947, Belize City) is at 6 Marine Parade. Its attractive ambience makes it popular with European visitors. It has a fine restaurant as well as conference facilities. Housed in a former mansion, it has been renovated and rooms have a/c, cable TV, and phones. Rates are around BZ$140 s, BZ$160 d, and BZ$180 t, plus tax.

Overlooking the mouth of the Belize River and only two blocks from town at 5 Southern Foreshore, the **Bellevue Hotel** (☎ 02-77051, fax 02-73253; e-mail fins@btl.net) has 42 a/c rooms with phones, an upstairs bar, and a disco. Rates are around BZ$130 s, BZ$150 d. In the US ☎ 800-223-9815.

The gaudy, 120-room **Fiesta Inn Royal Reef Hotel** (☎ 02-32670, US 800-528-6481; fax 02-32660; PO Box 1248, Belize City) opened along the sea at 2A South Park St. in 1991. It has two restaurants, a pool, marina, and meeting room.. It was formerly named the Ramada Royal Reef Hotel.

out of town: The Best Western Biltmore Plaza (☎ 02-32302, fax 02-32301; 800-528-1234 in the US and Canada – ask for "International Desk"; PO Box 959, Belize City) is at Mile 3 on the Northern Hwy. This 90-room luxury hotel offers rooms with a choice of a/c or fans, TV, and radio. Other facilities include meeting halls, a pool and sunken pool bar, and a business center.

The mahogany-constructed **Belize River Lodge** (☎ 888-275-4843, 025-2002, fax 025-2298; PO Box 459, Belize City; e-mail worldfishn@worldnet.att.net) is set in a garden environment on a secluded portion of the Belize River. Its four

rooms can accommodate up to 16. Fishing is done from 18-foot skiffs. A seven-night/six-day all-inclusive fishing package is around US$1,895, based on double occupancy; the single rate is US$2,232. The Lodge also operates three live-aboard vessels: 40-foot *The Permit*, 50-foot *Christy Ann*, and 52-foot *Blue Yonder*.

Featuring a/c, the **Riverbend Resort** (☎ 025-2297; PO Box 48, Belize City) is at Mile 9½ in Ladyville.

houseboats: River Haven (fax 02-32742; Box 78, Belize City) features an unusual way to see Belize on its floating 10-by-15 foot houseboats, which hold up to four in two bedrooms. On board are CB and AM-FM radios, and a kitchenette. Prices run around BZ$1,200 pw or BZ$400 pd for a charter cruise with captain and lunch; shorter-term rentals are also available.

yachts: Cruise Belize (☎ 800-371-7475; www.belize.net; e-mail belize@nashville.net) offers a live-aboard 58′ Hatteras for fishermen.

MODERATE: Fort Street Restaurant and Guesthouse (☎ 02-30116, fax 02-78808; www.belize.net; e-mail fortst@btl.net) is at 4 Fort Street. Set in a restored colonial house, it's probably the classiest of the city's guest houses. Room rates are around BZ$90 s, BZ$120 d, BZ$150 t, and BZ$170 quad for rooms with shared bath and ceiling fans; tax is added, and breakfast is included. In the US, contact MAGNUM Belize at 800-240-FORT, fax 218-847-0334, or write Box 1560, Detroit Lakes, MN 56520.

Opposite the Radisson Fort George at 9 Cork St. is **Colton**

Belize City

House (☎ 02-44666), an intimate, family run four-room guest house. Features here include complimentary coffee and access to a videotape library. Their one a/c room is luxury priced at around BZ$90 d plus tax. Other rooms start at BZ$60 s, BZ$70 d. There are plans to serve breakfast; it may now be available. Environmental videos are shown in the living room. The rooms are quite attractive, and Mr. Colton has a lot of singularly controversial opinions to share. Whether you agree with him or not, he's quite interesting to talk to. This place is best suited for serious, quiet types. Party animals should stay away. **Glenthorne Manor** (☎ 02-44212; PO Box 1278, Belize City), located at 27 Barracks Rd., offers a charming interior and attractively furnished, if small, rooms with high ceilings. The kitchen and refrigerator are available for use. Rates are from BZ$60 s and BZ$70 d with breakfast in season; tax and service are added. Group rates and church- and Peace Corps-affiliated discounts are available. Do note, though, that it is in a bad neighborhood.

The 12-room a/c **El Centro** (☎ 02-72413, fax 02-74553; PO Box 122, Belize City) is at 4 Bishop St.

The **Downtown Guest House** (☎ 02-39012, ☎/fax 02-32057; 7 Eve St.) has 15 comfortable rooms with hot water. Rates are around BZ$15 s and BZ$25 for a room with a bunk bed or BZ$20 s and BZ$30 d for a room with a double bed.

The 22-room **Royal Orchid** (☎ 02-32783, fax 02-32789; PO Box 279, Belize City) is at 153 New Road (corner of Douglas). Rooms have a/c and fans, cable TV, and phones; there's a parking lot, res-

taurant, and meeting room. Rates are about BZ$90 s, BZ$110 d, plus BZ$20 for each additional person; children under 12 are free.

The **Mopan Hotel** (☎ 02-77351/73356, fax 02-75383; 55 Regent St.) is run by environmental activists Jean and Tom Shaw. Ask them about Shawfields, their own nature reserve, which is still in the planning stage.

The partially a/c 24-room **Golden Dragon Hotel** (☎ 02-72817/72067) is at 29 Queen St; it charges around BZ$37 s or d plus tax. It is in a bad neighborhood.

Offering bed and breakfast, four-room **Alicia's Guest House** (☎ 02-75082) is at 8 Chapel Lane (corner of Dean St.).

Featuring both partial a/c and a swimming pool as well as private baths, the **Bliss Hotel** (☎ 02-72552, 02-73310) is at 1 Water Lane.

New Archie's Hotel (☎ 02-73303, fax 02-74159), at 74 Euphrates Ave., offers a choice of a/c or fans. **Venus** (☎ 02-77390/22132, PO Box 11482, Belize City) is at 2371 Magazine Rd. by the Venus Bus Station.

out of town: The a/c **Rio-Haul Motel** (☎ 02-44859) is at Mile 5½ Northern Highway. The partially a/c **International Airport Hotel** (☎ 02-52150; PO Box 1253, Belize City) is, as you might suspect, near the airport. Located on Miami Rd., the 16-room partially a/c **Estell's Airport** (☎ 025-2282) is in Ladyville.

BUDGET AND LOW-BUDGET: Plan on paying at least BZ$15 for the least expensive room. Other than price, one factor to consider is safety; the Fort George area is probably the safest.

At 7 Eyre St., **Eyre St. Guest House** (☎ 02-77724) is one of the better low-priced guest houses. Rates range from around BZ$30 s to BZ$45 d, with BZ$8 breakfasts. Another fine place to stay is the **Sea Side Guest House** (☎ 02-78339; e-mail jself@ucb. edu.bz) at 3 Prince St. near the Swing Bridge. It is safe and secure. Reportedly, it can be noisy. A disadvantage is that the office is open only from 7-11 AM. Prices are around BZ$33 for a single, BZ$48 for a double, and BZ$61 for a triple; dorm beds are also available. There's a common area with tables, and breakfast can be ordered. It is run by Friends Services International, a volunteer project of the Quakers. To reserve, send checks payable to Friends Services International. P.O. Box 2060, Belize City, Belize, Central America. If you include an e-mail address, manager John Self will confirm as soon as the check is received.

North Front Street Guest House (☎ 02-77595) is at 124 North Front Street. The recently remodeled rooms are around BZ$15 s and BZ$25 d. Baths are shared. Nearby are **Bon Aventure** (☎ 02-44248), at No. 122 next door, and **Dim's Mira Rio** (☎ 02-44970) across the street at No. 59. Its rooms all have a private bath. And don't overlook five-room **Bell's Hotel** (☎ 02-31023) at 140 North Front St., offering fans and shared bath.

Freddie's Guest House (☎ 02-44396; 86 Eve St.), has only three rooms but is secure and peaceful. Comfortable, quiet, and clean, **Marin's Travelodge** (☎ 02-45166) is at 6 Craig St. – in a bad neighborhood. **Vinats Hotel,** 8 Gabourel Lane, is under the same management as **Vinats Guest House,** 59 Regent St. W., but the latter is in a

less safe area. Equipped with fans and shared bath, six-room **America Hotel** (☎ 02-77384) is at 11 Dean St. Offering similar facilities, the **Annis Louise** (☎ 02-44670) is at 3 Freetown Road. Others include the **Belcove Hotel** (☎ 02-73054; 9 Regent St.); **Dianne's Hotel** at 65 George St.; **Eden Sweet Hotel** (☎ 02-74043; 137 Regent St. West); two-room **Isabel's Guest House** at 3 Albert St.; **Jane's Hotel** (☎ 02-44240) at 64 Barracks Rd.; **Simon Quan's "Luxury" Hotel** (☎ 02-45793) at 24-26 Queen St.; **Kitty's Travelodge** (☎ 02-44966) at 58 Daly St.; the 17-room **Las Palmeras Hotel** (☎ 02-73345, PO Box 299) at cor. George and Bishop Sts.; **Riverview Hotel** (☎ 02-73392; 25 Regent St.); **Violet's Hotel** (☎ 02-44171) at 41 Barracks Rd.; **R-B's Hotel** (☎ 02-30510) at 162 Freetown Rd.; **Fairweather Guest House** (☎ 02-72866) at 9 Rectory Lane; **The Taj Mahal Hotel** (☎ 02-72931) at 16 Albert St.; **The Gold Star Guest House** (☎ 02-33160) at 114 New Rd. (it charges BZ$20 for rooms with a fan and shared bath). Don't try smoking pot in your room. The owner will call the fuzz, as he did on one British lad.

camping: The only alternative is mainly for trailer vehicles. **The Caribbean Trailer Court** (☎ 02-45086; 5224 Barracks Rd.) has RV and regular camping. It is a long way out of town, however, and security is poor.

Food

DINING OUT: Four Fort Street has a pleasant atmosphere as well as unusual cuisine. Its Sunday brunch features everything from seafood quiche to mosquito toast

Belize City

(French toast stuffed with cream cheese and served with fruit). Another swank bistro is **Chateau Caribbean**, 6 Marine Parade. Formal **Fort George Hotel** offers American and European cuisine in an a/c setting; its sister hotel, **The Villa**, across the road, also offers fine dining. **The Bellevue**, 5 Southern Foreshore, serves European food with an extensive wine list. **The Gourmet** is at 13 Prince St. and serves Italian dishes, including pizza. **The Barracks Restaurant and Bar**, 136 Barracks Rd., is at Barracks Green, a short taxi ride from town on the way to the Municipal Airport. It serves lunch and dinner from Monday to Saturday; dinner only is served on Sunday. At 164 Newtown Barracks Rd., **The Grill** (☎ 02-45020) offers charcoal-grilled fish, chicken, and beef. In addition to gourmet fare, the **Ramada Royal Reef** also has a business lunch special daily, except Wednesday. At 3580 Sittee St. near the Civic Center by the river, the **Red Roof Lounge** (☎ 02-77158) is open for dinner late, has live music, and offers "a personalized drink mixed by the reading of your psychic." At Mile 4½ on the Northern Hwy. facing the seafront, the **Privateer** bar and restaurant features live music on weekends.

BUDGET DINING: Reasonably priced (BZ$10-18 for entrees) **Sea Rock** (☎ 02-34105) is an East Indian restaurant with wonderfully spiced vegetarian and other dishes, such as vegetable samosa, nan, biryani, tandoori, and vegetable curries. It's open daily from 11-10:30 except on Monday, when it opens at 6. The former location burned down, and it is now just past The Grill on the waterfront. If you eat only one meal in Belize City (and you appreciate spicy food), you should dine here. **Marva's**, on Collet Canal right near the river, is Belizean to the core (right down to the fact that you might not think it is a restaurant if you pass it by).

Unique, unforgettable and reasonable, the **Ark Restaurant** is on the lower part of North Front St. at Gabourel Lane. Featured are Spanish dishes, lobster, pancakes, waffles, juices, and fish dishes, including *séré*, a traditional Garifuna fish and coconut milk soup rarely found in restaurants. All this comes with the accompaniment of a hissing radio blaring gospel programming and the companionship of a merry ex-marine. Located up from the Ark and resembling a metal aircraft hangar, the orange **Temporary Market** is your best bet for truly cheap food. Food stalls sell fried fish, fried bread, and beans for breakfast, as well as various meat dishes; lunches run about BZ$3.50. You can also buy Iron Man Seaweed drink.

At the Belize Commercial Center across the Swing Bridge and to the left, you'll find **Kadel's** on the second floor, which serves reasonably priced Belizean-style food with lunchtime specials. The **Picadilly** at 35 Queen St. has reasonable prices, a/c interior and an outdoor patio with ceiling fans and an epiphyte collection suspended from metal grills. One excellent place for local food is the **Black Orchid**, 48 Albert St., which is open daily from 9 AM-10 PM and Sunday from 9-5. If you want to eat fish, get there before noon. It consistently sells out. At 50 King St., **Dit's** offers pastries, patties, conch fritters, and conch and cowfoot soups on Friday and Saturday. Acclaimed by some as the best place to eat local food, **Macy's Cafe**, marked by a flickering sign at 18 Bishop St., is dark, with plenty of whirring fans and laminated placemats featuring fruit plates and flowers. Sadly, it also serves sea turtle. One of the few places where you can dine in an outdoor atmosphere, **G. G.'s Cafe & Patio** is at 2-B King St. Prices are low (except for fish), and fresh brewed coffee is served. **The Marlin** is at 11 Regent St. West. Featuring daily happy hour from 6 to 7 and live entertainment every Thursday from 5:30, it specializes in seafood. **Dominique and Rochelle's**, 161 George St., serves Belizean and American food. **Big Daddy's** on Pickstock St., (two blocks from North Front St.) serves good vegetarian food. **Hotel El Centro's** restaurant at 4 Bishop St. offers lunch specials for BZ$6-8.

At the corner of King St. and East Canal, the **Mexican Corner** offers *escabeche, chimole, tacos, sabutes,* and other dishes. Bring your own wine or beer, as only soft drinks are available.

The most reasonably priced place for pizza (including slices), **Pizza House**, is on Albert St. near the BTIA office; it's closed Mondays. More expensive, **Buenas Pizzas** at 16 Albert St. features pizza and breakfast specials. **Bel's Taco** is a hole-in-the-wall Mexican spot on Hyde's Lane. Opposite the technical school on Freetown Rd., **Trev's** features Jamaican-style food. Located across the street from Save U, where the Northern Highway comes into town, **Raoul's** offers Mexican and Belizean food. **Mom's** – a longtime popular restaurant – has closed its doors.

CHINESE RESTAURANTS: There are so many Chinese restaurants in

town that you could spend days visiting them all. Some give new meaning to the word kitsch.

One of the best is the **Chaan Saan Palace**, 1 Kelly St., which is named after the proprietors' home village in China. There are over 100 items on the menu, and it seats 120. Dark and cool **Friendship Restaurant**, 2 King St., is decorated with Christmas lights. **Ping Woo** at Cinderella Square, curiously enough, has good rice and beans. **Chon Saan II**, opposite the Texaco station at 184 North Front St., has large servings of vegetables. Chinese videos show in the "dinning room." Attached to the Kiss Hotel, the **Mandarin House** has daily buffets.

Also try the **Caribbean Restaurant**, 36 Regent St.; **New Archie's Restaurant**, 74 Euphrates Ave. (Dim Sum served on Sundays from 10-3); **Hong Kong Restaurant**, 50 Queen St.; **Golden Dragon**, 29 Queen St.; **New Chon Saan Restaurant**, 55 Euphrates Ave.; **Lotus Garden Restaurant**, 81 Cemetery Rd; **Tam Yi**, cor. Magazine Rd. and Vernon St.; and the **Ocean**, 96 Barracks Rd. at Pickstock St.

BAKERIES AND SNACKS: There are a number of bakeries around town, including one near the Environmental Center. The **Eve St. Mini Mart** sells cupcakes, cookies, and crackers. **Scoops** on the same street sells ice cream from BZ$1. Bananas and peanuts are sold near the Swing Bridge, and **Creamy Corner** on Albert St. is just across from the bridge. **Blue Bird**, 35 Albert St., has burgers, sandwiches, and tropical fruit drinks. **The Play Boy Restaurant** on King St. has good sandwiches. A number of other places are in this same area of town. Across from the Budget Store on

North Front St., **Ding Ho** sells ice cream. The snack place **"Hello Amigo"** is opposite the Farmer's Market near the Belcan Bridge.

MARKET SHOPPING: Visit the **Temporary Market,** which is where the inhabitants of the original market were "temporarily" moved when it was rebuilt. Here, in addition to the usual piles of vegetables, bunches of garlic, cabbages, greens, herbs, and spices are sold. There are also corked bottles of coconut oil and bottles of "honney."

Rebuilt in 1991, the **Belize Commercial Center** stands next to the Swing Bridge. The original market dated from 1845 and the area was originally known as Mule Park because local vendors and farmers would tether their mules and buggies in front to be watered. Inside, besides vegetables and the like, you'll also find the Daiquiri Factory, which dispenses expensive (BZ$6-10) mixed drinks from machines that resemble front-loading washers. You can buy sexy panties at PJ's Modern Romance, and Laurine Chocolates sells pricey handmade chocolates. However, if you want atmosphere, you're better off at the Temporary Market. Hops and other items are sold at a small shop on the right-hand side of the Swing Bridge. Hops are claimed to "bringeth down women's courses, and expel urine."

Also visit the **Farmer's Market** near the Belcan Bridge. For a good selection of alcohol try **Gonzalo Quinto & Sons**, 11 Queen St.

Doubling as a sort of department store, **Brodies** is one of the largest supermarkets. Sample average prices: 75¢/lb. for potatoes; 90¢/lb. for onions; 30¢/lb. for brown sugar;

75¢/lb. for rice; 85¢/lb. for cabbage; fresh eggs BZ$2.80/doz. (including tray); three apples for BZ$4.50; tomatoes for BZ$3.50/lb.; fresh milk, BZ$1.85/qt.; sliced bread, BZ$1/loaf; cassava bread, BZ$1.25/pkg.; ground steak, BZ$4.50/lb.; ground sirloin, BZ$5.30/lb; Rye Crisp crackers, BZ$5/8 oz.; 12 Nature Valley granola bars, BZ$10; Hershey's Cocoa, BZ$19/lb.; Taster's Choice instant coffee, BZ$10/4 oz.; grated parmesan cheese, BZ$4.15/3 oz.; McCormick Garlic powder, $3.50/1.3 oz.; Baby Ruth bar, BZ$1.30; can of Diet Coke, BZ$1.25; bottle of Belikin beer, BZ$2.25; 12 oz. can of Old Milwaukee beer, BZ$4.50; 15 fl. oz. of Alberto VO5 Shampoo BZ$6.75; Crest toothpaste, BZ$6.30/6½ oz.; Kleenex tissues (250, 2-ply), BZ$8; Lightning Anise, BZ$9/750 ml.; Ginger Wine, BZ$4.25/750 ml; Fandango Papaya and Banana Wines, BZ$5/bottle; Dewar's Scotch, BZ$33/750 ml.; Marlboro cigarettes, BZ$41/carton; Independence cigarettes, BZ$15.50/carton; Kodak 36 Gold 100, BZ$13; month's strip of Ovral contraceptives, BZ$4; one condom, BZ$1.65; Deep Woods Off, BZ$7; Scotch tape 30½ yds., BZ$3.20; and patron saint votive candles from BZ$4.50.

Other markets include **Romac's**, 27 Albert St., and the huge **Save-U** at the Belcan Bridge.

Entertainment

Evenings bring quiet to town. Along the seafront in the Ft. George area it's all quiet, with rustling palm leaves and gentle lapping surf – save for an occasional passing car blaring *LA*

Woman. The streets are nearly deserted on Sundays when the main distractions to your solitude will come from hustlers and religious radio and TV broadcasts. However, there are a number of places to go and boogie at night.

The **Calypso** is a popular club; It is on the waterfront and is located inside the Fiesta Hotel.

The Bellevue, 5 Southern Foreshore, has a disco on weekends. Popular with locals, the **Big Apple** (☎ 02-44758), 67 North Front St., features live bands. The **Red Roof Lounge** (☎ 02-77158), 3580 Sittee St. near the Civic Center by the river, has live bands. The **Lumba Yaad** is a popular eating, drinking, and dancing club. It's located along the Haulover Creek river bank just outside town on the Northern Highway.

bars: If you dare to go, the Fort George has the **Paddle Lounge,** where sports afficionados will find a wide-screen TV. Located at the southern end of Foreshore St., **Sea Breezes Bar** is a pleasant spot. **Dim's Mira Rio's** bar has a veranda overlooking the ocean and is a favorite with boat owners. Also try the **Pub**, 91 North Front St. Out of town, the Best Western Biltmore Plaza has the **Squires Lounge**, which features (gasp! groan!) karaoke. Sing along to the insipid song of your choice.

concerts: The 5,000-seat **Belize City Civic Centre** has occasional events. Check the newspapers and watch for posters.

Information

The **Belize Tourist Bureau** (☎ 02-77213/73255, fax 02-77490; PO Box 325, Belize City) is located at 83 North Front St., just a few blocks down from the Swing Bridge, past the PO and on the right. The **Belize Tourism Industry Association/BTIA** (☎ 02-78709/75717, fax 02-78710; Box 62) has its offices at 99 Albert St. The **Belize Center for Environmental Studies** (☎ 02-45545, PO Box 666) is at 55 Eve St., just north of the Fort George area. It has a library containing a large amount of information on Belize, which may be used with permission.

The Economic/Commercial Section of the **US Embassy** (☎ 02-77161, PO Box 286, Belize City) dispenses handouts and information on trade and investment opportunites and procedures in Belize. The Commercial Library is open Monday to Friday, 8:30-noon, 1:30-4:30 and on Wednesday from 8:30 to noon. The **USAID Mission** (☎ 02-31066, PO Box 817, Belize City) has its office at the corner of Queen St. and Gabourel Lane. The offices of the **Belize Audubon Society** (☎ 02-34987/3504; PO Box 1001, Belize City) are in the Old Customs Bldg. at 12 Fort St.; it's readily identifiable by the toucan poster outside. Founded in Britain in 1989 with the intention of saving 250,000 acres of rainforest, the headquarters of the **Programme for Belize** (☎ 02-75616/7) is at 168 North Front St. Located at 63 Regent St., the **Chamber of Commerce** (☎ 02-73148/74394, fax 02-74984) offers a wealth of information on commercial opportunities in Belize. Selling a two-sheet 1:250,000 projection of the entire country, as well as 1:50,000 section maps, the **Lands Dept. Office** is on the second floor of the Paslow Building above the PO.

Services & Health

Change money at **Castleberry Ltd.,** ☎ 0272313; 63 Regent St. It is the local branch of Western Union and gives one the best exchange rates.

The **Post Office** is in the Paslow Bldg. on the Ft. George side of the Swing Bridge. It's open Monday to Thursday from 8:30 to noon and 1 to 4, closing at 5:30 on Friday. The parcel office is on Church St. just past Barclays Bank. **BTL**'s office is also on Church St.; overseas and long distance calls can be made from here. You must pay a deposit first, and the operator will dial the number. Although it's open daily from 8 AM to 9 PM, only collect calls can be made on Sundays. **TACA** (☎ 02-77257) is located in Belize Global Travel, 41 Albert St. At 13 Albert St., **Tropical Vision** will do faxes and photocopies.

The **Belize Laundromat** (☎ 23-1117) at 7 Craig St. does laundry for BZ$10/load, and the **Belize City Dry Cleaners and Coin Laundry** (☎ 02-75153), 3 Dolphin St., offers delivery service. Film can be purchased at **Venus Photo,** Albert and Bishop Sts. **The Acupuncture Massage Center** (☎ 02-31834) is at 8 Craig St. Chinese newspapers may be purchased at the **Bolinas Shop,** 158 North Front St. The **Belize Country Club** (☎ 02-33779) is out on the Western Highway at Mile 8.5. It has horseback riding, a pool, a tennis court, and a "gymnastic" room. It's chiefly open on weekends.

EMBASSIES: The **US Embassy** (☎ 02-77161) is at 20 Gabourel Lane. **Mexico** (☎ 02-45367) at 20 Park St. issues tourist cards the same day. **El Salvador** (☎ 02-44318) is at 120 New Road. **Honduras**

(☎ 02-45899) is at 91 North Front St.

BANKING: Atlantic Bank, Belize Bank, Barclays Bank, and the **Bank of Nova Scotia** have Automatic Teller Machines. At present, ATMs operate only in Belize City and accept only Belizean bank cards. In order to obtain a cash advance on your Visa card, you must go into the bank. Bank branches are found all over Belize, but moneychangers can be easier and offer a higher rate. Carry US dollars only for maximum ease of conversion.

HEALTH: Brodie's Pharmacy (☎ 27-7776, ext. 26) is one of the places to go for drugs. The five **Community Drug Stores** (Barracks Road, Market Sq., Albert St., Euphrates Ave., Farmer's Market) have a good selection; you can also send letters, make phone calls, or fax from any of them. **Central Drug Store** (☎ 02-44582) is at One Market Square. There are a number of others around.

One medical practitioner recommended by the US Embassy is **Dr. Manuel Lizama** (☎ 02-45138) at 13 Handyside St., Belize City. **St. Francis Hospital** (☎ 02-77068), 28 Albert St., is a small private hospital. **Belize Medical Services** (☎ 02-30303/30098), 5791 St. Thomas St., is a prominent private clinic. The **Belize City General Hospital** is on Princess Margaret Drive. It opened in 1995.

Tours

Most tour agencies run packages to the following destinations, often in combination: Cockscomb, Mountain Pine Ridge, Baboon Sanctuary, Altun Ha, Xunantunich and Guanacaste Park, Lamanai, and Crooked Tree. Some also offer excursions to Tikal for a hefty US$200-300. Prices average US$60 for a day tour.

Operated by the husband and wife team of Sarita and Lascelle Tillett, **S & L Guided Tours** (☎ 02-77593/evening 73062; PO Box 700, 91 North Front St., Belize City) offer the usual variety of trips. Their half-day tours to Altun Ha or the Baboon Sanctuary are a comparatively modest BZ$25. **Jal's Travel and Tours,** 148 North Front St., runs standard trips ranging from Bermudian Landing (BZ$25, half-day) to Mountain Pine Ridge/Xunantunich (BZ$60, full day).

Formerly Belize Mesoamerica, **Discovery Expeditions** (☎ 02-30625/30748, fax 02-30750); PO Box 1217, Belize City) offers a large number of tours including trips to all of the major ruins and reserves as well as reef trips and a "Manatee Experience." They also have a dive boat. Their main office is at 126 Freetown Rd.

At 41 Albert St., **Global Adventure Tours** (☎ 02-77185, ext. 40; www.belize.net; e-mail bzadventur@btl.net) offers a number of customized packages.

G&W Holiday (☎ 025-2661/2321) are at the international airport; trips include runs to Lamanai, Mountain Pine Ridge, Crooked Tree, and Blue Creek/Rio Bravo. Rates range from BZ$100 on up, depending upon the number of people.

At Mile 2½ along the Northern Highway, **Blackline** (☎ 02-44155) offers a "Manatee Magic" trip, as well as river and reef tours, fishing excursions, and dive trips.

Set in the Bellevue Hotel on 5 Southern Foreshore, **Maya Circuit Tours** (☎ 02-77051; PO Box 428,

Belize City) offers hotel-and-tour packages with optional rental car. **Aerobel Ltd.** (☎ 02-72692/31938; 12 Douglas Jones St.) specializes in group package tours to destinations such as Tikal and Cancún.

Gilly's Personalized Inland Tours (☎ 02-77630/77613; 31 Regent St.) features a range of trips from a walk along the Panti Trail to a visit to Lamanai. A full service travel agency, **Belize Global Travel** (☎ 02-77185/77363/77364) is at 41 Albert St. **Singing Woods Tours** (☎ 02-31070) is at 38 New Rd. The **Belcove Hotel** (02-73054; 9 Regent St.), offers day trips to the reef at Gallows Point. **Seven Candles Cab Service** (☎ 02-31979, VHF 152.975; Box 820, Belize City) offers a/c charters including lunch to destinations such as Xunantunich, Altun Ha, the Baboon Sanctuary, Lamanai, Crooked Tree, and others.

Other Belize City-based agencies include **Caribbean Holidays Ltd.** (☎ 02-73131/72593; 81 Albert St.), **Maya Land Tours** (☎ 02-30515; 64 Bella Vista), **Maya Mar Tours** (☎ 02-72262; PO Box 1234, Belize City), **Mayaworld Safaris** (☎ 02-31063; West Landivar or PO Box 997, Belize City), **Native Guide System** (☎ 02-75819/78247; 1 Water Lane or PO Box 1045, Belize City), **Oswald Gillett** (☎ 02-78736; 66 Dean and Euphrates Ave.), **Gilly's Inland Tours** (☎ 02-77630/77613; 31 Regent St.), **Melmish Mayan Tours** (☎ 02-45221; PO Box 934, Belize City), **Pancho's Guided Tours** (☎ 02-45554; 5747 Lizarraga Ave.), Rosy Tours (☎ 02-30341; 194 North Front St. or PO Box 1681, Belize City), **Royal Palm Travel Services** (☎ 025-2534; Belize International Airport), and **Thrifty Tours** (☎/fax 02-75491; PO Box 1678, Belize City).

DIVING: Contact Frank Bounting at **Belize Diving Services** (PO Box 667, Belize City; ☎ 02-22143). He rents equipment and offers instruction and diving. At Mile 2½ along the Northern Highway, **Blackline** (☎ 02-44155) offers dive trips.

Events & Festivals

There are three important holidays. On March 9th the death of the somewhat eccentric British baron with a Portuguese title, Baron Bliss, is commemorated by a formal ceremony at his tomb followed by fishing and sailing regattas. The holiday commemorating the Battle of St. George's Caye (on Sept. 10, 1798) is spread over an entire week and includes religious services and carnival celebrations. A parade takes place in Belize City on the 10th. Commemorating the nation's independence on Sept. 21, 1981, National Independence Day includes a variety of food, music, and cultural activities.

Shopping

Most businesses are open from 8 to noon and from 1 to 4; some reopen from 7 to 9. The entire city closes down on Sunday. The shops are generally small. Compared to Guatemala, Belize does not have an impressive variety of crafts, but Belize City is a good place to shop for what is available. On the Ft. George side of Fort St. across from the Audubon and Maya offices in the old TACA warehouse next to the BDF Maritime Wing, the **National Handicraft Center** is a great place to shop.

They have an excellent selection of cassette tapes (BZ$12) by local artists including Pupa Curly and Bella Caríb, a number of books including copies of this guide, and an intriguing selection of craft items.

Out by the river and near the Swing Bridge, the **Maritime Museum** sells crafts, and zericote woodcarvings are sold at **Brodies Dept. Store**. At 39 Albert St. West, **Rachel's Art Gallery** offers paintings, novelties, and art supplies. The **Philatelic Bureau**, inside the General Post Office on the western side, sells stamps, which you can give to your stamp-collecting friends or relatives. At 93 North Front St., the **Budget Store** sells an extensive collection of T-shirts, jewelry, and used books and clothes. **Go-Tees** on Regent St. has an assortment of T-shirts and other souvenirs. Featuring photo processing, photo accessories and Belizean music, **Venus Photos and Records** is at the corner of Albert and Bishop Streets. Other photo supplies are available at **Brodie's** on Regent St. and at **Rosales Ampli-Foto**, 42 Albert St. Practical items such as Coleman fuel and machetes can be purchased at **Habet & Habet** at the corner of West and Basra Streets. **Hofius Hardware** is at 19 Albert St. Out of town at the Best Western Biltmore Plaza, **El Papagayo Gift Shop** has a fine selection of crafts and other items.

BOOKSTORES: If you want a book to read, you should buy it while you're here. If other travelers have ogled your guide book, tell them to get it at one of the following places. The nation's largest selection of books and magazines is to be found at the **Book Center** (☎ 02-77-457; 4 Church St.). **Angelus Press Ltd.**

(02-35777; angel@btl.net; 10 Queen St.), sells a wide variety of books, maps, and videos. The **Budget Store,** 93 North Front St., has used books. Books can also be found in the gift shop of the **Audubon Society** on Fort St., **National Handicraft Center**, and at **El** **Papagayo Gift Shop** at the Belize Biltmore Plaza.

The Reef & The Cayes

You can travel the world over and not find anything like the cayes. Australia has its barrier reef but no islands; the Caribbean and Indonesia have islands galore but no comparable reefs. Stretching south of Chetumal Peninsula, these offshore islands are without a doubt the most striking feature on the Caribbean coast of the Yucatán Peninsula. Although locals maintain there are as many of these islands as there are days in the year, they actually number around 450. Over 150 miles of barrier reef form the edge of the coastal shelf block, with cayes strewn along this block as well as the deep sea banks just offshore. Most are uninhabited; the major settlements are on Ambergris Caye and Caye Caulker. Traditionally, these villages have subsisted through fishing and cocals (coconut plantations), but they are becoming increasingly dependent upon tourism for their livelihood. Underwater visibility is seldom less than 50 feet, and during March, April, and May, you may be able to see as far as 100-200 feet. The clearest area is around Lighthouse Reef Atoll.

> **ⓘ Did You Know?**
> The Belize barrier reef system is one of five new sites the United Nations has added to its list of natural places with "outstanding universal value."

Geographical Features

With a combined area of some 212 square miles, the cayes run the length of the country and lie 10-40 miles offshore. There are three types. Densely covered with mangroves, the **wet cayes** are partially or fully submerged at times and resemble bizarre floating forests sailing on the Caribbean. Barren **coral outcrops** comprise the second category. Finally, **sand cayes** are like miniature South Pacific islands, with coconut palms and white sand beaches. The three **atolls** are Turneffe Reef, Glovers, and Lighthouse. Although the area (including coastline, reef, and islands) has been proposed as a World Heritage Site under UNESCO protection, Belize is not a signatory to the World Heritage Convention. Only about 20 of the 450 cayes have been developed at all for tourism.

LAYOUT: Two tiers of atolls lie outside the Barrier Reef area. The Turneffe Island group is the first one to the east; the two groups further out are Lighthouse Reef and Glovers Reef. Their northeast-to-southwest tilt is due to a block-fault system which shapes the shelf and the Bahía de Chetumal. They are set apart from the Barrier Reef and from one another by sharply sloped submarine trenches. The first cayes you reach traveling from Belize City are The Drowned Cayes, a chain of wet cayes.

FORMATION: For the most part temporary, a caye is formed when a mangrove seedling takes root at a shallow point on the coral rock of a continental shelf. As the red mangroves grow, silt and debris accumulate, soil forms, and the caye grows. Always tenuous, it may be wiped off the map by a tropical storm or hurricane, or even by a change in the currents. Islands split apart by hurricanes include St. George's Caye and Caye Caulker. Atolls are circular or horseshoe-shaped coral reefs with slender, sandy islets formed by wind, storms, and surf.

History

The first people to reach the cayes were Maya, who settled on a number of the islands. Probably the most important settlement was on Ambergris, but ancient middens (shell heaps) are found on a number of cayes. The area was first charted by Spaniards arriving between 1528 and 1532. After the battle of St. George's Caye in 1798, English names were permanently applied to the territory. Today, except on the islands developed for tourism, the standard of living remains extremely basic. Of the three main traditional livelihoods (fishing, coconut farming, and sponge cultivation), only fishing remains prominent, and lobsters and conch are becoming increasingly scarce. There's generally no electricity, and rainwater remains the only water source. Chickens and pigs supplement the inhabitants' diet, but everything else must be brought in by boat.

Environmental Problems

Although from the air the cayes may appear to be bits of paradise, domestic sewage frequently washes back onto the windward side of the inhabited islands, and tar may be a problem on some beaches. The islands and the reef are part of a complex and highly fragile ecosystem,

one which fishermen and tourists alike have affected with devastating consequences. On Ambergris the construction of so many hotels has drawn down the water table to the point where, until the recent completion of a new water system, locals have had to drink sewage-laced salty water. Overfishing has threatened the fish population, and lobsters may become extinct in the area if the illegal harvesting of pre-reproductive ones continues. Out-of-season fishing, meanwhile, threatens the fish population.

Another problem has come from land developers who have transformed protective mangrove reef habitats into beachfront lots as on the south end of Ambergris Caye. This reduces fish and wildlife habitats, cutting down the amount of organic material released into the surrounding water, and exposing the coastline to erosion. These same developers are creating a series of canals and lots in an area of dwarf basin mangroves downwind of the San Pedro airport, using material suctioned from seagrass beds. This area is apparently not high enough or stable enough to support homes. If homes are built, they will have a negative effect on the surrounding seagrass beds. In tourist areas, the presence of nutrient-rich effluent from overloaded septic tanks and garbage dumps is fostering algae growth, posing a mortal threat to reefs and seagrass communities. Another threat comes from spills of fertilizer, oil, and other materials by ships coming in and out of Belize City.

Cayes Near Belize City

Moho Caye

A half-mile offshore from St. John's College on Princess Margaret Drive, this island once quarantined victims of smallpox and other contagious diseases. A cemetery contains some of their remains. It's the home of **Maya Landings** (☎ 02-45798, fax 02-30263), a yacht rental operation that also features diving; excursions are offered to the Río Dulce and to the Blue Hole.

It also has **The Quarter Deck Restaurant,** which provides a welcome respite from Belize City. Jack Chivers, President of Magnum Belize, writes: "For a special treat, catch the no-fee ferry that departs from the Landings every half-hour for Moho Caye. Just a quarter-mile off the coast of Belize City, the private island has 57 exclusive lots and a large, upscale marina where the 'big boys' dock. Serving such a clientele, the Quarter Deck is, as you might expect, a world-class restaurant that rivals everything in Miami or Chicago. Seafood dishes are the specialty. the Quarter Deck seats only 40, so reservations are recommended. Sunday brings live music and an outdoor barbecue from 11-8." (Jack rates it five stars!)

Gallows Point

Set seven miles east, this is the nearest point to the town where you can snorkel. Moderately priced, the **Wave** (☎ 02-73054) offers fishing, scuba, and glass bottom boats; airport transportation and meals are included in the rates. For information write 9 Regent St.,

Belize City. **Weir Dow Marina** is also on the island. Set just to the south of Gallow's Point Reef, **English Caye** has a lighthouse marking the entrance to English Caye Channel. Feel free to drop in and visit; it may be possible to stay overnight if you're camping.

Spanish Lookout Caye

The very expensive **Spanish Bay Resort** (☎ 02-77288/72725, fax 02-72797, ☎/fax 02-31960; Box 35, Belize City) offers a restaurant/bar and an attractive ambiance. This diving resort's 10 rooms are in five cottages on stilts; they have fans. It's about a 20-minute boat ride and some two miles from the barrier reef. Offices in Belize City are at 71 North Front St., and dive packages are available from US$500 all-inclusive for three nights. In the US, ☎ 800-359-0747.

The Bluefield Range

Set some 21 miles southeast from Belize City, this small set of three mangrove cayes hosts five-unit, moderate/expensive **Ricardo's Fishing Huts** (☎ 02-44970 or VHF Chan. 68). There are no baths. You may be able to accompany Ricardo on his fishing rounds. Tent sites (around BZ$6 pp, pd) are also available. Write PO Box 55 or contact Anna Lara at the Mira Río Hotel (Box 55, 59 North Front St., Belize City).

Middle Long Caye

Located near the Bluefields Range inside the barrier reef, southeast of Crayfish Caye and southwest of

The Reef & The Cayes

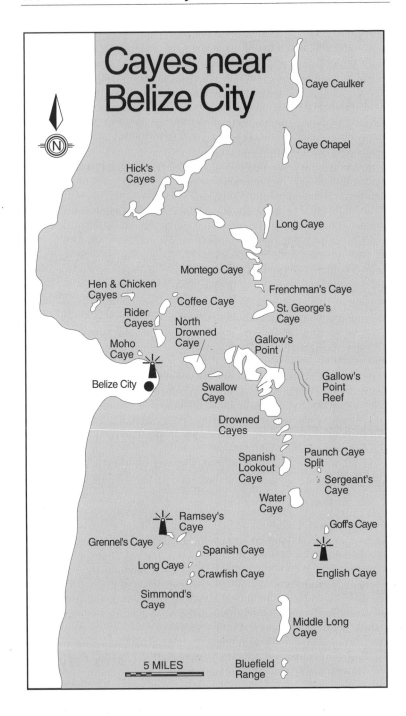

Cayes near
Belize City

Caye Caulker

Caye Chapel

Hick's
Cayes

Long Caye

Montego Caye

Hen & Chicken
Cayes

Frenchman's Caye

Coffee Caye

Rider
Cayes

St. George's
Caye

North
Drowned
Caye

Moho
Caye

Gallow's
Point

Belize City

Swallow
Caye

Gallow's
Point
Reef

Drowned
Cayes

Spanish
Lookout
Caye

Paunch Caye
Split

Sergeant's
Caye

Water
Caye

Ramsey's
Caye

Goff's Caye

Grennel's Caye

Spanish Caye

Long Caye

Crawfish Caye

English Caye

Simmond's
Caye

Middle Long
Caye

5 MILES

Bluefield
Range

English Caye, this mangrove island hosts the two-room budget **Moonlight Shadows Lodge** (☎ 08-22587). Write 5 Mahogany St., Belmopan for more information. Wendy Berkelman, an American residing in San Francisco, (☎ 415-584-9384; e-mail cantor@calon.com) runs a seasonal educational camp called **Mangrove Manor** on Montego Caye. A visit must be arranged in advance. Costs are very reasonable.

Ambergris Caye & San Pedro

👹 One of the most famous of the cayes, Ambergris remains the nation's major tourist destination. Over half of visitors to Belize come here only, and a sizeable number of visitors are divers.

Although it's the largest caye (about the same size as Barbados), most of the island is composed of mangrove swamp, and most of the residents live in the attractive seaside village of San Pedro at its southern tip. Some are descendants of British and French buccaneers, but most are of Yucatec Maya-Spanish (mestizo) descent and are remarkably bilingual.

Once this was a fishing village, with no traffic signs or vehicle regulations. Now the sandy streets abound with locals and tourists driving golf carts, and Belizean law applies. There are 23 stop signs and a few one-way streets.

If you're a middle-class North American or European, you'll feel right at home in San Pedro. But if you're a backpacker or low-budget traveler who likes lots of local flavor, you may find San Pedro to be a bit sanitized for your tastes. In any event, San Pedro – even with the recent surge in development – wins out any day over a sterilized resort environment such as Cancún.

History

The island was formed from the accumulation of coral fragments. First, a shoal patch appeared. Such patches tend to build up in long lines paralleling the mainland. It is believed that their orientation may correspond with submarine geological strata, rather than being solely the product of sea current flows. Little is known about the first Maya residents, except that they routed the Spanish in 1508. Presumably Ambergris was a stopover point for Maya traders. Pirates settled here during the 17th century. Artifacts and even skeletons, which have been unearthed all over town during the course of construction projects, attest to San Pedro's long historical roots. Although it is believed to have been named after the sperm whale secretions washed ashore on its beaches during the 19th century, the true origin of the island's name is unknown.

During Yucatán's War of the Castes (1848-49), an initial four families migrated here from Bacalar in Quintana Roo. Mexico tried to annex the territory in 1851, but the locals protested, and the matter was amicably settled by an 1893 treaty. In 1874 James Blake purchased the entire island (save for one parcel controlled by the Catholic Church) and began collecting rents. Nearly a century later the Belizean government stepped in and made a "forced purchase" of the island, selling parcels and lots to the islanders. Over the years, the local

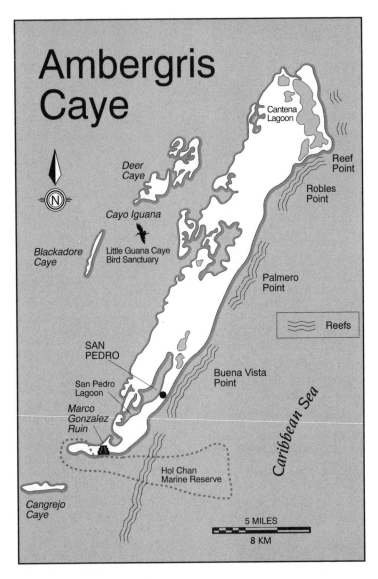

Ambergris Caye

Cantena Lagoon

Reef Point

Robles Point

Deer Caye

Cayo Iguana

Palmero Point

Blackadore Caye

Little Guana Caye Bird Sanctuary

Reefs

SAN PEDRO

Buena Vista Point

San Pedro Lagoon

Caribbean Sea

Marco Gonzalez Ruin

Hol Chan Marine Reserve

Cangrejo Caye

5 MILES

8 KM

economy has shifted focus from logwood to chicle to coconuts to lobster. The last became a valuable export item beginning in the 1920s. After a protracted struggle, the islanders established fishing cooperatives, which effectively protected them from exploitation. As a result, income levels rose.

The island was devastated by Hurricane Hattie in 1961, but the population recovered in succeeding years. The earliest tourists arrived in the 1920s, and the first real hotel, Celi McCorkle's San Pedro Holiday Hotel, was established in 1965. It charged US$10 for a room, three meals, and laundry service.

Tropic Air began flying to the island in 1979. In 1990, the government announced its intention to purchase the 22,000-acre Pinkerton Estate, which embraces more than the upper two-thirds of the island, excluding the beach frontage. Tentative plans call for two new town sites in the area, with plots to be offered to Belizeans at reduced rates. These days, San Pedro is in the midst of a tourism boom, with correspondingly high property prices. One sign on a vacant beachside plot near town reads, "Price went down from $200,000 to $140,000 US. Terms available."

In recent years, the property boom has continued, with most of the northern part of the island now slated for development. The new Bacalar Chico Marine Park was inaugurated in 1997. In Feb. that same year around 250 pounds of cocaine was found by San Pedro police in the Basil Jones/Rocky Point area north of San Pedro Town; another 40 pounds was found two days later in the Bacalar Chico area.

Natural Features

Flanked by a long beach, the island's windward side is straight in comparison with the leeward. The largest of the 12 lagoons is the Laguna de San Pedro to the west of the village. About 2½ miles long, it's fed by 15 creeks. Navigable channels at the island's south end traverse mangrove swamps and a number of the lagoons. Except at Rocky Point, the beach parallels the reef. The Boca Bacalar Chico – a six-foot-wide, 2½-foot-deep tidal channel said to have been dug by the Maya so that they could bring their canoes through – separates this caye from Mexico. It was en-

larged and deepened by the Mexicans in 1899. Approximately 20 miles long, it is now two to four miles wide.

The passage between Ambergris and the mainland has served whalers, pirates, and smugglers through the ages. Many of them wrecked. The most famous is the British frigate, *Water Witch*, which went down off the island's southern tip along with a cargo of gold and silver bullion, some of which is still believed to lie below. The nation's richest fishing waters are found around the caye, and the Barrier Reef is approximately 500 ft. offshore; channels or breaks in the coral permit the local fishermen to pass through safely.

Environmental Problems

Marring the island's placid atmosphere, there is a degree of hostility to expatriates and developers, whom the locals hate "because they always talk in six figures." One current conflict is whether or not to build the North-South Road. Advocates claim that it will relieve the population pressures on the southern six miles, allowing expansion to the north 20 miles. Opposition comes from landowners, who wish to keep their property secluded, and from environmentalists, who charge that the road will devastate the delicate environment.

Flora & Fauna

On the main part of the island, which is still separated from San Pedro by a waterway, a great deal of wildlife survives. You might see frigatebirds, herons, or egrets. Ocelots have been sighted in the mangrove forests, and sea turtles still come ashore to nest. Nearby Bird Caye hosts the nesting grounds of some 30 species, including the cormorant, spoonbill, various ducks, avocets, and both the greater and the reddish egret.

Transport

GETTING HERE: Most travelers arrive by air. Reliable San Pedro-based Tropic Air (☎ 02-45671, 026-2012, 800-422-3435; www. belize.net; e-mail tropic@btl.net) flies. **Maya Island Air** (☎ 02-31348/ 31362/31403; 800-257-8802; e-mail mayair@btl.net) flies direct from Belize City, Belize International, and Corozal. Expect to pay around BZ$70 each way from Belize International and BZ$40 each way from Belize Municipal. The *Andrea* leaves from the departure dock at the Maritime Museum near the Swing Bridge at 4 PM Mon. to Fri. and at 1 PM Sat., returning at 7 AM. The *Triple J* (☎ 02-44375/33464) generally departs at 9, returning at 3 from the Texaco Pier in San Pedro. The *Thunderboat Express* leaves at 1 PM from Mon. to Sat. Fare is BZ$25. (The *Triple J* stops at Caye Caulker to and from San Pedro). It may also be possible to catch a ride with one of the cargo boats departing from the Customs Wharf near the Fort George Lighthouse.

FROM SAN PEDRO: The *Andrea* (☎ 026-2578, 02-74988) departs Mon. to Fri. at 7 for Belize City and on Sat. at 8 from the Texaco wharf near Lily's Hotel. The *Triple J* (☎ 02-44375/33464) generally departs at 3 (BZ$20 OW); it stops at Caye Caulker. Leaving from the Lagoon Side Marina (a white house near the soccer field), the *Thunderbolt Express* (☎ 026-2217) travels from San Pedro Mon.-Sat. to Caye Caulker, Caye Chapel, and Belize City. It departs at 7 and 2, returning at 11 and 4. You may also be able to hitch a ride with a yacht. Be sure to reconfirm departure times with any of these three as they may be subject to change. Any boat with "CC" prefacing the serial number on its side is from Caye Caulker. They arrive in early afternoon, docking beside the Tackle Box. If they take you, expect to pay around BZ$20. One expensive trip (BZ$240-300) is a charter for the 26-mile run to Xcalak, Mexico. Unfortunately, there isn't much to do there save stock up on groceries or, perhaps, stay in the one budget-priced hotel.

> ☞ *Traveler's Tip*
> *Don't let a taxi driver steer you to a specific hotel when you arrive. They collect a substantial commission for doing this!*

Keep in mind that the boat trip from Ambergris to the mainland takes 1-1½ hrs. and is not for those who are susceptible to seasickness. There is no transport to the mainland at all after 5:30 PM.

Sights

Given San Pedro's reputation as a "resort," one might expect a wide, wonderful beach. Instead, what you have is a narrow ribbon of sand that has – owing, perhaps, to dredging of sand that has damaged the reef – receded dramatically over the past decade. Nevertheless, the beach does run along the island's length.

If you want, you can wade (or take the new ferry: BZ$1, daily until 8 PM) across the river and follow the beach all the way to Mexico. Note the extensive mangroves. Be on the lookout for such messages as, "Don't mess with the baby conchs" and "Our mangroves forever." Barking dogs will keep you company much of the way.

Set in Island Plaza, the **Ambergris Caye Museum** opened in 1997. It tells the history of the island, from the Maya to the arrival of the Mestizos and their founding of San Pedro. Japan has promised to supply two interactive computer terminals, and videos enlarge upon the exhibits. Its first curator is British Volunteer Service Overseas (VSO) member Peter Laws, a museum curator for the past 15 years. Exhibits focus on the caye and its heritage – exploring links between modern San Pedro and that of the Maya. The sea is a theme, and displays center around such topics as the Maya, shipwrecks, and the fishing and coconut industries.

A spot of some interest is the **Island Academy.** Established in 1995 by Dixie Bowen, wife of Belikin-Coca Cola magnate Barry Bowen,

the grounds sport three blue, yellow, and green circular cabins on stilts. Students are taught by seven full-time teachers, and class sizes range from 4-12. Tuition is BZ$5,000 per year.

Otherwise, unless you are a snorkeler or diver, there is not much to do here. You can visit the park in town or the relatively new **Boca Del Rio Park** next to the ferry. It has a swimming area with a slide as well as a playground and picnic area.

note: USAID funding having terminated, the Conch Hatchery has closed.

☞ *Traveler's Tip*
Many visitors do not realize that San Pedro may be used as a base to explore the mainland. Both Tropic Air (☎ 02-45671, 026-2012, 800-422-3435; www.belize. net; e-mail tropic@btl.net) and Maya Island Air offer trips to Tikal. Air flights to Lamanai are available, and a popular boat trip runs to Altun Ha and the Baboon Sanctuary.

MARCO GONZALEZ RUINS: Named after the island boy who

Ambergris Caye Suggested Itineraries

- **If you have one day:** Relax and enjoy yourself. Do as little as possible.

- **If you have two days:** Do as little as possible one day. Take a snorkeling trip the next.

- **If you have three days:** If this is your only stop in Belize, also take the "Howler Monkey" trip or visit Lamanai.

- **If you have four days or more:** Sail to Capricorn's one evening, take a day trip to Caye Caulker, visit Tikal, snorkel at Hol Chan or Shark-Ray Alley, bicycle to the north of the island, go birdwatching, get certified as a diver, or take a mainland excursion.

discovered them, the compact Maya ruins of Marco Gonzalez sit on the southern tip of the island. They were excavated by Canadian archaeologists Elizabeth Graham and David M. Pendergast from 1986 to the present. Once located on the beachfront, the site is now a swamp. You have to get there by boat, unless it's dry. Dating from 200 BC to 1500 AD or later the city came under the cultural influence of Lamanai. It appears to have blossomed between 1150 and 1300, after which it faded. All of the site's structures contain shells, and the three large 13th-century structures are built largely of conch shells. The site is thought to have been one of the major coastal trading centers of the Maya world (others in Belize included Moho Caye and Cerros).

DIVE SITES: The most famous of these is Hol Chan (see the section on *Diving*, page 156) at the island's southern end, which features the Hol Chan Cut. Other dive sites include The Pillars, Tackle Box Canyons, Pescador Tunnels, Mexico Rocks, Rocky Point Canyons, Victoria Canyons, and Mata Canyons. A new site is **Shark-Ray Alley**. This shallow cut to the south of Hol Chan was named by *Skin Diver* as one of the seven great sea creature dives of the Caribbean. Trips are often made to the Blue Hole and the Turneffes.

Accommodations

LUXURY: There are now plenty of places to select from in this price range. The **Mayan Princess Resort Hotel** (☎ 026-2778, fax 026-2784; Box 1, San Pedro) has 23 suites with kitchen and living room. All are beachfront, with a/c, queen bed and day bed. High season prices are BZ$220 s and BZ$250 d plus tax.

The island's oldest, the 16-room **San Pedro Holiday Hotel** (☎ 026-2014/2103, fax 026-2295; PO Box 1140, Belize City; www.ambergriscaye.com; e-mail holiday@btl.net) features a saltwater pool, a restaurant (Celi's) and a deli, as well as water sports and diving. Rates are around BZ$190 s or d for a/c rooms. More expensive apartments are also available (17% tax and service charge are added). In Belize City, ☎ 02-44632.

south from the airport: Set right across from the airport, the a/c **Belizean Reef Suites** (☎ 026-2582) has two bottom units (one and two) that open directly out to the beach. Rates are around BZ$250 for a one-bedroom, and BZ$500 for a three-bedroom unit plus tax. Suites have full kitchens, a/c in bedroom, cable TV, ocean views from roof and balconies.

The 34-room a/c Spanish-style **Sun Breeze Resort** (☎ 026-2347/2191/2345, fax 26-2346; PO Box 14, San Pedro) is near the airport. It has a beachfront bar & grill and a restaurant, the Coco Palms. Also on the premises are a dive shop and boats, windsurfers, volleyball, and electric carts. Rooms rent from around BZ$180 s and BZ$300 d in-season, with tax and 5% service added.

☞ *Traveler's Tip*

The Sun Breeze is the only resort on Ambergris with fully accessible rooms for disabled guests.

The expensive 52-unit **Belize Yacht Club** (☎ 026-2777, fax 026-2768; Box 1, San Pedro; e-mail bychotel@btl.net) is a group of modern Spanish-style condos that are being rented out. The resort offers diving, and a health club. It has a pool and the grounds are immaculately manicured. Each unit has choice of a/c or fan, queen bed, day bed, kitchen, and living room. Rates are from BZ$330. In the US, ☎ 800-44-UTELL.

Coconuts Caribbean Hotel (☎ 026-3500, fax 026-3501; reservations 800-324-6974; e-mail coconuts@btl.net) is one of the more popular newer hotels. Rooms have a/c or fans, and breakfast is included. Rates are around BZ$190 s, BZ$210 d, plus tax; children under 12 are free.

On the beach at the town's southern edge, **Ramon's Village Resort** has 60 thatched-roof cabanas, saltwater pool, and complete services including diving and fishing. From a distance, the resort has an authentic Maya look to it. Expect to pay from BZ$230 (plus tax) on up; rates are highest from Dec. 17-Jan. 1. ☎ 026-2067/2074, fax 026-2214, 544-443-2100, 601-649-1990; in the US, 800-443-8876 or 601-649-1990.

Caribbean Villas (☎ 26-2715, fax 26-2885; Box 71, San Pedro; e-mail c-v-hotel@btl.net; www.ambergriscaye.com) has attractive apartment suites just 1½ miles to the south of town (a 20 min. walk). Constructed in 1991, they are owned and operated by the affable Will and Susan Lala. You can expect that Will, the town's volunteer dentist, will greet you at the airport and take you on a superbly informative town tour in his golf cart.

Caribbean Villas' attractive and functional a/c suites have fully equipped kitchens with electric stoves. They are large enough to feel roomy while still being compact enough to feel homey. The atmosphere is laid back and unpretentious, so if your needs revolve around a blaring TV and chocolates on the bed at night accompanied by a hibiscus blossom, you'd better seek elsewhere. In contrast with other resorts, the two Jacuzzis truly live up to the name "hot tub." A hammock and sunning stations are stationed at the end of the long and breezy wooden pier, which affords complimentary stellar stargazing at night.

A towering wooden "people perch" provides birdwatching across a lovely littoral forest. Lovingly constructed, it's a great place to take in a sunset. You may catch owner Susan up here with her binoculars. Tours are arranged, and you may take their bikes out for a spin: use from 6-6 is complimentary! As numerous positive entries in the guest books show, the place is a winner with honeymooners. Winter rates run from BZ$170 plus tax for the single room with private bath, to BZ$300 plus tax for the one-bedroom villa, and up to BZ$500 for a deluxe suite, which has two bathrooms and houses up to six. In the US, ☎ 913-776-3738.

Set about 10 minutes walk from the airstrip, the **Hotel Playador** (☎ 026-2870/2872, fax 026-2871; in the US, ☎ 604-469-6317 or fax 604-469-6321; Box 11, San Pedro; e-mail harryb@cyberstore.ca) offers 10 cabanas with fan and one a/c cabana, as well as nine a/c rooms. Rates run from BZ$190 s or d to BZ$250; 17% tax and service is added. A great feature of the place is its Rasta Pasta restaurant: see *Food*.

At Woody's Wharf, **Corona del Mar Apartments/Hotel** (☎ 026-

2055, fax 026-2461; Box 3758, San Pedro; e-mail corona@btl.net; www.belize.net) has suites with kitchen, bedroom with two double beds, sofa-bed in living room, plus a/c and fans. Rates range from BZ$150 d off-season to B$250 d during Christmas and New Years; 17% tax and service is added. Diving (with instruction), fishing, windsurfing, and glass bottom boat tours are available. Excursions can be arranged. In the US, ☎ 800-426-0226.

On a secluded beach about two miles south of San Pedro, **Victoria House** (026-2067/2240/2304, fax 026-2429; e-mail victoria@btl.net) offers rooms (some with a/c) and stucco-and-thatch cabanas with tile floors, as well as diving and fishing. In the US, ☎ 713-662-8000, 800-247-5159, fax 713-661-4025; or write Box 20785, Houston, TX 77225. Rates start from around BZ$190 s and BZ$210 d, not including 17% tax and service. A variety of packages (diving, fishing, and "lovers") are available. They also operate Fantasea Watersports (☎ 026-2576).

EXPENSIVE: Formerly the Coconut Cottages, **Casa Solana** (☎ 026-2100, fax 026-2855; PO Box 19, San Pedro; e-mail casasolana@btl.net; www.ambergriscaye.com) is *the* place to stay if you would like to recapture the feel of San Pedro as it used to be. Hosts Mary and Henry Beissner are long-time residents who offer affable personalized services to their guests. With a fully equipped kitchen you have the advantages of a condo environment without a hint of sterility.

Located right by the airport and bordering the beach, the relaxing garden environment is ideal to hang out in. Unlike most hotels, Casa Solana does not impose a surcharge for the use of credit cards. Rates for the five efficiencies run from BZ$140 s, BZ$170 d. Two comfy long-term apartments (BZ$1000 winter, BZ$800 summer plus electricity) are also available.

to the north of town: The 41-unit **Paradise Resort Hotel** (☎ 026-2083, fax 026-2232; PO Box 25, San Pedro) lies at the end of Front St. The wood-and-thatch structures are old, yet attractively funished. Other rooms are more traditional but well appointed, with kitchenettes. The hotel has a distinctive sand, thatch, and wood ambience, and – with sand spread about everywhere on the grounds – is about the only resort in town where you really feel you're on the beach. Prices run from around BZ$100 s and BZ$140 d on up; 11% tax and service are added. For more information, ☎ 800-537-1431 or 713-850-1664, fax 713-850-1664; or write PO Box 42809, Dept. 400, Houston, TX 77242.

There are 24 units available at **Paradise Villas** (☎ 026-2822, fax 026-2592; PO Box 1922, Belize City; e-mail e_gomez@btl.net). In the US, contact owner Bob Howard (☎ 312-427-3600, fax 312-427-1850; e-mail rchrch@aol.com). These recently constructed condos rent for about BZ$250 pd. The one-bedroom units accommodate up to four people; two-bedroom ones sleep three to six. Rooms may have queen-size beds or twins, or a veranda bedroom; a Murphy bed is also available. There are fully equipped kitchens, a/c, daily maid service, a large pool, and fax, phone, office and conference facilities.

Belize Tradewinds owns and op-

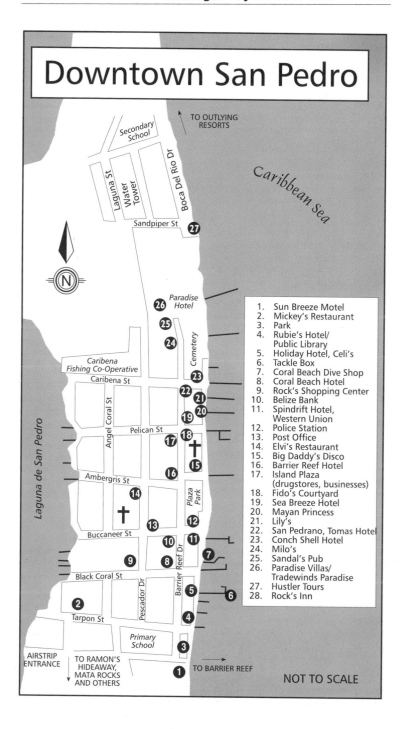

Downtown San Pedro

TO OUTLYING
RESORTS

Secondary
School

Caribbean Sea

Laguna St

Water
Tower

Boca Del Rio Dr

Sandpiper St

Paradise
Hotel

Cemetery

Caribena
Fishing Co-Operative

Caribena St

Angel Coral St

Pelican St

Ambergris St

Buccaneer St

Black Coral St

Pescador Dr

Barrier Reef Dr

Plaza
Park

Tarpon St

Primary
School

Laguna de San Pedro

AIRSTRIP
ENTRANCE

TO RAMON'S
HIDEAWAY,
MATA ROCKS
AND OTHERS

TO BARRIER REEF

NOT TO SCALE

1. Sun Breeze Motel
2. Mickey's Restaurant
3. Park
4. Rubie's Hotel/
   Public Library
5. Holiday Hotel, Celi's
6. Tackle Box
7. Coral Beach Dive Shop
8. Coral Beach Hotel
9. Rock's Shopping Center
10. Belize Bank
11. Spindrift Hotel,
    Western Union
12. Police Station
13. Post Office
14. Elvi's Restaurant
15. Big Daddy's Disco
16. Barrier Reef Hotel
17. Island Plaza
    (drugstores, businesses)
18. Fido's Courtyard
19. Sea Breeze Hotel
20. Mayan Princess
21. Lily's
22. San Pedrano, Tomas Hotel
23. Conch Shell Hotel
24. Milo's
25. Sandal's Pub
26. Paradise Villas/
    Tradewinds Paradise
27. Hustler Tours
28. Rock's Inn

The Reef & The Cayes

erates **Tradewinds Paradise Villas** (☎ 800-451-7776, fax 414-258-5336; e-mail bze@msn.com), a set of subsidiary units in the same complex. They can book you all over Belize, but are particularly expert where San Pedro is concerned. An off-season "7-Night/8-Day Island Dive Special" runs a mere $455 per person with accommodations in a two-bedroom condo for six; airfare, taxes, RT inter-island flights, and land transfers are included in the cost. If there are just the two of you, a week in a one-bedroom condo costs $679 pp. Other packages, diving, and tours are offered: call for a brochure. Their mailing address is 8715 West North Avenue, Wauwatopsa, WI 53266.

Offering horseback riding, partial a/c, and a pool, popular 14-unit **Rock's Inn Apartments** (☎ 026-2326/2717, fax 026-2358; PO Box 50, San Pedro) is designed for those who plan to do cooking. It's to the north of town along the beach. In the US, ☎ 800-331-2458.

One of the nation's most attractive small hotels, **Changes in Latitude** (☎/fax 026-2986) is run by an extremely friendly Canadian woman. Its logo – a melting igloo amidst palm trees –exemplifies the climate change she came here for. Room rates are BZ$160 d for rooms with fans, and BZ$190 d for a/c rooms. Tax is added, and breakfast is included. It's next to the Belize Yacht Club, a half-mile south of the airstrip. Call for complimentary pickup.

Also set to the south of San Pedro, **Mata Rocks Resort** (☎ 026-2336, fax 026-2349; PO Box 47, San Pedro) offers expensive accommodation ranging from BZ$150 s, BZ$170 d, BZ$200 t, and BZ$260

quad on up; 17% tax and service are added. The nine hardwood, stucco, and tiled suites, which vary in price, have kitchenettes, ceiling fans or a/c (some units), and sun decks. An outdoor bar is on the beach. For reservations contact Accent on Travel, ☎ 800-288-8646 or 503-645-7323, or fax 503-690-9308.

others: The five-room, expensive **Casa Tortuga Villa** (☎ 026-2386; 16 Mosquito Coast) has a/c or fan-cooled rooms. For further information, ☎ 303-925-3268 in the US. The seven-unit, expensive **Mosquito Coast Villas** (☎ 026-2531; fax 026-2331) feature fans and offer diving. The four-room, moderate-to-expensive **Tres Cocos** (☎ 026-2531; fax 026-2331) has fan-cooled rooms and also offers diving. Located in town, the expensive, six-room **Alijua** (☎ 026-2113/2791, fax 026-2362) features fans or a/c cottage-style accommodation, with kitchens and cable TV. Rates are around BZ$100 s or d on up, with weekly and monthly discounts. Others include the 10-room **Seven Seas Hotel** (☎ 026-2382/2137), the 10-room **Conch Shell Inn** (☎ 026-2062; around BZ$70 s, BZ$90 d), and the six-unit **Del Mar Garden Cottages** (☎ 026-2170, fax 026-2214; PO Box 89, San Pedro).

MODERATE: Hideaway Sports **Lodge** (☎ 026-2141, fax 026-2269; PO Box 43, San Pedro; e-mail hideaway@btl.net) is the least expensive hotel with a pool. Unpretentious, it has a laid-back character, which reminds you that you are on the Caribbean coast of Central America and not in Miami. The recently remodeled rooms are simple yet comfortable; most have fans but a few have a/c. There is a good restaurant. Rates (which include breakfast, but not tax) run from BZ$90 d up to BZ$180 for a suite that holds six. Children under eight are free.

The small **Hotel Casablanca** (☎ 026-2327, fax 026-2992) has a/c or fans and rooms from BZ$100 with breakfast. Its attractive rooms have bold decor, including bright red sheets – perfect for libidinously inclined couples. It is situated above the Lagoon restaurant. Bargain for values off-season. Also centrally located, the 20-room, unpretentious **Coral Beach Hotel and Dive Club** (☎ 026-2001/2013, fax 026-2864; Box 16, San Pedro) charges from BZ$60 s and BZ$90 d, plus 17% tax and service. It operates a restaurant and the Tackle Box Bar. Set in an elegant three-story building, the **Barrier Reef Hotel** (☎ 026-2075/2049, fax 026-2719; www.belize.net; e-mail barriereef@btl.net) offers 14 a/c rooms and is across from the plaza. It has a restaurant and charges BZ$100 s and BZ$130 d, with substantial off-season discounts available. The 24-room **Spindrift Hotel** (☎ 026-2174, fax 26-2551, 800-327-1939) is a reinforced concrete structure, with rooms starting from BZ$100, plus 11% tax and service.

BUDGET: If you're on a budget, don't expect much here in the way of luxuries. One of the best bargains is the 16-room **Martha's Hotel** (☎ 026-2053, fax 026-2589; PO Box 27, San Pedro), which charges from BZ$30 s and BZ$55 d in the off-season, or BZ$46 s and BZ$69 d in the winter months. Triples and quads are also available. Rates include taxes.

Nine-room **Milo's** (☎ 026-2033) – which charges BZ$20 s, BZ$25 d, and BZ$35 t – is the least expensive. Naturally, the rooms are a bit dark, and baths are shared. **Ruby's Hotel** (☎ 026-2063/2434, fax 26-2434; Box 56, San Pedro; e-mail Rubys@btl.net) charges from BZ$30 for simple rooms with wooden floors and shared baths. More expensive rooms are around BZ$50. Some rooms overlook the ocean.

The unpretentious and laid back **Hotel Del Rio** (☎ 011-501-26-2268) has rooms from BZ$48 s or d plus tax. These have rooms with fans and cold-water shared bath. More expensive units offer more amenities and top out at BZ$170 pd plus tax. In the US, call Gale Willis at 318-984-9655 or fax 318-988-0373. Their web site is www.connecti.com/~altonhah/hotle_del_rio/hotel.htm.

The a/c **San Pedrano Hotel** (☎ 026-2054, fax 026-2093; 4 Barrier Drive) charges BZ$50 s, BZ$60 d, BZ$75 t, and BZ$85 quad, plus tax and service charge for its wooden-floored rooms; off-season is less expensive. Meals are served upon request. They also have an apartment.

Ten-room **Lily's Hotel** (☎ 026-2059) is on the waterfront. Rooms are large and wood-paneled, with fluorescent lighting and fans; some have an ocean view. Charges are from BZ$80 in season.

The attractive eight-room **Tomas Hotel** (☎ 026-2061) charges from around BZ$60 s or d. Other budget hostelries include the 10-room **Cruz Apartments** (☎ 026-2091); the four-room **Islander Hotel** (☎ 026-2065); four-unit **Laidy's Apartments** (☎ 026-2118); eight-room **Lourdes Hotel** (☎ 026-2066) on Middle St.; and four-unit **Palm's Condominiums**

(PO Box 26, San Pedro). Finally, if staying for an extended period, houses are available for rent. For starters, try Mary Hawthorne (☎ 026-3077).

NORTHERN AMBERGRIS AREA: All of these are relatively expensive and can only be reached by boat. The closest of the resorts on the island's north end, at three miles, the colonial-style 22-room **El Pescador** (☎/fax 026-2398, 800-628-1447; PO Box 793, Belize City; e-mail pescador@btl.net) offers "a special fishing experience" for the devoted fisherman. Fish in the area include sailfish, wahoo, snook, lady fish, tarpon, bone fish, and jack crevalle. If you don't fish, there's *nada* to do here! A number of all-inclusive packages are available; they range in price from around US$1,400 pp, double accommodation.

Captain Morgan's Retreat (☎ 026-2567, fax 026-2768; Box 38, San Pedro; e-mail information@captainmorgans.com; www.captainmorgans.com) is three miles north of the river. It has 21 thatched-roof, wooden cabanas with fans and bath; there's a pool with a wooden deck and restaurant. Rates start from BZ$190 s and BZ$240 off-season and rise to BZ$260 s and BZ$340 d during the winter. Service charge of 5%, plus 6% hotel tax, are additional. Fishing, diving, and snorkeling are available. In the US, ☎ 800-447-2931 or 218-847-3012; fax 218-847-0334.

On the beach at the north end is **Journey's End Caribbean Club** (☎ 026-2173; PO Box 12, San Pedro; www.traveling.com/belize/journeyend; e-mail jorneyend@ncosoft.com). A self-contained resort, it features a combination of cabanas and villas, with French cuisine, tennis courts, TV, sailboards, and sailboats. If you're looking for a truly Belizean atmosphere, this isn't the place: you could be anywhere in the tropical world when you're here. Once devoted to the "rich and famous," it has been transformed into a "family-style" resort. In the US, ☎ 800-447-0474 or 305-899-9486.

Some six miles north of San Pedro, the moderately priced **Green Parrot Resort** (☎ 01-49163, fax 026-3293; Box 36, San Pedro) has six secluded beachfront cabanas with fans, plus boating and fishing. It is the project of Stuart Corns, a retired engineer from California. Leave a message at 026-2147 or fax 026-2245.

Where the exclusive resort The Belizean once stood are the imposing grounds of the **Essene Way** (☎ 888-297-8950, 407-297-7544, fax 407-290-2788). Funded by National Health Products, the 17-unit resort offers a/c rooms, a hot tub, pool, basketball, tennis, and volleyball courts, restaurant, recreational center with movie room, conference center, large gym, and watersports. And – yes – there is a seaside chapel where you can confess your sins. Opened in 1997, it is a charitable nonprofit foundation established to provide all-expenses-paid, week-long vacations for terminally ill cancer patients and their families. The resort is nondenominational, and outside visitors are welcome to stroll around. It was the subject of a cover story in the May/June 1997 issue of *Solar Today* because it is said to have the largest solar power installation S of the US border.

Owned and operated by Clarence and Annabel Burdes, **Capricorn**

Resort (☎ 026-2809, fax 021-2091; e-mail capricorn@btl.net; www. ambergriscaye.com) is currently Ambergris' preeminent gourmet restaurant. It has a few simple yet lovely units. Rates run from BZ$150 s, BZ$200 d; an a/c suite is more expensive. Breakfast is included, and meal plans are available. (See restaurant review below, under *Food*.)

When completed a decade from now, the planned **Royal Belize Village** at Punta Azul will consist of a 200-acre mixed-use development. The project will include some 350 residential units, 250 hotel rooms, restaurants, a casino, golf course, marina, a new airport, and other amenities as well. Developers are Dolphin Development International Ltd. and McIntosh Alliance International Hotel Development, Inc. Land for the airport will be donated free-of-charge by the Belize government. An investment of BZ$90 million is planned for the first three years.

CONDO CITY: Condo development is growing rapidly all over the island. Prices start at US$185,000 for two-bedroom, two-bath villas, with daily rentals under the "condotel" concept going for $175 a day double. Others include Casa Caribe, the Caribe Island Resort, Mayan Princess, The Palms, and the Belizean Reef.

The **Casa Caribe** (☎800-365-6232, 281-996-7800, fax 281-996-1556; e-mail star@ghg.net) is a condo development with 10 1,000-sq.-ft two-bedroom units and 19 one-bedroom units. Each has phone, cable TV, and daily maid service. The resort's swimming pool is lit by lasers, which make it change color at night.

There's a restaurant, two bars, shuffleboard, horseshoes, volleyball, a pier, and free shuttle service to San Pedro. Diving, fishing, snorkeling, day tours are available. There is a shuttle boat that offers complimentary transfers to San Pedro for shopping during the day. Set 1½ mi. south of the airstrip, **Royal Palm Villas** (☎ 026-2148, fax: 026-2329, 1-888-423-5403; Box 18, San Pedro Town; e-mail royalpalm@btl.net) are individually owned one-bedroom apartments of concrete construction. Plans are to have a total of 35 villas (each with four apartments) along with a health spa, restaurant, pool, marina, tennis courts, and other facilities. An artificial beach extension is planned as well. Rates are around BZ$320 s or d; BZ$20 pp for each extra person (max 4). Prices start at US$119,900.

The **Palms** (☎ 026-3322, fax 026-3601; e-mail palms@btl.net) consists of 12 one- and two-bedroom suites with kitchen. It has a pool. Rates are around BZ$320 s or d and up; extra people are BZ$40 pp; there is a maximum of four people in a one-bedroom and six in a two-bedroom. Reputed to be the most luxurious, **Villas at Banyan Bay** (☎ 026-3739, fax 026-2766; Box 91, San Pedro) is a set of 80 a/c 1,000-sq.-ft. condo units with two bedrooms (one with Jacuzzi) and two baths; a pool is on the property. Rates are around BZ$350 s or d, BZ$400 t. Tax is added Formerly the Chateau Caribe, the **Caribe Island Resort** (☎ 026-3233, 800-508-5620, fax 501-26-3399; www.belize.net; e-mail ccaribe@btl.net) is a condo complex of 26 suites on the S end of the island. The a/c units (which hold from two-10 each) have TVs and phones;

there's a pool, pier, gift shop, and a bar-restaurant. Use of bicycles, kayaks, and sailboats is complimentary. Local bands play on occasion. Rates run from BZ$180 pn plus tax for a small two-bedroom suite.

Food

San Pedro is an expensive place, where you may spend BZ$20 or more to eat a basic meal. As in other areas of Belize, for some strange reason seafood is more expensive than meat or poultry here.

☞ **Traveler's Tip**

Most restaurants are closed after 2 PM on Sun., so it's wise to plan ahead for an evening meal on that day.

One very popular spot is **Elvi's Kitchen** on Pescador Drive (Middle St.). It has good seafood and reasonable prices. In the Spindrift, **Mary Ellen's Little Italy Restaurant** (☎ 026-2866) offers Belizean and Italian dishes. The classy **Lagoon Restaurant** is in the Hotel Casablanca on Pescador Drive.

Moncho's Ice Cream and Deli offers sandwiches, 20 varieties of ice cream, pastries, and other snacks. It serves homemade tamales on Sat. They are in the Island Galleria.

Located in Fido's Courtyard, **Mojo**'s serves tasty California nouvelle cuisine, Dishes range from a seaburger (served on a whole wheat bun) to grilled pizza (a thin crust spiced with herbs and sesame seeds) to sautéed fresh fish. Prices range from BZ$8.50-29. **Reality Cafe** is upstairs here.

Run by personable David McGaughey – a "self-displaced" Paddy – **Cannibal Café** serves three meals including hearty breakfasts and subs. It's between the Holiday Hotel and the Coral Beach Hotel.

Big Daddy's has a nightly beach BBQ. **The Holiday Hotel** and **Mata Rocks** also have beach BBQs. Informal and excellent value, **The Reef** on Middle St. has seafood and daily specials, as well as *sabutes* and tacos. Food is served in an informal atmosphere to a reggae beat.

The Hideaway is reasonable and has good food. Its fried chicken, shrimp creole, and conch dishes are popular; breakfast here is good value.

The Emerald is a reasonably priced Chinese restaurant; it has cheap rice and bean dishes as well. Often packed and very attractive, the **Jade Garden** has an inexpensive vegetable fried rice; it's open daily from 7:30 AM to 10 PM.

Celi's Restaurant, attached to the Holiday Hotel, is one of the most famous bistros. It serves three meals, and dinner includes lobster, shrimp, and fish. Try the fish stuffed with cheddar and in beer batter.

The a/c **Coco Palms Restaurant** at the Sea Breeze serves elegant seafood and hearty Mexican dishes.

Set south of the airstrip and across from Ramon's, **Duke's Place** serves moderately priced Belizean, Caribbean, and Mexican food in a romantic atmosphere. The shrimp fajitas are recommended, as well as the breakfasts: try the Maya eggs, the fry jacks, or the eggs Benedict.

The Tex-Mex restaurant, **La Margarita** (☎ 2222), is in an attractive setting near the new Rock's grocery S of town. It serves lunch and dinner and 40-oz. margaritas!

Sit upstairs on the veranda here.

Formerly at the Hotel Playador, **Mickey's Place** is now near the Five Asides Sport Ground by the elementary school. Open daily and serves *huge* (recommended) burritos for lunch on Wed. Mickey's is also great for breakfast; try their fry jacks with tropical jam sauce.

Set atop the Hotel Playador, a cool and breezy spot, **Rasta Pasta** (☎ 027-3855) is the creation of Maralyn and Albert Gill, an American-Belizean couple who hooked up at the Oregon Country Fair of all places. It is open from 7 AM-9:30 PM and is closed Wed. Food ranges from appetizers (conch fritters) to enormous burritos, vegetarian lasagna, and a wide variety of pizzas including pesto. A meal can be topped off with a "decadent dessert." All breads are baked in their kitchen. Ask about their wines, as well as Genesis in the Jungles, their unique herb packages that come complete with recipes. Many people find the food so good that it is the only place they eat while on island. It's open daily (except Wed.) from 7-9:30. Albert and crew pump out Rasta drum rhythms most evenings.

Victoria House (☎ 09-22067) has buffet service and a special "Queen Victoria Brunch" on Sun. from 8-1; free transportation is provided.

to the north: Across from the river cut, **Sweet Basil** (☎ 027-3870) is a gourmet grocery and cafe. It serves lunch "all day" and is open 9:3-5:30; closed Mon. **Palapa Hut** is a popular place to have lunch.

Intimate **Capricorn Restaurant** (☎ 026-2809) is currently Ambergris' preeminent gourmet restaurant. It is owned and operated by Clarence and Annabel Burdes, a Canadian-Tanzanian couple, whose motto is "you aren't eating in a restaurant but dining in our home!" The cuisine is excellent and quite imaginative. Appetizers include sun-dried tomato pesto over cream cheese served with slices of Cajun baguettes, roasted garlic with extra virgin olive oil, and fresh snapper ceviche. There is one evening special as well as standards such as the chilled stone crab – large claws served with creamy garlic sauce. Another popular entrée is the seafood in mushroom and sherry sauce, which is served in a clamshell. Desserts (such as creamy rum chocolate cake) may be accompanied by espresso or cappuccino.

☞ *Traveler's Tip*

The best way to get to Capricorn for an evening meal is to sail aboard the Rum Punch II (☎ 026-2817, 2340). The gaff-rigged 32-ft. sloop will take you across the starswept seas to the north. If the moon is below the horizon, there's wonderful stargazing, and it's a very special experience. The sloop also offers a sunset cruise and travels to Caye Caulker and Mexico Rocks for snorkeling excursions.

LOW BUDGET DINING: El Parque, down from the Spindrift. serves the cheapest meals around. There are also a few lower-end restaurants, and you can always load up on fresh hot tortillas (from Tortillero el Patio across from Lourdes) and combine them with cheese for a snack.

snacks: Several shops have baked goods and pastries. **HL Burgers** is on Middle St. **Manelly's**, on Barrier Reef Drive across from the Lion's Den, has ice cream. **Celi's Deli** in the Holiday Hotel offers take-out items from 6-6 daily. **The Casa de Café** serves expensive coffee (BZ$2), muffins, and scrumptious slices of cake (BZ$2.50). **The Barrier Reef** has sandwiches for lunch. **Luigi's** serves Mexican food. **The Splash Bar** is in the Belize Yacht Club; it serves healthy dishes. In the park at night a lady sells rice and beans, chicken, and salad for BZ$5; a hotdog vendor stands right by her.

FOOD SHOPPING: Stores are packed with overpriced imported US processed food. The prices reflect high import duties, as well as added shipping costs. The largest store is **Rock's Supermarket** just down from the Coral Beach Hotel. The large food store below **Milo's Hotel** has space invader machines, which add audio ambience. Another store with similar prices is run by the same people who bring you **Martha's Hotel** above. **Super Jenny's** has cabbages (BZ$3.35), packages of two bell peppers (BZ$2.24), two tomatoes (BZ$5), and other items. **Patty's** – located directly across from HL Burgers on Pescador Drive/Middle Street – has the best variety of produce, ranging from kiwi fruit to snow peas to broccoli. Most are kept in the rear, which is air conditioned to the point where a polar bear might feel at home. A second, much smaller branch of **Rock's** is out of town right near Caribbean Villas.

Entertainment

At night the village is quiet, save for the sounds of Spanish language TV pouring into the streets. Most visitors are tuckered out and turn in early; here it is the locals who party all night! There are a few rollicking places to go, and the action starts late.

Frequently featuring live bands, **Big Daddy's Disco** is the mainstay. Located next to the park and marked by an unforgettable sign, it has a sand floor bar with a thatch peaked roof, booths, dartboard, maps, and a disco papered with checkerboard-style painted egg cartons that glow under the blacklight. Free snacks are dispensed during happy hour, which runs from 7 to 9 daily. Its "two for one" cocktails are largely fruit juice.

A newer venue, **Tarzan's**, is set across the road. It's an impressive disco, complete with tropical backdrop. Set at the end of the pier by the Coral Beach, the **Tacklebox Bar** offers live bands during tourist season. Thankfully, the sea creatures once imprisoned in the back have been freed.

The **Purple Parrot Too Bar** at Ramon's offers live music from Thurs. to Sunday. The **Sandal** has dartboards. The **Casablanca** has a romantic rooftop bar at The Playador, which has a happy hour from 5-7; try a mango colada.

Also try **Barrier Reef**, **Fido's Bar**, and the outlying resort called **Journey's End** (accessible only by boat), which has bands on weekends. Finally, visit the **Pier Lounge** in the Spindrift for the Mon. crab races and the Wed. evening Chicken Drop, where locals bet which number a chicken will defecate on first. Numbers from one to 100 are marked on a large board. It's a winner-take-all jackpot.

Events & Festivals

The **San Pedro Carnival** is held from the Sun. to Tues. preceding Ash Wednesday. Processions are held at Christmas and Easter. The **Fiesta of St. Peter**, the town's patron saint, takes place on June 29 and, as an added treat, the fleet is blessed the same day. The anniversary of the town's 1985 incorporation is celebrated on Nov. 27.

Another huge event (and the most recent in conception) is the **Sea and Air Festival**. Generally held in mid-August, it includes volleyball, windsurfing, waterskiing, a beauty pageant, mountain biking, kiting, greasy pole climbing, cardboard bat racing, tug-of-war, catch & release fishing, a grand parade, and other events. Each night is customarily dedicated to a Central American nation.

Because of the recent influx of Garifuna, **Settlement Day** is celebrated here on Nov. 19.

Information, Services & Health

The hole-in-the-wall **PO** (open Mon. to Fri. 8-noon, 1-4:30) is in the Alijua Building. The small **library** is open Mon.-Fri. from 5 to 8 and on Sat. from 1 to 4. Amazingly in this day and age, the library operates on the honor system: just leave your name and the title of the book at the counter.

Belize Bank is in the same building as the Spindrift Hotel. A branch of the **Atlantic Bank** is next door on Barrier Reef Drive. These are the only two banks that will change Canadian dollars. **Castleberry Ltd.** (☎ 026-3140), the local branch of Western Union, gives the best rate for changing money. They're in the Spindrift and open Mon. to Sat. 8-4 and Sun. 8-noon.

There are now four **doctors** in residence on the island; a **pharmacy** is located in the Spindrift Hotel. Gecko Graphics, next to The Reef, will make **photocopies**.

Hol Chan Marine Reserve Office (☎ 09-22420), Caribena St., is chock full of information. An informative window into expat existence on the island, *The San Pedro Sun* is the weekly newspaper. **J's Laundromat** (09-22373), Pescador Drive, is open daily.

rentals: Bicycles can be rented for around BZ$15 pd. Golf cart rentals are also available. With one office in Fido's and another next to the Catholic Church, **Joe Miller Photography** (☎ 026-2577/2556, fax 026-2568; Box 74, San Pedro) has underwater cameras for rent and other services. They are on Middle St.

Tours

Formerly Universal Travel & Tours, **Travel & Tour Belize** (☎ 026-2031/2137, fax 026-2185) has three offices – by the airport, in the Alijua Building, and on Barrier Reef Drive in the Spindrift Hotel lobby. They offer a wide variety of tours, diving, and excursions as far afield as Caracol, Tikal, and to Mexico's Kohunlich.

Also offered is bird watching, river and deep sea fishing, sailing, and snorkeling. Located on Barrier Reef Drive (Front St.), **Amigo Travel** (☎ 026-2180/2435) has moped and bike rentals, glass bottom boat and snorkeling trips, horseback riding, and tours to the cayes and other places.

Located in Fido's Courtyard, **Island Rentals** (☎ 026-2697 and

026-2488 eve., fax 26-2597) has a variety of water sports, water taxi service, beach cookouts, night snorkeling, excursions and tours to many spots, including Altun Ha. They also rent all types of equipment, from golf carts to underwater cameras, kayaks to bicycles. **Excalibur Tours** (☎ 026-2051/2604) offers fishing, snorkeling, diving, waterskiing, and other activities.

Also try **Hustler Tours** (☎ 026-2279/2538/2075), which will take you to Altun Ha, Lamanai, and other excursions.

Diving

Run by dive master Changa Paz, the **Amigos Del Mar** (☎ 026-2706 and 026-2261 eve., fax 026-2648; Box 53, San Pedro) has diving, instruction, rentals, and excursions, including trips to the Turneffes, the Blue Hole, and a night dive at Hol Chan. Changa's favorite dive sites include a 60-ft. tug that he deliberately sank and the caverns at Punta Arena (not for the claustrophobic). If you arrive at his pier towards dusk, you'll find him feeding the rays he has befriended.

---

66 *Reader's Comment*

"Probably the best diving company we had the pleasure of snorkeling with was Amigos del Mar. The staff was very helpful."

Larry Parker's Reefdivers Ltd. (☎ 026-3134, reefdivers@btl.net) are in the Royal Palm Villas. They offer courses as well as a variety of dives, snorkeling, and fishing.

The **Blue Hole Dive Center** (☎ 026-2982; e-mail bluehole@btl.net) runs trips to Sandbore Cay, Half-Moon Cay, and the Blue Hole.

Ramon's Reef Resort (☎ 026-2439) operates the *Sailing Fantasy* catamaran. In addition to diving, they can arrange birdwatching trips.

The **Hideaway Sports Lodge** (☎ 026-2141, fax 026-2269; e-mail hideaway@btl.net) offers a variety of snorkeling, fishing, and diving packages. **Fido Badillo** (☎ 026-2286) operates day trips to Altun Ha, fishing trips, and beach BBQs. **Heritage Navigation** (☎ 026-2394) runs its 66-foot *Winnie Estelle* on day trips to Caye Caulker for around BZ$90 pp. They depart from the Paradise Hotel dock at 9 AM. Rates include two snorkeling stops, but do not include lunch; however, snacks are served and there is a bar on board.

The *Nicola* (☎ 026-2255) runs river trips to Altun Ha, Caye Caulker excursions, fishing, diving, and other trips. The trip to the Community Baboon Sanctuary is particularly popular.

Gonzalez Adventures (☎ 026-2165, cellular 0149629) offers fishing, diving, snorkeling, and practically everything else one might imagine.

Expeditions are available from San Pedro to **Ian Anderson's Caves Branch Adventure Co.** for around BZ$275 pp for a one-day excursion. Flights depart Tues. and Fri. at 7 AM sharp. Featured are the Ancient Maya Crystal Cave Expedition, the Ancient Maya River Cave Tubing Expedition, the Rain Forest Expedition, and the River Cave Rafting. Finally, **Bill Henkes** will take you out on his yacht, *The Yanira*, for BZ$50 pp, pd. Write him c/o General Delivery, San Pedro.

dive boats: Several of the nation's live-aboard dive boats are based in San Pedro, although they

Popular Excursions From Ambergris Caye

- ▪ River trip to the Community Baboon Sanctuary (air return possible)

- ▪ "Jungle River Trip" to Altun Ha

- ▪ Seaplane (or boat) trip to Lamanai

- ▪ Plane and road trip to Xunantunich

- ▪ Manatee watching

- ▪ Diving the Blue Hole

- ▪ Sailing to Caye Caulker

- ▪ Snorkeling at Shark-Ray Alley and Hol Chan Reserve

The Reef & The Cayes

generally must be booked well in advance. The **Bottom Time Dive Shop** (☎ 026-2348, 800-382-7776; e-mail divebze@compassnet.com) is affiliated with Bottom Time Divers. They offer day trips to the Blue Hole and other trips.

The *Manta IV* (☎ 014-7443) is a live-aboard featured in the film *Cocoon: The Return*. Her specialty is trips to the Blue Hole. Five dives are allowed per trip, and an overnight is spent in a tent on Half Moon Caye. Rates are around BZ$500 pp for divers and BZ$350 pp for snorkelers.

Fantasea Watersports (☎ 026-2576) runs out of Victoria House and offers scuba instruction, fishing, and a variety of excursions and rentals. Note: Dive trips are frequently cancelled at short or no notice when the minimum number of divers doesn't show up. On all trips, you pay an insurance fee and this entitles you to free use of the recompression chamber near the airport should you need it.

Hustler Tours (☎ 026-2279/2538/2075) offers a Blue Hole dive

tour as well as a visit to Christ of the Abyss & The Ten Commandments. This shallow "dive site" was created after statues destined for the Essene Way fell off the boat that was carrying them.

Alfonso runs the *Lil' Alfonso* (☎ 026-2584), and knows how to attract sharks and rays at Shark Ray Alley. He's described by one couple as a "master bullfighter." There are more sharks in the afternoon and camera rental is cheaper. If you rent an underwater camera and dive, Alfonso will bring plenty of sardines. He can also take you snorkeling at Hol Chan; he knows where to find the crabs and moray eels.

Fishing

For flat fishing, contact **Romel Gomez Jr.** (☎ 022-2063) or **Tomas** (☎ 022-2134); expect to spend around BZ$200 for a half-day and BZ$300 for a full day. For deep-sea fishing, contact Tom Thomas at **Sea Boots Sportsfishing** (☎ 022-2911). For supplies, visit the shop in the Villa.

Shopping

Prices are generally higher than on the mainland. Postcards sell for BZ$1 instead of the usual 75¢, and other prices are set accordingly.

The small **art gallery** at Fido's Courtyard features a fine selection of arts as well as the work of Garifuna artist Walter Castillo. Castillo, a native of Nicaragua, is married to the gallery owner.

Set in the Hotel Playador, **Rasta Pasta** has an unusual gift shop. In town, **Hot Stuff** is a gift shop with a wide selection of books and other items. One of the more memorable shops here is **Iguana Jack's Island Art**, which has painting, sculpture, and ceramic iguanas. **Hummingbird Rattan**, on Coconut Drive between Rocks II and Mar de Tumbo, sells rattan-and-wood furniture. Other gift shops are in hotels such as Ramon's.

Hol Chan Marine Reserve

Contact the Reserve office for information at ☎ 09-22420. Set along the northern section of the barrier reef approximately four miles southeast of San Pedro, this reserve's central feature is its namesake – a natural break or cut (Hol Chan means "Little Channel" in Maya), which has produced striking coral formations. Established in 1987, its five sq. miles feature mangroves, a sinkhole and underlying cave in the seabed – a smaller version of the Blue Hole found in Lighthouse Reef – as well as a portion of the barrier reef. Some 40% of the diving that goes on in Belize takes place here, and significant damage has been done to the reef through snorkelers and divers either standing on coral or hanging onto outcroppings. Except for the gripes of a few disgruntled fishermen, the reserve has been well received by conservationists and hotel owners alike. Ironically, the developer responsible for the devastation of fringing mangroves at the south end of Ambergris Caye presently promotes the reserve in his brochure.

☞ **Traveler's Tip**
Night snorkeling is a great experience to try here. Expect to spend BZ$40 pp.

GETTING HERE: When planning a trip, be sure to stop by the Visitor's Center in San Pedro. Many companies offer excursions to the reef for around BZ$25. It's a 2½-hour trip. Either bring your own gear or you can rent it. Night dives are also an ideal way to see the reserve, and you may find the waters bathed in bioluminescence.

ORIENTATION: At either side of the reserve near the reef crest, signs inform divers that they are entering a protected area. The reserve is divided into three management zones, each of which has separate regulations.

Zone A, **The Reef** (Cut) is just for snorkeling, and no fishing or collecting is permitted. Boats should moor at the buoys. All visitors must obtain an entry ticket before entering the zone and all boats operating here must register with the administrator. Both sides of the cut are lined with long, narrow banded forests of elkhorn, finger, and leaf corals. Out in the open, ghostlike tilefish guard the entrances to their burrows, which are piled high with broken pieces of staghorn coral. A large cave hosts green moray eels and anemones, and purple-headed and bright orange-bodied fairy basslets hover beneath rocky overhangs and outcrops.

Zone B, **The Seagrass Beds** (Lagoon), covers a three-square-mile area and is for both snorkeling and diving. A license is needed to fish, and no netting or spearing of fish is permitted within the Boca Ciega Blue Hole. No trawling is permitted, and all fishing boats operating here must register with the administrator. Consisting chiefly of sand and seagrass, the zone hosts a wide variety of marine life – from sponges to small coral formations to surgeon fish, parrotfish, manatees, turtles, lobsters, and conch. The area is excellent for a warm-up dive and for practicing underwater photography techniques.

Zone C, **The Mangroves**, covers one square mile and is also for both snorkeling and diving. It is composed of seven mangrove cayes separated from Ambergris by the Boca Chica Cut. Red, white and black mangroves can be found here. Be careful not to disturb the sediment at the bottom of their channels or the plants and wildlife on the surface. Fish found here include French and grey angelfish; blue striped, French, and white grunts; four eye and banded butterflyfish, schoolmasters, and grey snappers.

other rules and regulations: Tickets for diving and fishing in Zones B and C are required. Feeding or touching of fish is prohibited, as is touching or standing on live coral heads. Inexperienced snorkelers must wear a life jacket. A maximum of eight divers/snorkelers per guide is the limit, and the guide must join the group in the water. While Zones B and C are open 24 hours, Zone A is open only from 6 AM to 9 PM.

safety precautions: Only certified scuba divers can dive in the reserve. Never dive alone, and avoid sea urchins and fire coral. Wear a T-shirt to prevent sunburn. Be cautious of the channel's strong current. Obtain prior clearance from the reserve manager before entering the cave in the Boca Ciega blue hole.

Bacalar Chico National Park & Marine Reserve

Accessible only by sea, Bacalar Chico is set at the north tip of Ambergris and overlooks the Bay of Chetumal. The ranger station here is set in part of **Chac-balam**, a Maya ruin being excavated by groups from the Royal Canadian Museum. The location was originally part of the Pinkerton Estate. The park was inaugurated on Aug. 23, 1996. From here, the small Mexican village of X'calak is approximately a half-hour by boat. A ferry (4½ hrs.) is scheduled to connect the village with Chetumal.

Caye Caulker

Also known as Caye Corker, the island's Spanish name is Cayo Hicaco, after the coco plum, now found only on the southern part of the island. Once synonymous with the island, the spiny lobster has been severely depleted. Surrounded by a shallow placid blue-green sea, this island contains

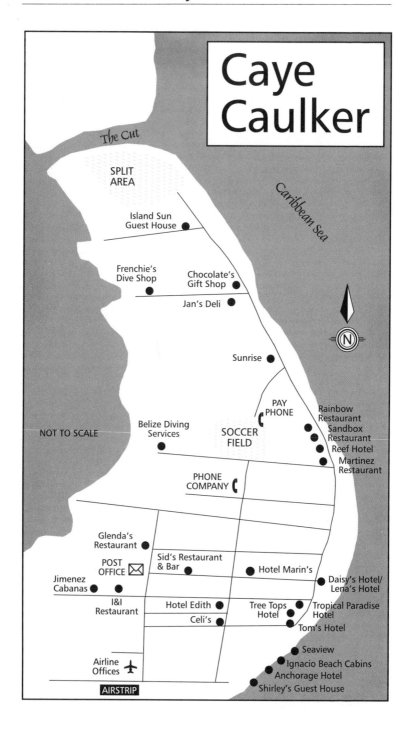

Caye Caulker

The Cut

SPLIT AREA

Island Sun Guest House

Caribbean Sea

Frenchie's Dive Shop

Chocolate's Gift Shop

Jan's Deli

N

Sunrise

PAY PHONE

Rainbow Restaurant

Belize Diving Services

SOCCER FIELD

Sandbox Restaurant

Reef Hotel

NOT TO SCALE

Martinez Restaurant

PHONE COMPANY

Glenda's Restaurant

POST OFFICE

Sid's Restaurant & Bar

Hotel Marin's

Daisy's Hotel/ Lena's Hotel

Jimenez Cabanas

I&I Restaurant

Hotel Edith

Celi's

Tree Tops Hotel

Tropical Paradise Hotel

Tom's Hotel

Seaview

Airline Offices

Ignacio Beach Cabins

Anchorage Hotel

Shirley's Guest House

AIRSTRIP

a peaceful fishing village. Satellite dishes are now in evidence, as are new homes that clash with the traditional architecture. Once a backpacker's haven, Caye Caulker's prices have risen dramatically. But it still remains relatively affordable for the low-budget traveler. Although golf carts have grown in number on this once vehicle-free island (more than 70 at last count) and development is increasing, today's slow-paced lifestyle still resembles San Pedro a decade ago.

Despite a certain amount of environmental devastation (partially brought on by mangrove cutting), the island has seen a growing spirit of ecological awareness and cooperation spurred on by problems that have become evident to all. A tour guide association has now been established, reef mooring buoys have been installed, and an offshore reef reserve is planned. Other island features are the sand flies and mosquitoes, which zero in for attack on calm days and make life a misery.

History

Visited by pirates and Mexican fishermen, the island was uninhabited as late as the 1830s. The first permanent residents were refugees from the Caste War in the Yucatán, and most of today's Jicacquenos can trace their ancestry directly back to Mexico. The initial industry was cocal, growing coconut palms and harvesting their nuts for oil. Lobster fishing became important from the 1920s and, after a struggle, a cooperative was formed in 1960 to assure reasonable prices. In a good year they can catch 1,000 lbs. of lobster tails, with an average

of 50-70 lbs. per day during the height of the season. Today, the 600-member Northern Fisherman's Cooperative supplies nearly 10% of all the lobsters sold in the Red Lobster chain's 650 restaurants. Unlike other lobsters – which must be kept alive until they are cooked, lest a strong chemical reaction turn the meat into a putrid jelly – rock lobster can be frozen. However, it lacks sizeable claws, so the meat is all in the tail.

Nearly every home standing on "Main Street" was demolished by 1961's Hurricane Hattie; the new version of town was built farther inland using more hurricane-resistant building techniques.

> ⚡ *Warning!*
> *The island has been plagued by Rastaphonians. Coming from as far away as Roatan, most of these dreadlocks-with-attitude people are thoroughly obnoxious, and their presence is resented by locals. Many of the men supplement their income by playing gigolo to naive visiting foreign women and by selling drugs, including crack. Don't let this ragamuffin posse spoil your visit. The Jicacquenos are still friendly and hospitable in the extreme, and you can really have a fine time talking to them.*

The "hippies" discovered Caye Caulker during the 1960s. Over the years it has metamorphized and these days appears to be following in the footsteps of Ambergris. With overfishing and catching of undersized specimens rampant, lobster fishing appears doomed and tourism may soon become the island's sole source of income. As each lobster takes four to five years to mature, it is not practical to farm them.

Unfortunately, the quiet charm and pristine environment that has given the island its touristic appeal over the decades is in danger as well. Bizarrely, condo developments have started to sprout on both ends! A more inappropriate form of development for this island could not be imagined, but such is the power of greed! A host of mangroves has been cut, and newly built sea walls are intended to stave off the erosion produced by past mangrove felling.

Events

Commemorating the introduction in the mid-1800s of the vitally important coconut palm, a three-day coconut festival is held in May. A Catholic mass inagurates the festivities, followed by activities such as a food fair, processing tour, crowning of a Coconut King and Queen, and various coconut competitions, such as husking, tree climbing, grating, tossing, and chipping.

Transport

GETTING HERE: The preferable way to visit the island is still by boat. Boats (BZ$15 going, $10 return) depart from the new terminal near to the S of the Swing Bridge. About a dozen boats in total now make the run.

by air: An airstrip was completed in 1991, wreaking ecological devastation on the southern part of the island and starting a decline in the island's serenity. Tropic Air (☎ 02-

45671, 026-2012, 800-422-3435; www.belize.net; e-mail tropic@btl.net) will stop here if requested on its flights to Ambergris Caye and from both Belize International and the domestic airport. Maya Island Air (☎ 02-31348/31362/31403; 800-257-8802; e-mail mayair@btl.net) also flies.

from San Pedro: The *Andrea* departs at 7 AM from San Pedro and stops here before heading to Belize City. Some tour operators run day trips, and it's also possible to fly with Tropic Air (☎ 02-45671, 026-2012, 800-422-3435; www.belize.net; e-mail tropic@btl.net) and other carriers.

FROM CAYE CAULKER: Most boats swing by the "front bridge" in search of passengers from around 6:30-7 AM. You can reach the international airport from the Belize City dock by 8:30 if you take a taxi. Boats also depart about the same time for San Pedro (BZ$20 or less); ask around. In addition to the morning run, there are generally trips at 8, 10, and 3.

for San Pedro: A water taxi departs to San Pedro at 10 and returns at 3.

by air: Tropic Air (☎ 02-45671, 026-2012, 800-422-3435; www.belize.net; e-mail tropic@btl.net) and Maya Island Air (☎ 02-31348/31362/31403, e-mail mayair@btl.net) fly. Both have offices at the airstrip.

Group Tours

The only group tour currently visiting the island is the one offered by the **American Littoral Society** (Highlands, NJ 07732; ☎ 908-291-0055). It is co-sponsored by the Siwa-Ban foundation. Of the tour's eight days, five are spent on Caye Caulker. The cost is around US$1,400, not including airfare, and the tour generally takes place at the end of April or early May.

Orientation

With only a few streets and numerous but short sidestreets, it's nearly impossible to get lost on the island. To the north, the village ends at The Cut, a swimming hole created by 1961's Hurricane Hattie. The swift current can make it dangerous for children and poor swimmers. Separated from the rest of the island by this barrier, the island's north doesn't have much in the way of development. It remains a preserve, with swamps, mangroves, and a lot of coconuts gone wild.

A nice path leads along the southern shore, dividing the hotels from the piers. Along the way, you might see a hummingbird or an iguana basking in the sun or descending from a palm. You'll also note the lobster traps piled atop one another. Each year, they are beached for longer and longer periods. From Shirley's near the airstrip, a seaside path wends its way past iguanas, small anoles, and seabirds, until it terminates in mud, muck, and mosquitoes. Near here, the toxic village dump has bred a population of crocodiles. Island residents are working on the declaration of an offshore marine reserve, separate from the Siwa-Ban Nature Preserve and larger than the one at Hol Chan

Sights

SIWA-BAN NATURE PRESERVE: On the northern end of the island, this proposed reserve, to be modeled after Hol Chan Preserve, will protect the flora and fauna of the littoral forest, mangroves, seagrass, and barrier reef. The littoral (seaside) forest will protect coco plums, seagrapes, and areas of red mangrove. The seagrass habitat will extend from the littoral forest and mangrove zone into part of the barrier reef. The preserve's name comes from the black catbird (siwa-ban in Yucatec Maya), which is a relative of the tropical mockingbird. Also present in the area are over 125 species of birds and the endangered American crocodile. For more information or to make a donation, contact Ellen McCrae at Galeria Hicaco (e-mail sbf@ btl.net) or send a tax deductible donation to The Siwa-ban Foundation, 143 Anderson, San Francisco, CA 94110-5602.

☞ *Traveler's Tip*
Despite whatever deceptive signs you might see (such as "no trespassing"), access to the shoreline within 36 ft. is guaranteed by Belizean law. So, all of the island's shore is public right of way.

SWIMMING: The water's too shallow to swim from shore. You must go to The Cut – a deep channel at the village's north end created by Hurricane Hattie in 1961, when it sliced Cay Caulker in half. You can see the erosive damage done here from cutting down mangroves. Note that saltwater crocodiles are sometimes seen in this area. Be-

The Reef & The Cayes

ware of fire corals. There's also a new area for swimming created by the new dock opposite The Reef.

DIVE SITES: It's about a mile to the Barrier Reef. Hol Chan is another popular destination. The Sponge Avenue, North Cut, and Swash are snorkeling and diving locations off the east coast. Mackerel Hole and George's Cut are near the South Cut. A difficult and potentially dangerous cave system is located off the island's west coast. Diving services are listed below under *Tours.*

Accommodations

There are still a lot of relatively cheap digs around, although prices are rising and newer, more upscale accommodations are being built. The most deluxe is the 12-unit **Tropical Paradise Hotel** (☎ 022-2124; PO Box 1573, Belize City), which charges from around BZ$45 s to BZ$130 for a triple suite. Rooms have ceiling fans. Don't smoke pot in your room: busts have occurred here.

Right nearby is **Morgan's** (☎ 022-2178; e-mail sbf@btl.net), cozy if simple cabanas run by Ellen McCrae and her husband Morgan. Rates are around BZ$80 pn.

Popular with budget travelers, **Tom's Hotel** (☎ 022-2102) overlooks the water, and one room even has an ocean view. Tom charges about BZ$20 for a room and BZ$50 for a cabin.

The **Seaview**, run by Ray and Carolyn Avila, is just down from Tom's and charges around BZ$60 d.

One of the best budget hotels is the small **Hide-A-Way** (☎ 022-2103), which features five comfort-able rooms with fans. Located behind the evangelical church and on the same street as the Health Center, the hotel is around the corner from Daisy's Hotel.

The Tree Tops Hotel (☎ 022-2008, fax 022-2115; Box 1648, Belize City) has five spacious and attractive rooms for around BZ$60 d. Rooms have cable TV, refrigerator, ceiling fan, tiled floors, and high ceilings. The rooms are kept in immaculate condition by the owners Terry and Doris Creasy. Terry will sit down with you and give you the lowdown on where to go and what to do. It's a pleasure just to sit up on the breezy balcony and shoot the breeze. If it's within your budget, this may be the best place to stay.

The Anchorage (☎ 02-45937) has four white cabins with thatched roofs from around BZ$40. Rooms go for BZ$70 d, with BZ$10 for each additional person.

Ignacio's Cabins (☎ 022-2212; PO Box 1169, Belize City) are cute and have private bath. Charges are BZ$30 d; triples are also available. Ignacio has the following notice by his pier: "IF YOU DO NOT STAY HERE AT IGNACIO CABIN, DO NOT GO ON MY PIER BECAUSE I, IGNACIO WILL RUN YOU OFF OR CHASE YOU AWAY. Don't say that you have not been warned!" (This should give you an idea of the place's atmosphere.)

Run by a hospitable local woman, **Lorraine's Guesthouse** (☎ 02-2002) charges around BZ$35 for its cabins, which have hot water.

The attractive **Shirley's Guest House** (☎ 022-2145), run by expatriate Shirley Young, charges BZ$32 s and BZ$41 d. The **Caye Caulker Guest House** (☎ 02-2249) charges around BZ$35 d.

near The Cut: The **Castaways** (☎ 022-2295) charges around BZ$25 d with shared bath. The **Mira Mar Hotel** (☎ 022-44307) is next door and the **Sandy Lane Hotel** is behind it. Formerly the Hotel Martinez, 16-room **The Reef** (☎ 022-2196) is next. The unspectacular **Rainbow Hotel** (☎ 022-2123) follows, charging around BZ$50 s and BZ$55 d. It has been accused of environmental violations.

Chocolate's (☎ 022-2151; PO Box 332, Belize City) has one room for BZ$100, with a great view and a small refrigerator. Cheaper rooms (some of which may still be under construction) are BZ$35.

Attractive **Island Sun Guest House** (☎ 022-2215; Box 1698, Belize City) charges BZ$50 for a simple room with a bath. They rent bicycles and snorkel equipment. Note: Theft is more likely if staying in the north end. Watch your possessions.

Sobre Las Olas is a set of simple rooms with showers not inexpensively priced (for what they are) at BZ$53.50 and BZ$70 w/tax. These rooms have fans; more expensive rooms have a/c.

Barbara's (☎ 022-2005) is a six-room, budget-priced establishment where single women will feel comfortable. Rooms rent for around BZ$20.

others: Other hotels include eight-room **Edith's Hotel** (☎ 022-2150); nine-room **Hotel Marin** (☎ 022-44307); six-room, moderately priced **Sea Breeze** (☎ 022-2176); **Daisy's Hotel** (☎ 022-2150; PO Box 196, Belize City); the three **Jiminez Huts** (☎ 022-2175); the 15-room **Lena's Hotel** (☎ 022-2106); **Johnny's Rooms** (☎ 022-2149); the **Caribe Hotel** (☎ 022-2159); and the **Trend Hotel** (☎ 022-2321).

Northern Long Caye: This small island has the budget-priced, basic, eight-room **Castaways** (Box 1706, Belize City).

rentals: Ask around if staying a long time. Houses may be rented from around BZ$800 per month. Camping on the beach is prohibited. Contact **Heredia's Apartment & House Rentals** (☎ 022-2132; Box 1018, Belize City); or the four-unit **M & N Apartments** (☎ 022-2111).

Food

Food prices here are climbing, with many restaurants charging BZ$1.50 just for a cup of coffee. **Glenda's** is famous for large bottles of fresh-squeezed orange juice for breakfast, along with fresh-baked cinnamon rolls. For lunch there are burritos and ganaches. Nearby, another excellent place is **Syd's Bar**, which unfortunately is legendary for the long wait in the evening. Either go here for lunch or bring a thick novel. **Marin's** has a nice atmosphere but fairly high prices. For Chinese food, the only choice is the nearby **Chan's Garden.**

Just up from the soccer field, **Mrs. Paquita** sells cake and fresh brewed coffee inside her blue-green wooden house. **Pinx Diner** is an informal restaurant.

The **Oceanside** is known for its breakfasts. It serves dishes as diverse as lasagna (BZ$12) and a wide variety of seafood. **Razzle Dazzle** is a thatched roof bar and coffee shop with a tropical ambience. The budget **Little Kitchen** is right across from Vega's.

In a new location but still relatively near The Split, the **Sandbox** is another fine restaurant. It's run by the affable Mary Jo Prost, a former manager of the Seaside Guest House in Belize City. Dishes include snapper almondine, ceviche, and both vegetarian and meat lasagna.

On the main drag by the sea and just up from Dolphin Bay Travel, **Claudette's Fast Food** has inexpensive handmade burritos: fish, chicken, or vegetable. It's strictly take-out, but you can sit at the tables in the back of the house and watch as the fishermen clean off their catch by the pier and the pelicans fight for the cast-off remains.

Sobre Las Olas is also right on the shore and has outdoor dining; dishes are pricey for the island but attractively prepared. It has vegetarian and other dishes, including breakfast with fried jacks and omelettes.

Right on the shore, **Popeye's Pizza** has pizza and other light dishes. They offer free delivery. Their full moon parties have a DJ or band and feature limbo contests.

Attractive **Castaways** serves lasagna, Thai shrimp, fried rice, and other dishes in an outdoor area. It's one of the more romantic places to have dinner.

Located near the soccer field, **J&L**'s has ice cream and coffee. Also try the **Martinez Restaurant**, and the **Tropical Paradise**, famed for its seafood. Located in a blue house on the second street inland from the ocean at the island's western end, **Emma** sells lobster pies for BZ$1; they're ready at noon and gone by two. Also try her chocolate coconut. Across the street from Marin's, **Mrs. Rodriguez** serves meals at 5 PM; she also has limited accommodations. **Koko Riko** has seafood, as well as pizza specials on the menu. There's also a pastry shop that serves good coffee and rents snorkel gear. But you'll have to find it on your own, as the owner threatened to "sue the author's ass" if he were included.

> ⚡ **Warning!**
> The lobster that Caye Caulker is so famous for are being over-fished out of existence. You'll notice that the lobster you receive is undersized. The reason is that lobsters of nonreproductive size are being caught en masse and sold to local restaurants throughout Belize. A legal lobster tail must weigh at least four oz. and should measure no less than 3½ inches from eye to carapace. It's up to you whether to eat them or not, but the islanders are undoubtedly killing the goose that laid the golden egg. Someday there will be no lobsters at all!

MARKET SHOPPING: There are a number of small stores, including **Chan's Mini Mart** – which has a variety of goods including pasta and bread. Sample prices in stores: onions, BZ$1/lb.; carrots BZ$1.40/lb.; Campbell's Vegetable Soup, BZ$2.15/can; Del Monte Peach Halves, 16 oz./BZ$3.95; Joy dishwashing detergent, 22 oz./BZ$6.50; and Head & Shoulders shampoo, 7 oz./BZ$8.75.

New to the island is the **Harmouch Supermarket,** which offers a variety of goods. The **bakery** is just down the street. Tortillas are sold at the **Tortillera del Mar,** across from Edith's Hotel.

Entertainment

Down near The Cut, the **Reef** is the popular hangout, a favorite of Rastaphonians. The multi-leveled **I&I** is also popular and has a special atmosphere. You'll also note the ubiquitous television sets. In this village of 600 there are two cable companies: one controlled by the UDP, the other by the PNP. Sadly, whereas entire families of Jicacquenos once sat out on the pier at night, enjoying the night air and shooting the breeze, today they stay glued to the tube.

Services & Shopping

A tourist information center is planned. Be sure to shop around before taking a tour or going snorkeling: a wide range of trips is available. You don't even need to ask. They'll ask you – 16 times a day. Caye Cauker now has a **post office** to call its own. And even better, the island now has its own **BTL office** with a pay phone outside; a second pay phone is at the soccer field.

One of the best places to visit – both for information and for shopping – is marine biologist Ellen MacCrae's **Galerie Hicaco** (☎ 022-2178; e-mail sbf@btl.net). Ellen has a good collection of photos for sale, as well as Maya handicrafts from all over the nation. She also offers reef tours (BZ$29) and bird walks (BZ$12). Her husband rents out windsurfers and cozy cabins. You can view her "Life Strategies in Barrier Reef Environments" slide show upon arrangement. Unfortunately, she is often away leading International Expeditions

tours, but you may be lucky and catch her at home.

Friendly Cindy Novelo runs **Island Designs**, a boutique with a wide range of original goods: check out the atttactive painted boxes with manatees, fish, and other creatures on them. (Look for it near Sobre Las Olas.)

Ernest Westby runs **Caye Caulker Gallery** (☎ 022-2289), which has a surprising assortment of art, including works by Dangriga's own loquacious local legend Benjamin Nicholas (see *Sights* under *Dangriga* for details).

Also visit **Chocolate's Gift Shop**. The semi-mythical Capt. Chocolate takes visitors to Goff's Caye (BZ$50 pp including snorkel gear), where you see manatees. Other excursions include a river trip (BZ$60 pp). Inquire at his shop. There are also innumerable other souvenir shops around. Don't find them; they'll find you.

Tours

Personable, long-haired **Jim Novelo** (☎ 022-2195, fax 022-2239), husband of Cindy from Island Designs (see above), runs trips on his boat, the *Sunrise*. Trips include excursions to Hol Chan, Goff's Caye, Half Moon Caye, Glovers Reef, the Turneffes, and other destinations. A long-standing favorite is the day-long excursion to the Turneffes, Half Moon Caye, and the Blue Hole. He can take you to see manatees or dolphins. Charters are also available. Stop by the shop and chat.

Daisy's Hotel (☎ 022-2150) rents kayaks. **Frenchie's Dive Shop** (☎ 022-2234) leads dives to all of the major sites. **Belize Diving**

Services (☎ 022-2143; West North Avenue, Wauwatosa, WI 53266).

BZ Travel Services (☎ 800-382-7776; Box 1723, Dickinson, TX 77539; e-mail bztravel@compass-net.com) is near the soccer field. Their packages include a stay at Tree Tops. NAUI and PADI classes are available.

Sea-ing is Belizing (☎ 022-2189) requests a donation for their slide shows of the jaguar preserve and coral reef ecology. Their shop includes a gift shop. photo gallery, and a bookstore.

Caye Caulker's School of Scuba (☎ 022-2292, fax 022-2239), the island's dive school, is next to Edith's. The **Martinez Restaurant** also has a glass bottom boat. **Emma Gill** charters her outrigger sailboats. Another operator is Charlie, whose **Turtle Tours** is based on Main St.

❝ Reader's Comments

"Went on snorkel trip with Harrison Catel to see manatees and also to Hol Chan. Excellent guide."

"Went on snorkel trip with Ras Creek on his boat Reggae Muffin. He feeds eagle rays, sting rays, sharks, etc. daily. Fishes for lunch, which he provides. Excellent guide and very fun."

Operated by Ramon Rosado and next to Daisy's Hotel, **Big Fish Little Fish** (☎ 022-2150/2122/2058) offers a variety of tours (BZ$20 and up), including one to a caye that has manatees. They also rent snorkeling gear and kayaks.

Jan's Deli rents golf carts. Also try contacting **Ricardo's Adventure Tours** (☎ 022-2138), as well as Allen Nuñez, Harrison, Indio, and Ras Creek about snorkeling and other trips.

Caye Chapel

Only 2½ miles long, this was one of the nation's most beautiful islands before development. Caye Chapel has always been protected from hurricane damage by a solid portion of the Barrier Reef. Its sloping two-mile beach faces east.

Situated 16 miles from Belize City, Caye Chapel is on one of the higher reefs – rising five to 10 ft. above sea level. The numerous coconut palms are reminders of the first planned venture on the caye, a coconut plantation. Some of the dead from the Spanish fleet battle of St. George's Caye in 1798 were buried here. A failed resort, the island (owned by a wealthy US citizen) is now in the process of radical transformation. Condos and a golf course are in the works and may have been completed by the time of your arrival. A new sea wall has been built as well.

GETTING HERE: Formerly, there were regular air flights. Once the resort opens, these will likely resume.

PRACTICALITIES: Expensive Pyramid Island Resort had 32 a/c beachfront rooms and beach houses. They also had a private airstrip, yacht marina, and restaurant. There were tennis, badminton, basketball, and volleyball courts, as well as a golf driving range, and water sports that included sailing, snorkeling, diving, and fishing. It had the best beach in Belize and a great Sunday barbecue. It is likely that some or all of features will be available again when the resort reopens sometime in the coming years.

St. George's Caye

Set nine miles northeast of Belize City, this caye was first inhabited by buccaneers, who used it as a base for smoking and drying manatee and turtle meat for sale to fellow pirates and logwood traders. For this reason the Spanish early on had named it Cayo Cosina (Kitchen Cay). According to the first known map of the caye, published in 1764, it had over 70 houses, next to which stood pens for storing turtles awaiting slaughter. In 1796 a group of fishermen and loggers, with the help of one British man-of-war, repelled an attack by 32 Spanish ships. This battle was the last attempt by the Spanish to forcibly expel the English from the area. Partly washed away by hurricanes and storms during the recent decades, an old colonial-era graveyard stands on the southern tip. Until Hurricane Hattie hit in 1961, St. George's Caye, along with nearby Sergeant's Caye, had summer homes for Belizeans and, in the case of Sergeant's Caye, for New Yorkers. Hattie turned Sergeant's Caye into a sandbar and divided St. George into four sections. Only two houses remained standing.

PRACTICALITIES: The best known lodging here is expensive 16-room **St. George's Lodge** (☎ 02-44190 or PO Box 625, Belize City). Among its features are windmill-generated electricity and a solar-powered hot tub. Two dives per day and meals are included in the rates. There are no phones, no TV, and no nightlife –making it the perfect getaway. Rates are around BZ$480 pp, pd and up including tax. In the US,

☎ 800-678-6871. The six-unit **Island Cottages** are under the same management.

Owned and managed by the Bellevue Hotel, the expensive 15-unit **Cottage Colony** (☎ 02-77051; PO Box 428, Belize City; e-mail fins@btl.net) offers attractive colonial-style units lined up in a row, with fan or a/c, plus a restaurant and diving. Rates are around BZ$170 s, BZ$200 d. It's run by the Bellevue Hotel, 5 Southern Foreshore.

diving: Among the nearby sites are a large cave that you can swim through, the Ice Cream Cone (which features humongous gorgonians), the Aladdins (spur-and-groove topography with immense variety), Bruce's Column (a large pillar with sponges and grouper), Little Finger (grouper concentrations), and Eel Gardens (lots of eels). You can also dive off Gallows Point Reef, Rendezvous Wall, or other southern Turneffe dive sites. And you can dive or snorkel off nearby Goff's Caye.

The Turneffe Islands

Situated a few miles to the east of the Barrier Reef, these islands lie approximately 35 miles from Belize City. Incorporating 32 islands and wet cayes, they form an elongated oval archipelago, around 30 miles long and four to 10 miles across. At their center is a placid blue lagoon. The nation's largest atoll, its area is some 205 square miles. The mangroves are so closely grouped that, when viewed from a distance, they give the appearance of being one continous flat island. Openings known as bogues lead into large interior lagoons that are four to eight feet deep and that are filled with turtles and fish. There is also a large population of American crocodiles, but they are difficult to spot.

cayes: Sparsely sheltered Calabash Caye is the center of the local coconut trade. There are three mangrove cayes in the northern end of the atoll: Three Corner Caye, Crawl Caye, and Mauger Caye. Mauger Caye's name derives from the Creole word for "meager," denoting a time when crops fail and everything falls into stagnation. Southern Lagoon and Northern or Vincent's Lagoon are the two interior lagoons. Captured females were brought to the atoll by pirates after the sack of Bacalar during the 17th century. These islands were famous around the beginning of the 20th century for their sponges, which were destroyed by a fungus in 1939.

fishing: The waters surrounding this atoll swarm with fish, including the smaller bonefish and permit and the larger sailfish, grouper, marlin, and blackfin tuna. Bonefish (averaging three to five lbs.) can be fished from the wadeable flats. While they peak in mid-June, tarpon can be fished in mangrove creeks from mid-May through December. Billfish are abundant from January to April.

diving: One of the best places to dive in Belize, the Turneffes offer challenges for every level of diver. There are 23 cuts punctuating the surrounding reef, and some of these offer superb snorkeling and diving. Unfortunately, the reef is still recovering from the effects of 1961's Hurricane Hattie; otherwise, there

would be even more sites. Accordingly, the major dive sites are on the **"Elbow,"** the atoll's southern tip and off the atoll's north end. Diving here is not for beginners.

Dives along the atoll's eastern side are wall dives. The more gradually sloping reefs on the west have large coral heads. Many boats from Ambergris also dive here off the north end. **Triple Anchors** is graced by three 18th-century Spanish anchors; one is to the northwest of the mooring buoy. Other sites include **Black Beauty**, whose highlight is an enormous black coral, the deteriorated condition of which makes the case for not purchasing black coral jewelry; the **Sayonara,** which features a deliberately sunk (in 1985) wooden skiff; **Cabbage Patch**, with concentrations of lettuce and other coral; **Cockroach Wall**, with garden eels residing in a sandy expanse, as well as large tube sponges; **Permit Paradise,** with a concentration of permit; **Dory's Channel,** which features large gorgonians and tube and barrel sponges; and **Myra's Turtles** (or Myrtle's Turtle), at which a hawksbill makes a perennial appearance. This last is one of the nation's best places to dive. Still **others** are the Dark Forest, Calabash Wall, Lefty's Ledge, Majestic Point, Vincente Wall, Rendezvous Wall, Gailes Point, and Black Rock Mountain.

DIVE SITES: There are some 40 dive sites in Lighthouse Reef. One of the nation's best dive sites is the **Long Caye Wall** (or Long Caye Ridge) at Long Caye here. It is named after its spur and groove formations. Gorgonians, sponges, and various corals are found here in

Turneffe Islands

Mauger Caye

Crawl Caye

Rendezvous Point

Three Corner Caye

① Dog Flea Caye
Pelican Caye
Cockroach Caye

Northern Lagoon

Pelican Caye

Snake Point

Shipwrecks
Reefs

Crickozeen Creek

Central Lagoon

Cross Caye

Douglas Caye

Ambergris Creek

Western Four Cayes

② Blackbird Caye
Soldier Caye

Crooked Creek

Crayfish Range

Harry Jones Point

Little Joe's Hole

Grand Bogue Creek

Soldier Bight

New Bight

Calabash Caye

Pelican Caye

Joe's Hole

Southeast Bight

③ Coco Tree Caye

1. Turneffe Flats Lodge
2. Blackbird Caye Resort
3. Turneffe Island Lodge

5 MILES

8 KM

The Reef & The Cayes

abundance. Getting its name from the schools of silver sides no longer found here, the **Silver Caves** give you a chance to view nocturnal sea creatures on a day dive. You might see basket starfish or the rare sclerosponges. Once considered extinct, they have been rediscovered only within the past few decades. Off Long Caye's northwest corner, the **Aquarium** is named for its wide variety of colorful fish and other marine life. Sharks are frequently sighted at nearby **Nurse Shark Lodge;** it also has a number of spur and groove formations with loads of sea life. Similarly, eagle rays reside at **Eagle Ray Wall.** Others include **Blue Hole, Half Moon Wall, The Abyss, Tres Cabanas,** and **Woody's Favorite Bight.**

ACCOMMODATIONS: The **Turneffe Island Lodge** (Box 480, Belize City; www.turneffelodge.com, e-mail info@turneffelodge.com) on 12-acre Caye Bokel (meaning "Elbow" in Dutch) is a diving and fishing resort. It's reached by a 1½- to two-hour boat transfer. Twelve guest rooms are furnished with with two beds, private bath, screened porches, ceiling fans, and a/c. There is 24-hour electricity.

A variety of packages are available. Dive packages (around US$1,450 pw) have a day trip to the Blue Hole, Half Moon Wall, and Long Caye Wall. The seven-night package includes 17 single-tank dives, tanks, and weight belts. Flats fishing is also available for US$2,200 pw. Included in packages are RT transfers from Belize City, three meals daily, and use of sea kayaks, wind surfers, Sunfish, and snorkeling gear. On-island facilities include volleyball and horseshoes. Three- and four-night

packages and fish/dive combos are also available. For more information, ☎ 800-874-0118 or 770-534-3210; fax 770-534-8290; or write Box 2974, Gainesville, GA 30503.

Very expensive **Turneffe Flats** (☎ 02-30116, fax 02-78808), a fishing and diving lodge, has six bungalow units with fans. It's set on Northern Bogue at the atoll's northeastern side. In the US, ☎ 605-578-1304, fax 605-578-7540; or write PO Box 36, Deadwood, SD 57732.

The expensive **Blackbird Caye Village** (☎ 02-32772, 02-30007, fax 02-34449) opened in 1991. Its ten thatched cottages are on stilts. It was sold in 1996 to Belizean entrepreneur Mike Feinstein.

Lighthouse Reef Lagoon

The outermost of the outlying banks, **Lighthouse Reef** was designated as "Eastern Reef" on old charts. Its lighthouse gave it the current name. With its northern end about 50 miles due east from Belize City, the 78½-square-mile, irregularly shaped atoll is about 28 miles long, varying in width from two to six miles. Almost totally bounded by a barrier reef, which is solid on the eastern side, the reef's southern edge forms a half-moon curve five miles in diameter. Scattered into two groups at the northern and southern ends of the bank, its six cayes are all widely separated. Being set at the northern tip of this near-perfect semi-circle gives Half Moon Caye its name.

Half Moon Caye Natural Monument

Across the atoll from Long Caye, this island is widely reputed to be the most spectacularly beautiful in Belize. Half a mile wide and 1½ miles long, Half Moon has white sand beaches with a drop-off on the north and a shallow lagoon on the southern end. The island is so remote that German subs were able to use it undetected as a WWII refueling station. Half Moon has long been the haunt of the nearly extinct booby bird, as well as conch and lobster poachers. It was first designated a "Crown Reserve" in 1928.

The National Park System Act of 1981 precluded further clearing of the island – protecting both the caye and Belize's only nesting colony of red-footed boobies (about 4,000-strong). Unfortunately, the "National Monument" designation protects only the caye and portions of the lagoon and barrier wall.

The 45-acre reserve contains two separate ecosystems: the eastern half has coconut palms, while the west, fertilized by seabird guano, is covered with lush vegetation. Nearly all of the birds are white. In most other colonies, red-footed boobies have dull brown plumage. Half of the island is their sea rookery – one shared with their chief adversary, the magnificent frigate bird. There are over 220 species of

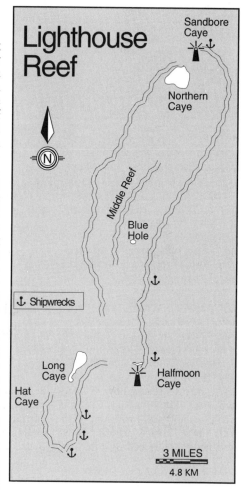

reef fish in the vicinity. Belize's largest land crabs share the southern sandy beaches with loggerhead and hawksbill turtles that come ashore to lay their eggs in season.

The 98 other bird species present include ospreys, white-crowned pigeons, and mangrove warblers. Other reptiles include the "bamboo chicken," a red iguana with black stripes on its back, and the smaller (up to four feet) "wish willy," yellow with black bars on its back.

The Reef & The Cayes

> ### ⓘ *Did You Know?*
> *Boobies are actually related to pelicans. Sailors, who gave them their name because they were too ignorant to fear men, would club them and throw them into the "booby hatch," where the ship's fresh meat was stored.*

SIGHTS: Set in the middle of the nesting area, a bird-viewing platform is accessible by a trail that begins on the island's northern side. Manned 24 hours a day by the National Customs Department, the solar-powered lighthouse offers a stupendous view; it's on the eastern tip. Along with the one on Sandbore Caye to the north, it gives the reef its name.

Originally constructed in 1820 (the current version dates from 1931), it has not always served its purpose – as several wrecks attest. Over the years, many have arrived in search of the Spanish galleon, *Juan Baptista*. It sunk about a mile off the reef in 1822 with a cargo of gold and silver bullion.

Also included in the park is **Half Moon Wall**, a dive site with a number of varied coral formations. Garden eels are numerous here. Numerous snorkel sites also lie offshore. In particular, check out the buttressed coral formations to the southwest.

practicalities: Day trips sometimes stop here. Trips also run from Ambergris; try the Blue Hole Dive Center (☎ 026-2982; e-mail bluehole@btl.net). Caye Caulker's James Novelo also comes here.

The Great Blue Hole

Proceeding eight miles north from Half Moon Caye, traveling through the lagoon in the center of Light-house Reef, you come to this great cylindrical hole in the sea bottom, popularized by a Jacques Cousteau television special. Appearing from the air as an indigo blue circle in the midst of a larger azure blue one, this is the nation's most famous dive site. Formed some 12,000 years ago, the hole is a geological phenomenon akin to a limestone sink, and its caves undercut the entire reef.

From surrounding ocean depths of five to 15 feet, this "hole" plunges to 412 feet and is 450 feet across. A giant cavern is reached at 140 feet, with enormous stalactites up to 10 feet in diameter hanging 20-60 feet down from the cavern roof. A "monster" was sighted in its depths in 1970, but you're not likely to see much more than sponges or worms.

diving it: This is a decompression dive and should be attempted by experienced divers only. The nearest recompression chamber is in Miami! Operators on Caye Caulker and dive resorts such as Lighthouse Reef Resort will make the dive.

dive boats: There are a number of choices. Some require scheduling before your arrival. Ambergris's **Blue Hole Dive Center** (☎ 026-2982; e-mail bluehole@btl.net) runs out here. **snorkeling:** Shallow coral reefs surrounding the perimeter make for fine snorkeling.

Peter Hughes Diving (☎ 800-932-6237; www.peterhughes.com; e-mail dancer@peterhughes.com) runs its luxurious *Wave Dancer* to the Blue Hole and surrounding locales every Sat. from Belize City.

Aggressor, a 100-ft. luxury yacht, runs trips here. Write Aggressor Fleet Ltd., P.O. Drawer K, Morgan City, LA 70381, ☎ 800-348-2648,

Altun Ha (opposite)

Cahal Pech *(above)*
Garifuna Girl, Seine Bight *(opposite)*
Market, San Ignacio *(below)*

504-385-2416, fax 504-384-0817, telex 784041; www.aggressor.com; e-mail divboat@aol.com.

Northern Two Caye

The attractive **Lighthouse Reef Resort** (PO Box 26, Belize City) features five private a/c cabanas, bar, restaurant, and private airstrip. The resort offers fishing, diving, volleyball, snorkeling, and windsurfing. Rates are around US$1,050 for the resort package, US$1,200 for the diving package, and US$1,400 for the fishing/diving package. Flights usually operate on Wed. and Sat. Divers must bring basic equipment such as weight belts. For more information, contact Blue Lagoon, Inc., PO Box 40915, Houston, TX 77240-0915, ☎ 800-423-3114 or 713-937-4045; worldwide ☎ 813-439-1486.

Glovers Reef Marine Reserve

Set south of the Turneffes about 20 miles off the coast and 70 miles southeast of Belize City, this circular chain of bare coral outcrops, about 20 miles long and seven miles wide, surrounds a crystal clear lagoon that shelters more than 700 patch reefs in its 80 square miles. It was once the abode of pirate John Glover. Uninhabited now, it is occasionally visited by fishermen. Southwest Caye is the only remaining Belizean nesting site for the brown noddy. All of the roughly 500 pairs nest in the branches of coconut palms.

Of its six small islands, Middle Caye was purchased by Wildlife Conservation International in

1990, thus protecting it from becoming the site of a tourist lodge. In an attempt to preserve the atoll for sustainable fishing and to protect recreational use, Glovers Reef was decared Belize's second underwater marine reserve in May 1993. Approximately 75% of the atoll is zoned for general use, but five of the six cayes have been designated as conservation areas. Middle Caye is also zoned as a wilderness area. Northeast Caye is not included, and the atoll's southeastern portion has been zoned for seasonal closure to allow its recovery from out-of-season fishing.

ⓘ **Did You Know?**
Glovers Reef Marine Reserve has perhaps the most developed reef growth as well as the greatest variety of reef types in the entire Caribbean!

ACCOMMODATIONS: The Lomont family operates **Glovers Reef Atoll Resort** on Northeast Cay. (After a 12-year legal battle, they were evicted from Long Cay in 1996.) Not a "resort" in the usual sense of the word, but rather a very basic set of accommodations, their establishment is on Long Caye. You must bring your own food, and there's well water, but no electricity. Be as prepared as you might be if you were camping. A stove is supplied, but a backpacking stove would be better. Washing is done using a bucket from a well, and outhouses serve as sanitary facilities. They charge around BZ$200-300 pp, pw for a cabin or tent and RT passage, and US$80 pw for transport and camping. It takes six or more hours to get out to the atoll on their slow boat, which rocks from

The Reef & The Cayes

Mask of Chac, Great Plaza, Tikal *(opposite)*

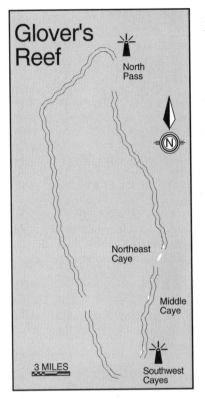

Glover's
Reef

North
Pass

N

Northeast
Caye

Middle
Caye

3 MILES

Southwest
Cayes

fishing. For more information, write PO Box 563, Belize City or call 0148351.

To the southwest, expensive **Manta Resort** (☎ 02-31895/45606 or VHF Chan. 70) offers cabanas, as well as a two-bedroom house, set on 12 acres. They have nine fan-equipped rooms. A spacious, thatched-roof restaurant and bar are built over the water. They specialize in fishing and diving; other activities include snorkeling, volleyball, canoeing, and windsurfing. Eight-day, seven-night packages run from US$1,050 to $1,595 pp based on double occupancy. Write PO Box 215 or 3 Eyre St., Belize City.

DIVE SITES: Glovers remains one of the least explored sites for diving in Belize. Offering both a shallow reef area and an exhilarating drop-off, Long Caye Wall has a stand of coral that can be reached from shore on calm days. Near Southwest Caye and Manta Resort, **Southwest Caye Wall** offers excellent wall diving down a steep drop-off.

Along the atoll's western side, **Emerald Forest Reef** has excellent diving as well as snorkeling. You can see large stands of elkhorn coral here. Also on the same side are Split Reefs, which has both shallow and deep areas, as well as Baking Swash Reef, a narrow, coral-lined channel, also with shallow as well as deep reefs. Named after the diminutive palm- and mangrove-covered island to its rear, **Middle Caye Reefs** host a wide variety of marine life contained within a small area. Be sure to explore the turtle grass beds, which house a number of creatures. Sea life is most diverse near the dropoff. Named for its abundance of

day, but departure or arrival may be delayed by bad weather. Otherwise, you'll have to charter. Canoes, rowboats, motorboats, snorkeling and diving gear are available for rent. The Lomonts will sell you conch, lobster, and fish; water is also sold for BZ$4/gallon. They have a small store and will accept orders for goods from town for a 20% markup. Meals are BZ$8-10.

If you arrive ahead of time in Sittee River, you can overnight in their **Glover's Atoll Guest House** for BZ$10.50. That gets you a bunk berth. Camping is BZ$4 pp. Group rates are also available. **Belize's Wall Divers** (Box 448, Belize City) also operates out of here and offers courses, including reef ecology, snorkeling instruction, and sports groupers, **Grouper Flats**, set along the northeast side, has both shallow and deep reefs. **Shark Point** is known for its sharks and is not for the timid soul.

RENT AN ISLAND: From December to May, **Slickrock Adventures** (☎ 800-390-5715; Box 1400, Moab, UT 84532; www.slickrock.com, e-mail slickrock@slickrock.com) rents out Northeast Caye for US$3,500 from Sat. to Sat. subject to availablility. Rates include one staff member, sea kayaks and accessories, radio system, cabanas, hammocks, tents, and other facilities.

KAYAKING: Slickrock Adventures, Inc. (☎ 800-390-5715, fax 801-259-6996; Box 1400, Moab, UT 84532; www.slickrock.com, e-mail slickrock@slickrock.com) offers four- to 10-day adventures on Northeast Caye. Prices run from $835 to $1395, and accommodations are in tents or cabins on Northeast Caye, an island owned by Fred Dodd of International Zoological Expeditions. The Lomonts (see page 173) formerly leased this island, but were evicted following a 12-year legal battle. Diving (with **Living Reef Divers**) is optional and additional.

It's about a two-hour high-speed boat ride out to the small caye where you will base yourself. Along the way, you will pass by Tobacco Caye and perhaps visit Man O'War Caye. It's not unusual to find dolphins following your boat. After arrival, you will be assigned a cabin or a tent and be given linen. Cabins command ocean views, are very simple but comfy, and are recently built. (Several were destroyed by a freak water funnel that arrived in Feb. 1997). There are hanging vinyl shower bags and composting toilets. Although the main dining area is generator-lit, the cabins are supplied with kerosene lamps.

The reason to come here is to sea kayak and snorkel, not necessarily in that order. Accordingly, you need snorkeling and other basic equipment. Kayaks are provided, and instruction is expert. Owners Cully and Lucy (as well as other instructors) are patient with beginners, and it is not as difficult to learn as you might think. The hardest thing is probably clambering up into a kayak from the water. Excursions go out several times per day. You may kayak over to another island or go to a patch reef. Where you go depends upon wind and sea conditions: there are no guarantees.

There is a small island library in the dining room with a number of titles. Not surprisingly, Paul Humann's superb fish and creature identification series (see booklist) is the most popular. Meals are tasty but simple. Desserts range from key lime pie to banana-chocolate mousse. Coffee is brewed by 6:30; breakfast follows at 7. Dishes range from fried jacks and beans to pancakes; fresh fruit is served on the side. Lunch might be handmade wholewheat tortillas and conch ceviche; dinner might consist of conch stew with rice and beans and fried plantains or baked fish with mashed yams; chocolate is a frequent desert. Dinner entrées include poached fillets in horseradish baste accompanied by parsley potatoes and cucumber salad, or open-pit BBQ fish with black beans and Greek salad. A refrigerator and ice chest provide an endless and varied supply of complimentary cola

The Reef & The Cayes

drinks and Belikin beer and stout. Owner Cully may deliver a lecture after dinner or Lucy may foist a game on you. Generally, life follows the early-to-bed-and-early-to-rise pattern: everyone is too exhausted to do otherwise.

Gilligan's Island or Robinson Crusoe this is not. The island has a few squatters, a caretaker couple down at the south end, and some occasional fishermen and even Belize Defence Force members on patrol drop by from time to time.

There's a marvelous reef just offshore on the south end. At lowest tide (and provided the surf is still), you can tiptoe around the sandy bottom, observing reef life at your leisure. This would be a great spot to bring an underwater camera. To get to it, cross the sandy bottom, emerge onto the outlying seagrass plateau, and then head straight on.

The tidepool also merits a visit at this time. It's off the east side and near the cabins. Anything might turn up here, provided it can fit under a rock. Turn over the rocks to find brittle starfish or adorable scowling morays. The small sea-urchins can be handled; avoid contact with the others unless you have a remarkable degree of self-hatred. You can visit here at any time, but the sea is calmest at low tide.

others: One of the best known kayaking companies, **Island Expeditions,** arranges trips here. They have a base camp on Southwest Caye. Contact them at ☎ 800-667-1630 or 604-325-7952, fax 604-325-7952, e-mail island@ whistler.net; 368-916 W Broadway, Vancouver, BC, Canada V5Z 1K7.

The North

Largely a plain, once covered by the sea, the nation's north still retains traces of its past existence underwater in the form of shallow valleys and low ridges – ripples in a seabed eons ago. As it does along most of the country's eastern perimeter, the coastal land is largely swamp, suitable only for seabirds. The north is the main agricultural center, producing most of the sugar, corn, and beans. But vast areas have remained untilled since Maya civilization lapsed over a thousand years ago.

Sights

In addition to three natural reserves, the north has a number of Maya ruins, including Lamanai, an archaeological reserve. The area serves as a gateway to the wonders of Mexico. A two-lane highway runs north, serving the main towns of Orange Walk and Corozal, en route to the Mexican border town of Chetumal. Public transportation heading off the main road is scarce, but distances to most attractions are not substantial.

Bermudian Landing

Community Baboon Sanctuary

Established in 1985 by zoologist Dr. Rob Horwich and a group of local farmers (with assistance from the World Wide Fund for Nature), this reserve, comprised of privately owned land, protects 1,800-1,900 "baboons" (black howler monkeys). These are an endangered sub-species of the howler that lives only in Belize, Guatemala, and Mexico.

Combining tourism, conservation, and education, the project coordinates more than 150 landowners and eight villages. Its lowland forest parallels the Belize River and is bordered by cohune palm forests to the east and pine forest and savanna to the west. The reserve also provides a home for some 250 species of birds (which makes it a paradise for birders), deer, coatis, anteaters, peccaries, and iguanas.

History

An old logging camp, Bermudian Landing dates back to the beginning of the 17th century. Once called Butchers Landing, it is thought the name change in the late 18th century was either because of Bermudian settlers or because Bermuda grass was grown for cattle. The large number of Scotsmen settling in the area is reflected by the name of the settlement, Scotland Half Moon, across the river.

The area remained an unvisited backwater until recently, when zoologist Robert Horwich was conducting a survey of howler monkey habitats in Mexico, Guatemala, and Belize. He came upon a stable and healthy population only here and recognized the need for action to preserve howler habitats. Realizing that without community participation such a reserve would be doomed to failure, he sought to mobilize local support. Along with botanist Jon Lyon, Horwich laid the ground work for the reserve, surveying each villager's land and establishing ownership. Villagers were asked to avoid cutting 66 feet on each side of a waterway to spare figs, roseapples, sapodillas, trumpet trees, and hogplums, which the monkeys feed on, and to leave small forested strips between pathways as aerial avenues. The reserve was officially established on Feb. 23, 1985, and it currently receives some 5,000 visitors per year.

COMMUNITY BABOON SANCTUARY

Transport

GETTING HERE: Buses leave Belize City for the sanctuary at noon-12:30 PM daily except Sunday. Mr. Oswald McFadzean's bus or truck leaves from the corner of Orange and Mussel Streets, and both Mr. Sydney Russell's and Mr. Valentine Young's buses depart from the intersection of Euphrates and Cemetery Streets. The bus returns from Bermudian Landing at 5:30-6 AM. Fridays and Saturdays are busy, so arrive early to be sure you get a seat. Check with the driver well in advance to confirm the departure time; times and days may be subject to change.

by car: From Belize City proceed 13½ miles along the Northern Highway. Go left at the Burrell Boom cutoff, traveling 14 miles past Burrell Boom and Mussel Creek until you reach the Belize River again. Take the right fork to cross the new bridge into Bermudian Landing. On the way, you pass over railway trestle bridges and slow-moving Black Water Creek (its color is due to tannin). The large building on the right after Burrell Boom was intended to be a sewing factory. The Chinese investors pulled their support after the Belizean government recognized Taiwan. It remains closed. The homes you pass on the way have neither electricity nor running water. They do have television, however: the sets run on car batteries.

At another bridge constructed by USAID, where you cross over the Belize River again, there's a sign marking the entrance. You'll soon see a rope bridge stretched over the road from the famous fig tree that starred in the documentary, *El Amate*. At first, Dr. Horwich had only a single rope across the road. One monkey was crossing when the rope started to spin. After that the monkeys preferred the road. It took some time for the troop to trust the bridge again. One troop still resides in this area; another is near the school. **donations:** Send these to Howlers Forever, c/o Dr. Robert Horwich, RD 1, Box 96, Gays Mills, WI 54631.

Tours

The best preparation for your visit is the excellent field guide, which sells for around BZ$30; it's available at the Audubon Society bookstore on Fort St. in Belize City. You'll want to have your mosquito repellent with you, as well as a camera flash for the trails. Begin your visit at the Visitors' Center, which has a number of very informative displays. You can view a sample planned agreement for the reserve, a map showing how the sanctuary has grown, the throat bone that gives the howler its howl, a grison skeleton, a mummified baby armadillo, gibnut and tapir skulls, a mummified marine toad in a box, various pickled snakes, turtle shells, and a display about crocodiles. After you visit the sanctuary, a guide can take you around on a trail. He might point out the sensitive plant, which closes at noon, show you cohune palms and nuts and describe their uses, and tell you about trees and their medicinal or other uses. An example is the ringworm tree, which can cure ringworm. One highlight is a gigantic "wee wee" ant nest, guaranteed to put you more in awe of nature than you were before. Your visit can be as short as half an hour or as long as 90 minutes. Canoe trips on the Be-

lize River, fishing, and horseback riding can also be arranged.

> **ⓘ Did you know?**
> *If scaled to human size, leafcutter ant workers each run the equivalent of a four-minute mile for some 30 miles with 500 lbs. slung over one shoulder.*

Accommodations & Food

Camping at the Visitor's Center costs around BZ$3/tent; rooms are BZ$20 d, and meals are BZ$4 for breakfast, BZ$5 for lunch, and BZ$4 for dinner. Basic food and supplies are available from local stores. Vegetarians can be catered to. Guides cost BZ$5/hr., BZ$20/half-day, and BZ$40/day. Suggested admission to the reserve is BZ$10 and this includes the services of a guide. Guides for canoeing the Belize River may be available for the same price. For more information and reservations call Sanctuary Manager Fallet Young at 02-4405. State the number in your party, when you will arrive, whether coming by car or bus, if overnight meals are needed, if you have a tent, and if you wish to dine with a local family (at the prices above).

Another alternative is the **Jungle Drift Lodge** (☎ 02-32842, fax 02-78160; PO Box 1442, Belize City). It has cabins (BZ$30 s, BZ$40 d, BZ$60 t) overlooking the Belize River. Each holds up to three and has a fan; the bathroom is detached. Discounts are offered to students and for extended stays. They run a number of tours and provide transport to the lodge.

The North

The **El Chiclero** (☎ 028-2005) is in the village of Burrell Boom and boasts the "best food" in Belize, a/c, and "spacious" rooms. Another alternative is to stay at the moderate two-room **Little Eden Guest House** on Burrel Boom Road (currently for sale but it may have reopened by the time of your visit). **The Olde River Tavern & Inn** (☎/fax 028-2213) is a five-room bed and breakfast at Mile 3 on the Burrell Boom Rd. Its motto is "This place will spoil you!" Canoes or kayaks can be rented at **Baboon River Canoe Rentals** (☎ 028-2101) in Burrell Boom. If you are looking for something to eat, rice and beans are generally served next to the gas station at Burrell Boom.

The public phone is 021-2001 in Bermudian Landing and 021-2004 in Double Head Cabbage.

Crooked Tree Wildlife Sanctuary

Set approximately halfway between Belize City and Orange Walk, just off the Northern Highway, this 3,000-acre reserve, consists of lagoons surrounded by marshes and logwood swamps. It is administered by the Belize Audubon Society and only the reserve's western portion is open. The fishing and farming village of Crooked Tree, across a causeway two miles from the main road, is in its center. This six-by-three-mile island is connected by a ¾-mile causeway to the mainland. There are three neighborhoods (Crooked Tree, Pine Ridge, and Stain) in the village. The total population is 650.

In addition to a fishery, there are a number of small farms.

A strong relationship exists between the locals and the Baymen: many have blond hair and blue eyes. A close community, many residents are related to each other; it's rather like one extended family. Locals plant corn, cassava, cacao, and rice. Logging, fishing, hunting, cashew cultivation, and charcoal making are traditional activities. Note the mango and cashew trees in the area, some of which are believed to be several hundred years old.

Of the thousands of birds wintering here, the most prominent transient resident is the **jabiru stork**. It nests and rests in these lowlands from November to April or thereabouts. This is the largest nesting population of these magnificent birds in all of Central America (see description under "birds" in the *Introduction*). Its relative, the wood stork, is a smaller version with black on its wings and tail and a grey head. Other frequent flyers include black-collared hawks, tiger herons, snowy egrets, ospreys, and snail kites. Also present are howler monkeys, turtles, coatis, iguanas, and crocodiles.

---

66 Reader's Comment

"Crooked Tree was an odd place; it is really a place where rich people go on a day trip. Being there for two nights we got to experience a small town, which was interesting but frustrating for students who can't spend US$70 for a three-hour lagoon ride! We had fun there, however: lots of laughs."

Back on land, you may see spider monkeys. Although they prefer higher trees, they do come to feed on the breadfruit trees. The best times to see wildlife are in April and May. The nearby community of Spanish Creek, located in the reserve's southwestern corner, has turtles and crocodiles.

Transport

GETTING HERE: Until recent times, Crooked Tree was accessible only by boat. Today, at Mile 33 of the Northern Highway, a dirt road leads off to a causeway traversing the Northern Lagoon and ends four miles later at the village of Crooked Tree. Some residents rent their boats out, but in April and May the water level may be too low to launch a boat. There is now bus service from Belize City running two or three times daily into Crooked Tree; inquire about times at Orange Walk or at Batty's in Belize City. You can also hitch or walk from the junction to the village, where you can rent a boat. But be sure to leave yourself enough time. Many tour companies will also arrange excursions.

Festivals & Events

An Agricultural Show is held in mid-March, and a Cashew Festival was held for the first time in May of 1993.

Sights

Birds, birds, and other wildlife. There are a number of trails through the village, and it may be possible to see jabiru storks nearby. The best are the **Jacana Loop Trail** and the **Trogon Trail**. The **Limp-** kin Trail is good in April and May. The Muscovy duck and the black-bellied whistling duck nest in trees by the side of the lagoon. Aside from walking around the village or on the paths near Chau Hiix Lodge, the best place to see birds is on the lagoon itself. Charter a boat or rent a canoe. En route, you may see local cows in the river munching on water lilies.

Chau Hiix

Aside from the birds and other wildlife, the only notable attraction in the area is **Chau Hiix**, an archaeological site to the west of the village in a cohune palm forest known as Blackburn Ridge. Originally named Indian Hill, it has been known to the community and protected for more than 150 years. It was renamed Chau Hiix (meaning "jaguarundi" in Kekchi Maya) by American archaeologist, Dr. Anne Pyburn. A professor at Indiana University, she had seen one of these elegant cats on an initial visit to the site. Dr. Pyburn was approached by the village council, who wanted to excavate, preserve, and increase visitation at the site. Thought to have been a stop on the trading routes, Chau Hiix is the only known source for a type of black-colored chert. Chalcedony and jasper found in the area are also thought to have been likely barter items.

Along with her students, Dr. Pyburn began test excavations in 1992 and major excavation work began in May 1973. To date, most excavation has been in the form of test trenches to determine the dates of each structure and check on its preservation. Although some of the stone tools found along the shores of Crooked Tree Lagoon date back

Crooked Tree Wildlife Sanctuary

CALABASH POND

Northern Highway

REVENGE LAGOON

To Orange Walk (22 miles)

----- Sanctuary boundary

Village

WESTERN LAGOON

CROOKED TREE LAGOON

To Belize City (33 miles)

JONES LAGOON

BLACK CREEK

Biscayne

MEXICO LAGOON

SPANISH CREEK

May Pen

SOUTHERN LAGOON

BELIZE RIVER

6 MILES

The site's center is dominated by the "Kinichku," an enormous 80-foot-high pyramid. Constructed of stone blocks, it was once covered with a layer of blood-red painted plaster. It overlooks the Great Plaza, which covered a 180-by-300-foot area. The entire plaza was raised 15 feet above the ground with a layer of earth, stone, and plaster. Two tiny square platforms, constructed from blocks and rubble, are thought to have been used for sacrifices as well as burial services for their leaders. A number of other structures are grouped around the plaza.

TOURING THE SITE: You can hire a boat in the village to bring you here. You will spend around BZ$140 RT for up to seven passengers. If you come by canoe, expect to spend three to four hours each way. After arrival, the caretaker will give you a brief tour, after which you'll be free to explore on your own. The area is a superb birding site and has many animals. One good place to observe them is in the central main open-space area during the early morning hours. You may see a coati come to forage or any one of a number of birds – including trogons, toucans, and red bellied woodpeckers. Some birders enjoy this site so much that they have trouble tearing themselves away.

to 500 AD, the earliest structures here are believed to date from the Early Preclassic (1100 BC). The most recent buildings probably date from 800-900 AD, but the site is believed to have been occupied right up through the Postclassic period (1000-1500 AD). English loggers, working in the area during the 1700s may have driven away the last remaining Maya residents.

Chau Hiix could be the only Maya site of this size in Belize that has remained free from looters.

The site largely consists of ruined mounds in the midst of forest composed of cohune palms and pocono boys. Strangler figs are also found. Orange strips tied to stakes delineate the corners of buildings. The holes you see on the ground are left by fallen cohune palms. Keep your eyes to the ground to spot armadas of leaf-cutting ants struggling with their burdens down the trees and across the paths. Palm leaves rustle eerily in the wind, and shadows play on the vegetation in the subdued light. Back near the dock, be sure to observe the wild papaya tree with its miniature fruit and the snail egg colonies attached to the trees; the pink ones still have snails inside. note: If you see an artifact here, please leave it *in situ*. And take care not to dislodge stones.

Information & Services

The modest **Visitor's Center** is on the right side of the causeway at the end; they have information, including a brochure about accommodations and other facilities. Make sure that you don't just get the flyer for Molly's! The village now has 24-hour electricity. There are three larger shops, as well as three smaller ones. The village **community telephone** is 02-44333. Dolls are made to order by the **Crooked Tree Women's Group**. A gift shop is planned and may be there when you visit.

Accommodations

Sam Tillett's Hotel & Tours (☎ 02-12026) is run by Sam Tillett, one of the area's best known guides.

He offers atttractive rooms in a thatched-roof wooden home for around BZ$60 db and will provide meals. For BZ$60 (for up to four; BZ$30 for each additional person), Sam will take you out to see nesting Jabiru storks, to "converse" with howler monkeys, or to watch crocodiles. He calls the area his "backyard."

Featuring four rooms and a dorm, **Bird's Eye View Lodge** (☎ 02-32040, fax 02-24869; Box 1976, Belize City) looks inauspicious, but is hospitable. Dorm beds are BZ$20 and rooms are around BZ$130 d for bed and breakfast. Canoe rentals, horseback riding, nature walks, and boat trips are offered. Pickups from the airport and Belize City are available. In the US, contact Dino Jones at 718-845-0749.

The Paradise Inn (☎ 025-2535, fax 025-2534; e-mail ptlgreg@aol.com) has cabanas for BZ$70 s and BZ$90 d plus tax. Inexpensive meals are offered in the restaurant, and fishing, birding, horseback riding, and boat trips are offered. In the US, ☎/fax 718-498-2221 or write Box 153, Vanderveer Station, Brooklyn, NY 11210.

Offering seven cabanas and a restaurant/bar, eight-room **Crooked Tree Resort** overlooks Crooked Tree Lagoon, about 30 miles northeast of Belize City. Write PO Box 1453, Belize City or ☎ 02-77745. Horseback riding is available here. Adventurous and hardy travelers can stay with a family and experience local life directly.

The four-room **Rhaburn's Rooms** is operated by Pastor Owen and Miss Maggie Rhaburn. Mr. Rhaburn will take you on a three-hour buggy ride of the village for BZ$60. **Others** include those run

The North

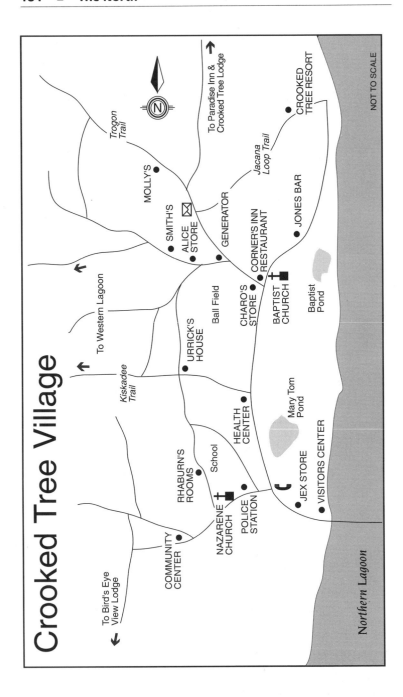

Crooked Tree Village

by Mr. Richard, Alma Smith, Ruby Crawford and Miss Kelly. A small restaurant has been opened, and additonal accommodations are planned. Contact these and other small hotels through the community phone: ☎ 02-44101 or 021-44101.

---

66 Reader's Comment

"We would really recommend Rhaburn's Rooms to everyone. It's just like a bed and breakfast in the US. The rooms were clean, wonderful view of palm trees.... The food was out of this world!"

---

outlying areas: For a very different and quite special experience visit **Chau Hiix Lodge** (☎ 02-77891, 021-2036 fax 02-77891). A former fishing lodge now geared towards birdwatchers, Chau Hiix is off by itself – a 40-minute boat trip along the lagoon. It is generally accessible by road only during April and May. Surrounded by trails and facing the lagoon, the lodge has one of the best locations for birdwatching in all of Central America. While quite comfortable, the rooms are nothing spectacular. They are wood-paneled, with two beds and a bathroom. But the outdoors is why you're here. You can see an amazing amount of birdlife on the trails, and you might see jaguar or ocelot tracks, and even spot a wild peccary. Jabiru stork nest upriver.

Nearby, you can see an airstrip where two small planes were torched by drug smugglers in 1989 and 1991. Having been loaded, they were too heavy for takeoff. A rusting British Army vehicle, shot full of holes from target practice, stands nearby. A generator runs at

night, and there's a comfortable living/dining area to relax in. Because the lodge can only hold eight to 12 occupants, you're guaranteed intimate service. The home cooking is hearty, and vegetarians can be catered to. A trained guide is always at the lodge, and some packages include your choice of a trip to the Community Baboon Sanctuary or to Lamanai.

Packages start from US$525 pp, double-occupancy, for three nights and four days. Prices range up to a high of US$1,175 pp, single-occupancy, for seven nights and eight days. The package includes RT transportation from Belize International, room and three meals, drinks, snacks, tours, and guiding. Airport departure tax, alcohol, and tips are not included.

Lamanai Archaeological Reserve

Lamanai's ruins are set along the New River Lagoon within the 950-acre Archaeological Reserve. Lamanai is one of the nation's most impressive Maya sites, as well as one of the longest continually occupied, Its name (originally "Lamanyan," meaning "Submerged Crocodile") is one of the few original Maya city names known. It accords well with the large number of crocodile carvings found here and the crocodile bones found in burial sites. Lamanai remains a great "lost city." Over the square mile area, not even 5% of its 718 structures have been excavated!

History

One very notable feature of Lamanai is the site's longevity: it was occupied by the Maya from 1500 BC until the 19th century – some 200 years longer than most of the other sites in Belize. Lamanai is believed to have been on the main trade route from the Yucatán to the central Maya areas. The Spanish arrived here in the 17th century and the English in the 20th century via the New River. It is believed that at one time 60-70,000 Maya lived here. The earliest mention of Lamanai is on Nicholas Jannson's map of the Yucatán peninsula. It shows "Lamanay," but incorrectly labels it as being on the shore. Lamanai was excavated by Canadian archaeologist David Pendergast during the 1970s and 1980s.

Flora & Fauna

In addition to the wildlife passed on the New River Lagoon en route (page 187), the reserve is rich in howler monkeys and various bird species. You might spot black oropendolas roosting around the Temple of the Mask and the High Temple. Black vultures may be spotted soaring off

Lamanai Self-Guiding Nature Trail Key

1. Santa Maria *(Calophyllum brassiliense)*. Its anise-flavored leaves can be used to cook and wrap fish.

2. Cohune Palm *(Orbignya cohune)*. Its leaves are used for roof thatching and for walls.

3. Trumpet Tree *(Cecropia peltata)*. A food source for the howlers, the hollow trunks are said to have been made into Maya trumpets.

4. Tubroos *(Enterolobium cyclocarpum)*. The trunks are used to make dugouts.

5. Cotton Tree *(Ceiba pentandra)*. Considered sacred by the Maya, who gave it a place at the center of the cosmos, with its roots in the ground and its leaves in the sky.

6. Allspice *(Pimenta dioica)*. A popular dish for howler monkeys.

7. Red Gumbo limbo *(Bursera simaruba)*. Its leaves and bark are used as a tonic..

8. Pimenta Palm *(Acoelorraphe wrightii)*. This tree can be recognized by its stout and prickly trunk.

9. Bucut *(Cassia grandis)*. This tree is notable for its large black seed pods, which may grow up to three feet.

10. Cedar *(Cedrela Mexicana)*. The scent of its bark repels insects.

11. Rubber Tree. Cuts in the tree show where rubber has been extracted.

12. Breadnut Tree *(Brosimun aicastrum)*. This tree was used as food source by the Maya.

13. Copal Tree. Its sap was used for incense by the Maya.

14. Cordonica. Its roots can be used to treat snake bites.

in the distance from the top of the High Temple. The double tapping sounds of the Guatemalan ivorybill make its presence evident. A variety of toucans may be found at structure N10-9 and, at the High Temple, the collared aracari cries out shrilly through the forest. Generally found near the area of Stela 9, pairs of rufous-tailed jacamars are slender and medium-sized birds whose iridescent coloring and needle-like beaks cause them to resemble overgrown hummingbirds. Spotted around the lagoon's edge, the northern jacana has pale green legs, yellow-paneled wings, and a brown body. Seen near the ground, the citreoline trogon has a bright yellow chest, a black-and-white tail, and a blue-and-green back.

Less common are agoutis, spider monkeys, tarantulas, peccaries, nine-banded armadillos, and jaguarundis.

Transport

GETTING HERE: The bus runs to Indian Church but, as there's no daily run, it's not practical. Despite what you may have read elsewhere, it can be difficult to find a boat to rent and boats are not commonly available in either Guinea Grass or Shipyard! You may approach by road from San Felipe during the dry season.

☞ Traveler's Tip

It's now easy to visit Lamanai as a day trip from San Pedro. Maya Island Air tours (☎ 02-31348/31362/31403; e-mail mayair@btl.net) is among those offering a day trip for around BZ$330 pp.

Tours

Unlike other sites, which can easily be visited on your own, this is probably best seen as part of a tour. One of the best tour operators is **Herminio Novelo's Jungle River Trips** based in Orange Walk (☎ 03-22293; 20 Lover's Lane or PO Box 95, Orange Walk Town). An active promoter of ecotourism in Belize, Mr. Novelo is a lively and enthusiastic guide who knows his subject. His usual pickup site is from Orange Walk's toll bridge, where he meets passengers arriving from Belize City.

Maruba (☎ 03-22199) and *Lamanai Lady* (☎ 02-31063, fax 02-30263) leave from Jim's Cool Pool. **Lamanai Mayatours** (☎ 03-23839) also operates out of Orange Walk. Plane tours leave from San Pedro; see that section for details. From the departure point, you travel along the river, with the jungle on both sides, passing the Mennonite settlement of Shipyard to the right. You could be in Pennsylvania (watch for Mennonites fishing). Eventually, you reach the wide New River· Lagoon. On the way you might spot black oropendolas, collared aracaris, citreoline trogons, immature blue herons, rufous-tailed jacamars, northern jacanas, fishing bats, herons, purple gallinules, and turkey vultures, as well as ubiquitous crocodiles sliding into the water on your approach. You'll also pass immense termite mounds on tree branches. The entrance to the park is a series of huts on the right.

TOURING THE RUINS: A small but excellent museum is up from the pier. It contains primarily ceramic artifacts. Dating from the 6th cen-

The North

tury, pyramidial N9-56, the **Mask Temple**, has a 12-ft.-high mask carved on its side, the largest such carving discovered so far in the entire Mundo Maya. Note his crocodile headdress and classic Olmec features – thick lips and broad nose. The deteriorated **stela** of a Maya ruler stands in front under a corrugated zinc shed. The temple was constructed from the early to late Classic Maya eras. To the rear of the temple, there's a grove of ramon (breadnut) trees and a view of the lagoon. The closed-off tunnel here enters an excavation that disclosed another large mask 15 feet inside.

Back on the path there's a **throne** with a symbol vaguely resembling either a yin and yang sign or a bow tie (depending upon your inclination) and an excavated tomb. There's a small, well-preserved temple dating from 100 BC at its base. The **Stela 9,** also in good condition, shows the ruler Smoking Shell, along with hieroglyphs portraying his title and reign. Done up in the Late Preclassic style and the largest of its kind in the entire area, the massive N10-43, **The High Temple**, faces a small ball court and provides a breathtaking 360° view of the surrounding wilderness from its 100-foot summit. Excavations here have uncovered thousands of blades, a dish dating from 700 AD, which contains the skeleton of a bird, a giant bowl, and numerous Preclassic vessels, as well as other finds. It is the largest securely dated Maya structure.

Back on the road, note the woodpecker holes in the surrounding cohune palms. When the gigantic marker disc was raised at the small **ball court** in 1980, lidded vessels containing miniature vessels were uncovered, as well as a number of shells and small jade objects found floating on top of a pool of mercury. Little is known about the rules governing the game played on this court, but it is certain that they held great ritual and cultural significance. Dating from around 500 AD, with modifications in the 700s and 1200s, **Temple N10-9** has yielded numerous finds, including jade earrings, a jade mask, a bowl with an animal motif, and a large black-on-red bowl.

Nearby at Indian Church are the remains of two 16th-century **churches**. Incorporating Maya temple blocks, the older one has only its lower walls remaining intact. Next to it stands a Maya stela, possibly erected by Maya who had destroyed the church as an affirmation of their age-old beliefs. Ruins of the second church, destroyed for the same reason, are in the vicinity. A bit more of it remains intact.

To the west are the ruins of a **sugar mill** – with flywheel and a sunken brick-laid reservoir – built by Confederate refugees. Part of the British Honduras Estate Company that had several sugar operations around Belize, the mill's machinery was imported from the Leeds Foundry in New Orleans and installed in 1869. The bricks used for its construction had been brought in as ship's ballast. Its laborers are thought to have been Maya as well as Chinese (because of the Chinese coins found at the site). After the owner died of yellow fever, the mill was abandoned in 1875 and now a strangler fig has overtaken the flywheel.

Accommodations

The only place to stay is at **Lamanai Outpost** (☎/fax 02-33578, 02-2012; Box 63, Orange Walk; e-maillamanai@btl.net; www.belize.net), a 13-cabaña facility with 24-hour electricity and fans. Two-night packages (US$340 pp, double-occupancy and up) are available. The four-night package (US$640 pp, double-occupancy) includes a day trip to La Milpa ruins as well as Blue Creek and the Programme for Belize. Accommodation only is BZ$140 s and BZ$180 d. Children under 12 are free; children 12-16 are BZ$20. Extra persons (four max. in rooms) are BZ$40, not including 6% tax and BZ$5 pp, pn service charge. The lodge offers wind surfing, canoeing, massages (BZ$16 per hour), and night river trips, where they shine a light on the crocs. To get here, you must either charter a plane to land at the airstrip, cruise up the river, or drive. Contact the lodge for details.

Altun Ha

Thirty miles to the north of Belize City and just a few miles from the coast, Altun Ha is a rare example of a Maya coastal center. Built on limestone rising just above sea level, the site is separated from the Caribbean by a swamp. Its name derives from the Maya words for the nearby village, Rockstone Pond. That, in turn, takes its name from the large freshwater pond, a reservoir lined on the bottom with yellow clay. At its peak, Altun Ha occupied almost 4½ square miles, and as many as 8-10,000 may have lived here, with some 3,000 residing at its center. There are about 500 mounds or structures in total.

History

Many inhabitants collected shells and worked them into beads and pendants. The presence of jade, obsidian, and shells suggest that it was an important trading as well as agricultural center. It is thought that there may have been a settlement as early as 1000 BC and that a culture existed here by the end of the first century. The first major structures date from that time. They appear to have been occupied until the 10th century – possibly until the 14th-15th centuries. Although it was once supposed that this was on the fringe of Maya influence during the later periods, excavation has proved that Maya inhabited the area from ancient times onward. It was thought that, as the area's soil is largely inappropriate for agriculture, the excellent water supply must have been what lured the Maya.

Current theory holds that the Maya fed themselves through a system of raised fields and canals built in swampy areas. While tombs at other sites were constructed in the form of vaulted and plastered crypts, Altun Ha's were built simply, using walls of boulders and

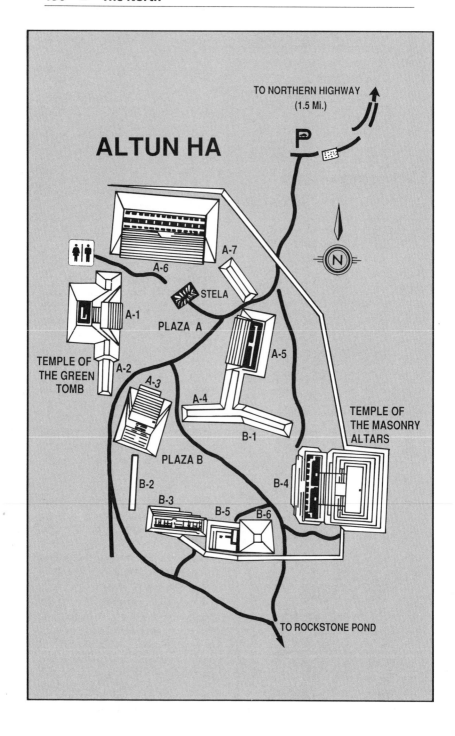

ALTUN HA

flint slab ceilings. Each crypt held spectacular jade objects.

LAYOUT: Altun Ha is similar in design to other sites. Five pyramids and a palace surround **Plaza A**, the northernmost of the two central plazas. The solid pyramids were once topped by altars or chambered structures made of masonry or wood and thatch. Plaza A contains Pyramid A-1, the **Temple of the Green Tomb,** which yielded over 300 jade pieces. Badly damaged **Temple A-6,** to the right as you come in, has two parallel 157-foot-long rooms, each with 13 exterior doorways. **Plaza B** was added around 550 AD, rising 59 feet.

The most spectacular find was the carved jade head of the sun god (Kinich Ahau) found in the seventh tomb at the summit of the **Temple of Masonry Altars**. Also known as the Sun God Temple because of the images of the Sun God carved on either side of its bottom set of steps, as well as the carved jade head, this is the site's tallest building. This temple's circular stone altars date from around 600-700 AD. Remains of incense and blackened jade beads and pendants were found around the base.

Fed by rain runoff and springs, and dammed by the ancient Maya, **Rockstone Pond** is 1,500 feet south of Plaza B. The medium-sized temple (200 AD) standing next to it was used to receive offerings from Teotihuacán in the Valley of Mexico.

Transport

GETTING HERE: Unfortunately, the road here is the former Northern Highway, and there is now not much in the way of bus service. But you may be able to take a bus from Belize City to Maskall; Altun Ha is a few miles further. Tour and taxi are the easier ways to visit. Many visitors fly in to Corozal or Belize City and make day trips here from San Pedro. If you are a low-budget traveler and can't afford a tour, there are a number of ruins that equal or surpass Altun Ha in interest (notably Xunantunich) and are more readily accessible.

Tours

Entering, you register and pay. A guard will show you around. First, you pass Plaza A; a strangler fig is to your left and a large mound is to the right. Straight ahead is a large structure, A-3, which has a representation of Chac, the Rain God. To its right are cohune palms. From the top, you can see the Temple of the Masonry Altars. The stairs of the latter are slippery and steep, so watch your step on the way up. This is the temple where the jade head (see above) was discovered, and the views are well worth the somewhat strenuous ascent.

From the base, a slippery trail leads back through cohune ridge terrain to Rockstone Pond. This is where the mosquitoes move in for the kill. On this trail, you'll see trees such as pocono boy, hog plum, sea grape, and trumpet. When you arrive at the pond, you might be able to spot a croc or two in the water. In 1993, one nine-footer took a dog that was swimming in the water! It's common to see Salvadorians fishing here. Bird-watching is good during early morning or late afternoon hours. You might see wildlife such as brocket deer. The site is open from

9 to 5. Entrance fee is BZ$3. There are a few souvenir stands nearby.

Colha: Although not an attraction for visitors, this ancient archaeological site along the highway north of Maskall shows evidence of Maya habitation dating back 4,500 years.

Accommodations

OUTLYING: The **Maruba Resort** (☎ 23-22199) is a health spa located at Mile 40½ on the Old Northern Highway near Maskall. It's run by youthful Nicky Nicholson and his older sister Franzisca, who designed the resort. The uniquely decorated rooms are adorned with hibiscus flowers. Specially prepared vials of body oils, insect repellent, and anti-itch cream are provided.

Well-suited for those who want something more adventurous than Cancún but aren't prepared to rough it, Maruba has grounds adorned with bromeliads, blooming heliconias, and coconut palms. The majority of guests are women seeking a spa experience. A small zoo has a kinkajou and a peccary. The comfortable and atmospheric thatched-roof restaurant and bar has eclectic local art, including wood carvings and masks, and a wide variety of world music plays in the background. There's a large outdoor hot tub, a pool with a fountain, and a variety of services, from pedicures to facials. Massages and wraps are given with New Age music soothing the atmosphere. While two types of massage oil are provided, there's little apparent difference between the two except the price.

A variety of tours and excursions are available, including a trip to nearby Altun Ha and a visit to Lamanai aboard the resort's private boat. A resort exclusive is a hike through the bush led by a local, who explains the area's natural history. A visit to a looted Maya mound may be included. You'll learn about the pocono boy palm, the trumpet tree, the mountain cow rib, and the water tea time vine. Rates are around BZ$170 s, and BZ$215 d, plus 17% tax and service. In the US, write Box 300703, Houston, TX 77230; ☎ 800-627-8227 or fax 713-799-2031.

note: Maralyn and Albert, who formerly sold their wines and herbs at Maskall, have relocated to San Pedro, where they run the wonderful Rasta Pasta.

Orange Walk Town

Situated on the left bank of the New River, Orange Walk Town (pop. 11,000) is 66 miles north of Belize City and 30 miles south of Corozal Town. Orange Walk isn't a particularly attractive place to stay. It is a major sugarcane and ganja center. Sugarcane trucks rumble through the town continually during the harvest season, spilling pieces of cane here and there. Cane-laden trucks line up at the sugar mill to the south of town. From its center, roads branch off in four directions – linking the 20-odd outlying villages.

The town is best used as a base to visit the Cuello and Lamanai ruins. There are a large number of low-life bars here – seemingly more per capita than anywhere else in Belize. At night you may be offered a piece of rock – and they don't mean Gibraltar. In direct contrast, Mennonites, visiting from the outlying settlement of Blue Creek, abound and almost 20% of the stores are owned by East Indians.

History

One of the nation's first settlements, it began as a timber camp. Mestizos arrived en masse in 1849. The local Icaiche Maya attacked the town in 1872 but were defeated. Today their descendants reside in the village of Botes, near the Río Hondo on the Guatemala border. Once this was mainly a center for chicle tapping and maize growing, but the sugarcane industry has grown substantially in recent years and has come to dominate the local economy.

Sights

The ruins of **Ft. Cairns** (now the new town hall) and **Ft. Mundy** (near the police station; now the government rest house) serve as reminders of the days the town warded off Maya attacks. In 1872, an outnumbered detachment of the West India Regiment fended off an attack by the Icaiche Maya; an **obelisk** by the taxi stand commemorates the encounter. Just past the police station is a park and children's playground. Here, you will find the statue of a soldier, though no one seems to know who he is or why the statue was erected. In the area you're likely to hear the sound of barges blowing their horns on the river.

Accommodations

The best place to stay is undoubtedly 31-room **D'Victoria Hotel**

(☎ 03-2518/2364). The BZ$45 s or BZ$50 d you pay here entitles you to use the swimming pool and enter the disco. The comfortable rooms are equipped with private shower and fans; more expensive (around BZ$85) double rooms come with a/c. The management and staff are friendly and helpful. There's a cable TV in the lobby, along with complimentary coffee.

The two **Jane's Hotels** (03-22473), at 2 Bakers Street and on Market Lane, charge around BZ$15 for spartan rooms. The latter is in a bad location – near the sleazy, hustler-ridden Club America, a bar-brothel nicknamed "Vietnam."

Next up in price and above the restaurant of the same name, **Tai San's Hotel** (☎ 03-22752) is at 30 Queen Victoria Ave. and charges BZ$20 s and BZ$30 d. All other hotels are higher priced but still in the budget range. Next to a gas station on the northern side of town, **Chula Vista Motel** (☎ 03-2365) has seven rooms from about BZ$40 d.

Also try the 11-room **Nueva Mi Amor Hotel** (☎ 03-2031) at 19 Belize/Corozal Rd. or the nine-room **La Nueva Ola Hotel** (☎ 03-22104), 73 Otro Benque Rd. Near the center of the town, but on the water, **Lamanai Mayatours** (☎ 03-23839; Box 90, Orange Walk) has bungalows renting for around BZ$110 d. Outside of town, **Circle K Lodge** (☎ 03-22600), at Mile 48½ along the Old Northern Highway, is not particularly recommended.

Food

One of the few places serving fish is the attractive lounge next to the Hotel Baron. Log-cabin-style **Eddie's Cabin**, 46 San Antonio Rd.,

The North

features gibnut. Also try the **Lover's Lane Restaurant**, right by the park, run by the friendly Novelos. **Julie's**, near the police station, features good inexpensive creole cooking. Others to try include **La Favorita**, 15 Lover's Lane, the **Golden Gate Restaurant**, 10 Main St., and **El Beliceño**. The classiest place is **"The Diner,"** which is behind the former general hospital building on Clark St., a good walk (or short taxi ride) from the north of town. For bread, **Panaderia La Popular**, Beckie's Lane, sells onion bread and sweet "Chop Suey Bread."

CHINESE FOOD: Orange Walk has a large number of Chinese Restaurants. Cool and spacious **Lee's, New Light, Kingfa**, and **Golden Gate** are all nearly in a straight line on Yo Creek Rd. **Jane's Chinese Food Corner**, 21 Main St., also has burgers and "lobster thermidor." Next to the park, **Happy Day's Ice Cream Parlor and Restaurant** has the monthly pages from a calendar of Chinese movie stars pinned up on the wall. **San Martin Bar and Restaurant**, 4 Park St., and the **New Chinese Restaurant**, 1 Park St., offer good value. Just around the corner, **Happy Valley Chinese Restaurant** has similar prices, allegedly "in air conditioned and romantic atmosphere." Still another choice is **Tai San** on Belize Rd.

Services

There are three banks. **Schnookles Travel Services and Postal Agency** is on the southern outskirts, along the Belize-Corozal Rd.

    tours: **Herminio Novelo's Jungle River Trips** is based in Orange Walk (☎ 03-22293; 20 Lover's Lane

or PO Box 95, Orange Walk Town). They offer good tours of Lamanai. Also try the **Godoy family** (☎ 03-22969) at No. 4 Trial Farm to the north of town on the right. They can take you on a tour of their orchid farm.

Transport

GETTING HERE: Any bus running between Belize City and Corozal will stop in Orange Walk.

FROM ORANGE WALK: Buses run hourly toward Corozal and Chetumal and half-hourly toward Belize City. Since the town is a way station, there's no telling the exact time a bus will pass. Just wait at the gas station up from Baron's in the center of town.

Vicinity of Orange Walk Town

El Posito

This is about four miles west of Guinea Grass. It was once partially excavated and, although it has been largely reclaimed by the jungle, you can see a wide range of Maya ruins.

Shipyard

Visible along the river if you travel from Orange Walk to Lamanai by boat, this Mennonite community makes furniture. Locals here are a mixture of progressive and traditional.

Cuello

This is a later site than Lamanai and not developed for visitors. There's not much to see here save for a small pyramid and a few mounds. Archaeological indications are that it was founded by 2500 BC and continuously occupied for the next 3,000 years. It is believed that many of the pyramid-plaza architectural techniques originated here. Excavations at this site have demonstrated that, by the end of the Early Preclassic (1000 BC), the pyramid-plaza ceremonial architecture, house design, a social structure, staple foods, and ceramics were well established, laying the path for further development.

The site also contains the earliest known Maya masonry building, a rectangular plaster-covered limestone structure in the central courtyard dating from 650 BC. Typically glazed a monochrome red-orange, Swazey ceramics, the earliest ceramics found in Belize, have been found here.

Not all of the discoveries here indicate an easy existence. Over 20 skeletons showing evidence of torture and sacrifice have been found in a mass burial site dating from 400 BC. Containing five individuals believed to have been part of the same family, the oldest known human burial plot (dating from 3,000 years ago) was excavated here in 1993. A total of 180 graves have been unearthed. As with nearly all Maya sites, the original name is unknown and the site's current name comes from the property owners.

GETTING HERE: To get here, follow Bakers St. west from the center of town for about an hour. A taxi will charge around BZ$10 RT. To the left as you enter through the pasture, there are a set of completely unexcavated ruins amidst a thick grove of ramon trees. The site is open Monday to Saturday, and is closed on Sunday. As the site is on private property, ask permission inside the first building you come to (a soap factory) and pass through the gate to the left of the rum factory. Turkey buzzards scatter as you approach down the road. It's pleasant enough just to sit atop the pyramid and watch the cows munching grass.

Nohmul

This major ceremonial center, whose name means "Great Mound," rises atop a limestone ridge extending from the west of the Orange Walk/Corozal boundary to the west of San Pablo village. There are two "twin" ceremonial groups, spread widely apart, surrounded by several plazas and connected by a raised causeway, or *sacbe*. The main building is an Acropolis-like structure on which a pyramid has been mounted, and is the tallest building in the Orange Walk/Corozal area. Abandoned during the Classic Period (350 BC-250 AD), it was reoccupied during the Early Postclassic (600 AD-900 AD). Unfortunately it has been extensively plundered, and one structure was even used for road fill!

GETTING THERE: The site is situated among sugarcane fields a mile to the west of San Pablo village, 7½ miles north of Orange Walk on the Northern Highway. All Orange Walk-Corozal buses from Belize City or from Orange Walk pass by. Ask the driver to let you off at the entrance to Nohmul in San Pablo, which is at the Keystone Bar. Before visiting you might try contacting the caretaker, Estevan Itzab, who lives in the house across from the village water tower. Just knock on his door.

TOURING THE SITE: From the road, keep walking straight in. A bit up to the right from the first road intersecting at right angles, you come to a wood-fired bakery and then a school. Keep straight on the road, passing sugar cane fields and corn until the road bends sharply to the left. At this point, take the road to the right, heading off into the trees and then the smaller road off to the right again. You'll see a hill covered with vegetation. To the right, you'll see an excavated grotto; to its left, there's a path. Climb up, and you'll come to a stone platform. Descend from there and head up the other, vegetation-covered hill, and you will see where artifacts have been looted. The top – surrounded by cecropia trees – affords great views of the lush area. Everything is still save for the sounds of clattering martins. From the top, you can continue down the other side, see more trenches, and take a path to the right, which leads back to your starting point.

Blue Creek

There are Mennonite settlements around the progressive community of Blue Creek Village, about 30 miles from Orange Walk. As you approach, sugar cane fields give way to fields of sorghum and corn. The small hydroelectric dam and plant here is an example of the ingenuity of this remarkable people. Having dammed the Rio Bravo and cut the channel to provide water for the plant's operation, they still lacked hydraulic equipment to control the water's flow. After a Constellation cargo plane crashed at the international airport, the Mennonites purchased the wreck. They converted its fuselage to a barn and its hydraulic gear was used to control the flow of water! There are also furniture-making operations in the village.

Half of the community here belongs to the Evangelical Mennonite Mission Church (EMMC), while the remainder have joined the slightly more conservative Kleine Gemeinde. The Old Colony church, which monopolized the village's religious industry until 1966, has disbanded. Its remaining members moved elsewhere in Belize or even as far afield as Bolivia. Shop at the **Linda Vista Shopping Center**.

BLUE CREEK PROJECT: Sponsored by Texas's St. Mary's University, the **Blue Creek Project** (www.qvision.com/MRP) is excavating the Blue Creek ruin, a mi. S of the Mexican border near the junction of the Azul, Bravo, and Hondo rivers. Work has been going on (usually from May to July) since 1992. Volunteers pay around $1,350 for a two-week session; additional sessions are discounted. Work is rough, and you must be Mennonite-tolerant (because that is who lives in the area). For more information, call 210-431-2280, fax 210-436-3500, e-mail guderjan@netxpress.com, or write Maya Research Program, Box 15376, San Antonio, TX 78212-8576.

Corozal Town

On the edge of attractive Corozal Bay is the small town of Corozal (pop. 8,000), which abounds with flowering flamboyants and coconut palms, as well as a number of old buildings. Safer than Orange Walk, this attractive community is also just 20 minutes from Chetumal, Mexico. Lying 96 miles north of Belize City, it is nine miles from the Río Hondo, which delineates the Belize-Mexico border.

As is the case with other Belizean towns, it's not so much a destination in itself as a base from which to visit the surrounding area. Santa Rita, one of the most important Post-Classic Maya ruins, is just east of town, and Cerro Maya or Cerros, another archaeological site, is at the head of the bay across from town. The surrounding area depends upon the sugar industry. Other major products include rum, corn, citrus, and coconuts. Among the holidays celebrated here are Carnival, Columbus Day, and many other fiestas.

If you're looking for an attractive town to visit, Corozal is an apt candidate. Its only drawbacks are that the bay is too polluted for swimming and that a number of indolent locals think all gringos are Daddy Warbucks and will try to get a handout. Politely refuse; don't encourage dependency.

History

Originally a private estate named after the cohune palms found in the area, the town was settled largely by mestizo refugees from the massacre at Bacalar, Mexico during the Caste Wars (La Guerra de las Castas, 1848-1880). In this war the Maya struggled to drive mestizos and Spanish Creoles from the Yucatán. The town was largely rebuilt after 1955's Hurricane Janet wreaked devastation, destroying its Mexican-style adobe walls. It has been largely rebuilt and now has parks and modern streets.

Transport

ARRIVING BY AIR: If flying in from Ambergris with Tropic Air (☎ 02-45671, 026-2012, 800-422-3435; www.belize.net; e-mail tropic@btl.net) or with Maya Island Air (☎ 02-31348/31362/31403; e-mail mayair@btl.net) you sweep over the ocean and across a vast expanse of jungle, swamp, and more swamp. There's no habitation as far as you can see. As you approach the landing strip, you fly over milpas (cornfields) hacked from the jungle. At the strip, taxis (BZ$5 pp) await to speed you the two miles to town. Or you can take the short walk out to the road and flag down a passing bus. It will take you either to Chetumal or to town, letting you off at the small bustling market.

FROM COROZAL: Buses for Belize City and Chetumal, Mexico pass through the town approximately once an hour. While the Venus bus station (☎ 04-22132) is near the northern edge of town across from the Shell station, Batty buses (☎ 04-23034) stop at their own station by the road just around the corner from the park. For Chetumal, Batty runs at 7, 8, 8:15, 9, 10, 11, noon, 1, and 2; Venus runs at 2:45, 4, 4:30, 5, 5:30, 6, 6:30, 7, 7:30, 8, 8:30, 9, and 10.

For Orange Walk and Belize City, Venus departs at 6:15, 6:45, 7:15,

Corozal Town

TO SAN ANTONIO
①
⑫

TO FOUR MILES LAGOON,
MEXICAN BORDER & CHETUMAL

RICAIDE
STADUIM

TO CONSEJO SHORES

HOSPITAL

SANTA RITA ROAD

SPORTS GROUND

7th St. North
6th St. North
5th St. North

4th St North

11th Ave.
10th Ave.

3rd St. North

2nd St. North

2nd Ave

③
⑤
④

1st St. South

2nd St. South

1st St. North

3rd Ave

②

G St. South

9th Ave.

7th Avenue

6th Avenue

⑨

⑧

3rd St. South

⑥

TO XAIBE
VILLAGE

⑩
⑫
4th St. South
5th St. South
6th St. South

⑦

5th Ave
4th Ave
1st Ave

N

10th St. South

F St. South

E St. South
D St. South
C St. South
B St. South

8th Ave.

⑪

COROZAL BAY

TO ORANGE WALK TOWN

NOT TO SCALE

1. To Santa Rita Ruins
2. Batty Bus Terminal
3. Venus Bus Terminal
4. Post Office, pay phone
5. Belize Bank
6. Town Hall
7. Market
8. Bookstore
9. Nestor's Hotel
10. The Capri
11. Taxi Stand

7:45, 8:15, 8:45, 9:15, 9:45, 10:15, 11:15, 11: 45, and at 12:15; Batty leaves at 12:15, 1:15, 2:15, 3:15, 3:30, 4:15, 5:15, and at 6:15. Maya (☎ 02-31348/31362/31403, 025-2336) and Tropic Air (☎ 02-45671, 026-2012, 800-422-3435; www.belize.net; e-mail tropic@btl.net) both fly to Belize City.

Sights

The old fort harks back to the era when there were frequent Maya attacks from across the border. In typical Latin style, the Catholic and Protestant churches, the library, the town hall, and other governmental buildings surround the main square. Interlaced with diagonal foot paths, the park has a broken fountain as its centerpiece. Nearby, a **mural** by Manuel Villamor Reyes in the town hall depicts the area's history. Villamor originally painted the vibrant mural in 1953 and, when asked to restore it in 1986, he decided to redo it entirely. Among other things, it portrays an owner whipping his slaves, snobbish nobility, deforestation, a Maya temple, a great hurricane, chicle tapping, and sugarcane processing. If the town hall is closed, you may view the rear wall mural through the side windows.

Constructed to ward off Maya attacks, the ruins of a small fort stand in the corner of the plaza. Located on private land, the **Aventura Sugar Mill** is seven miles from town on the Northern Highway just past the village of the same name. The chimney is the most prominent feature remaining. Sugar processing began here during the 1800s. The ruins of a 16th-century church are also found here.

Santa Rita ruins: Completely ringing Corozal are the ruins of **Santa Rita Corozal**. It's not nearly as impressive as other Maya sites, with only one partially restored structure still standing. Located about a mile to the northeast, the Maya Santa Rita ruins were first explored by British medical practitioner, Thomas Gann, at the beginning of the century. Originally the mighty Maya city known as Chetumal, it was still thriving in 1531 when conquistador Alfonso Davila was booted out. While it is linked by pottery styles to the Yucatán, some of its murals resemble those found at Tulum. The site was extensively excavated by the Chases of the University of Southern Florida from 1979 through 1985. Most of the exciting finds have been removed to Belmopan's Archaeological Vault.

To get to the largest Classic Period construction at the site, take the road heading north and then continue left on a smaller road as the highway veers to the right. The site's largest remaining **pyramid** is set across from the Coca-Cola factory. The site's **Structure No. 7** dates from 350 AD. The purpose of the temple's construction was ceremonial, to provide both living quarters and, later, a tomb for the chief. Six murals from No. 1 were destroyed by superstitious Indians in 1900, before Gann could copy them.

The site is open from 8 to 5 daily; BZ$2 admission. To get here, turn left at Hilltop Bar and follow the road. Pedro, the one-armed guard, will show you around and give you a wonderful description. It's worth the trip alone just to meet him.

Cerro Maya ruins: Cerro Maya or Cerros ruins were excavated by

David Freidel of Southern Texas Methodist University. They are now partially underwater. Admission is BZ$2. One temple is 64 feet high. Its masks have been covered with plaster to stave off erosion. The center blossomed in the Late Preclassic. Abandoned around AD 100 – probably because the growth of inland Maya centers had made it economically untenable – it was not remodeled like other sites. A canal 4,000 feet long, 20 feet wide, and six feet deep – part of the raised terrace agricultural system – surrounded the site, enclosing some 90 acres. Two ball courts and a pyramid-plaza group were in the center. Its pyramids displayed stuccoed and painted masks. Structure 5C has four masks: two representing the sun and Venus, with two others not positively identified.

It was acquired during the 1970s by Texas-based Metroplex Properties, Inc. The Cerro Maya Foundation was formed to excavate the site, reconstruct it as a tourist attraction with a museum, and to build a hotel with a swimming pool. This all came to naught when the foundation went bankrupt. It can now be reached by boat from Corozal or by a roundabout dry-season-only land route though Chunox, Progresso, and Copper Bank. Taking the shore route on foot, it is necessary to find an accommodating boatman to ferry you across the New River's mouth.

Four Miles Lagoon is set by the road to the Mexican border, about seven miles from Corozal; it's possible to camp here if you contact the owners. There's good swimming.

Festivals & Events

The liveliest times of the year are when the Mexican-style fiestas punctuate the day-to-day monotony. The three major events are Carnival, Columbus Day, and Christmas. The latter features colorful posadas in which the nativity is re-enacted.

Accommodations

Located in the town, the cheapest hotel (around BZ$11 s) is the 30-room **Capri** (☎ 04-2042) at 14 4th Ave. (cor. 5th). It's ideal only if you're truly on a low budget; a blaring TV is by the bar downstairs, bugs are plentiful, and weekend dances can keep you up late. Conveniently located **Nestor**'s (☎ 04-22354), 123 5th Ave., is also low-budget and very popular. Rooms, which are being refurbished, have private baths with hot water. It's not a yuppie spot but neither is it a dive: value by Belizean standards is reasonable for what you get. Room rates are around BZ$20 s, BZ$25 d, BZ$29 d with twin beds, and BZ$35 with double twin beds. There's a BZ$5 key deposit, and tax is added. It also has a restaurant.

Just past the southern entrance to town, the 20-room **Hotel Maya** (☎ 04-22082/22874, PO Box 112) is pricier, at around BZ$33 s and BZ$58 d. Rooms have a/c or fans; group rates and conference facilities are available. (Less expensive rooms are available.) The **Caribbean Village** (☎ 04-22045; PO Box 55), located at the South End on the main road to the south of town, charges BZ$10 for a campsite and rents seven cabins for BZ$30.

On the sea a bit over a half-mile south of town, attractive 26-room

Tony's Inn and Resort (☎ 04-22055, fax 04-22829; PO Box 12, Belize City) charges in high season from around BZ$70 s and BZ$90 d for its cheapest rooms on up to BZ$160 for a "deluxe" quad; 17% for tax and service are added. Popular with tour groups, it is the most upscale place to stay and has a good restaurant. Rooms have both a/c and fan and the "deluxe" rooms have a/c, cable TV, and fan.

Budget-priced eight-room **Hotel Posada Mama** (☎ 04-22107) is on G St. in southern Corozal and is partially a/c.

On Air Strip Rd., the **Ranchito Hotel** (☎ 04-23744) is near the airstrip and offers rooms with fans, cable TV. It offers bicycle rental as well. Rates are around BZ$40 s, BZ$50 d with breakfast.

In the village of the same name, the **Santa Cruz Lodge** (☎ 404-22441, fax 04-22442; Box 84, Corozal) was once the private compound of sugar estate execs. It's by the New River and has 18 rooms; boat trips are offered. It has a restaurant, pool, and conference room. Rates are around BZ$120 s, BZ$140 d plus tax; there is a three-night minimum stay. Pickups from Chetumal and Belize City Airport are available.

Opened in 1996 and set by the sea, **Hok'ol K'in** (☎ 04-2239, fax 04-23569) has rooms with two queen-sized beds. One room is equipped for the disabled. There is an upstairs lounge with TV, VCR, coffee pot, and library; dining rooms are available for use. Rooms are around BZ$120 s, BZ$160 d plus tax.

Some 3½ miles from the Mexican border, the **Camino Real Hotel** offers a restaurant and four rooms in the inexpensive price range. You can also camp along the shore of Four Mile Lagoon near the border. **note:** The Adventure Inn closed its doors forever in April 1994. The Don Quixote has also closed.

in Copper Bank: The **Last Resort** will pick you up in Corozal and ferry you out to the village of Copper Bank. It offers stays in cabanas or camping, a restaurant, and stupendous birdwatching.

Food

Nestor's has reasonably priced food, real coffee and espresso, two TVs, and a decor that includes mannequins and posters of bikes, Randy Travis, and a young Elvis crooning. **Club Campesino** on 4th Ave. has fried chicken in the evenings from 7 to midnight. Try **Donna's Cafe** near the Texaco station for breakfast and local food. The market has plenty of good food (rice and beans with beverage for BZ$4.50) and ambience aplenty. It is set right on the dock, and both fresh and dried fish are sold here. **Dubie**'s is exceptionally good value for rice and beans and for fish dishes. **Splendique** is at the northern edge of town. The **Chula Vista** is another alternative. For pastries try the **Flamingo** at the northeast edge of the park.

out of the center: Set at the northern end of town on the sea front, **Crises** features good local food. In the opposite direction from the plaza, you can try the **Hotel Maya** for Spanish cuisine. For hamburger and steak, try inexpensive **Miss Joe's Caribbean Restaurant** in the middle of the Caribbean Village. It closes during the afternoon. **Tony**'s has the nicest ambience (and some of the highest prices) of any local restaurant.

The North

CHINESE FOOD: As in Orange Walk, there's no lack of choice here. **Bumper** Chinese restaurant is on the main road opposite the Capri. You can also try the **Mayflower** on 4th Ave., **King of Kings** on 3rd Ave., **Hong Kong** on 4th Ave., and the **Rexo** at 9th and 6th St. North.

Entertainment

Located by the cemetery to the north of town, next to the Adventure Inn sign, **Gonz Z Roses** is a popular bar. On 1st Ave by the waterfront, the **Cascada Maya** has dances on weekends, as does the **Capri** to the south of town. Also visit the **Sky Top** and the **Blue Dahlia** in town.

Services

The town's banks (open Mon. to Fri. 9-1, plus 3-6 on Fri.) are the **Belize Bank** across from the park, the **Bank of Nova Scotia**, and **Barclays.** Travel agents are **Menzies Travel and Tours** (☎ 04-22725/23415, fax 04-23414, VHF 148-600; Ranchito Village or PO Box 210) and Manuel Hoare's **Malan's Tours** (☎ 04-2274/22055) at No. 13 6th St., southern Corozal Town. Also contact **Leslie's Travel Service** (☎ 04-22377; 57 7th Av.), which offers charters and other services. For plane tickets contact **Jal's Travel Agency** (☎ 04-22163) on Fourth Avenue. **Johnnie's Auto Repair** is at 23 8th Ave. Sincerely.

Chetumal, Mexico

Founded in 1898, this modern city today is the capital of Quintana Roo and the gateway from Belize to Mexico. Once a somnolent tropical port, its designation as a duty-free port (6% duty as opposed to the usual 15%) has brought development galore, and this is a major shopping spot. The waterfront is a 10-minute walk from the marketplace, and most of the hotels are centrally located. While the city doesn't have much of a traditional Mexican air about it, it does serve as a good introduction to the country and as a base to get acclimated before moving on. There's really nothing to do in town, but the surrounding countryside has a good deal to offer. It makes a much more interesting day trip than, say, visiting Melchor from Benque Viejo.

Transport

ARRIVING: If you're going farther, it would be a good idea to get a Mexican visa stamp and visitor's card (free for US citizens) at the embassy in Belize City. In any case, when you cross the border, pass beyond the two desks at the front (where Belizeans wait) and go straight ahead to the desks at the back, where you'll be stamped in. The bus will be waiting for you on the road. If you have your own car, you'll have to pay to have it fumigated for medflies when entering Mexico. Moneychangers at the border give a lower rate than you'll get at the bank. However, if you need Belizean dollars and have cash, you can get around BZ$2.03 per US dollar when you return. Buses arrive at and leave from the large, ultramodern terminal on the outskirts of town; either take a taxi or walk half an hour. If you haven't changed money at the border, you can change at Banamex (open 9-1:30) at the corner of Juárez and Obregón.

by air: Aerovias flies between Belize City and Chetumal for around US$30 OW.

Sights

The best area to explore is the back streets, but the main sight is the **Zoo** (Zoológico Payo Obispo) along Ave. de los Insurgentes on the north side. Take a taxi or the ISSTE bus from the rear of the market on Ave. Héroes. There is a wide variety of wildlife indigenous to the area on display, from a manatee to spider and howler monkeys to ocelots and jaguarundis. **Calderitas**, five miles north of the city, is a great spot for a picnic. There are also RV hookups and camping. Public beaches are nearby. Isla Tamalcas, about a mile offshore from Calderitas, is home to the capybara, the world's largest rodent. With its partially webbed toes and coarse hair, it can weigh up to 110 lbs. Renowned for their swimming ability, capybaras are referred to locally as water pigs.

Accommodations

EXPENSIVE: A 15% tax applies to all meals and accommodation. Equipped with swimming pool and a/c rooms, the **Hotel Los Cocos** (☎ 20544; Ave. Héroes at Chapultepec) is the city's best hotel. Less expensive is the **Hotel Continental Caribe** (☎ 20441; Ave. Héroes 171), also with a pool. Less expensive still (approximately US$30 d)

are the **Hotel Real Azteca** (Ave. Belice 186), the **Caribe Princess** (☎ 20900; Ave. Obregón 168;), and the **Hotel Príncipe** (☎ 25167, 24799) at Prolongación Ave. Héroes 326.

BUDGET: Expect to spend about US$10 pp. Alternatives include the **Posada Pantoja**, Lucio Blanco 95, a half-mile northeast of the market; **Hotel Quintana Roo**, Obregón 193; **Hotel Baroudi** (☎ 20902), Obregón 39; the **Hotel Ucum** (☎ 20711), M. Gandhi 167; the **Hotel Jacaranda** (☎ 21455), on Obregón; **The Colonial** (☎ 21520), Benjamin Hill 135; **Tabasco** (☎ 22045), Ave. Zargoza 206; the **Hotel María Dolores** (☎ 20508), Obregón 206; and the **America**, Orthon P. Blanco 11. The **CREA Youth Hostel** is at the corner of Calz. Veracruz and Obregón (☎ 205255).

Food

For pizza try **Sergio**'s at Obregón 182. The hotels also have good restaurants. Another good restaurant under the same management is **María Restaurante,** which serves pasta, seafood, and other dishes in an attractive environment. The **Restaurant Pantoja**, at M. Gandhi and 16 de Septiembre, serves inexpensive meals, as does the nearby restaurant in the **Hotel Ucum**, M. Gandhi 167. There are a large number of cheaper restaurants, and the market is good value for dining.

FOOD SHOPPING: If you're driving your own car, you may wish to load up on food before returning to Belize. **Conasuper** supermarkets are at Independencia (two blocks west of the main drag) and on Zara-

The North

goza. Set at the corner of Ave. Héroes and Zaragoza and open 24 hours, the **Supermercado y Restaurante Arcadas** serves light food and sells groceries. If leaving by bus, you can stop in at the enormous **Blanco** department store-supermarket next to the bus station.

Entertainment

Discos here include the **Focus** at the Hotel Continental, Ave. Heroes 171; the **Sarawak** at the Del Prado, Ave. Héroes and Chapultepec; and the **Huanos Astoria**, Ave. Reforma 27. There are also a number of cinemas; check the newspapers.

Events

An international road race takes place annually in Dec.

Shopping

Shops are open 8-1 and 6-10. The market is well worth a visit. Located on the town's outskirts, the prison has a gift shop selling jewelry, hammocks, and other handmade wares.

Services

The **Tourist Office** is on Avenida de los Heróes, on the 2nd floor of the Government Palace across from the Parque Central downtown. The **Correos** (post office) is at Plutarco Elisa on C. 2A. The **Telégrafos Nacionales** (telegraph office) is at Ave. 5 de Mayo s/n. The **Biblioteca Central** (central library) is at the corner of Ave. Primo de Verdad and Ave. Hidalgo.

Vicinity of Chetumal

The **Chetumal Manatee Refuge** has been created off the coast; contact local travel agencies for information about visiting.

The **Lagunas de Siete Colores** ("Lagoon of Seven Colors") lies 23 miles north at Bacalar, which also features a 17th-century fort with a small museum. Also known as Laguna de Bacalar, the 36-mi.-long lake is the second largest lake in Mexico; its persistent breezes make it suitable for windsurfing.

On Hwy. 307, 20 miles north of Chetumal, **Cenote Axul** (admission charged) is a beautiful deep-blue watering hole, the Yucatán's largest sinkhole. On Hwy. 186, 45 miles west of Chetumal, the Maya site of **Kohunlich** (open daily 8-5) was built between AD 100 and 900. Its main attractions are the two six-foot masks in the Temple of the Masks. There were eight originally, but six have been destroyed by looters.

ACCOMMODATIONS & FOOD: Moderate **Hotel Las Lagunas** is here. Set on the lake, **Rancho Encantado** (☎ 800-748-1756; write Box 1644, Taos, NM 87571) offers eight *casitas* accommodating a total of 29 guests; they also have a villa for rent. Breakfasts and dinners are included in the rates. Dine at **Restaurante Cenote Azul,** which overlooks Cenote Azul on Hwy 307.

FROM CHETUMAL: Long-distance buses run to Tulum (four hours), Merida (five hours), and Mexico City (22 hours). For Belize, Batty buses depart daily at 5, 6, 6:30,

8:30, 10, noon, 1, 1:30, 3, and 5. The noon bus is an express, stopping only in Orange Walk. Also an express, the 1:30 bus stops only at Orange Walk and Corozal Town. There's an additional bus on Monday at 2. Venus buses depart at 4:30, 8, 9, 11, 2, 4, and 6 daily. If you want to proceed directly to Guatemala and Tikal, Batty buses leave at 2:30 and 4 AM for the Guatemalan border. Don't try to bring cigarettes and alcohol bought in Mexico into Belize; it's officially forbidden – although Belizean customs seldom searches you.

by air: Aerovias flies directly to Belize City. Note: West German and Japanese nationals require a visa for Belize, which can be obtained at the consulate in Chetumal.

Shipstern Wildlife Reserve

Established in 1981, this reserve protects 31 square miles and 22,000 acres of tropical moist forest, an area devastated by Hurricane Janet in 1955. There are also vast areas of savannah and the Shipstern Lagoon, which is sprinkled with mangrove-covered islands. Taking its name from the abandoned village of Shipstern in the reserve's south, this is the nation's only protected area that contains both the more seasonal northern hardwood forests as well as saline lagoon systems and mangrove shorelines. Wide belts of savannah – containing saline mudflats, limestone hillocks crowned with palms and hardwoods – separate the forest from the lagoon. Tracks between the hillocks show the variety and quantity of animal traffic. Shallow and barely navigable, the Shipstern Lagoon provides an important habitat for many birds, including migrants during the winter months.

Fauna

The area is a naturalist's nirvana with over 200 species of birds. Warblers, keel-billed toucans, flycatchers, collared aracari, and at least five species of parrots reside in the forest. Lesser scaup, American coot, 13 species of egret, Yucatán jay, black catbird, and blue winged teal fly over the lagoon. Other dwellers include manatees, coatis, jaguars, ocelots, tapirs, deer, peccaries, pumas, raccoons, 60 species of reptiles and amphibians including the Morelet's crocodile, plus innumerable butterflies and other insects.

butterflies: The butterfly breeding center at the reserve's headquarters exported pupae to Britain until 1991 when the operation was suspended because of time constraints. Because butterflies become quiescent on overcast or rainy days, it's best to visit on a sunny day.

Transport

GETTING HERE: A bus departs from Belize City around noon (from the Shell station on North Front St. by the Caye Caulker dock). The trip to Sarteneja Village is three hours (including a stop in Orange Walk), and the bus returns at 3, 4, and 6 PM. A direct bus from Orange Walk generally leaves at 6 PM, but you should ask.

by car: From Orange Walk, it's a one-hour drive. Pass through San Estevan and take the turn to the Mennonite community of Little Belize just before Progresso. From there proceed to Chunox. The reserve is three miles before Sarteneja.

Hiking

The **Chiclero Botanical Trail**, a self-guiding nature trail, leaves from the visitor's center. It displays three different types of northern hardwood forest, along with 100 or so species of trees. You'll see sapodillas, ceibas, and strangler figs.

tours: Prices are BZ$12.50 for one to four, and an additional BZ$2.50 for each extra person. Belizeans receive a 50% discount.

Sarteneja

Founded in 1849 by settlers from Valladolid, Mexico, who were later joined by groups from Tulum, the Maya name (tza-ten-a-ha) literally translates as a request for water, and this small fishing village (pop. 1,000) is built over an archaeological site. Situated on the largely uninhabited northeast peninsula of the same name, it once could be reached only by boat. The town was leveled by Hurricane Janet in 1955. Once this was the nation's boat building capital, but only two boat building operations survive today. The ruins of a 19th-century sugar mill stand a mile south of town. A bat-filled cave is next to the airstrip. The airstrip was closed in the mid-1980s after suspicions arose that it was being used for cocaine transshipment. Even today, it is alleged that boats transport drugs offshore for seaplane pickup. Locals can take

you horseback riding and canoeing down the river.

where to stay: Inexpensive 11-room **Diani's Hotel** (☎ 04-22154) is in Sarteneja Village; other – very basic – rooms are also available.

Blue Heron Cove

This getaway lodge at Catfish Bight is run by Anne K. Lowe, and she provides the best description: "This place is my retirement home. My family now consists of five dogs, five cats (good snake detectors), and a bilingual parrot. [It] is very quiet and not suited to those who like the night sounds of a town or city. The night sounds here are a Pigmy Owl, the cries of other night birds, and my five dogs chasing animals out of my vegetable garden. What I have here is 317 acres of forested land with about five acres cut. There is a lawn of sorts and flower beds with tropical shrubs. There is a house, three small cottages, and two large cottages, plus one that I use when the archaeology students who are working at Cerros come in the summer. Last summer there were 30 students and teachers. There is a trail of more than two miles behind my house to the ruins. Right now we do not have a proper water system so you will have to haul water buckets to flush your john and bathe, unless you want to jump in the bay. Although there is mud, white and sticky on the bottom, it is possible to swim. If you need to arrange transportation, Miro Tzul, who works for me part-time, has the village community phone in his house in Copperbank: ☎ 04-22950, best after 6." The five-room lodge is moderately priced; rates are around BZ$20 for dorm, BZ$50 s, BZ$60 d.

The Rio Bravo Conservation Area

Managed by the Programme for Belize, this 250,000-acre tract has been preserved for research and sustained-yield forestry. The plan is for it to become part of the proposed tri-national Maya Peace Park, which would also encompass the Maya Biosphere Reserve in Guatemala and Mexico's Calakmul Biosphere Reserve.

History

In 1989, the Programme for Belize purchased 110,000 acres in the area, and it is currently managed as a large, regional resource management and conservation area. An additional 42,000 acres has been donated by Coca Cola Foods. Nearby landowners have cooperated, so the total land under management is nearly 300,000 acres.

MAYA RUINS: Over 40 ruins have been discovered in the area between Gallon Jug and Blue Creek. The largest is **La Milpa** (see below).

Flora & Fauna

Subtropical broadleaf forest predominates, covering some two-thirds of the area. It has been a source of mahogany, cedar, and a dozen other hardwoods, so most of the old growth has been harvested at some time.

Mammals include 80 species of bats, all five species of cats, tapirs, tayras, monkeys, peccaries, Mexican porcupines, anteaters, and grey foxes. Up to 367 bird species live here, although only 200 have been noted so far. The best time to see wildlife is in June.

Transport

GETTING HERE: Drive here in the dry season from the village of Orange Walk near Belmopan (not the other Orange Walk). Ask for Iguana Crick bridge. There's a private airport at Gallon Jug.

For more information contact the Programme for Belize (☎ 02-75616/7; fax 02-75635; PO Box 749, 168 North Front St., Belize City). Or write Mr. William F. Burley, Director for Planning, Programme for Belize, PO Box 1219, McLean, VA 22101; ☎ 703-506-0175.

Accommodations

Stay at the inexpensive six-room Research Station, which offers cabanas and dorm-style digs. Package tours are also available. A second research station has opened at Hill Bank. For information contact the Programme for Belize (see above).

Chan Chich Lodge

One of the most famous "jungle" lodges in Belize, Chan Chich is owned by Belikin beer magnate and Belize Coca-Cola distributor Barry Bowen. It sits atop the plaza of an ancient Maya temple, a fact that has engendered much controversy in the past. The lodge is surrounded by rainforest and has some three miles of trails. You can also canoe and ride horses. There's a restaurant, bar, upstairs gift shop, and a small library.

The North

Opened in 1988, Chan Chich's 12 thatched cabanas have ceiling fans. Winter rates are around $100 s, $115 d, and $35 each additional person, plus 7% tax. For full American plan meals, add $40 per person and $30 for children under 12. The lodge's all-inclusive plan is around $135 pp d, $190 s, including soft drinks and beer, as well as a variety of activities and guiding. A pool is a new addition. Gratuities are additional. The main attraction is the fauna in the surounding forest. There are some 300 species of birds along with a resident flock of ocellated turkeys, howler and spider monkeys, ocelots, deer, puma, peccaries, and jaguars. In Belize, ☎ 02-75634, fax 02-76961; PO Box 37, Belize City. In the US, call 800-343-8009 or 508-693-0856, fax 508-693-6311, or write PO Box 1088, Vineyard Haven, MA 02568.

GETTING HERE: You can either fly or drive four hours from Belize City. Javier Flying Service offers round-trips from Belize City's Municipal Airport on Mon., Wed. and Fri. at around US$100 per person. You may charter from International but that will be more expensive. Chan Chich is situated in a remote area of Orange Walk District near the former logging settlement of Gallon Jug. This is south of the Rio Bravo Conservation Area and quite near the Guatemala border. The plane lands at Barry Bowen's farm, a few miles from the lodge. After you reach Orange Walk, the road is largely unpaved but in fair condition.

La Milpa

The area's largest archaeological site, La Milpa has some 84 structures. It ranks below only Caracol and Lamanai in size. It is midway between the sites of Lamanai and Río Azul, both of which were occupied from the Late Middle Preclassic (600-400 BC), an dis believed to demarcate the northeastern limit of the Petén's cultural influence. Much of the site is thought to have been built during the Late Preclassic period. Its center stands set atop a limestone ridge some 600 feet above sea level.

In addition to two reservoirs to the south of the Great Plaza, a 300-foot-wide waterhole has been found beyond the southwestern edge of the ridge.

GETTING HERE: The site is a three-mile hike from Chan Chich.

ARCHAEOLOGICAL HISTORY: La Milpa was first noted, and named, by Sir J. Eric Thompson in 1935. He speculated that it might well be the largest site in what was then British Honduras. Archaeologists David M. Pendergast and H. Stanley Loten visited in the 1970s, and archaeology officials inspected the site in 1979, following reports of looting, and again in 1985. During this period, looting (which mainly destabilized the ruins) went hand in hand with ganja growing.

Other surveys of the site took place in the late 1980s, and Norman Hammond identified Stela 1 as dating from the Early Classic period. Mapping of La Milpa, under the La Milpa Boston University-National Geographic Project (La-Map) began in Feb. 1992. Its intention is to map the area and construct a picture of the ancient Maya community through examination of the available plants and mineral resources. The site's relationship to its landscape will be studied, and excavations will be conducted. As the site is located in a biosphere reserve, an effort will be made to minimize the environmental impact. Other sites, on outlying ridges, are being investigated by a team from the U. of Texas.

TOURING: La Milpa's **Great Plaza**, one of four, is among the largest in the Maya world. Three buildings on its eastern side rise over 70 feet above the plaza. Structure 1, the largest, looms nearly 100 feet, and another building in the Great Plaza's center exceeds 80 feet. Looters' trenches are clearly visible by Structures 1 and 5. The Plaza's southern side is dominated by **Structure 8.** This collapsed masonry building appears to have 13 rooms, a number with cosmic significance for the Maya. To its west stands an acropolis with an enclosed courtyard; it probably contained residences for the elite. Stelae in front of the structures commemorate important events in the lives of the city's rulers. These date from the Early Classic (300-600 AD) and Late Classic (600-900 AD) periods.

There are also at least 20 courtyard groups that housed the elite, as well as two large reservoirs, which, if filled with six feet of water, would have held over 1½ million gallons. South of the main plaza, a second group of buildings consists of three open plazas juxtaposed with enclosed courtyards.

There are no stelae and only one pyramid in this area.

So far, some 16 stelae have been located throughout the complex; most line the eastern side of the Great Plaza in front of the pyramids. Mutilated **Stela 1** and eroded and broken **Stela 2** and **Stela 5** are probably of Late Classic origin (AD 600-800); **Stela 3** lies in the same area. **Stela 4** is believed to have been buried under looters' rubble and lies just north of Stela 5. The best preserved and least eroded of the lot, **Stela 7** has been dated to Nov. 30, 780. **Stela 8** stands in front of Structure 2. **Stela 12** is on the ground in front of Structure 3; it is least weathered on its lower portion and side. Pick out the legs and loincloth as well as the left arm outstretched and holding a circular shield. Uncarved **Stela 13** lies opposite the east end of the northern ballcourt. Stela 14 and 15 lie outside of the Great Plaza. While **Stela 14** – standing in front of Structure 16 – is both uncarved and split into three parts, highly eroded **Stela 15** has been raised to the front of a looted mound to the south of Reservoir A. Carved in Early Classic style, diminutive **Stela 16** is beyond the ballcourt's western end next to a much larger altar.

The West

Belizeans claim "the west is best," and visitors in the know will agree. Heading west from Belize City, the land is swampy for about 10 miles, after which it gives way to a vast sandy heath, once pine forest and now denuded through logging and forest fires. Past the capital "city" of Belmopan, the landscape changes, and the surroundings turn to "pine ridge" – stretches of pine-covered hills.

This area is easily accessible by bus from Belize City, with frequent service along a good road that runs all the way to the Guatemalan border. The Cayo District is extremely popular with overseas visitors, providing the "turf" end of what is termed a "surf and turf vacation." Cayo is also the stepping stone to Guatemala and the Tikal ruins. The Mountain Pine Ridge, one of its main scenic attractions, is less accessible, as are the extensive ruins of Caracol.

Belmopan

The devastation caused by Hurricane Hattie in 1961, coupled with a growing population, housing scarcity, and the lack of modern sewage and water supply systems, convinced the government that the establishment of a new capital city was a necessity. Begun in 1965, Belmopan was built with British grants and loans on land purchased with the Baron Bliss legacy.

The name combines the "Bel" from Belize with the name of the Mopan indigenous people, a group that successfully defied the Spanish conquerors. Like its hemispheric cousins, Washington D.C. and Brasilia, it was designed and built from scratch. With the main governmental buildings grouped around a central plaza, its layout is intended to resemble a Maya City. On the city's opening day, it had 1,000 residents, mostly governmental employees. Its population was projected to rise to 5,000 for the first few years and then onward and upward to 30,000. However, the population remains stuck at around 6,000. It will probably take another hurricane to make Belmopan flourish.

Transport

GETTING HERE: Buses leave from Belize City frequently and also run from Dangriga, Placencia, Punta Gorda, and San Ignacio. One way to visit is just to stop by for a couple of hours, heading for San Ignacio. Store your luggage at Batty Bus Terminal or at Novelo's. Z-Line buses are higher priced than Batty.

FROM BELMOPAN: Buses to Belize City include Batty's, Novelo's, and Z-Line. Batty Bus runs to San Ignacio (one hour, BZ$2.25, 28 miles) and then on to Benque Viejo and Melchor. Novelo's runs to San Ignacio and Benque Viejo from their terminal building. Z-Line runs along the Hummingbird to Dangriga and Punta Gorda.

Sights

The city still has an unfinished feel to it. The concrete government buildings, designed by London ar-

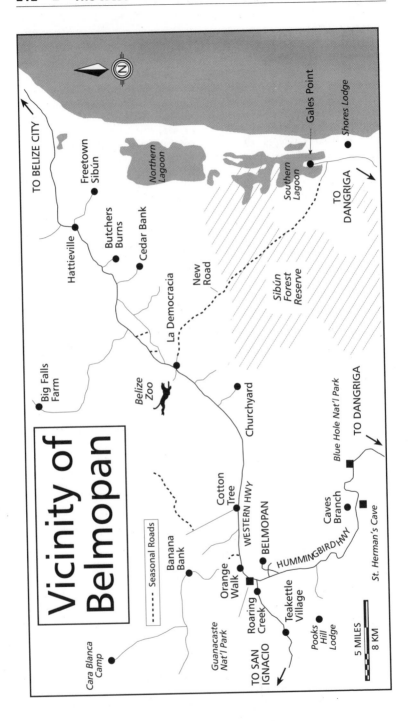

Vicinity of Belmopan

----- Seasonal Roads

chitectural firm Norman and Dawbarn, play on the Maya theme. The most impressive of them is the National Assembly Building. You can go inside and watch the debates when they are in session. The hideous painted "avant-garde" painted metal **sculpture** was donated by the Mexican government. One theory is that it actually a set of two giant magnets drawing Taiwanese to Belmopan.

THE ARCHAEOLOGY VAULT: The last edition of this guide reported that visitors could view an extensive collection of Maya artifacts at the Archaeology Vault inside the Department of Archaeology, and that ground had been broken for the National Museum of Belize, which would eventually display these Maya artifacts in all their glory. Unfortunately, the Archaeology Vault has been closed to visitors due to petty theft and staff cutbacks, and prospects for the establishment of a museum appear slim. Why is anyone's guess. The Department of Museums has been absorbed by the Department of Archaeology, and there is no word of where and when such a museum is planned.

Cynics maintain that some influential souls in Belize made a great deal of money from the export of Maya artifacts and such a museum – which would highlight these treasures and their importance to Belize's rank in the world – would be an embarrassment to them.

Accommodations

There are no true low-budget places to stay in Belmopan and, given the proximity of Cayo, travelers would be well advised to stay there. If you should need to stay in Belmopan itself, the least expensive place is the **El Rey Inn** (☎ 08-23438), 23 Moho, which charges around BZ$36 s and BZ$46 d. Its 12 rooms have fans, private baths, and desks with reading lamps. The restaurant has cable TV.

The plushest place to stay is the expensive **Belmopan Hotel** (☎ 08-22340, fax 08-23066; PO Box 237, Belmopan). Located at 2 Bliss Parade near the bus station, it features 20 a/c rooms, meeting facilities for up to 150, and an a/c restaurant and bar.

Located on the other side of town, a short taxi drive or a fair walk away, are the seven-room **Bull Frog Inn** (☎ 08-22111/23425; PO Box 28, 25 Halfmoon Ave., Belmopan); and the **Circle "A" Lodge** (☎ 08-22296; 35-37 Halfmoon Ave., Belmopan).

OUT OF TOWN: Located in Teakettle at Mile 56 on the Western Highway, 10-room **Warrie Head Ranch and Lodge** features a restaurant and offers excursions. A former colonial logging camp, it is now tastefully decorated with 18th-century furniture and has a variety of trails and activities including swimming, horseback riding, and canoeing. Its restaurant is a screened-in porch on the main building's second floor.

The lodge takes its name from a nearby creek whose curves appear to imitate the head of a peccary. It caters to groups, but individuals are also welcome. Rates are around BZ$100 s, BZ$115 d plus 17% tax and service. ☎ 02-77257/77185/75317, fax 02-75213; or write PO Box 244, Belize City.

The West

OTHER ACCOMMODATIONS:
Set on five landscaped acres at Mile 62 about 10 miles before San Ignacio, **Caesar's Place** (☎ 09-22341, fax 09-23449; Box 48, San Ignacio), is a cafe and bed and breakfast. The large rooms have fans and private bath. They are priced at around BZ$72 s and BZ$84 d; camping is BZ$6 pp. There's a swimming hole, and arts and crafts are offered. Well to the south at 30½ Hummingbird Highway, Palacio's inexpensive two-room **Mountain Retreat** offers a roadside bar, swimming, horseback riding, and fans in its rooms. **note:** Also see the descriptions of Banana Bank Ranch and Pook's Hill, beginning on page 217.

Food

There's a tienda near the market area and you can also buy food in the market. Most of the restaurants are right near here as well.

You're certain to feel right at home at the **International Café** (☎ 08-20203). Owners Dewey and Lily are former Canadians who have refurbished a wonderful home nearby, where they reside. The cafe has cappuccino, fruit drinks, sandwiches, and other light fare. They are a good source of information. (Closed Wed. and Sat.)

Also open on Sundays, **Caladium Restaurant** has a nice atmosphere, is inexpensive, and provides newspapers to read. Right around the corner, the **Chinese Bar & Restaurant** isn't very interesting but it is reasonable. **Yoli's**, an open-air roofed restaurant next to the Shell station, is the only nightspot in town, Behind the semi-circular bar are mottos such as "Yer, ya! Mr. Credit is dead! Dig?" If you arrive here on a swinging Saturday evening, you may find locals boogieing away. To the rear of Shell, the **Little Dragon Restaurant** has its name in Chinese above the door. Inside are the typical pinup calendar girls, two sets of Taoist deities flanking a tapestry portraying elephants on a rampage, and one of those classic, aged Belizean Chinese menus that appear to have been blockprinted. It's more interesting to look at than to eat there; there have been negative reports. **Circle "A"** also has a restaurant, as does the **Bullfrog**.

On the outskirts of town, the **Art Box** is an anachronism. It is an avant-garde cafe that would be at home in Taipei (where its owners grew up), in Paris, in Montreal, or in San Francisco. It is not, however, what one might expect in colorless Belmopan. It has a gift shop, art exhibit, and special artsy menus (designed by daughter-in-law Jill). If you have to eat in Belmopan, this is the place to try first!

Services

Barclays Bank is open 8-3, Monday to Friday and 3-6 on Friday. The **PO** is in the BTL Belmopan Earth Station. The **British High Commission** (☎ 08-2146/2147) is at Embassy Square. For information about agriculture, contact the **Agricultural Department** (☎ 08-22241). Obtain statistical data from the **Central Statistical Offices** (☎ 08-2207, 22353), located in the Public Buildings. They publish annual reports. The **Economic Development Office** (☎ 08-22526, 22527) reviews development concession applications. The **Land and Surveys Dept.** (☎ 08-224499) sells the same maps as in its Belize City office; it conducts surveys and holds land titles.

Vicinity of Belmopan

The capital is a convenient place from which to explore the Cayo District. A rough road to the right from the junction with the Southern Highway leads to the Valley of Peace, a UN-sponsored refugee resettlement camp, which houses landless Belizeans and Salvadorian and Guatemalan refugees.

Guanacaste Park

Where Belmopan Rd. meets the Western Highway, 52-acre Guanacaste Park lines the Belize River and Roaring Creek. The park area was originally the home of the British City Planner, who was commissioned after Hurricane Hattie to plan the relocated capital. He recommended that it be set aside as a reserve. Established in 1973, it was declared a National Reserve in 1988. There are four or five trails totaling about three miles.

Its centerpiece is the huge 120-foot-high guanacaste tree, which supports some 35 other species. An enormous variety of orchids, bromeliads, strangler figs, and cacti hang from its limbs. It escaped being felled because of the three-way split near the base of its trunk. Sadly, despite the park's name, there are no other equally impressive guanacaste trees standing, though you will find cohune palms, young mahogany trees, ramons, raintrees, hog plums, quamwoods, and a silk cotton tree.

Although not easily spotted, there are also jaguarundis, white-tailed deer, agoutis, and opossums in the area. The over 50 species of birds include black-faced ant thrushes, red-lored parrots, squirrel cuckoos, and blue-crowned motmots. If you gaze down at the ground, you're sure to see wee wee ants struggling with their loads.

GETTING HERE: Board any bus heading towards either San Ignacio or Belize City from Belmopan and get off at the junction of the main road and the beginning of the Hummingbird Highway – only a few miles from Belmopan.

HIKING: Ask for information at the recently constructed visitor's center. As many of the trees are labeled, the park is a great primer on the splendors of the tropical forest. Entering the park, proceed across the grassy field, then turn left for the trail that leads to the guanacaste. The tree, laden with epiphytes and bromeliads, resembles a one-tree botanical garden. It gives an indication of the area's splendor in the pre-logging days. Further on, the park intersects with emerald green Roaring Creek, the park's westernmost boundary.

Back at the park entrance, cross the meadow and head right on the **Riverview Trail**, bordering the Belize River, which runs along the north of the park. The **Agouti Trail**, which follows, runs into the Ceiba and Cohune trails. A nice place to take a break is at the junction of these two trails. **note:** Unfortunately, there have been muggings in this park. Always walk in a group or with a warden. Stop at the Visitor's Center.

The West

The Belize Zoo

One of the most unusual in the world, the Belize Zoo strives to recreate a natural habitat. When Sharon Matola found herself with a collection of animals after filming *The Path of the Raingods*, she established the original zoo in 1983. Sharon, a naturalized Belizean citizen, is one of Belize's most outspoken environmentalists.

Believing that exposure to the nation's wildlife will spur concern for their protection among locals, the zoo works to inspire community interest. One of its most important functions is community outreach. Children are educated about the local wildlife, and it's a fascinating experience to join a visiting school group if you have the opportunity. Many Belizeans have learned much about their nation's wildlife here and have benefited immensely. It's a wonderful place to visit.

CAST OF CHARACTERS: All told, there are some 130 animals here, including 18 species of mammals and 12 of birds. All of the animals in the zoo have their own names and personalities. You'll meet Betty and Bambi the deer, Tanga and Henry the scarlet macaws, Zuni and Inca the pumas, Angel the jaguar, Pancho and Gracie the spider monkeys, growling Sugar the ocelot (tigrillo), and other creatures – including a roadside hawk, a sleeping great horned owl that can rotate its neck up to 270°, an Aztec parakeet, and a woodrill that's so persistently noisy you feel like telling it to shut up.

The most famous resident is April, a Baird's tapir well-known to the nation's schoolchildren. April was originally discovered dying by a riverbank and was nursed back to health by Matola, who fed her fortified banana shakes. Her birthday celebration – featuring cake and entertainment by a clown named Rose Tattoo – is a major annual event here. Her 1990 engagement to a tapir from the Los Angeles Zoo was headline news in Belize, but the suitor was found to have inappropriate bloodlines.

Along with the proper identification (range map, habitat, food), handpainted humorous signs grace the cages. The sign in front of the peccary enclosure states that "We are the waries, and we like the way we smell." Another informs the visitor, "We are great currasows. What's so great about us? Well, first of all we are great looking!"

The Zoo's latest incarnation opened in 1991; it is spacious and entirely solar-powered. There are gravel walking paths and a boardwalk for bird watching, It also has a children's playground with a model flower to crawl through and an enormous climbing net where rug rats can fantasize they are spiders.

GETTING HERE: The Zoo is at Mile 32 on the Western Highway. All buses headed from Belize City toward Belmopan will stop here. Entrance (an extortionate BZ$20 for foreigners, BZ$5 for locals) includes an hourly personal tour. Pre-arranged student tours are free for bona fide Belizean groups. The Zoo (☎ 02-45523) is open daily from 9 to 4:30; the last tour is at 4. It's closed on Good Fridays.

VICINITY OF THE ZOO: The home of conservationist Dora Weyer, now the new solar-powered education center, is next to the Zoo. It includes a dormitory for visitors, lecture rooms and offices, and 140 acres of wilderness with trails. After the Zoo, at Mile 32, is the road to the village of **Churchyard** and **J.B's Bar.** British army relics adorn the walls. They have (reportedly) good meals and rent rooms for around BZ$50. **Cheers Restaurant and Bar** is farther down the road towards Belize City.

Monkey Bay Wildlife Sanctuary

This wildlife sanctuary (☎ 08-23180, fax 08-2333161; Box 187, Belmopan) is near J.B.'s, at Mile 31 on the Western Highway and named for its Tokyo nonprofit affiliation. It encompasses 1,070 acres of pine ridge, cohune ridge, lagoons, and wetlands. The Sanctuary runs along the Sibún River for 1½ miles.

There are over 250 species of birds. Pumas, peccaries, jaguars, and coatis (but no monkeys) have been sighted here. River bathing and camping (overnight is inexpensive; day use is free) are available. One of the trails (45 minutes) leads down to the river. Student groups camp here; there are no permanent facilities. In the US, write Monkey Bay, PO Box 31032, Seattle, WA 98103.

Jaguar Paw Jungle Resort

Named after the Maya ruler, *not* the jungle cat, Jaguar Paw Jungle Resort (☎ 081-3023, fax 081-3024; 888-77-JUNGLE; cyoung@btl.net) was constructed with quality as the primary concern and cost taking a back seat. Owners Cy and Donna Young spent years building it. It is

nothing if not singular! "You don't expect to see a two-story concrete structure modeled after a Mayan ruin in the middle of the Jungle," Young relates. "It is for people who want a comfortable living experience with proximity to nature."

The resort has 16 specially designed a/c rooms. Features include a waterfall in the dining room, a pool, satellite TV at the bar, and night binocs for wildlife viewing.

A variety of tours are offered, including one to Five Blues, a caving expedition, and other trips and hikes. The resort is on a private road seven mi. back from the Western Highway; the turnoff is at Mi. 37. Winter rates are around BZ$270 s and BZ$310 d, including hotel tax, 10% service charge and breakfast.

Banana Bank Ranch

One of the most unusual destinations in the nation is this ranch (☎ 081-2020; fax 081-2025; e-mail bbl@pobox.com; www.belizenet. com). It is run by John and Carolyn Carr, an American expatriate couple. Their specially designed, two-story house has many unique touches, including an intricately carved door and stained glass, both by ultra-talented Carolyn. Her remarkably detailed oil paintings, famed nationwide, show her love and respect for Belize, nature, and – most of all – jaguars.

The Carrs have a menagerie of animals, acquired largely through happenstance over the years. There's Simon the baby howler; Tika the jaguar, who might gently lick your palm through the mesh fence; Juanita the collared peccary; Bucky the whitetailed deer; Festus the spider monkey (who appeared

The West

in the film *Heart of Darkness*; and Joe the Toucan.

There isn't much to do at night, but John will gladly show you his telescope. Hoping to avoid the bumptious boozing that sometimes characterizes other resorts, the Carrs have instituted a BYOB policy with respect to alcohol.

ACCOMMODATIONS: There are five guest cabanas with private baths that can accommodate up to six persons. Of the four rooms in the house, one has a waterbed and private bath. Another is a special loft designed for younger guests. Delicious meals (BZ$15 for breakfast; BZ$20 lunch, BZ$30 for dinner) are available and are served in a new restaurant. For private bath, rates are around BZ$190 s, BZ$230 d, BZ$275 t, and BZ$308 for four. Group rates for accommodation and three meals run around BZ$110 pp, pd for eight to 30 people. Accommodation tax is added to rates. Packages are also available.

EXCURSIONS: The specialty here is horseback riding, with 20-25 horses on hand. The two-hour excursions pass through pasture and bush, sometimes visiting Maya ruins. John and Carolyn also offer canoe rentals and a river trip in a 15-foot launch. Trips to Tikal and other sites are also available. For more information write PO Box 48, Belmopan.

GETTING HERE: If there are two or more of you, call and they will pick you up in Belmopan. If you're driving, the all-weather road to the ranch is at Mile 47, Western Highway, across from the Silva airstrip, one mile before Roaring Creek Village. Follow the signs. It's 1.25 miles to the river from the highway. Once there, you'll have to cross in a boat, pulling yourself across with the overhead cable.

Pook's Hill Jungle Lodge

Jabbering toucans will serenade you at dawn and dusk at this unusual and distinctive "high bush" lodge. **Pook's Hill** (☎ 08-12017, fax 08-23361; Box 14, Belmopan; e-mail pookshill@pobox.com) is 5½ mi. in from the highway at the small village of Teakettle, 12 mi. W of Belmopan. Its name comes from the Rudyard Kipling children's tale called "Puck of Pook's Hill." The Snaddons gave it this name after purchasing the property from Svea Dietrich-Ward in 1991. Although they tried to find a snazzier title when they built the lodge, the name had taken root. After it made its way into the phone book, they started receiving calls from other Pooks around the country who were checking up on what they thought must be long lost relatives. As it turns out, Pook is a Mayan name meaning – of all things – hill!

Unlike other self-styled "jungle" lodges, Pook's flyer contains only pictures shot on location; there are no shots of distant waterfalls, caves, and ruins that require you to shell out an additional hefty sum for a tour! Indeed, there is enough activity on the premises and surrounding area to keep you happy for some time. Birdwatchers needn't go far, and the trails (although limited) should provide hours of pleasure. The property is surrounded by virgin tropical broadleaf forest that hosts innumerable birds and other (less frequently seen) wildlife.

Each of the white cottages has a Maya-style thatched roof that extends African-style, down over the walls – enhancing privacy and helping to keep the fanless rooms cool. The baths have hot water heated by burning cohune nuts in a central furnace, and each unit has low-wattage electricity, a double and single bed, and a table and chair.

Activities are not limited to guests. You are welcome to come for a gourmet lunch (advance reservations required), may swim in the large natural pool (on the Roaring River), or take one of their legendary eight-mile horseback rides.

Meals are among the best found in Belize. Vicky supervises, and she has a way with spices. Breakfast includes fruit, granola, toast, eggs, and coffee, and dinner runs the gamut from lasagna done Belizean-style, to beans, to a spicy ratatouille. Dietary preferences will be catered to (although fish is hard to obtain locally), and Pook's Hill is one of the few lodges in Belize where vegetarians will feel totally comfortable; the choice of meatless dishes is extensive. Delicious homemade bread and pastries are also served.

Two of their sons have gone off to the concrete jungle, but you may be lucky enough to meet up with younger son Jake (whose phenomenal boxed insect collection graces the central lounge area), or jeweler and iguana breeder Kara – if either one is home from their studies abroad.

Rates are around BZ$180 d with full breakfast; tax is added but not service charge. Dinner is BZ$30 per person additional. Outsiders are welcome to reserve meals.

From Belmopan to Dangriga

The bad news is that this stretch is accessed by the Hummingbird Highway, which, unless it has been resurfaced when you arrive, is a bumpy road. Moreover, buses using this stretch tend to be scarce, especially now that some buses are using the "New Road," which passes by Gales Point and circumvents Belmopan. The good news is that this is a lovely area, well worth visiting if you can make the time.

Blue Hole National Park

At Mile 45 along the Hummingbird Highway from Belmopan, this natural pool lies about 100 feet from the road. Steps lead down to the "hole," which is actually a short, remarkably peaceful stretch of emerald blue river. There's a changing room on the path to St. Herman's Cave, and a new **visitor's center** as well. It's great to swim in (although now limited to just five persons at a time) – or just to sit and watch the fish go darting about beneath the shimmering surface.

The nearest food is at the **Oasis Bar and Restaurant**, a short drive away on the western side of the road opposite the Texaco station. Offering swimming, dancing, and horseback riding, the restaurant is run by the Alpuche family.

The West

note: Thieves have been known to hide in the bushes and raid unattended, unlocked cars. A rape and assault on a couple occurred in 1989. The opening of the visitor's center should help to prevent any problems now.

St. Herman's Cave

Off the Hummingbird Highway and within walking distance from the Blue Hole, this dark cave has long passages and a stream. To get here, take the unmarked road, about a mile south of the Road Dept. depot, which leads to the west. After about 3,000 feet, take the path up and then down to the cave. If you are coming on foot from the highway, take the trail just beside the entrance to the Blue Hole and climb up the wooden staircase. Buses between Dangriga and Belmopan will get you here, but check what time the next one will be along so you don't get stuck! Be sure to register in the warden's hut at the Blue Hole before visiting.

Caves Branch Adventures Jungle River Camp

Run by **Ian Anderson's Adventure Tours** (☎/fax 08-22800; 02-33903, fax 02-33966; Box 332, Belize City; e-mail caves@pobox.com), this jungle river camp runs some of the most truly adventurous excursions in Belize. A privately owned estate, Caves Branch covers more than 55,000 acres of pine ridge and rainforest, with caves, Maya ruins, pools, waterfalls, and underground rivers. Plentiful wildlife includes kinkajous, margays, howler and spider monkeys, and toucans.

The camp is a mile off the highway just south of the entrance to the Blue Hole and on the opposite side of the road (Mi. 41½). Its screened and thatched cabins and bunkhouses lack private baths: you bathe in the river. There's no electricity, and food is cooked over an open hearth. Activities include tubing through three different caves, horseback riding, Maya ruin exploration, wildlife treks, and one- and two-night jungle treks, as well as longer guided walks and off-site excursions. Prices range from BZ$45-375 with the river-cave tube float at BZ$80, a jungle trek for BZ$60, an overnight caving expedition at BZ$150, and a four-day three-night "jungle quest" for BZ$375. There are a large number of others to choose from!

Camping is around BZ$10 pp; a stay in the bunkhouse costs BZ$230; and cabanas run from BZ$38 s to BZ$150 for six. Meals cost BZ$11 for breakfast, BZ$11 for lunch, and BZ$16 for dinner. Packages are also available.

> ☞ **Traveler's Tip**
> *Expeditions are available from San Pedro for around BZ$275 pp for a one-day excursion. Flights depart Tues. and Fri. at 7 AM sharp. Featured are the Ancient Maya Crystal Cave Expedition, the Ancient Maya River Cave Tubing Expedition, the Rain Forest Expedition, and River Cave Rafting.*

Jaguar Creek

Jaguar Creek is a "Christian environmentalist" project in the heart of Belize. As director Mike Egusa (e-mail jagcreek@btl.net) tells the story, "the philosophy behind the design of Jaguar Creek was to have as little impact on the local environment as possible. So here you do not see the cabanas in the middle of a clearing that has been carefully landscaped. Rather, you find yourself literally in the middle of it. There are many things about Jaguar Creek that continue to reflect this philosophy from the self-composting toilet systems, to the saving of office paper to be recycled into decorative cards, to the use of state-of-the-art solar energy systems. The academic program here, called the Global Stewardship Study Program (GSSP) pulls students from all over the US and Canada – mainly Christian universities – to participate in an integrative study program that is intense, strongly academic, and life-changing. Although we have limited space available for guests during the semesters, the off-times are available for academic groups and visitors to stay here at JC. You can visit our Web site at rgetearth.org for further info."

This "Environmental Research and Education Center" is near 10 acres of protected virgin rainforest that is owned by the Christian Environmental Associations's Eden Conservancy Program.

Currently, the lodge accommodates up to 40 in dorms and double rooms. In addition, there is ia a main dining and meeting room, a library and study area, and a burgeoning laboratory/museum building.

Five Blues Lake National Park

Five Blues Lake National Park is a 4,050-acre park whose centerpiece is a pristine 200-foot-deep, 10-acre lake fed by underground springs. Near St. Margeth's (or Santa Marta's) Village on the Hummingbird Highway and some 30 mi. S of Belmopan, it is accessed by the newly constructed gravel-capped Lagoon Road.

Five Blues is named for its varied shades of blue and green; during the dry season it appears to have five different colors. Orchids flourish on Orchid Island near one side of the lake, and there are hiking trails and a picnic area. The newest National Park, it was inaugurated on Earth Day in 1991. Leon Wengrzyn has organized the Friends of Five Blues Lake National Park here. The association aims to maintain community control over tourism in the area, a difficult task requiring endless writing of grants by Peace Corps volunteers. The village's population has doubled in the past decade, drawn by the citrus industry. But plummeting prices have created an incentive to clear land for cash crops and cattle grazing. Many are also turning to hunting paca (gibnut), which may put pressure on the species.

There is a bed and breakfast association here that will put you up at a very reasonable cost. This is a great way to have a truly Belizean experience. You may also stay at Tamandua (see below).

Tamandua Wildlife Sanctuary and Tropical Fruit Farm

Tamandua Wildlife Sanctuary (PO Box 306, Belmopan) is bordered on three of its sides by the Five Blues National Park. It's approximately four miles in from the Hummingbird Hwy. turnoff, which is three mi. from the entrance to Five Blues

National Park. Some 60% of the land is limestone karst, replete with sinkholes and caves. A number of trails range from short walks along creeks to full-day undertakings. The tropical fruit orchards contain over 60 species, ranging from carambola to soursop to pomegranate, and cows, sheep and horses roam the range. Accomodation is in three Maya-style cabanas along the creek; each is equipped with a private rock-lined plunge pool where you might find your bath shared with a duck or turtle. Four-poster beds are equipped with mosquito netting. Meals are served daily, and packed lunches are also available. Day trips and expeditions may be arranged on request. **note:** The lodge changed ownership in April 1997; contact the Tourist Board for current details.

Poor Man's Fridge

This small waterfall is at Mile 26 (from Dangriga), 22 miles from Belmopan. The peaks rising above are called the Sleeping Giant, and are found on the watermark of the national currency.

Between Belmopan and San Ignacio

Barton Creek

This traditional Mennonite community ("Old Colony" or *Kleine Gemeinde*) is reached by a locally maintained road to the east of San Ignacio. Here, women wear bonnets and long dresses. Their husbands wear long beards, drive horse-drawn buggies, and till their fields with horse and plow. Other prohibitions include garments with zippers (buttons are substituted) and the use of flashlights instead of kerosene lamps. While they may ride in vehicles and do use manufactured goods, no one will own a car. Don't take photos here!

The nearest accommodation is expensive 5,000-acre **Cool Shade Resort** (☎/fax 09-22146, Barton Creek Farms), which is set amidst citrus groves. Features include satellite TV and horseback riding.

Barton Creek Cave

Barton Creek Cave is Cayo's newest attraction. Although the cave has been known for decades to current residents of the area, it has only recently become an attraction for visitors. A local named David pioneered tours here, and others have followed in his wake. Sometimes too many others – it may be necessary to wait a bit before entering!

To get here, you drive through the village of Barton Creek. You may offer locals a lift (they will accept rides but will not drive themselves) and strike up a conversation. The cave entrance is beautiful. To reach it, canoes must be lifted up and over a rocky formation and then down again. In order to really appreciate the staggering beauty of the cave, you should have a car battery and headlight on your boat. If not, you can make do with flashlights.

Floating along in eerie silence, you will pass any number of weird and wonderful formations: stalactites and stalagmites galore, each with character and color. In several places you must duck down in order to get through. In still others, the canoe is a tight fit. At one point bats, burrowed in the rocks, are only inches above the top of your head. In other parts, flycatchers cry in the darkness. You travel around a mile each way down the cave.

There are two optional stops for the adventurously nimble. At one you must climb up and through in order to view a bridge and ledge with pots and skeletal remains. At the other you can climb up a bit into a passage. Both prove how true the old axiom is that if liability insurance were necessary in Belize, many of the nation's attractions would cease to be!

At present, in the best Belizean style, there is some confusion as to the tour's legal status. At David's instigation, each vehicle pays BZ$5 to a Mennonite family at the entrance. The community maintains the road at their own expense (and with no little effort, given the fact that they shun machinery). However, the landowner has recently sold the property, and the new owner has not been contacted yet. By the time you visit, this murky issue will likely have been resolved.

If you come here with Maya Mountain Lodge, you will likely lunch at the ruined abandoned house nearby. The story goes that it was built by a "back to the land" type couple from California during the 1970s. Being so far in, they found it difficult to make a living. The husband had to leave to work, which the wife did not like. And she felt that her children were growing up culturally deprived. Eventually, he began hanging out with his cronies in San Ignacio and not returning home at night. The couple left

and has since separated. It is this woman who has sold the land. Tours here are also available through David (**David's Adventure Tours** at Martha's Kitchen; ☎ 09-23647) as well as through other lodges and agencies.

> ### ⓘ *Did you know?*
> *Bats are the most numerous mammal found in the rainforest. Believed to have evolved from lemurs some 65 million years ago, they are the only mammals that are actually able to fly. Most bats use echolocation – a high-pitched sound emitted via their nose and throat – to feed. It echoes off objects, thus allowing them to navigate in the dark. Bats also pollinate many fruits, including mangoes, cashews, figs, and bananas.*

Spanish Lookout

The turnoff for this non-traditional Mennonite center (pop. 600) is at Mile 59; it's six miles to the north. There are two major poultry operations here. The Friezen hatchery produces 40,000 chicks per week using eggs imported from Gainesville, GA. Kept in incubators for 18 days, the eggs sit in the hatcher for another three days. The newly hatched chicks are packed a hundred to a box and sent largely to chicken farms in Blue Creek and Shipyard. Full-grown chickens are repatriated to Quality Poultry Products here, where they make the journey from truck to refrigerator in just 20 minutes. The plant's motto is "Dis Da Fu We Chicken" ("This Is Our Chicken"). It also processes some 50,000 turkeys annually. A dairy and cheese factory operate here as well. If you're hun-

The West

The Hawkesworth Bridge

Some compare it to San Francisco's Golden Gate or New York City's Brooklyn Bridge. Others call it the longest suspension bridge in Belize – symbol of the "twin towns" of San Ignacio and Santa Elena. It spans the Macal River, which separates the two. Its wooden deck was replaced in 1991 by a set of slotted metal sheets welded together. Named after the former governor who served from 1947-49, the bridge now has lights, as well as one of the nation's few traffic signals (installed in 1994). Tourists have dubbed it "the roller coaster bridge" owing to the clanging sound as vehicles roll across it.

What makes the bridge truly worthy of note is that it is single-lane, a situation that provides plenty of opportunities for the Belizean human circus to come into its own. Columbus Park, across from the Police Station, is a prime spot for watching bridge scenarios.

In the days before the traffic lights, the following were possibilities:

- Two motorists would simultaneously approach the bridge from different sides and one would yield. The other driver would express his gratitude.

- Two motorists would simultaneously approach the Bridge from different sides and one would yield. From one to four vehicles would then take advantage of the opening to sneak across.

- Two motorists would simultaneously approach the bridge from different sides, and each would race across towards each other. The one who had managed to cover the least amount of territory would fire up in reverse.

- Two motorists would simultaneously approach the bridge from different sides, and each would race across towards each other. Neither would yield until blaring horns summoned the police in to referee.

- Two motorists would simultaneously approach the bridge from different sides, and each would race across towards each other. The policeman would decide in favor of the car that reached the bridge first but had covered less ground by the time of gridlock. Tempers would flare, and the drivers would get out and argue.

While the traffic lights helped for a while, they soon began malfunctioning, which produced fresh scenarios:

- The lights go out for some time, and motorists return to the previous habits described above. They get accustomed to ignoring the lights and race across – only to meet up with a motorist who had the green light!

- The motorist on one side finds a red traffic light. Stopping, he waits and waits before deciding to cross, then realizes that the light on the other side must also be red!

Repairs are being done to the bridge, which means that vehicles must line up for an hour or so on each side. The bridge is closed for hours at a time, so a temporary road has been built over the river.

gry while in the area, dine at **Three Flags**, Mile 61. Those heading back to Belize City by car should take the Iguana Creek Rd. as an alternative.

Baking Pot

This little-publicized Maya site is on the grounds of Belize's Central Farm and Agricultural College. Mapped initially by a Carnegie project during the 1930s, it was given some attention by a Peabody Expedition during the 1950s and was excavated during the 1960s. In order to reach the site you must walk through the cattle farm's pasture areas. The two structures are connected by a causeway.

San Ignacio

San Ignacio, Western Belize's major town (pop. 8,000) is also called Cayo or El Cayo de San Ignacio. It lies in a valley – 72 miles from Belize City and 22 miles from Belmopan – surrounded by lush, rolling green hills. Set on the banks of the Macal River, a tributary of the Belize River in the heart of the Cayo District, San Ignacio's rewards for the visitor encompass Maya ruins, rainforests, rivers, caves, and a cornucopia of hotels and lodges with different price ranges and facilities. This hustler-free, relaxed, and prosperous agricultural center has fresh days and cool evenings.

History

The town probably began as a logging camp. San Ignacio lies sandwiched between two rivers – the Macal and the Mopan. El Cayo, its

first name and the one frequently still used, was also the Spanish name given to the offshore cayes. The nearby Maya town of Tipu was a center of Maya resistance until 1707, when its inhabitants were forcibly relocated to Lake Petén Itzá. No trace of the settlement remains today.

San Ignacio's earliest inhabitants were mostly *mestizos* and Maya from Guatemala, along with a few Lebanese who conducted trade with the area's indigenous people. Today, an expanded range of inhabitants includes Maya, Creoles, Chinese, Mennonites, East Indians, US expats, and Sri Lankans. San Ignacio has now grown to incorporate the neighboring settlement of Santa Elena, lying across the Hawkesworth Suspension Bridge (see sidebar). In recent years, it has been transformed into a tourist town, and the numerous travel agencies and souvenir shops that now line its streets have corroded its innocent charm.

Events

Usually held in May, the three-day **Cayo Expo** features a parade and motorcade to Columbus Park, live music, fireworks, booths, and events such as the "greasy pole." For more information, contact Mr. Godsman Ellis at the Piache Hotel (☎ 02-2032).

Transport

GETTING HERE: As travel here was once limited to either mule or water (10 days by canoe from Belize City), the town was isolated until the construction of the Western Highway in the 1930s. Today, it's a pleasant

The West

San Ignacio

1. Venus Hotel
2. Buses/Sand Castle
3. Eva's Bar & Restaurant/
   Tourist Information
4. Blue Angel/Post Office
5. Gas station
6. Mystic Moon
7. San Ignacio Hotel
8. Piache Hotel
9. Maya Mountain Lodge
10. To Cahal Pech Ruins

300 YARDS
275 METERS

San Ignacio Suggested Itinerary

■ If you have one day: Relax and enjoy yourself. Stroll around the town if that is where you are staying or hang out on your lodge's grounds. Do as little as possible.

■ If you have two days: Visit Xunantunich or Caracol, tour the Mountain Pine Ridge, visit Chechem Hah or Barton Creek Cave, or spend the day by the river.

■ If you have three days: Do some of the above and/or take a horse-back ride, visit Tikal, or birdwatch.

■ If you have four days or more: Do some of the above and/or visit Cahal Pech or El Pilar, canoe the river, or take a day trip to Melchor and/or Benque Viejo.

2½ hr. bus ride from Belize City along a good road.

Batty buses (☎ 02-72025/73929/77146) and **Novelo** buses (☎ 02-71160/71161) run from Belize City to Belmopan and then on to San Ignacio. Batty buses leave at 5, 5:30, 6, 6:30, 7 (express and regular), 7:45, 8, 9, 9:45, and 10:15, Monday to Saturday, and at 6, 6:15, 6:30, 7:30, 8:30, 9:30, and 10:30 AM on Sunday. These buses continue on via Benque Viejo to the border at Melchor. Novelo buses leave hourly from 11 to 9.

A good way to approach would be to get off the bus at the Belize Zoo (about an hour from Belize City) for a visit before continuing. If coming from Dangriga or further south, you will need to change in Belmopan (unless the bus travels the New Road and skips Belmopan). Although the bus is a good and very inexpensive way to travel, most lodges have pickup service from either the airport or in town. Ask your hotel about details.

Sights

Although it's a pleasant place to stroll, there's not much to do in the town itself. Recommended excursions include visits to the Maya ruins of Xunantunich and Caracol, canoeing up the river, horseback riding, and visiting the Panti Trail, and the Chechem Hah, Barton Creek, and Río Frio Caves. Hanging out at the Blue Angel on weekends is always fun if you like to dance.

But don't forget to take it easy: relax, read a book on the steps at Cahal Pech, commune with nature, and chat with locals. Don't try to do too much too fast. Remember there's always next time.

Accommodations

IN-TOWN BUDGET: There are new hotels downtown all the time it seems. Check with Bob Jones at Eva's Restaurant, 22 Burns Ave., for current recommendations. You might start with the six-room **Backpacker's Hotel** which is right above Eva's. The eight-room **Cen-**

The West

tral Hotel (☎ 09-22253), 24 Burns Ave., and the six-room **Jaguar**, 19 Burns Ave., are on either side. **Elvira's Guesthouse** is on Waight St.; it has rooms for around BZ$10 s, BZ$20 d.

Other low-budget hotels include the six-room **Hi-et** (☎ 09-22828) at 12 West St. (cor. Bullet Rd) and the seven-room **Riverview Hotel and Restaurant** (☎ 09-22166), 1 Wyatt St., next to the river.

MORE EXPENSIVE: The **Tropicool** (☎ 09-23052) has British and Belizean management, with comfy rooms for BZ$20 s and BZ$25 d; triples and quads are also available. There's a central sitting room with a TV.

The **Hotel Pacz** (☎/fax 092-2110, fax 092-2972; e-mail pacz@btl.net) is run by Pete and Diana Zubrzycki; it's at 4 Far West St. Rooms rent for around BZ35 d; they are famous for their caving tours.

The 15-room **Venus Hotel** (☎ 09-22186), 26 Burns Ave., is a reasonably good value. It has cable TV in its sitting room; more expensive rooms have private baths. The 13-room **Maxima** (☎ 09-23993, fax 09-23075), Hudson St., offers rooms with a/c (around BZ$45) or ceiling fan (around BZ$30). All rooms have cable TV.

The recently renovated **New Belmoral** (☎/fax 09-22024), 17 Burns Ave., has rooms with cable TV, fan, and continental breakfast for around BZ$50 s, BZ$60 d.

At 4A Burns Ave., the 12-room **Plaza Hotel** (☎ 09-23332/2040) is another option; it has rooms for around BZ$20 s, BZ$30 d; a/c is additional.

Martha's Guest House (☎ 09-23647), 10 West St., charges BZ$25 s, BZ$30 d. It's run by affable Martha August, who also manages the restaurant. "It's hard for Belizeans to get in these books, isn't it?" she asked the author. Well, Martha, here you are.

Run by Michael Wight, an American-raised Belizean, the **Snooty Fox** (☎ 09-23556/2150), 64 Price Ave., is an attractive and clean place to stay; it overlooks the river and has canoes, as well as a restaurant and bar. Rates are around BZ$35 s and BZ$60 d.

☞ *Traveler's Tip*

*If you lean toward small and locally run lodging, contact the **Cayo Small Hotel/Resort Association** (☎/fax 092-3231; e-mail daniels@ btl.net), which represents the Aguada, Five Sisters, Log Cab-Inns, Midas, New Belmoral, Rose's, the Snooty Fox, Venus Hotel, and others. They can help you with bookings and coordinate tours.*

UPHILL FROM TOWN: To get to one of Cayo's best hotels you must climb (or take a taxi) up a short hill. At 18 Buena Vista St., the **San Ignacio Hotel** (☎ 09-22034/2125, fax 09-22134; PO Box 33, San Ignacio; sanighot@btl.net) features conference room and convention facilities. It has also started to breed iguanas. The attractive wood-paneled hotel has a spectacular view. The staff is very friendly, and rooms come with fan, beds, desk, and large shower room. It can, however, be noisy in the morning. There are 25 rooms, a pool, and a basketball court. Rates run from around BZ$86 s and BZ$100 d; ba-

Selected Nature Lodges Near San Ignacio and Belmopan

sic rooms have fans; a/c rooms are substantially more expensive.

The **Piache Hotel** (☎ 092-2032, fax 092-2685; PO Box 54, San Ignacio; www.belize.net; e-mail piache.hot@btl.net) has a tropical garden that maintains more than 50 species of medicinal and nutritional plants. It is at 18 Buena Vista Rd., just up the road from the San Ignacio, and is run by the hospitable Godsman Ellis. Rates are BZ$44 s, BZ$59 d, BZ$100 for a/c suite (plus tax).

The **Log Cab-Inns** (☎/fax 09-22289/3367, 800-783-4400; e-mail logcabins@btl.net) offers six spacious mahogany cabins equipped with hot showers and TVs. They have a restaurant, bar and gift shop and offer tours.

Overlooking the city and run by the hospitable Creole lady of the same name, **Rose's Guest House** (☎ 09-22282) charges around BZ$60 s and BZ$80 d (plus tax) for attractive rooms in a congenial environment. A full breakfast is included and other meals are available.

Near the ruins, the attractive **Cahal Pech Cottages** (☎ 092-3740; e-mail daniels@btl.net) are available from around BZ$90 d. There is a restaurant, bar, conference room, and gift shop.

TOWARD BRANCH MOUTH: Named for the heavenly view at night, **Cosmos Campground** charges BZ$5 pp plus BZ$3 pp to rent a tent; sleeping pads are BZ$1/night. There are two gas ovens and other cooking facilities. They get guests who stay for a month or more. The campground is on the right a half-mile from town, heading towards Branch Mouth. The six-room **Midas Eco Resort** (☎ 09-22101/23172, fax 09-23845/23172) is on Branch Mouth Road. The lodge is comprised of four thatched-roof cottages renting for around BZ$80 s, BZ$90 d; less expensive rooms

The West

with shared bath as well as campsites are also available.

Santa Elena: Across the river in Santa Elena, hotels are generally cheaper. One good value is **The Aguada Hotel and Restaurant** (☎ 09-23609, fax 09-23573), 1 Aguada Ave., offering comfortable rooms with fans and handmade furniture for BZ$40 s or d; upstairs rooms are BZ$65 s or d. A conference room is available. It's a five-minute walk from the main road.

Off the Western Hwy. at Mile 63 in Central Farm, the **Grove Resort** (☎/fax 09-22421, 800-735-7273, 305-935-7273) charges BZ$200 s and BZ$250 d for accommodation in two-room a/c suites with refrigerators; tax is added. It has a pool, gym, landscaped grounds, a restaurant, and horses. Spa treatments range from massages (BZ$40) to jungle herbal wraps (BZ$90) and facials (BZ$90). Write Bob and Peggy Huffstatler, Box 1, San Ignacio.

OUTLYING RESORTS: San Ignacio has its own "cottage" industry providing places to stay for affluent visitors. Many "surf and turf" vacationers commute between San Pedro and here. With the exception of Maya Mountain Lodge, most of the lodges have been set in pastures, thus the nickname "cottage country." Most are hosted by expatriate couples and offer attractively furnished rooms, with prices to match. They usually offer cabana-type accommodations, typically with hot water and fans. Except for Maya Mountain and Windy Hill, none are within reasonable walking distance from town. That means you will be a bit isolated. If you want to try a lodge run by Belize-born natives, stay at Crystal Paradise or Clarissa Falls. Others may

have opened; ask at Eva's. (For descriptions see the following sections). Many of the other resorts are off the Benque Rd. between San Ignacio and Benque Viejo.

Food

Eva's Restaurant, Burns Ave. (☎ 09-22267), is the best place to socialize, to get information, and to wine and dine at reasonable prices. Bob Jones and his wife Nestora represent the tourist board in town, and they're chock full of tips. Bob says he "makes sure the tourist gets his money's worth." Try **Cayo's Own Frozen Yogurt** here; it's made by a Canadian family of Jehovah's Witnesses who have arrived to make the heathen see the light.

Tandoor (☎ 09-24221) is an a/c Indian restaurant offering authentic food at moderate prices. It's at 30 Burns Ave., and open from 11-11 daily. It has an all-you-can-eat buffet for BZ$17 on Wed. and Sun. Biryani, nan, and seafood dishes are available.

Martha's is a friendly Belizean-run restaurant that offers pizza, burritos, nachos, spaghetti, and other delights. Martha hosts a number of tour guides, including David of David's Tours. It's a comfortable place to hang out, and there's a guesthouse above.

Despite its reputation as a "Sri Lankan" restaurant, **Serendib**, 27 Burns Ave., offers little apart from the standard Belizean fare, other than a few (quite popular) curries. But, for a comfortable and inexpensive place to dine out, it can't be beat.

Located in Manta Plaza (right by where the buses come in) and overlooking the Macal River, the **Sandcastle Bar & Grill** (☎ 09-23213) is open from 6 AM to midnight and offers both Belizean and international dishes ranging from conch soup to ceviche. Batty bus tickets and information are available at the bar. Meet the memorable Remo.

Right in the middle of town, **Yesteryears** looks like part of a chain, but it isn't. It actually belongs to Windy Hill, the area's fastest growing resort. It's open from 6:30-11 daily, has a/c, and is reasonably priced.

Next to Scotia Bank and near the town's entrance, **Hannah**'s serves seafood and grilled dishes done up Spanish style. It's owned by the couple who brought you Nabutunich.

The **Mystic Moon** (☎ 09-3078) is a simple and inexpensive restaurant run by a US-expat artist couple who were married in Belize in 1996. It offers Italian dishes, broiled fish, milkshakes, and other delights. It is at 5 Messiah St., up the street from Eva's in the direction of the hill leading to Cahal Pech.

For inexpensive food, you can also try the restaurant across from the Belize Bank.

out of town: The plushest place to dine is the **San Ignacio Hotel**, 18 Buena Vista St., up the steep road to Benque from the town.

Around a mile out of town, the **Kon Tiki** offers American-style burgers and the like. (It goes through intervals of being opened and closed). Expensive, **Maya Mountain Lodge** is renowned for its innovative cuisine and friendly staff; reservations are a must. **Shal's Diner** is near the Maya Mountain turnoff.

The **Aguada,** popular with the locals and an excellent value, is at 1 Aguada Ave. in Santa Elena. It has good food and is about a 20-minute walk from the bridge and five minutes from the main road.

Finally, at Mile 58, **Mike's Paradise Club** is a popular and reasonably priced dining spot with has live music in the evenings; visiting musicians are welcome to drop in.

FOOD SHOPPING: There's a fruit and vegetable **market** every Saturday morning in town. There are a few other food stores but nothing large or special. One can buy produce from Mennonites at the traditional community of Barton's Creek (pop. 200) and ice cream and cheese can be found at Georgeville, five miles away.

CHINESE RESTAURANTS: There are no fewer than four. They are open all hours and are near each other: **Maxim's**, **Taisan**, **New Lucky**, and the **Oriental**. The last has the classiest atmosphere, with translucent flashing flower pots, poster girls above the bar, and schlocky music. Maxim's is the oldest and most popular.

Entertainment

Surprisingly, considering San Ignacio's small size, there are two major nightspots that are definitely the nation's best. Everyone hangs out every night at the **Blue Angel**, a great club featuring fairly good live bands, including the very danceable Blue Angel Band. There are a number of other bars in and around town, including **Amnesia**, a club with libidinously named drinks.

Set atop a hill above town, spacious **Cahal Pech** is world-class in atmosphere. To get here it's either a short taxi ride or a stiff hike up the hill. Bear left after the San Ignacio

The West

and follow the music; you'll see a trail marked for pedestrians. Try to find out if Gil Harry, who fronts Belize's best band, will be appearing during your stay.

Shopping

Eva's has a good selection of T-shirts and other items. Bob Jones here is an excellent source of information regarding accommodation, rentals, and tours. The Central Hotel next door has a good selection of things as do some of the other shops including the one run by the Windy Hill resort. Several shops in town near the river sell Guatemalan handicrafts at prices much higher than in Guatemala. Selling high quality wooden items and other crafts, the **New Hope Trading Company** is on the road to Benque just up the hill and past the San Ignacio.

☞ *Traveler's Tip*
For information on guiding services, smaller lodges, and other info, be sure to visit Eva's Online at www.webspawn-er.com/users/evasonline/ home.htm.

Services

Scotia, Atlantic, and **Belize Bank** are located in town. There's also a new **post office**. It's next to the Blue Angel and is open Mon. to Thurs. from 8-noon and 1-5; it closes at 4:30 on Fri. You can send and receive e-mail messages at Eva's (for BZ$3 each), and there will likely be competition providing this service by the time you arrive. The **gas station** is right near the town's entrance just as you come over the bridge.

TRANSPORT RENTALS: Contact **Maxima** at ☎ 09-22265 or ask at Eva's. As Bob of Eva's maintains, someone could do quite well operating a car rental service here. So far, no one has picked up the ball.

Tours

There are innumerable choices available. The cheaper way to go is with the local operators. David runs **David's Adventure Tours** (☎ 09-23647) from Martha's Kitchen. He'll take you to Barton Creek Cave or on a river tour. Competition is keen, and there are a lot of other options available. Many (ritzier and more expensive) tour operations are run by the "cottage country" set. All offer similar trips, horseback riding, river tours, canoe rental, etc. One of the best of these is operated by **Maya Mountain Lodge** (PO Box 46, San Ignacio; ☎ 09-22164; e-mail maya_mt@ btl.net), which offers tours with extremely knowledgeable guides to Tikal, Xunantunich, the Panti Trail, Mountain Pine Ridge, and other sites.

Others include **Chaa Creek** (☎ 09-22037; PO Box 53), **San Ignacio Hotel** (☎ 09-22034/2125), **Windy Hill Cottage Tours** (☎ 09-22017), and **du Plooys** (☎ 09-22188). Other reputable companies include **The Divide** (☎/fax 501-92-3452; General Delivery, Central Farm PO, Cayo); **Guacamallo Treks** (☎ 09-22076, fax 09-22060; Box 198, Belmopan); and **Mountain Equestrian Trails** (radio ☎ 09-23310, fax 082-3325/3505).

It has become fashionable to have your office right in town. The first to do so was **International Archaeological Tours** (☎ 09-23991, fax 09-22760; e-mail iatours@ btl.net) at 23 Burns Ave. It is a one-man operation headed by the personable Ramon M. Silva; his van travels as far afield as Tikal.

Slickrock Adventures (☎ 800-390-5715; e-mail slickrock@slick-rock.com; www.slickrock.com) rafts whitewater on the Macal river for BZ$190 pp from Dec. to Mar. Trips leave whenever a minimum is met.

Also right in town are **Yute Expeditions** (☎ 09-22076), 5 Fifth St.; **Hinterland Tours** (☎ 09-22475), 3 Eve St.; and **Toni Canoes** (☎ 09-22267), 22 Burns Ave. You can also find offices for **Crystal Paradise** and others.

HORSEBACK RIDING: Run by an affable German woman named Charlie, **Easy Rider** (☎ 09-2253, 14-8726, evas@btl.net) offers horseback rides from BZ$40; free pickup in San Ignacio is included. Her tours have been recommended by readers ("a great guide who really enjoys what she does"), and she owns the Central Hotel next to Eva's. Other alternatives include Crystal Paradise, Mountain Equestrian Trails, and Pooks Hill.

FROM SAN IGNACIO: Batty buses (☎ 09-22508) leave daily on the half-hour from noon-5. On Sunday they leave at 1, 2, 2:30, 3, 3:30, 4, and 5. Batty buses leave Belize City directly for the border at 6 and 6:30; they pass through San Ignacio between 9 and 9:30 and should meet the 11 AM bus to Flores, which will arrive around 2 or 3. Novelo's buses run from 1-11 PM.

Near San Ignacio

Branch Mouth

This is very pleasant excursion. From San Ignacio just head down along the river following the road for half an hour until you reach the scenic terminal point where the Mopan and Macal rivers merge to form the Belize. At the river's edge you'll probably hear disco music (often the tune "Jungle Life") pouring out from a compact cabin on a hill across the river. This goes on night and day, as long as anyone is home, ruining the otherwise serene atmosphere but reminding you that you are definitely in Belize.

Bullet Tree Falls and El Pilar

One of the largest Classic Maya centers found in Belize, the extensive but unexcavated ruins of **El Pilar** (Spanish for "watering basin," after the nearby falls) are seven mi. from the village of Bullet Tree Falls. El Pilar (e-mail ford@brass.org.bz) is comprised of palaces, temples, and at least 15 courtyards. One building rises 70 ft. above the plaza. A thick wall of unknown purpose, running westward from the site towards Guatemala, has also been discovered. Its relationship to Xunantunich is as yet unknown.

The earliest formal report on the site was in 1972 when the Archaeological Commissioner paid a visit after looting had been reported. Pilar was mapped by the University of California, Santa Barbara's Anabel Ford during 1982-84.

VISITING THE SITE: You will need your own vehicle to get here. In the village, cross the Mopan and then make a right, followed by a left, where you'll find a wooden gate at the entrance to a path leading to the site. Locals Teo Williams and Gus Manzanero have worked with Anabel Ford and can serve as guides upon request. The site has been left intentionally uncleared, so it still gives a sense of the wonder of initial discovery to visitors. Over 25 plazas have been identified so far in its 100 acres (38 ha.), and it is more than three times as large as Xunantunich. All in all, there are five trails ranging in length from 1/10 mi. to 1.5 mi. **Chorro**, a small waterfall, is about 1.2 mi. (2.3 km) E. Another minor center, named after the falls, is found here.

ACCOMMODATIONS & FOOD: The nearest place to stay is the **Parrot's Nest**. Fred Prost, former manager of Sea Side Guest House in Belize City, has brought a long-held dream to fruition with this budget-priced lodge (around BZ$35 d), which has innovative thatched bungalows on stilts by the river and near the forest. The lodge accommodates eight and has two separate shared baths. Three meals are around BZ$25 pp, pd or you can order individually. For more information, query at Eva's.

San Ignacio to Mountain Pine Ridge

Maya Mountain Lodge

Off the road heading from Santa Elena toward San Antonio, **Maya Mountain Lodge** is more integrated with the natural environment than the average Cayo resort. A self-guiding nature walk is in back of the premises, and occasional visitors include tayras, agoutis, and toucans. Be sure to use the trail guide. The more expensive rooms (BZ$140 s or d plus tax and 10% service) are in tiled and thatched cottages with porches. The less expensive rooms (with separate hot water bath – from BZ$80 s or d plus tax and service) are in the hammock-equipped Parrot's Perch Lounge. A two-story guest house (around BZ$1,150/wk. with maid service) is also available. Rates are discounted off-season.

A variety of packages (including a "Jungle Experience" and a "Ruta Maya Expedition") are offered. They also run a number of tours and operate educational summer workshops for elementary, junior high, and high school teachers. These include courses in rainforest ecology and Maya culture. They have a "Belize Night," with a Belizean-style meal and a lecture, slide show, or video on a Belizean topic; it's available on request.

The owner-managers, Bart and Suzi Mickler, are well-traveled, devout Ba'hais. Their specially prepared food is delicious. They are not vegetarians, despite reports to the contrary, and the staff is flexible enough to cater to your dietary needs. No alcohol is supplied, but they will serve your bottle of wine or beer if you bring it along. Dinner comes with home-baked bread, and coffee is available anytime during the day. Children under 12 are free. **All those who bring this book in hand will receive a discount.** For information, ☎ 09-22164, fax 09-22029; or write PO Box 46, San Ignacio. You can also e-mail them at maya_mt@btl.net or visit them on the Internet at www.belize.com/mayamountain.

☞ *Traveler's Tip*

*Just down the road from Maya Mountain, tour guide extraordinaire **Manfred Lohr** (☎ 092-2276; Box 1, San Ignacio) has a unique homestay under construction. He plans to serve fresh milk and eggs from his farm as well as fresh-baked bread. A refugee from the constrictive jungle of German society, Manfred came to Belize along with his English wife and settled down. For a time, they lived with the Mennonites, and Manfred can entertain you with wonderful stories. Rates are around BZ$50-60.*

Crystal Paradise

One of the few Cayo resorts operated by natives of the area, **Crystal Paradise Resort** (☎ 92-2823, fax 92-3075; VHF radio 147075), an attractive set of cabanas, is three miles from the Mountain Pine Ridge turnoff and about four miles from town, just before the entrance to Cristo Rey Village. First opened in 1992, the lodge is the concept of the Tut family. Mr. Tut has built many of the thatched-roof cabanas you see in the area, including the ones at Chan Chich and at Blancaneaux. He and his sons built the cabanas here as well as the ceiling for the lodge's attractive restaurant. The landscaped grounds include walk-through arbors and a path down to the river. A 100-acre reserve is across the river, and many of the plants and trees are labeled.

Meals are served family-style around a set of tables. Bread and tortillas are freshly made. The food consists of Belizean staples such as chicken and meat dishes. Efforts will be made to accommodate vegetarians as well, but it's not something they're used to yet. One of the best features of the resort is that you'll get a chance to meet the affable Tut family. Personable son Jeronie is one of the area's most popular guides.

Thatched-roof cabanas, which have private bath and two double beds, as well as hammocks in front, rent for BZ$150 s, BZ$190 d, and BZ$230 t. Less luxurious rooms with private bath go for BZ$110 s, BZ$150 d, and BZ$200 t; 17% tax and service are added. Breakfast and dinner are included in the rates.

A full range of excursions (including trips to Caracol and overnight camping at Laguna Aguacate) are available, as are fishing trips, rafting, river tours, and bird watching. Airport transfers are also available. In the US, ☎ 713-781-827 or 505-455-1021.

The West

San Antonio

The saga of the illustrious and world-famous Garcia sisters began in this small Yucatec and Mopan Maya village. Their artisanry began when Aurora, daughter number three, came upon a piece of slate while at work in a field in 1985. As if some force were telling her exactly what to do, she began to carve it at home. Following her example, the others – Maria, Piedad, Carmelita, and Sylvia – began to take up this nearly extinct Maya art form. Today, it has evolved to the point where one slate, which took all of them working together three months to finish, weighs 250 lbs. Their work is displayed in their charming **Tañah Mayan Arts Museum,** which charges BZ$6 admission.

The first edition warned eligible bachelors that the sisters had pledged to live with their future husbands in San Antonio and continue to develop their craft together. But love has begun to separate them. Aurora has married Ernesto Sacqui, Director of the Cockscomb Jaguar Sanctuary, and the happy couple are raising their children there. Another sister, Piedad, took her life in 1996 in connection with a relationship problem.

Feel free to talk to the remaining sisters, who are always ready to answer questions, and be sure to check out their gift shop. Ask about their 500-acre **Uxawal Reserve.**

Other than the museum, there isn't much to see in the village save the house of the sisters' uncle Dr. Panti of Panti Trail fame. But it's an interesting place to walk around. While in the area, visit the **Magana Art Center** – run by another (now married) Garcia sister Carmelita – which is off the road on the way back to town.

ACCOMMODATIONS: The Garcia Sister's **Chichan Ka Lodge** (Box 76, San Ignacio, Cayo) is the place to stay here.

Pacbitun Ruins

The Pacbitun ("Stones Set in the Earth") archaeological site is about two miles east of the village. One of the nation's oldest known Preclassic sites, this large ceremonial center dates from 1000 BC and has 24 or more temple pyramids, several elevated walkways, and a ball court. Before visiting, check in with the property owner, Mr. Tzul, at his home less than a mile from San Antonio. The surrounding hills accommodate Maya farming terraces and farmhouse mounds.

Green Hills Butterfly Ranch and Botanical Garden

At Mi. 8 on Mountain Pine Ridge Rd., the Green Hills Butterfly Ranch and Botanical Garden (☎ 092-3310; e-mail tfs@pobox.com) is run by butterfly expert Jan Meerman and damselfly expert Tineke Boomsa. It is open daily from Christmas thorugh Easter and by appointment at other times. Admission is BZ$5; two-person minimum.

Mountain Equestrian Trails

Established in 1986 and owned and operated by Jim and Marguerite

Slate Creek Preserve

Slate Creek is not a preserve in the sense one normally expects. Its lands include farm fields as well as forest, and its boundaries are being constantly redefined. It is actually an organization of local residents who have founded this nonprofit preserve in order to conserve habitats in the Slate Creek and Upper Barton Creek areas. It intends to train local representatives to make intelligent decisions on conservation issues as well as increasing involvement on a local area. An educational center is under construction. For more information or to make a contribution, ☎ 09-23310, fax 082-3361, or e-mail met@pobox.com.

Bevis, Mountain Equestrian Trails (radio ☎ 09-23310, fax 082-3325/3505; Mile 8, Mt. Pine Ridge Rd., Central Farm PO; general e-mail met@pobox.com, reservations e-mail Aw2trav2bz@aol.com; www.belize.net) is an acclaimed center for riding through more than 60 miles of old logging roads and trails.

Featuring Maya decor, the four thatched-roof hardwood and stucco cabanas have comfortable beds with handmade quilts, hammocks on the porches, and are lit by kerosene lamps. Commanding great views of the area, their open-air cantina serves as a restaurant, bar, and leisure area. The varied cuisine includes freshly baked bread and tortillas, as well as locally grown fruits and vegetables. They cater to vegetarians.

Their **Chiclero Trails Campsite** affords a true "bush" experience. Each of the eight tents is on a platform and has two twin size beds with mattresses, linens and pillows and is spaced for privacy and seclusion. Showers are in a common area. The dining area features a large tent with an insulated roof for indoor dining, as well as a Chiclero-style camp kitchen where the cooks use a traditional comal

(griddle) and fire to prepare excellent barbeques and local dishes. From here you may hike to a nearby pristine valley and up a meandering mountain stream to a pool at the base of a small waterfall.

MET also offers "Turf & Surf" packages and a large number of excursions, including a horseback trip to Caracol, caving, and overnight camping on horseback. MET conducts jungle treks and rainforest workshops in conjunction with **The Divide Ltd.** (☎/fax 501-92-3452; General Delivery, Central Farm PO, Cayo), a "Rainforest Resource Company" offering very special tours to the rainforests in the Chiquibul and Slate Creek Preserve areas. Trekking and rafting expeditions run from US$400 (three days, four nights). Room rates are around BZ$150 s or BZ$180 d, BZ$190 t, and BZ$210 quad. In addition, there is a 7% room tax and a BZ$10 pn, pp service charge. MET is at Mile 8 on the Mountain Pine Ridge (Chiquibul) Road.

Huru Kaan

Huru Kaan (☎ 09-2755) in Slate Creek Canyon is owned and operated by locals (who control and protect 1,600 acres). It offers accommodations in thatched hut cabanas. Rooms are lit by kerosene lamps but have hot and cold water. Meals are served. Rates (including breakfast) are around BZ$100 d. A full-day "safari" is BZ$40 pp with a minimum of two. Tours can be arranged. It's 8½ mi. from Georgeville; access to the final ¾ mi. is by four-wheel-drive only.

Blancaneaux Lodge

Famous because its owner is film director Francis Ford Coppola, Blancaneaux opened in 1993 and features luxury thatched cabanas furnished with Maya and Belizean handicrafts in a beautiful setting. Coppola has spent a lot developing its infrastructure – from the hydroelectric plant to a commercial-grade water purification plant for river water to a wood-burning pizza oven. You may swim in the Privassion River.

GETTING HERE: Expect to spend about 2½ hrs. driving time, or charter a plane to land you at the private airstrip.

ACCOMMODATIONS & FOOD: The five two-bedroom luxury villas are complemented by seven thatched-roof cabanas, and three small rooms in the lodge. The restaurant serves Italian specialties, including pizza and pasta, along with garden-grown vegetables. Espresso and cappuccino are served, as are wines from the owner's vineyards. The impressive bar countertop was fashioned from slate by the Garcia sisters. Rates are around BZ$220 s and BZ$300 d for cabanas and BZ$550 d for villas. Rooms are less expensive. A 17% tax and service charge is added, and

a 5% surcharge is applied for payment by credit card. A lunch and dinner package is BZ$80 pp. While a continental breakfast is included, à la carte breakfasts are additional. Expect to spend around BZ$40-60 for dinner, not including drinks. Rates are lower off-season. Packages are available, some of which include charter airfare. Contact **Blancaneaux Lodge**, Mountain Pine Ridge, Central Farm Post Office Box B, Cayo District, Belize; ☎ 09-223878, fax 09-23919.

Five Sisters Falls and Lodge

Five Sisters Falls and Lodge (☎/fax 09-22985; fivesislo@btl.net; www.belize.com) is located near the pretty, petite, and pristine waterfalls of the same name. During the few years that it has been open, it has gained a good reputation. Accommodations are available in 10 thatched cabanas; swimming, horseback riding, and biking are offered, as is a "moonlight madness" party. It is a 286-step walk down to the falls, which may be seen from an observation platform at the lodge. Rates for cabanas are around BZ$160 s, BZ$190 d plus tax. Less expensive rooms are also available. A conference center is planned.

Mountain Pine Ridge Area Lodges

At Mile 4½ on Pine Ridge Rd., **Maya Ranch** (☎ 09-22076, fax 09-22060; Box 198, Belmopan), a working cattle ranch, has a small guest house with a kitchen; rooms are also available in the owners' home. **Guacamallo Treks** is based here. Expensive **Mount Pleasant**

Hidden Valley Inn (PO Box 170, Belmopan; ☎ 08-23320) is at Mile 4 on Coona Carin Rd., on a 19,000-acre estate near the Hidden Valley Falls. Cabins have fireplaces, and there are extensive hiking trails on the property. Rates are around BZ$210 plus tax and service. Visits may be arranged to include a stay at the Manatee Lodge in Gales Point. In the US, ☎ 800-334-7942 or 904-222-2333, fax 904-222-1992; or write 1220 E Park Ave., Ste. 12, Tallahassee, FL 32301.

Nearby, on the main road, **Pine Ridge Lodge** (☎ 09-23310, PO Box 2079, Belize City) has Maya-style thatched cottages with private bath, hammocks, a restaurant, and tours. Prices run from around BZ$90 d plus tax.

Mountain Pine Ridge Forest Reserve

The branch road from Georgeville, 66 miles from Belize City, leads to this 300-square-mile controlled logging reserve, an enthralling area of rising hills and craggy crests, which are among the oldest geological formations in Central America. Caves in the surrounding area include the Río Frio Caves near Augustine. On the western slope of the Maya Mountains there are numerous caves surrounded by abundant foliage.

Twenty miles inside the reserve, at the Río On, are the 1,600-foot falls, also known as the **Hidden Valley Falls**. Across from the caretaker's hut at the overlook is the privately funded Hidden Valley In-

stitute for Environr
an aspiring resea
There is a four-mile
down to the base of
full day for the trip. Your
will be the pool at the bottom.

GETTING THERE AND TOURING:
There's no public transport. If you don't have your own vehicle, you must hitch or rent a car (four-wheel-drive necessary in wet season only). Two access roads lead into the reserve: one from the village of Georgeville on the Western Highway and the other from Santa Elena – running along the Cristo Rey Road and passing through San Antonio. The two roads converge soon after San Antonio. The slightly graded but bumpy road passes mango trees and cohune palms. Citrus groves are visible to your left. As you proceed up to 2,500 feet, a shimmering water hole is just past the Maya Ranch. Mountain Equestrian Trails is on your left. Then you reach the junction with the San Antonio Rd. The road twists and turns as you continue on past the forest reserve boundary. The thatched-roof huts along the road belong to recent immigrants from Guatemala. You begin to see scattered pine trees on the side of the road. Turning to the left, follow the road (off-limits for military vehicles because they tear up the road) past new-growth pine forest and termite nests, then past Hidden Valley Inn, which has its own path to the waterfall. The thick broadleaf forest gives way to pine. Another 2½ miles leads to a pavilion and lookout point.

The paths off of the roads actually function as culverts. The San Miguel Line leads to a sawmill. Oak Burn Line gives access in case of a

Mountain Pine Ridge Reserve

forest fire. Pinol Creek and Pinol Line are named after the Spanish word for pine. Granite Cairn Rd. to the left leads to the British Soldiers Communal camp, which has a large cairn. The **Río On Falls** are to the right. After less than two miles, a road to the left leads four miles (1½ hours walk) to a point over-looking the falls. Continuing on the main road, the Río On is an-other 11 miles. The river here forms pools before plunging down a gorge. It's an absolutely gorgeous picnicking and swimming spot – one of the finest in Central America.

The reserve headquarters, once known as Augustine – after a soli-tary *mestizo* who used to haunt the site – was renamed **Douglas Silva** in 1990, after a local politician's grandfather, who was the first ranger. The 30-family settlement has a grocery store, police station, and chickens strutting on picnic ta-bles; there's no disco, but the store has a boom box blaring on a table underneath a circular pavilion out front. The peak-roofed, low-lying sheds you see house pine seeds.

The Río Frio Caves are two miles farther, down a bad road. Another mile down the vegetation changes dramatically. Fiddlewood, hog plum, and mahogany emerge by the side of the road. Sapodillas are scarred from tapping. The Novel Line, which you pass on the way, is named after a now-bankrupt com-pany that exported gum collected from pine trees. The road to the small Domingo Ruiz Cave, five miles farther off the main track, is impassable by vehicle. There's also a short nature trail heading off the road to the right.

From the parking lot, a trail leads down to the main **Río Frio Caves**, one of the nation's great scenic at-tractions. It lies at the base of a small hill. Follow the river through the cave and out the other side. Sandy beaches surround both sides of the river on either side of the cave. Enter and climb for a view of the stalagmites and stalactites – some of which resemble a bizarre Martian fungus, others the clumped-up stalks of oyster shell mushrooms. Others hang from the ceiling, thin and wispy like petrified Spanish moss, or jut upward like the spires of a Gaudí cathedral. Climb down to the sandy base. You could easily spend a day here. Pris-matic light is reflected on the ceil-ing from the pond as though some Stephen Spielbergian creature were about to materialize. On the way back you can stop at the small **Cue-vas Gemelas**. The entrance is short and slippery. Follow this trail for about 20 minutes, hiking at a good pace, and you will come to another spectacular cave.

☞ *Traveler's Tip*
From the Rio Frio Cave you can follow a trail along the river, on the same side as the parking area, downstream for about 100 yards. The trail on that side of the river terminates and you cross the river to continue.

PRACTICALITIES: Camping is per-mitted at the Douglas Silva (Augustine) reserve headquarters, where a shop sells food and basic supplies. Although you officially re-quire permission from the Forestry Department in Belmopan, you may also camp at the Pincherichito gate near San Antonio; ask politely upon arrival. There's also a

The West

budget-priced cabin near the falls that you can rent by prior arrangement. See Mr. Green at the Forestry Dept. in Belmopan two days in advance.

Back in Georgeville and near the beginning of the road, **Back to My Roots** (☎ 09-24139) rents low budget rooms and offers campsites. **Sandal's Restaurant and Bar** in Cristo Rey Village offers canoeing.

Tapir Mountain Nature Reserve

Originally owned by Svea Dietrich-Ward and known as Society Hall, the 6,741-acre Tapir Mountain Nature Reserve is now under the control of the Belize Audubon Society. Located in the karst hills north of the Mountain Pine Ridge Forest Reserve, it has no facilities or services. Although the reserve has been selectively logged for mahogany and Spanish cedar, it remains largely virginal tropical forest, interlaced with karst terrain and Maya middens. To visit the reserve, you must be a credentialed researcher or part of a student group. You can walk in or go on horseback.

Caracol National Monument

Set in the Chiquibul Forest, this archaeological site's highlight is the beautiful Caana ("Sky Place") pyramid, which rises more than 128 feet above the jungle floor. Some of the other pyramids

are over 61 feet high. But the ruins do not compare with those at Tikal because excavation and restoration are just beginning. So if you're looking for souvenir stands and a sort of ruined stone Disneyland, then Caracol is not for you. Caracol is a spectacular Maya city in the process of being recovered from the jungle.

Lost for centuries and rediscovered by *chicleros* only in 1936, Caracol (Spanish meaning "snail") was so named by archaeologist A. H. Anderson either for the curving road to the site or for the many snail shells found there. There are thousands of large structures, with at least five main plazas and several outlying ones.

Originally thought to be a minor site, Caracol covers an area larger than Tikal, though it is only 48 miles away. Population peaked around AD 700, at which time the Caracol region held more people than currently live in all of Belize. It appears that Caracol spans two distinct Maya sub-cultures. For example, the practice of burying multiple bodies in tombs and placing tombs at sites is one found in the Maya heartland and not at Tikal or Tayasal to the west. In contrast, the burial practices as well as structural designs here mimic those found at western sites. Unlike other Maya sites, there are buildings that actually touch each other. Another notable feature are the many causeways. At least 700 years old, an enormous ceiba tree with wondrously huge buttress roots stands just north of the site's epicenter.

The most recent excavations, conducted by teams under Arlen and Diane Chase from the University of Central Florida in Orlando, were initiated in 1989 and con-

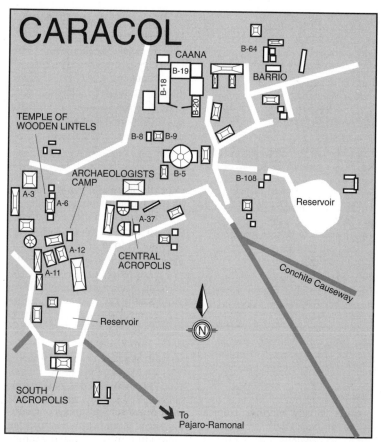

CARACOL

CAANA

B-64

B-19

B-18

B-20

BARRIO

TEMPLE OF
WOODEN LINTELS

B-8   B-9

ARCHAEOLOGISTS
CAMP

B-5

B-108

Reservoir

A-3

A-6

A-37

A-12

CENTRAL
ACROPOLIS

A-11

Conchite Causeway

Reservoir

N

SOUTH
ACROPOLIS

To
Pajaro-Ramonal

tinue right through to the present. The site is now guarded by a team of resident custodians, and the Belize Defense Force patrols frequently. Unfortunately, this has not prevented theft on a grand scale. One recent band of looters was driven off in 1993 only because they were stupid enough to light a fire. British soldiers thought they were peasants burning land to make *milpas* and came in to investigate.

GETTING HERE: Although far from great, the road has been much improved and is a far cry from the nightmare it was only a few years ago. You no longer need to reserve for a permit from the Dept. of Archaeology, but a BZ$10 admission fee has been imposed. If you don't have your own vehicle, ask at Eva's Bar in San Ignacio about trips; many lodges also run trips.

ALTARS AND STELAE: Altar carvings relate the tale of the power struggle between Caracol and Tikal. One altar's hieroglyphics mark Caracol's victory over Tikal in AD 567. A number of altars and stelae were damaged when logging trucks ran them over during the late 1930s on their way to the region's only waterhole. While Stela 18 depicts a feathered serpent, Stela 17 as well as Altars 10, 12, and 13 appear to depict meetings between Caracol's rulers and outsiders. These suggest that Caracol may have had contact with Maya cities in the Yucatán.

RECENT DISCOVERIES: Archaeological digs at Caracol are doing much to further understanding of the Maya world. There are more than 40 inscribed monuments covering a span of more than 500 years – from the dynasty's foundation in 331 AD through its 9th-century conquests. A ballcourt marker discovered in 1986 describes Caracol's defeat of Tikal in 562 AD. An incomplete frieze discovered on the Caana pyramid details a series of conquests and power successions.

ⓘ *Did You Know?*

Sir Eric Thompson, a famous archaeologist who dominated Maya studies until his death in 1995, believed that the Maya inscriptions were about gods, not kings. Said Sir Eric, "I do not believe that historical events were recorded on the monuments." He died in 1975 and so did not live to see his theory disproved.

There are numerous burial sites: close to 60 tombs have been discovered. A large tomb, unearthed in May 1993, may be that of a woman. If so, it may change the traditional ideas regarding women in Maya society. Unfortunately, this tomb is the only one from this temple that had not already been looted prior to the first excavations in 1985. Tombs unearthed here show that there is little apparent difference between the burial of royalty and commoners. In contrast to the Western practice of isolating the dead in cemeteries, the Maya brought their dead to live with them by burying them inside everyday structures. The Chases believe that Maya society included a large middle class, which may have arisen following the spoils garnered through Caracol's conquest of Tikal in 562 AD.

TOURING THE SITE: Two-hour tours are generally given at 10:30 and 1 daily when the archaeologists are in residence (during the winter dry season from February to June). The tours do not overlap. It's possible to see actual reconstruction of a site going on if you visit during the dry season, and your guide will be a knowledgeable young archaeologist. Caretakers give tours the rest of the time. Right by the entrance you might see a crenelated turkey or a pair of slatey-tailed trogons. The Caana Sky Pyramid is to your right as you come in. After being admitted to the site, you drive into the thatched picnic area. Don't count on getting any water here: it's in short supply. If necessary, you wait at this point for the next tour to depart.

You'll be assembled in a group and then leave for the ruins. The highlights are too many to detail here, but it's very much a tour of a working archaeological site. Along the way, you'll see a circular ballcourt marker that has been enclosed in a shelter. This is because one careless visitor kicked a piece of it out of place. The initial damage to the marker was done by years of logging trucks running over it. You'll also see the remains of the reservoir, which still serves as a water source for visiting archaeologists. Caracol is set far from any major water source, as is Tikal. The reasons for this are unclear. You'll also stop at one of the two replica stelae, which are copies of those taken to the University of Pennsylvania Museum. These copies were funded by the La Ruta Maya Conservation Foundation. You'll see a lot of beautiful old-growth forest along the paths.

The last stop is generally the Caana (Sky) Pyramid. From the top of the pyramid, you can can see as far as Guatemala. Many glyphs and drawings are explained during the course of the tour. One of the most memorable sights is a passage that goes directly back into the rock: an excavation by looters. Because the thieves knew precisely where to dig, they were thought to have been supervised by someone who had been the right-hand man of an archaeologist. Fortunately, they didn't find anything. The Caracol team extended the tunnel farther in and found the undisturbed tomb. As the site is not officially open, there's no admission charge. You can give your guide a donation at the end if you wish. There's no refrigeration on site, so your guide would likely appreciate a cold soft drink or beer should you have one on hand.

Chiquibul Forest Reserve / Chiquibul National Park

Split in November 1991, the Chiquibul Forest Reserve covered 714 square miles (456,000 acres). In order to protect the endangered species found here (forest reserves may be logged), 265,894 acres have been re-designated as **Chiquibul National Park**. Both the rare keel-

billed motmot and the scarlet macaw are found here. Said to be the largest such network in the Americas and one of the five largest in the entire world, the **Chiquibul cave system** is nine miles to the south and is part of the park, as is Caracol National Monument (described above).

San Ignacio to Benque Viejo

Cahal Pech

Situated west of the Macal River and commanding a panoramic view of San Ignacio and the Belize River valley, medium-sized Cahal Pech has 34 structures covering just over two acres. Given its natural setting, which offers such a contrast to the bustling town spread out below it, Cahal Pech is a real find for visitors. Discovered in the 1950s, the site was vandalized from 1970 to 1985, and was finally surveyed in 1988. Its name (meaning "Place of the Ticks" in Mopan Maya) was given during the 1950s, when it was used for pasture. This ancient Maya settlement has undergone excavation by a team from Canada's Trent University. While nothing spectacular, the ruins are a good place to escape and perhaps spend some quiet time reading.

touring the ruins: To get here, continue straight up the hill past the Hotel San Ignacio and continue on ahead where the main road turns to the right. The surrounding area is devoted to pasture. Entrance is BZ$3. You'll see a **Visitor's Center** (and its small museum) as you approach. The ruins have been "restored," which means that layers of

CAHAL PECH

Edge of Acropolis

North Access

Stela
Stela
PLAZA B
Stela
Stela
PLAZA A
PLAZA D
PLAZA E
PLAZA F
PLAZA G
West Ball Court
Stela
PLAZA C
Altar
East Ball Court
Stela
Stela
South Access

100ft.
30 M

N

concrete have been put on them so that they resemble recent constructions. Along the peaceful sidepaths you can see butterflies and birds.

Most of the buildings are grouped around seven plazas. **Structure A-1** is the tallest, at 77 feet. Although **Plaza A** is the site's center, **Plaza B** is the largest. Six plain stelae, two ball courts, and an altar have been unearthed. Climb on top of **Structure 9**, which has been topped off with concrete. Cahal Pech differs from many other sites in that you can see the remains of **residences**. You'll find these in the relatively more spacious Plazas B, C, and F.

Windy Hill Cottages

Set at Graceland Ranch, expensive **Windy Hill Cottages** (☎ 800-Windy-95, 09-22017, fax 092-3080; e-mail windyhill@btl.net; www.belize.net) are at Mile 1½,

Benque Viejo Rd. and is one of the more popular lodges. Facilities here include table tennis, a pool table, TV, and hammocks. Less adventurous visitors who value their creature comforts and desire a familiar environment will be happiest here.

Chaa Creek Cottages

Chaa Creek Cottages (☎ 09-22037, fax 09-22501; PO Box 53, San Ignacio, Cayo), one of Cayo's premier nature lodges, is on the shores of the Macal River to the west of San Ignacio. It first opened in 1981 and is operated by Mick and Lucy Fleming. Chaa Creek features elegant accommodations. Romantically lit by lamps, the resort's adobe and wood-walled, palm-thatched cottages are decorated with Maya weavings. The 10 units have two rooms each. Field trails are marked near the lodge and some pass by Maya ruins. Chaa Creek opened a new **Natural History Center** and its small **Blue Morpho Butterfly Breeding Center** in 1996.

The famous **Panti Trail** borders the lodge. Chaa Creek operates three programs: Belize Explorer, Belize Adventure, and Inland Expeditions. In addition to river canoeing, trips run everywhere from Xunantunich to Caracol and the Chiquibul area, where they have a remote camp. Rates run from around BZ$200 s and BZ$230 d. BZ$10 pp service charge and tax are added; a 5% surcharge is applied on credit cards. Expect to spend around BZ$15 for breakfast, around the same for a boxed lunch (restaurant meals are also available), and around BZ$50 for dinner. Their all-inclusive rate (accommodations, meals, and activities) is around BZ$250 per person per day with a three-day minimum.

The Macal River Camp: Owned and operated by Chaa Creek, the Macal River Camp has been designed with students and adventurers in mind. It has 10 raised covered wooden platforms, which have tents with cots, chairs and bed linens. Meals are served at the thatched recreation and dining center. The camp offers courses on rainforest ecology and has hiking trails nearby. Rates around BZ$100 pp, pd, not including taxes.

Panti Trail

Named after the Mayan healer Eligio Panti, the trail (☎ 08-231280, fax 08-23235) is located at Ix Chel, a farm owned by American expatriate and Panti follower Dr.

Rosita Arvigo and her husband, Dr. Greg Shropshire. It is right next to Chaa Creek cottages and can be reached by boat or by taxi from San Ignacio. The trail's most remarkable feature is that all the plants and trees along it were found *in situ*, that, is none of them were planted by Rosita. This in itself best illustrates the natural biological diversity found in the rainforests.

Along the path are jackass bitters, cohune palm, hogplum, basket tie tie bay, cockspur (acacia), bullet tree, Spanish elder, bay cedar, and chico loro vine (used as a purgative). Brought back to Europe by returning sailors, the bark of the negrito, or "dysentery bark," was sold for its weight in gold in European apothecaries for over two centuries. Various trees have products displayed to illustrate their uses. In reference to its Spanish name of *escoba*, the "give and take" has a broom (made by Dr. Panti himself using leaves from the tree) next to it. It is so named because, while it will wound you with its spikes, the fibers from the base of its leaves will staunch the flow. There is copal, with some varnish, the allspice (once used as embalming fluid), wild pineapple, wild grapevine, which serves as a water source, bullhoof, used in birth control, fiddlewood, used by Maya for making musical instruments (its name comes from the Latin *fidele*, indicating toughness). The white ramon or breadnut was a staple for the ancient Maya.

Controversial to say the least is Rosita's "Doctrine of Signatures," which maintains that a plant has been marked by some supernatural power to indicate how mankind might use it. Examples of this, she claims, are the cocol meca, whose heart-shaped root vines branch out as if they were arteries, and which can be used to cleanse your blood. Another example is poisonwood, whose black oozing resin warns of its toxicity. Also on the premises is a reconstruction of a typical healer's hut with all of the necessary utensils. The gift shop offers a variety of herbs, tinctures, and other souvenirs.

Terra Nova: Dr. Arvigo's Belize Association of Traditional Healers (fax 09-22057) supervises the 6,000-acre Terra Nova Medicinal Plant Reserve in the Yalbac Hills. The intention is to transplant medicinal plant seedlings that are endangered in other areas. Medicinal healers will cull the reserve in a sustainable fashion, and field trips will be conducted.

about the owners: Drs. Rosita Arvigo and Greg Shropshire are narapaths, graduates of the Chicago National College of Narapathy, a Czechoslovakian combination of folk medicine and modern chiropractic. Rosita apprenticed for 10 years with Dr. Panti, an elderly Maya *curandero* (healer) in San Antonio, who introduced her to the local herbs.

Rosita and her husband are currently studying local remedies in collaboration with the New York Botanical Garden and accumulating medicinal plants for the National Cancer Insititute's program, which is searching for AIDS and cancer cures. They also offer a number of seminars every summer. For more information, write Rosita Arvigo, General Delivery, San Ignacio, Cayo or ☎ 09-23870.

GETTING HERE: If you're staying at Chaa Creek, it's a short walk. If you have your own vehicle, it's an easy drive. Otherwise you have three choices: 1) rent a canoe and come on your own, 2) take public transportation to Chaa Creek and make the long walk in or hitch, or 3) go on a tour – in which case you'll go upriver in a canoe, motorized or not as you prefer. The river trip is one of the most beautiful in Belize and is highly recommended. Maya Mountain (☎ 09-22164) and many others arrange tours.

Black Rock

Owned by Caesar Sherard who also operates Caesar's Place, former "eco-lodge" Black Rock has grown more and more conventional with each passing year. Tents have been replaced by thatched-roof cabins, which are now getting regular roofs. The solar-powered resort has cottage accommodations (BZ$84 d), along with an open-air dining pavilion. Rooms in the more expensive Slate Lodge are BZ$120 d. Activities offered include hiking, horseback riding, canoeing, and excursions. Camping (BZ$10 pp) is also available, as are RV hookups. To get here, turn off at the Chaa Creek junction and follow the signs. Caesar put in a highly controversial road here in 1997. In the process, he destroyed part of the trail to Vaca Falls. (You must pass through his property, opening and closing barbed wire fences, in order to reach Vaca Falls.) Caesar's view is that eco-tourism is "nonsense" and that he needed the road to attract visitors. For more information ☎ 09-22341, fax 09-23449, or write Box 48, San Ignacio.

Ek' Tun

Billed as "a distinctive destination for discriminating adventurers," Ek' Tun (Maya for "Black Rock") is an intimate nature lodge set below a 200-acre reserve. To get here you must drive and then cross the river by boat; there is no direct road access. It is run by Ken and Phyllis Dart, former Coloradians who have made a new life for themselves in Belize. They labored for over five years to build the resort, living in a tent and hauling in all materials and goods by boat. The impressive result (world class by any standards) are two lovely thatched-roof cabanas and a main dining area and lounge where the Darts also live. The view is spectacular, one of the prettiest in Belize. You look down into the Macal river basin and gaze across at towering hills with open limestone cave entrances. The water supply comes from pumps next to a small, pretty waterfall. There is a small sand beach down by the river. It is intended as a small paradise – a retreat for honeymooners and for those who need to relax.

If you can afford it, you should stay here for at least three nights, and preferably longer. Ken and Phyllis see Ek'Tun as a destination in itself rather than as a base camp from which to explore the wider Cayo area. What you pay for here is the luxury of isolation in a lovely environment with gourmet cooking. However, they offer a wide variety of tours and excursions ranging as far afield as Tikal. Were the author staying here, the only trips he would make would be one of Ken's delightful guided hikes (which are full of surprises) and possibly a hike to Vaca Falls. The surrounding area is rife with Maya ruins traversed by hiking trails though lush secondary forest. You are unlikely to see many mammals, but there are hundreds of species of birds, including the snowy egret, the collared aracari, and the rare spectacled owl.

Finely crafted meals are cooked with fresh vegetables gathered from the garden. Phyllis is a talented cook who will try to meet your needs and tastes.

The cabin holds up to four comfortably: a double bed downstairs and one up the stairs; a third single bed can be supplied upon request. Rates are around BZ$305 s, BZ$450 d, BZ$570 t, and BZ$700 quad, including tax and three meals. There is a two-night minimum stay (which may soon change to a three-night minimum). Children ages 2-12 are charged $32.50 pp pd. Pickups in the Darts' Land Rover are available. For reservations and further information, in the US, ☎/fax 303-442-6150, PO Box 20935, Boulder, CO 80308-3935; or write c/o General Delivery, Benque Viejo, Cayo, ☎ 091-2002 (cellular). In the US, e-mail ektunbelize@msn.com; in Belize, e-mail ektunbz@btl.net. Their Web page is www.ektunbelize.com.

> 66 **Reader's Comment**
> *"I cannot recommend Ek'Tun highly enough. The food is out of this world, especially considering the difficulty of obtaining and transporting everything from San Ignacio." – J.E.B.*

du Plooy's

A quiet, exclusive 12-room resort, du Plooy's (☎/fax 09-23301, in the US 800-359-0747) is at Big Eddy on

The West

the river's edge. Since opening in 1989, they have launched a reforestation project – planting over 2,500 trees in the their original 20 acres. A botanical garden and tropical fruit orchard is planned for an additional 40 acres. All rooms have generator-powered fans; kerosene lamps are provided for use after the generator shuts off at 10 PM.

They have a variety of rooms. The least expensive rooms are in "The Pink House," a six-bedroom and two-bath guest house. They rent for BZ$60s, BZ$80 d, and BZ$100 t, plus tax. The entire house is also available for rent. "The Jungle Lodge" is luxury-priced, and three bungalows – designed to resemble deluxe vacation villas – are also available in that same price range. Horses and canoes are for rent, and custom-planned tours can be arranged.

Nabitunich Lodge

A 400-acre cattle farm, Nabitunich Lodge (☎ 093-2096/2309, fax 093-3096; Central Post Office, San Lorenzo Farm, Cayo) is run by a British-Belizean couple. This set of eight thatched-roof cabanas with either stone or white stucco walls is an easy walk from the road. The lodge originally was built to house doctors coming from the US to do volunteer work. Horseback riding is available, there's good birdwatching, and you can cool off in the river. Rates start at around BZ$90 pp, with dinner and breakfast; tax is included.

Clarissa Falls

Near the falls of the same name and run by a local woman, the simple and inexpensive three-cottage Clarissa Falls Cabins (☎ 093-2424; Box 44, San Ignacio) are off of Mile 5½, Benque Viejo Rd. Meals are served under a thatched-roof pavilion.

Vaca Falls

These attractive low-lying falls are about nine miles south of San Ignacio on the east branch of the Belize River, surrounded by karst hills. Difficult, but worth it. Take the Negroman Farms road from Chial, turning off the road before San José Succotz. It's a two-hour walk to the falls. It used to be a beautiful trail but much of it has been turned into a road by a man who required access to his "eco" lodge. A second approach is via Chechem Ha (see below).

Xunantunich

The famous Mayan ruins of Xunantunich mean "Maiden of the Rock." The site was named after the Maya maiden seen, according to legend, by one of the temple's earliest visitors after its discovery. Following a pattern established in 16th-century Spanish, the Maya "X" is pronounced "sh." Thus, the site is pronounced "Shoo NAN-too-NEECH." Stress is on the last syllable, as in all Maya words.

To reach the ruins, you cross the Mopan River using the hand-pulled cable **ferry** about 10 minutes walk from the village of Succotz. The ferry (free of charge) operates daily from 8 to 5, with a break from noon to 1. If you're coming from Benque Viejo, it's a peaceful and pleasant walk along the river, past women washing clothes, marred only by the occasional pile of garbage and a vine-covered overturned car – a re-

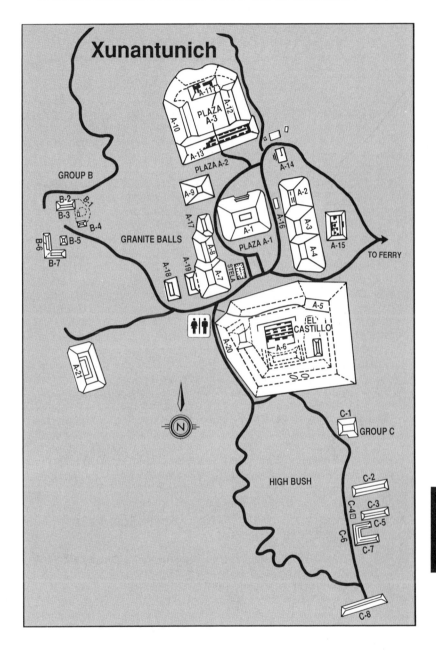

Xunantunich

minder of the perils of the road. From the ferry stop it's a 20-minute walk uphill along a thickly forested paved road to the top.

From the entrance, there's one large site you can climb. Then you pass by a couple of stelae, so worn and weathered as to be indecipherable. In **Plaza A-1** there's a pavilion sheltering three well-worn horizontal stelae with barely decipherable carvings of warriors. From here you can climb **El Castillo**, following a trail that winds back and forth along its face. There are stairs to the front, steps to the huge, ornate glyphs, representing jaguars, on the side. One set of stairs leads up to the top. From here, the towers that give El Castillo its name resemble coke chimneys. Back down at the base, you can walk to the right, down to the remains of a ball field and farther on to the residential area excavated by Jes Thompson.

HISTORY: Xunantunich was first explored in the 1890s by British medical officer Thomas Gann. The Peabody Museum's Teobalt Maler photographed El Castillo in 1904. Returning in 1924, Gann unearthed large numbers of buried items and made off with the carved glyphs of Altar 1, which have since disappeared.

It was excavated again in 1938 by archaeologist Jes Thompson. Although a Cambridge University team exploring the site in 1959-60 surmised that a 900 AD earthquake apparently precipitated its abandonment, discoveries in 1993 show that it survived and apparently prospered until around AD 1100. The fact that it was on a river (as with Lamanai) may have helped it to survive longer than other such sites. Recent excavations have

cleared the preserved sections on the western side of the building, which match the famous one found on the east side. Dangerous cracks have been uncovered, and steps are being taken to strengthen the structure. The southern group has now been opened up, and three stelae are now housed in the Visitor's Center.

LAYOUT: Three adjacent plazas run from north to south along its center. Rising at the southern end is 130-foot-high El Castillo, an enormous pyramid that even today is the tallest building in all Belize, save for the Sky Palace at Caracol to the south. Most of the friezes have been destroyed by natural elements. A 9th-century one that shows through from a previous layer, uncovered by archaeologists but intentionally covered by the Maya, has carvings representing astronomical symbols including the Sun, Moon and Venus. All of these can be seen in the east during the morning hours. The mask with the "big ears" and the ornaments represents the Sun God. The sign for the moon is next, and the border's signs stand for Venus and the different days.

San José Succotz

The village of San José Succotz is named after the succotz trees found here. The big fiestas here are St. Joseph (March 19) and the Holy Cross (May 3). The local dances ("hog head," "mañanitas," "quinceaños," and "el baile de los mestizos") are all performed to the accompaniment of marimba music. An annual fair is held in April. Because its inhabitants sided with the British, the Icaiche, a rival indigenous group, burned the settlement to the ground in 1867. The 12-room, moderately priced **Xunantunich Hotel** (☎ 093-2264) is located in this village. A number of souvenir shops now line the area near the ferry to Xunantunich.

Tropical Wings Nature Center, The Trek Stop (☎ 09-32265; www.tbcnet.com/dyaeger/susa/ trekstop.htm; e-mail susa@btl.net) is on 22 acres of second-growth tropical forest near San José Succotz. Opened at the beginning of 1998, the center has interpretive facilities and ecological exhibits, a large screened butterfly house, hummingbird garden, signed nature trails, Maya ruins, snack bar, and gift shop. The Trek Stop, lodging associated with the Nature Center, offers simple but comfortable, clean, and hospitable accommodations. Facilities include cabins (BZ$20 pp), small A-frames (BZ$15 pp), tents (BZ$12 pp), and tent sites (BZ$7 pp); kitchen facilities; dining and lounge area; self-service laundry facilities; and shared composting toilets and solar-heated showers.

Chechem Ha Cave and Resort

One of Belize's most accessible true remaining adventures, this one-of-a-kind site features a cave containing Maya pottery galore in a beautiful setting. It's also a starting point for a visit to Vaca Falls. Although not for arachnophobes, claustrophobes, nor those who have a fear of ladders, Chechem Ha is well worth a visit. It's one of the only sites in Belize (and one of the few in Central America) that is under the control of locals who are profiting

directly from it. The Morales family discovered the cave after they found their dogs were periodically disappearing for 15 or 20 minutes at a time. Following the canines, they discovered the cave. Although the cave is on their property, since it is an ancient site it belongs to the Belizean government. The cave has been investigated by archaeologists, who have dated the pottery and carted the better pieces off to storage. Judging by the remains of corn and other items found within the urns here, it was used for storage, although it is likely that one area was also a ceremonial site. For the Maya, who knew nothing of geology, the cave must have seemed a frightening and bizarre place – an entrance to the underworld. While visiting, try to imagine the cave as they might have seen it.

GETTING HERE: From San Ignacio, take the Benque bypass and then the road past a basketball court and the Chinese-built hydroelectric dam. If asking directions, ask for the road to Bob Dole's place. On the way, you must drive along a dirt road and pass by beautiful secondary forest. Following the sign to the right, follow the rough road (a four-wheel-drive is preferable) down to the Morales farm. Unfortunately, no public transportation is available, but it may be possible to hitch a ride. Lodges such as Chaa Creek and Maya Mountain Lodge will arrange transport. If you want to take a taxi, it should cost BZ$35. Be sure to bring a flashlight; otherwise, you'll need to rent one.

VISITING THE SITE: This is no sound-and-light experience, but a real adventure. Youthful and knowledgeable William Morales is likely to be your guide for the tour. He leads the way, pointing out flora and fauna en route. The entrance to the cave is secured from trespassers by a locked steel grating. Once inside the cave, you can climb up ladders to get a closer view of the pottery. In certain areas you must duck down pretty low to get through. The oldest pots date back 2,000 years; others were made 1,500 years ago. Most are unadorned. Although you're unlikely to encounter the nesting gibnuts, you might meet the three fruit bats. Pancho is the one who hangs from the ladder. There are some large stalactite formations. To reach the ceremonial chamber, you need to hold onto a rope and climb down a brief but narrow passage, which ends in a short drop-off. It's not as difficult as it might first appear.

PRACTICALITIES: If you're looking for a simple and inexpensive experience that is genuinely Belizean, Chechem Ha is an ideal place to stay. Facilities at the resort are very basic, but it has a great deal of charm for exactly that reason. Individuals who would not feel ill at ease staying in a log cabin in the mountains or camping will feel at home here. Those who want a/c and constant attention won't. The hospitable Morales family are your hosts, and they make a real effort to please. Prices are a reasonable BZ$44 pp for accommodation in cabanas and all meals. Otherwise, breakfast is BZ$10, lunch is BZ$12, and dinner is BZ$20. Meals consist of local dishes, including rice and beans, panades, fried plantains, and fish. A household specialty is handmade, piping-hot tortillas. The round,

thatched-roof cabins have two single beds and kerosene lighting; the bath is detached. There's no generator. A path leads down to the river where you can relax. Vaca Falls are nearby; visitors must pay to visit.

The tour to the **Pottery Cave** is BZ$50 for up to four. While this is not inexpensive (especially if you are alone), you are given a lot of personal attention. The more distant **Bat Cave** (four hours RT) is BZ$200 for up to six. Similarly distant, though less rough, the **Ghost Crab Cave** costs BZ$100 for up to three. The smaller **Gibnut Cave** is BZ$50 for up to six. For more information call Luis Morales at 093-2109; contact him on radio frequency 147.625, or write Antonio Morales, Elizabeth St., Benque Viejo del Carmen, Cayo.

Benque Viejo del Carmen

Set on the east bank of the Mopan tributary of the Belize River, Benque Viejo (pop. 3,500) lies at the nation's western frontier – 81 miles from Belize City and right next to the El Petén frontier of Guatemala. Its name probably derives from the Spanish translation of "old bank," with "bank" denoting a riverside logging camp. Its orderly layout makes it the best-planned town in Belize. This mestizo settlement has all the trappings of Guatemalan culture – marimbas, fiestas, spicy Hispanic food, and archetypal Catholic religious events. But its public services, including a firehouse, police barracks, and running water, make it abundantly clear that it is in Belize.

Catholicism predominates and Spanish is the tongue of daily life, but the streets have names like George, Churchill, and Baron Bliss. There's nothing in particular to interest the visitor here, but it's a pleasant enough place to stroll around in.

EVENTS: Held in July, "Las Alboradas" is the local celebration featuring Linda Beliceña, the local marimba band. Indigenous dances are performed.

GETTING HERE: Most buses heading from Belize City to San Ignacio also stop here; they board in the center of town.

ACCOMMODATIONS: Possibly the cheapest hotel in the country at BZ$5 pp, **Hospedaje Roxie** is across from the cemetery and near the police station at 70 St. Joseph St. Others include the **Okis Hotel** (☎ 093-2006, BZ$10), 47 George St., and **The Maya Hotel** (☎ 093-2116, BZ $10 s, BZ$18, shared bath), 11 George St. More expensive rooms with private bath are also available at the latter.

Run by the Hong Kong Chinese native who started Maxim's in San Ignacio, **Maxim's** (41 Churchill St., ☎ 093-2360, fax 093-2259) offers attractive rooms and good food. Room rates start at BZ$65 s and BZ$85 d plus tax. It opened in 1994.

The moderate 12-unit **Woodlands Resort** (☎ 093-2264) offers horseback riding, fans, restaurant, and camping facilities. The **Ahl Bahzil Hotel Cabinas,** on the road to Benque, may or may not be open. Behind them on the same hill, the **Vista del Carmen Resort** has a restaurant and disco. **Rancho Los Amigos** has closed.

FOOD: Long Lucky's is a cheap Chinese restaurant. Very inexpensive, the **Hawaii Restaurant** on Main St. features large commando pictures by the posted menu. Just above is a placard reading, "Enjoy yourself, it's later than you think." Also try the **Riverside Restaurant** on the water nearby, the cafeteria-style **Okis** up the street, and **Restaurant Los Angeles** on Church St. You'll sometimes find vendors around the square.

FROM BENQUE VIEJO: For Belize City, Novelo's buses depart from 119 George St., Monday to Saturday at 4, 4:30, 5, 5:30, 6, 6:30, 6:45, 7, 9, and 10, and on Sunday at 6, 7, 9, and 10. Batty's buses leave at 6-11:30 AM. Shared taxis or (less frequent) buses will take you to the Guatemalan border. Otherwise, it's a 20-minute walk.

The Petén, Guatemala

Occupying about a third of the nation but with less than two percent of the population, the Petén is Guatemala's last frontier – an area rich in Maya ruins and wildlife, combining tropical rainforests, lowland swamps, and dry savannahs. Part of an untamed and nearly virgin wilderness stretching from the Lacondon forest of southern Mexico across the Maya Mountains into Belize, the Petén is almost a country unto itself. It is a jungle environment ruled no longer by the jaguar but by the repressive Guatemalan military.

Everywhere you go you will see outposts manned by olive-green-uniformed youths brandishing automatic weapons, and signs featuring, among other things, a fanged military hunk posing with a submachine gun. As you travel on, the wooden structures on stilts of Belize are supplanted by thatched huts and miserable poverty.

Flora & Fauna

This is a major reason to visit. More than 250 species of birds have been sighted in the Tikal area alone, and mammals include jaguars, monkeys, coatis, deer, tapirs, and ocelots. There are also crocodiles, as well as innumerable species of insects.

History

Maya civilization spread to the area some 2,500 years ago. Of the total of 102 Maya sites reported in the Petén, many still remain buried beneath the jungle floor. The Maya civilization reached its architectural, artistic, and scientific zenith in this area during the Classic Period (300-900 AD). The area was abandoned at the end of the 12th century, and the Maya apparently moved north to the Yucatán. When the Spanish first arrived, the Petén had been partially colonized by the Itzá, a Toltec-Maya tribe from the Yucatán, who now lived in the Lake Peten Itzá area.

The whole of the area was not subdued by the Spanish invaders until 1697, more than 150 years after the rest of the nation had been brought under the conquistador's heel. Resisting attempts to Christianize them, the Itzá were finally conquered, marking the submission of the last independent tribe.

Under the Spanish, the area remained a backwater in which chicle collecting was the major economic activity. In recent years, it has become a shelter for the FAR (Rebel Armed Forces) and other guerrilla groups. Today it is under attack from loggers and recent emigrants, and the region is rapidly becoming deforested.

📖 **Suggested Reading**

Tom Barry's Inside Guatemala (IBSN 0-911213-40-6), published by the Inter-Hemispheric Resource Center, is good for background information. A number of guidebooks provide good information for travel in the nation. Passport's Mexico & Central America Handbook is one example.

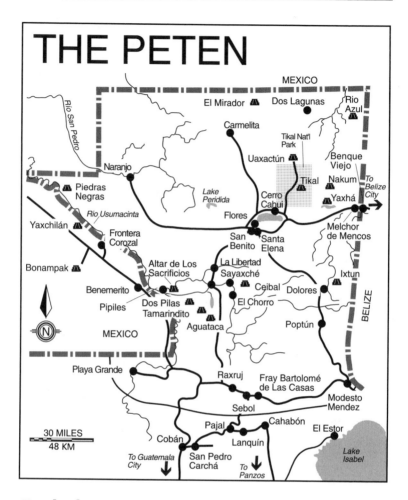

THE PETEN

MEXICO

Rio San Pedro

El Mirador ▲   Dos Lagunas   Rio Azul ▲

Carmelita

Tikal Nat'l Park

Naranjo

Uaxactún ▲

Benque Viejo

Piedras Negras ▲

Lake Peridida

Cerro Cahui

Tikal ▲   Nakum ▲   To Belize City

Yaxhá ▲

Rio Usumacinta

Flores

Melchor de Mencos

Yaxchilán ▲

Frontera Corozal

San Benito   Santa Elena

Bonampak ▲

Altar de Los Sacrificios

La Libertad

Sayaxché

Ixtun ▲

Benemerito

Ceibal   Dolores

BELIZE

Pipiles

Dos Pilas ▲
Tamarindito ▲

El Chorro

N

Aguataca ▲

Poptún

MEXICO

Playa Grande

Raxruj   Fray Bartolomé de Las Casas

Modesto Mendez

Sebol

Cahabón

30 MILES
48 KM

Pajal

El Estor

Cobán   Lanquín

Lake Isabel

To Guatemala City

San Pedro Carchá

To Panzos

Exploring

The Petén has been accessible by car only since 1970. Today there is a mere skeletal framework of roads – many of which are impassible during the rainy season. However, the chief attraction, the Tikal ruins, is readily accessible by road. The Melchor-Flores highway is in bad shape until the Tikal turnoff. Buses run from Melchor to Flores and from Flores to Tikal, Guatemala City, Poptun, and other locales.

Organizations

If you've been moved by the situation in Guatemala and wish to do something to help it, **Casa CAMI** is an organization founded by Rodolfo Robles, former secretary general of the union that led the historic strike against Coca Cola. It works with displaced refugees, runs cultural programs and projects to preserve traditional culture, and operates a sewing cooperative. Send tax deductible donations (made payable to "IF, A Nonprofit Corporation") to Friends of Casa Cami, 3105 Freedom Blvd., Lake Freedom, Watsonville, CA 95076; ☎ 408-724-5526. In Guatemala, their offices (☎ 2-515021, fax 83075) are at 2A, Av. 6-40, Zona 2, Guatemala City.

Melchor, Guatemala

If you are coming in from Flores, this small town's paved streets will be a refreshing relief. Just across the river from Benque, Melchor is equally placid, yet worlds apart. If you don't have the time to venture into Guatemala, a short trip here will at least give you some perspective on the national ambience.

Transport

GETTING HERE: Immigration will give US citizens a tourist card valid for a month for a US$5 cash payment. If you're only going to Flores/Tikal, the visitor's card may not be necessary but you'll still pay the same. From the border, it's an easy walk into town. The bus to Flores (three hours or more) generally waits at the border and then travels into the market area of town, where it waits some more before departing; make sure you get a seat. Minibuses for charter (bargain hard!) generally wait just past Immigration. The bank at the border, though closed on Sat. and Sun., offers a significantly better rate than the moneychangers, and no commission is collected. (A Western Union office may be opening on the Belizean side, which will also offer good rates).

RETURNING TO BELIZE: Heading through Immigration, US citizens pay 5 quetzales (Q5) to exit. From the border, there's a Novelo bus leaving at intervals for Melchor, San Ignacio, Belmopan, and Belize City. You can also take a shared taxi to Melchor (BZ$2) or charter one to San Ignacio.

Accommodations & Food

Many of the hotels here are for low-budget travelers and are around US$1-2. Try the **Maya**, **Zacaleu**, or the **Mayab**. More deluxe (but still reasonable at around US$12 s and US$14 d) is the **Hotel Palace**, which has attractive bungalows and a café that serves pizza, seasonal fruits, juices, and other items. Camping (around BZ$4 pp) is also offered. It's next to the Banco Café. You can change money here (which involves two forms being laboriously typed) or with the moneychangers at the border. There are a number of small restaurants around but, despite the proximity of the river, fish is in short supply.

Shopping

In addition to the souvenir stands near Immigration, there are several long rows of street stalls in the market where you can pick up basic items, as well as "Tikal" and other T-shirts for around US$3; it's generally easy to knock a dollar off the price by bargaining. There are many restaurants, including a Mexican one by the river. Not much nightlife exists here, save some bars with red lights over the doors. But during the daytime you can always take a dip in the river to cool off.

Guatemala

Flores, Guatemala

 Officially still the region's capital, Flores today is a small, poor colonial-style town on an island connected by a clay causeway to the mainland. There are a few nice streets on the island but nothing much to see. Across the causeway a dusty road leads to the contiguous towns of Santa Elena and San Benito; the latter has a cinema and some sleazy bars.

Transport

ARRIVING BY AIR: From Belize International, it's a beautiful 40-minute flight with Tropic Air. Along the way, you fly over stretches of virgin rainforest that contrast vividly with checkerboard-square Spanish Lookout, a Mennonite settlement, with its tin-roofed structures precisely lined up as though on a monopoly board. The effects of slash-and-burn are clearly in evidence, and it is striking just how little primary forest is left. Dipping down into Flores, you pass over Laguna Petén Itza before passing the island of Flores and descending to the airport. US citizens will be required to fill out a Visitor's Card form and pay US$5. While Europeans may not need a visa, they may be asked to show a return ticket. Curiously, there is no customs check at the airport because Flores is not considered to be a frontier.

You can change money with the moneychangers, who offer a slightly lower rate (US$=Q5.50) than the bank on Flores island. The departure section of the airport has a cafeteria and a number of over-priced souvenir shops. They do have some valuable books here – such as the Guatemalan edition of *Birds of Tikal*. If you're on a tour or headed for one of the hotels at or near Tikal, you will find a representative waiting for you at the airport. If not, you have three choices: a) bargain with a taxi driver for a ride (around Q10), b) take the cheap local bus from the main road, or c) walk to town – about 20 minutes.

FROM FLORES: Aeroquetzal, Aerovias, and Tapsa fly to Guatemala City. Although, as a foreigner, you pay much more than Guatemalans, flying is better than an excruciating 14-hour bus ride on bad roads. If you must take a bus be sure to take a *servicio especial*, which may whittle the trip down to 10 hours or so. Buses also run to Sayaxché. Check at the Hotel San Juan in Santa Elena for times. If you are returning to Belize, they may try to charge you three times as much bus fare as when you came in. Don't let them get away with it!

FOR MEXICO: If you wish you can skip Belize and go straight through to Chetumal the same day by catching the 5 AM bus. It costs around US$30. You will save more than half of this by taking local buses.

Sights

There isn't much to do in Flores itself. But the place is attractive to wander in, and its main plaza hosts some badly weathered Maya stelae. One thing you may do is take one of the local ferries – in a large, traditional-style canoe – from San Benito across to one of the lakeside villages. It will cost you a quetzal. Service is irregular. Boatmen also offer trips for tourists, at tourist prices. Don't find them; they'll find you! While walking around the lake, note how many of the structures are now underwater, thanks to rising water levels.

One interesting sidetrip is to the **Cueva de la Serpiente**, also known as the Grutas Actun-Can, a cave that features stalactite formations. To get here take the causeway road from Flores through Santa Elena, turn left when it forks in front of a small hill, then turn right. Admission is charged.

Accommodations

The best place to stay for low-budget travelers is probably functional and reasonably clean **Hotel Jade** by the causeway in Santa Elena. They charge US$2 s or d. It's attached to the neighboring **Hotel Leo Fu Lo**, which has an atmospheric Chinese restaurant. Both leave much to be desired in terms of sanitary facilities. The **Hotel Sac Nicté**, which offers rooms with private bath, is one block over.

The 60-room **Hotel San Juan** (☎ 081-1562) is priced around US$10 d; more expensive rooms have a/c. Expect to be awakened early in the morning by buses; use earplugs.

The best hotel on the Santa Elena side is modern, Spanish-style **Hotel Del Patio-Tikal** (☎ 081-1229; in the US, 800-327-3573), which has 21 rooms and a restaurant. Rooms have color TV and fan. There is an attractive garden and a restaurant that will prepare a box lunch for you to take to Tikal. Rooms run upward from US$60 s or d.

Under the same management as the identically named establishment in Tikal, the **Jaguar Inn** (☎ 081-002), Calzada Rodríguez Macal 879, has attractive rooms for US$30 d.

Near the bus station and also on Calzada Rodríguez Macal, the 17-room **Costa Del Sol** (☎ 081-1336) has a pool; some rooms have a/c and refrigerators.

Set on the lake, the 20-room **Hotel Maya Internacional** (☎/fax 081-1276) is a set of thatched bungalows priced from US$32 s and $38 d. Others include **Hotel El Diplomático** and **Hotel Don Quijote.**

Situated between the town and the airport, the 36-room **Hotel Tziquinaha** (☎ 081-359) has a pool, tennis court, and restaurant; it's popular with tour groups. Rooms have color TV and a/c. Rates run from around US$55 s, $65 d, and $70 t.

Five miles east of town at Lake Petenchel, the **Hotel Villa Maya** (☎ 081-086) charges US$100 s or d for attractive rooms; write 3 Calle 10-58, Zona 10, Guatemala City for further information.

across the causeway: Flores itself tends to be more expensive, and most of the hotels also have restaurants. The 21-room **Hotel Petén** (☎ 081-1692, fax 081-1662) is one of the best upmarket bets. Rooms go for US$25 d.

Opened in 1990, the **Posada El Tucán**, facing the water, has five rooms with shared baths for around US$5 s, $10 d, and $12 t. The 42-room **Hotel Yum Kax** (☎ 081-1686) has rooms from US$11 s and $15 d; more expensive rooms are a/c. Popular with group tours, the 23-room a/c four-story **Hotel Savanna** (☎ 081-1248) is set far from the causeway. Rooms at the rear overlook the water, and there's a small island offshore that is connected to the hotel. Rates are around US$22 s, $30 d, and $40 t.

Food

There are any number of restaurants, with more opening all the time. Restaurants across the causeway tend to be more expensive. Try **Cafe Maya** in San Benito, **Cafe Lago Azul** in Santa Elena, or **Café Doña Amantes**, which serves lasagna as well as pie slices. One place guaranteed to infuriate animal rights advocates, the **Restaurant Gran Jaguar** serves game.

Services

The only **tourist information** is at the airport. Representatives of the major hotels congregate nearby during flight arrival times. Guarded by rifle-equipped military, **the Bank of Guatemala** is in Flores. It's open Monday to Thursday from 8:30 to 2:30 and on Friday from 8:30 to 3:30. You can change money at a lower rate at the Hotel San Juan in Santa Elena. The **post office** in Flores doesn't have stamps; you must buy them at the stationery store nearby. Another Correos y Telegrafos is situated just west of Santa Elena's Hotel Patio. Be sure to carry a flashlight at night, as there are frequent blackouts.

LANGUAGE STUDY: Guatemala has long been a mecca for language study, and an innovative program has been established here in the Petén. Set in the village of San Andres, on the northwest shore of Lake Petén-Itza, the **Eco-Escuela de Español** (☎ 9-508-106, 928-

8106) combines language study with rainforest ecology. Costs are around US$50 per week for accommodation and food; tuition runs from US$60 (four hrs. pd) to $95 (seven hrs. pd). For more information, ☎ 202-429-5660, fax 202-887-5188, or write Conservation International Eco-Escuela, 1015 18th St. NW, Washington, DC 20036.

The Tikal Ruins

The most spectacular of the 102 Maya sites found in the Petén, and one of the oldest Maya sites, Tikal ("Place of the Voices") rises from the Petén jungles. Set some 40 miles from Flores and surrounded by 230-square-mile Tikal National Park, the ruins are dominated by five steep-sided granite pyramids that rise 120 feet from the ground. So astounding are the ruins to the eye that Director George Lucas used Tikal to represent the hidden rebel base on the fourth moon of the Planet Yavin in the classic film, Star Wars.

Originally, the city was stuccoed, and plastered red-painted temples with blue trim rose from the white plazas. Today, as there is little ornamentation and the stelae have been almost completely eroded, the imposing size and quantity of the structures is what impresses. Amazing as it may seem to the sore-footed visitor, only a small part of Tikal can be visited: over 3,000 structures and 200 monuments still lie under the forest. Still, stripped of their gaudy grandeur of yore, the temples have little of the ornate carving that makes Quiriguá and Copán so awesome. For some, the best part may be hunting for howler monkeys in the jungle or watching the parrots, toucans, or other birds. Crenelated turkeys stroll the lawn in front of the café near the museum.

GETTING HERE: The Tikal bus leaves at 7 from the front of the Hotel San Juan in Flores. Unfortunately, the bus company consistently overcharges foreigners – about US$2 instead of US$1. Pay only the correct fare, which will be reluctantly accepted if you insist. Slightly faster minibuses are available for about US$3.50 each way. Taxis may also be chartered from the town or the airport.

A paved, fairly smooth road from El Cruce, the crossroads, leads up past Laguna Petén Itza to the park entrance, where you are ordered out of the bus with the gruff pronouncement that foreigners must pay 30 quetzales (around US$6) to enter. Guatemalans pay US$2, but they generally remain on the bus! A final way to reach Tikal is to charter a minibus from the border (bargain hard!). You can also take the Flores bus and get off at El Cruce, but you risk getting stuck. Realistically, if you have the time, Tikal should be more than a day trip, and you should be prepared.

tours: Many of the lodges in the Cayo District and elsewhere offer package tours.

by air: While there is no airport at Tikal itself, many visitors first fly to Flores and then travel from there. **Tropic Air** (☎ 02-45671, 026-2012, 800-422-3435; www. belize.net; e-mail tropic@btl.net) runs an excellent day tour for US$200; this rate includes ground transport, guided tour, and lunch, but does not include departure taxes (add around US$20). The

flight alone costs US$80 OW and US$160 RT. **Maya Island Air** (☎ 02-31348/31362/31403; e-mail mayair@btl.net) has a similar package for around BZ$500, from either San Pedro or Belize City.

☞ *Traveler's Tip*

If you have the time (and especially if you are a birdwatcher), it is worthwhile to spend a few days around the ruins. Accommodations are a much better value in Flores, but you will have to commute from there. On the other hand, if you are merely interested in a once-over, then a day trip is the way to go.

PREPARATIONS: Be sure to wear good shoes, be prepared for rain, and take something along to eat and drink. As there is no water on site (only expensive soft drinks) and the lodges are reluctant to give you water (even with your lunch!), it's better to bring along a good supply. Bottled water is pricey but available from hotels. Bring a good supply of quetzales. You may have difficulty in changing a traveler's check here unless it's being used in payment for a hotel room.

HISTORY: Tikal's historical roots are fuzzy, to say the least. Its beginnings have been placed at 750 BC, during the middle Preclassic Era (ca. 1000-300 BC). Although inscriptions and burial paraphernalia provide information only after 300 AD, it is believed that Tikal's rulers migrated from the area of Kaminaljuyú some 2,000 years ago. The names of a number of rulers (including Curl Nose, Stormy Sky, and Ah Cacaw, and Chitam) have been identified with certainty. Oth-

Guatemala

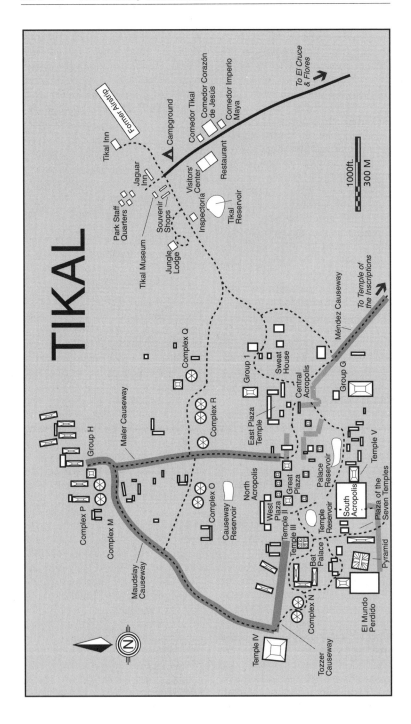

TIKAL

To El Cruce & Flores

Former Airstrip

Tikal Inn

Jaguar Inn

Campground

Comedor Tikal

Comedor Corazón de Jesus

Comedor Imperio Maya

Restaurant

Visitors' Center

Park Staff Quarters

Souvenir Shops

Inspectoría

Tikal Reservoir

Tikal Museum

Jungle Lodge

To Temple of the Inscriptions

Méndez Causeway

Complex Q

Group 1

Sweat House

Central Acropolis

Group G

Maler Causeway

Complex R

East Plaza Temple

Temple V

Group H

Complex P

North Acropolis

Great Plaza

Palace Reservoir

South Acropolis

Plaza of the Seven Temples

Complex M

Complex O

West Plaza

Temple II

Causeway Reservoir

Temple III

Temple Reservoir

Pyramid

Maudslay Causeway

Bat Palace

El Mundo Perdido

Complex N

Temple IV

N

Tozzer Causeway

1000ft.
300 M

ers are more speculative, and there are undoubtedly a number who have not been identified.

In any case, the names of the rulers are based on the shapes of their glyphs; their actual names are not known. For example, Curl Nose has a curly nose, and Chitam is named after the Maya word for peccary because that animal appears on his glyph. These rulers were believed to be living gods, and their forefathers were venerated as gods in turn. It is believed that this essentially feudalistic society operated from the Central Acropolis – specifically from Group G, and the Palace of the Windows. Jaguar Paw, the first ruler, was followed by Curl Nose and then Stormy Sky.

From the period between the death of Stormy Sky in AD 457 to the accession of Ah Cacaw in AD 682, little is certain. Ah Cacaw ushered in the Golden Age of Tikal, which was continued by his son, Ruler B (Half-darkened sun), and grandson, Chitam. During this period most of the great pyramids were constructed. It is believed that the city of Tikal declined around 900 AD. After that, all goes dark until Tikal was rediscovered in 1848 by a government expedition under Modesto Mendez and Ambrosio Tut.

Later in the 19th century, an expedition led by Gustave Bernoulli removed some of the lintels from Temples I and IV to Basel. Visiting in 1881 and 1882, Alfred Amudslay was the first to photograph the site. Work continued by Teobert Maler in 1885 and 1904 on behalf of Harvard University's Peabody Museum. Next to visit were Sylvanus Morley, who studied the hieroglyphic texts, and then Edwin Shook of the Carnegie Institution, who discovered Group H and the Maler and Maudslay Causeways.

In 1951, the Guatemalan military cleared an airstrip, making the area truly accessible for the first time. The Tikal Project, initiated by the University of Pennsylvania's University Museum in 1956, has been continued since 1970 under the auspices of the Guatemalan government.

ORIENTATION: Entering the area, you will pass the hotels and the museum on the way to the entrance. There are a number of places to eat, and there's a large market behind the museum. The **Tikal Museum** has a lot of weathered stelae with descriptions of them on the wall. It also displays photographs and has a number of rubbings on rice paper, metates (grinding stones for corn), jewelry, and stone tools. It's easy to spot a crenelated turkey strolling the grounds.

The ruins begin at the end of a path that cuts to the left of the Jungle Lodge. At the entrance to the ruins, you present your admission ticket (good for that day only) and enter the grounds. Be sure to note the large ceiba tree on the right, just before the guardhouse. Enclosed on the east by Temple I (The Temple of the Giant Jaguar) and on the west by Temple II (The Temple of the Masks), the Great Plaza is the center of the present-day site. To its west is Temple III (The Temple of the Jaguar Priest) and still further west is enormous Temple IV; the unexcavated Temple V lies to the south of the Great Plaza, and to the southeast – all by itself – is Temple VI (The Temple of the Inscriptions). From the top of the stairway flanking the plaza's southern side, the stelae and Northern Acropolis are in front, Temple I is to the east, and Temple II is to the west. Most of these restored structures date from the late Classic Period (AD 700-800).

EXPLORING THE RUINS: The best way to enter is to pass by Complex Q and R, and then either take the Maler Causeway around past Group H and down to Temple IV, or cut straight across and down to Temple IV. From Temple IV you can visit the Plaza of the Lost World, Temple III, the South Acropolis, the Great Plaza, the North Acropolis, and the Central Acropolis. From the Central Acropolis, it's a pleasant walk southeast to the Temple of Inscriptions. Visitors with less time may want to visit the Great Plaza first and then visit other locations as time permits.

TWIN-PYRAMID COMPLEXES Q AND R: The first major structures you come to heading in to the park are these, built to mark the beginning of a katun, a two-year period. These two complexes, part of a total of nine found at Tikal so far, were probably used in conjunction with large public functions relating to cosmic order and the passage of historical time.

TEMPLE IV: Measuring some 212 feet to the top of its roof comb, this magnificent structure incorporated some 250,000 cubic yards of rubble in its construction. Built by the order of Ruler B, the temple is thought to have been finished somewhere around AD 740. Its six lintels have now become naturalized Swiss citizens and reside in Basel. Climbing to the top of this temple is a true adventure: you grab hold of a couple of branches and head up wooden ladders. From the first level – which affords an amazing view – you must head around the corner and climb a steel ladder up to the uppermost platform.

☞ *Traveler's Tip*

While in Tikal try to imagine the city as it was a thousand years ago. See it in the morning before 10, when the fog sometimes makes the landscape resemble an East Asian painting, or savor the damp, faintly tart odor of the forest after an afternoon rainfall. Be sure to bring food with you and plenty to drink; vendors do sell pricey soft drinks at times, but they don't bring them to the top of pyramids. It's worth bringing a compass, as the routes are largely unmarked. Keep an eye out for wildlife (best seen early in the morning and in late afternoon), as well as for the lowly leafcutter ants.

LOST WORLD PYRAMID: To get here follow a path leading south from Temple IV on the west side of the Palace of the Windows. Built before AD 300 and stripped and stabilized in the 1980s, this Late Preclassic 100-foot-high truncated pyramid once had four stairways flanked by masks. Unlike many other temples, it was not created as an ancestor memorial but functioned as part of a calendar ceremony complex. Just north of the Lost World Pyramid, the unfortunate Temple 5C-49 or **Lost World Pyramid Plaza** was being stripped of trees and readied for reconstruction in 1979-80, when it collapsed after a series of heavy rainstorms.

TEMPLE III: This unrestored temple is known as the Temple of the Jaguar Priest, after the lintel depicting an unknown personage thought to be either a pregnant woman, the leader Chitam, or his brother. It may have been the last temple built. Right in front of the temple, **Stela 24** and **Altar 7** are also believed to be some of the last of their kind built. The altar depicts a woven mat (a symbol of authority) flanking each side of a deity head, depicting the God of the Eccentric Flint, which rests in a bowl. Extending out from the bowl are strips of paper used in the bloodletting ceremony. Entering the temple, you will see a passage going off to the side. Using a flashlight, you can follow the passage to see the Preclassic area inside.

THE GREAT PLAZA: Although today this is the most impressive part of restored Tikal, it was not the city's center. That lies to the east in the unexcavated E Plaza at the intersection of the Mendez and Maler Causeways. Instead, it appears to have been an elite ceremonial area erected on behalf of the ruling nobility. In its center are **Temples I and II** with the **North Acropolis** in the center background. To the south, the **Central Acropolis**, a huge palace complex, housed the elite and held their offices.

Temple I (the Temple of the Giant Jaguar) was built around AD 700 by Ah Cacaw, as was Temple II, which it faces. Temple I displays Ah Cacaw at its top; he was once painted a vividly contrasting red and cream.

The best known silhouette of any Pre-Columbian monument, the **Jaguar Temple** is a symbol of the Guatemalan nation. Its nine terraces have horizontal grooves on their lower portions, along with inset or recessed corners – architectural techniques used to create a shadowy chiaroscuro effect extending vertically and horizontally, thus enhancing the visual impact of the 145-foot pyramid. The steep climb up is well worth it. From its top, the Northern Acropolis is to the right, Temple II is across the plaza to the west, the Central Acropolis is visible to the left, and the Great Plaza's 70 stelae and altars, spread out across an area the size of two football fields, lie below. Underneath the pyramid, a vaulted grave chamber (now reconstructed in the site's museum) held Ah Cacaw's remains, along with assorted jewelry, ceramics, and bone artifacts.

Once adorned with a roof comb featuring a massive face with earplugs on each side, **Temple II** (The Temple of the Masks) takes its name from the two enormous masks set on each side of the third terrace's stairway. They flank a platform thought to have been used as a reviewing stand.

Lying between Temple I and the Central Acropolis Palace, the Great Plaza's **Ball Court** was built during the Late Classic era. Only partially excavated and stabilized, it is similar to others found in the Petén. Originally comprising some 42 structures, extending 700 feet east to west, and covering four acres, the **Central Acropolis**, or **Palace Group**, was built over a 500-year period. While the buildings facing the Great Plaza appear to have been used for administrative functions, the layout and construction of the rest make the term "palace" appropriate. The most palace-like structure of all is the **Great Eastern Court Palace** or Court 6, 5D-46.

Guatemala

Dating from 200 AD, the **Northern Acropolis** is a group of funerary structures built to honor the ancestors of the elite. They have been rebuilt time and time again. It contains as many as 100 structures and Jaguar Paw, Curl Nose, and Stormy Sky were buried here. Once partially painted a garish red, it was as impressive as any monumental structure anywhere before 700 AD.

THE EAST PLAZA: Just to the north of the Central Acropolis and to the rear of Temple I lies the East Plaza, which features a large rectangular conglomeration of buildings (Structures 5E-32 to 5E-36). This plaza functioned as a central market area. It's well worth your time to explore this area.

At the entrance to the **"Maler Palace,"** as the building facing the plaza is known, you can distinguish three masks – one over each entrance. Maya graffiti (a carved sketch of a head) can be seen inside, and archaeologist Maler's signature can be seen on the side of a doorway.

Structure 33 here provides the chance to view a wide variety of different layers and see how the structures have been built on top of one another. Note the false arch you can see here. The pigeon holes serve unknown purposes. Just to the west is a ball court. You can view the remains of the reservoir – now lined with lush vegetation – to the rear.

TEMPLE VI (THE TEMPLE OF THE INSCRIPTIONS): Thought to have been completed around 736 AD and later renovated, this temple is ┆ end of a path heading off to ┆ight from the path leading ┆the Great Plaza back towards

the entrance. The temple's glyphs, found on the east side of the roof comb, record a series of dynastic successions that began in Olmec times. Many of the rulers are probably mythic. **Stela 21** here is believed to represent Ruler B; the drops falling from his hand are thought to depict blood flowing from his incised penis. As the stela is not colored, it is impossible to ascertain if the blood is blue or not.

ACCOMMODATIONS: Because of the strong demand, it can be difficult to find a room here, and you may not find good value for what you get. **The Jaguar Inn** is the least expensive, but it only has a few rooms, so you need to reserve well in advance by writing them at Tikal; accommodation in tents is around US$20 d; rooms are US$40 d, including two meals. An interpretive trail runs past the property.

The renovated **Jungle Lodge** (☎ 501519) is now priced at US$35 s and US$50 d and is the largest hotel. The **Hotel Tikal Inn** charges from around US$35 s and US$65 d. With a pool, it is perhaps the best of the lot.

low budget: If you're on a tight budget, Tikal is bad news: it's one of the priciest places to stay in Central America. Cheapest is the once-free **camping area**, which now charges US$6 per person, per night for the privilege of hanging a hammock or pitching a tent. There are no facilities, not even water, but you can rent a hammock at a similarly inflated price. If you want to get more bang for your buck (and don't mind a bit of a commute) the village of El Remate (see page 271) is recommended.

outlying: Set along the road outside of Tikal, the luxurious, 128-

room **Hotel Camino Real-Tikal** (☎ 800-228-3000 in the US), a Westin Resort, has a restaurant, cafeteria, bar, pool, and conference rooms.

FOOD: There are a number of rather pricey restaurants, but several *comedores* are affordable, including an inexpensive and very popular one next to the campsite. Water is difficult to obtain from the restaurants; some will try to sell you bottled water with your meals. You should bring a good supply, along with snacks to munch on while atop the ruins.

ENTERTAINMENT: There's nothing to do at night save listen to animal sounds. However, if there's a full moon you might apply for permission to enter the ruins at night from the Inspectoria, climb a pyramid, and sit in the moonlight – perhaps you could bay at the moon.

TOURS: Tour guides can be shared at US$30 for a four-hour tour. An alternative is to pick up a copy of *Tikal, A Handbook to the Ancient Maya Ruins* by Michael Coe (possibly available in one of the shops) and do it yourself. The ideal itinerary would be to spend one day just wandering around on your own and the second in the company of a guide.

SERVICES: There's a post office, along with a couple of stores.

Vicinity of Tikal

While there's not a lot in the Petén, there are a number of other Maya ruins. To visit them requires time, flexibility, and stamina. One possible way to visit is with **Yaxha-Petén Tours**. They run

Campamento El Sombrero at Laguna Yaxha to the southeast of Tikal. There is a selection of four tours, which visit Nakum, Yaxha, Naranjo, Kinal, Río Azul, Topoxte, and other locales. Trips are by jeep or on horseback and they generally involve camping.

For more information contact Agencia Tivoli (☎ 0811-285/329) at 4 C. 0-43 in Santa Elena or Circus SA (☎ 314051) in Guatemala City at Ave. Hincapié 3-81 Z.13.

Uaxactún

Located 15 miles north of Tikal, these ruins and accompanying village line an abandoned airstrip. Beneath one of its temples, the oldest building ever found in the Petén, dating back to 2000 BC, has been excavated. The ruins have been stabilized – to prevent further deterioration – by plastering cracks with white mortar.

Group E and Group H are 15 minutes to the right from the airstrip; Group A and Group B are to the runway's left, about a 20-minute walk. You'll notice the damage to Group A. It was done by early archaeologists who simply dug into the temples, looking for graves but nearly wrecking the temples themselves.

GETTING HERE: It's a six-hour walk here from Tikal. The path begins between the museum and the Jungle Inn. Although beans and tortillas will be available, plan on camping or pitching a hammock. If you have a four-wheel-drive vehicle, you can also drive here.

El Mirador

Rediscovered in 1926, this site predates Tikal. There are a series of massive pyramid structures, which, in turn, support three smaller pyramids. **The Dante Complex,** the largest set, rises to 216 feet, the highest Maya building known. The Tigre Pyramid to the west is 132 feet high.

In order to get here you must make a difficult two-day jungle trek from the chicle-gathering village of Carmelita, 40 miles north of Flores. Carmelita can be reached by road from the village of San Andrés on the northern side of Lake Peten Itzá. The trek takes 5-7 days RT and should not be attempted during the rainy season.

Río Azul

Much smaller than El Mirador, this site is 104 miles from Flores to the northeast and was rediscovered in 1962. Covering some 750 acres, it has been extensively looted. It takes three days RT by jeep to get here along a barely passable road.

Lake Yaxjá

The Flores-Melchor bus passes five miles from the lake, which is located halfway to the border. You'll have to walk two hours. Rediscovered in 1904, the extensive, unrestored Yaxjá ruins are to the left. The ruins of Nakum are 12 miles to the north. There are two main groups of structures. You will also find some miniature ruins on the lake's island of Topoxte.

Sayaxché

Set 38 miles southwest of Flores along the Río de la Pasión, this town has a number of sites nearby, but you'll need to hire a boat or a horse to get at them.

To the north is **El Ceibal** (600-900 AD) with stelae and a circular temple. To the south are the ruins of **Don Pilas, Aguateca, and Tarmarindito** on the shore of Lake Petexbatún. Down the river is the Altar de los Sacrificios and the difficult-to-reach sites of **Yaxchilán** and **Piedras Negras** along the Mexican border.

Established in 1990 with the help of the German and Dutch governments, the **Parque Nacional de Laguna Lachua** is a macaw breeding area on a lake set inside a volcanic crater. It is 81 km (41 mi.) off of the Sayaxché-Cobán road. You will need a four-wheel-drive, and there are no facilities. It takes two to three hours to get here by bus, and the best place to stay is the **Guayacan.** Talk to Julian at La Montana restaurant about arranging trips to the ruins. El Ciebal is upriver and is the most accessible). **Posada de Mateo** is a six-cabin luxury-priced nature lodge on Laguna Petexbatún.

Biotopo Cerro Cahuí

Set up to preserve the crenelated turkey, the Cerro Cahuí Wildlife Reserve on the east side of the lake covers an area of old growth rainforest. To get here, take the Tikal bus to El Remate and walk or take the minivan to Jobompiche.

Stay either at the reserve or at the basic but attractive and hospitable **Gringo Perdido** (☎ 370674), a "Parador Ecologico," which has a restaurant. Rates, although not cheap for Guatemala, are reasonable, and you may camp here. You can swim in the lake or hike the trails. The **Hotel Camino Real Tikal** is also nearby, as is **Posada Casa Roja**.

El Remate

Still relatively undeveloped for visitors, the settlement of El Remate is set by Lake Petén Itza along the road to Tikal. The village is known for its woodcarvers. There are several low-budget places to stay, including **Hospedaje Maya, La Casa de Don David**, and the camping and bungalow spot of **Mirador del Duende**. Another alternative in the village is **La Mansión del Pájaro Serpiente** (☎/fax 501514 in Santa Elena), a resort composed of thatched-roof cottages on stone foundations. Pickup at the airport is available.

Onward in Guatemala

Many visitors to Belize will also want to visit Guatemala. What follows is a brief description, giving you an idea about some of the places you may want to visit. A good route would be to fly from Flores to Guatemala City (US$50), proceed immediately to Xela (Quetzaltenango) by express bus (four hours, $3), spend a week in that area, continue on to Atitlán, Antigua, and environs before returning to southern Belize via Guatemala City, Copán (Honduras), Quiriguá, Livingston, and Puerto Barrios. **note:** Livingston, Puerto Barrios, and Quirigua are described under the "Punta Gorda" section of the following chapter.

Tours

One major company operating in Guatemala is **Maya Expeditions,** ☎/fax 37466; 15 C. 1-91 Zona 10, Edificio Tauro Local 10, Guatemala City, Guatemala. In the US, write Section 66, Box 527270, Miami, FL 33152. They offer trips to Tikal, Quirigua and other ruins, turtle watching, birding, rafting, bungee jumping, volcano and jungle trekking, and other activities. They are dedicated to serving individuals willing to leave civilization's excess baggage behind to seek out unique adventures. These are true expeditions, providing "unforgettable experiences of discovery."

Guatemala City

The nation's capital, it is also one of the Americas' least inviting capital cities. The main reason to stay here is to visit the museums, and/or to make travel connections. If you should have time to kill, it's a fascinating experience to hop aboard any city bus and explore this vast and monstrous urban sprawl. Don't worry about getting lost. The bus will eventually come back to where you got on. But allow an hour or two because the routes can be extensive.

Antigua

This is the nation's tourist capital: every time you turn the corner you'll likely encounter another for-

Guatemala

eigner or someone who wants to sell you something, or both. It is a beautiful city, a restored ex-colonial capital with many churches and is surrounded by volcanoes. It also has the largest concentration of good restaurants and cafes.

Chichicastenango

This town is famous for its Thursday and Sunday markets, which have made it a tourist mecca. Another reason for interest is the potent mixture of animism and Catholicism prevalent among the Maya people in the area.

Lake Atitlán

A preeminent tourist attraction, this lake's chief resort town is Panajachel. Ferries traverse the lake, stopping at each village. The nicest village to stay at is **San Pedro de la Laguna** at the southern end.

Quetzaltenango

The second largest city (pop. 100,000), Quetzaltenango is popularly known as Xela (pronounced "Shey-la"). This small, pleasant, and sometimes chilly town is an excellent base for a highlands tour. Nearby places to visit include markets (there's an extraordinary one on Friday at San Francisco El Alto), the hot baths at Almolonga and the vapor baths in the hills close to town, Laguna San Cristobal near the village of San Martin, the wool center of Momostenango, and many other small villages and attractions. Xela also has a few English schools and is a better place to study than tourist-ridden Antigua. One good school to contact is **Ulew Tinimit**, 14 Ave. "A," 8-38 Zona 3. Apdo. 346, Quetzaltenango, ☎ 502-061-4886.

The South

Comprising tropical rainforest as well as coastal swamps, the long-neglected but treasure-filled South rewards nature lovers and amateur social anthropologists alike. The nation's highest point at 3,800 feet, Victoria Peak rises amidst the verdant and vibrant Cockscomb Jaguar Reserve. While the main Garinagu (Garifuna) settlements are around Dangriga and Punta Gorda along the coast, the Kekchi and Mopan Maya indigenous peoples reside in the interior, still retaining many customs.

Exploring

This long economically neglected area is rough but beautiful. A bad road – difficult and sometimes impossible to negotiate during the wet season and horrifically dusty during the dry – leads to Punta Gorda in the south. The reddish color of the rainforest soil is from the high iron and clay content. As the trees have been cut on both sides of the road, the soil has been free to blow about everywhere. (If you're headed toward Cockscomb directly, a rough road leads off from the Western Highway in the Sibún area.) Along the way are nature reserves, and a separate branch road leads to Placencia Peninsula. Its fishing village is fast becoming the nation's major tourist destination after San Pedro on Ambergris Caye. In the Toledo area around Punta Gorda, it's preferable to have your own vehicle, but you can get around by bus and hitchhiking if you have patience. The area's temples are unique in that they, virtually alone among Maya structures, were built

without mortar. Last but not the least of the area's charms, the few spectacular cayes off the coast are worth a visit, if you're willing to travel the distance and pay the cost. The most unusual is Wee Wee Caye, which has been transformed into a biological field station and welcomes guests.

Dangriga
(Stann Creek Town)

With its clapboard houses on stilts and relaxed lifestyle, this small Garifuna settlement (pop. 7,700) resembles something straight out of a Somerset Maugham novel. A smaller but more placid version of Belize City, relaxing Dangriga is fun to visit for a day or two. In this town everyone checks you out upon arrival, and everyone knows just what you're doing.

History

Around 1640 a group of English Puritans from the ill-fated island settlement of Providence in the Bay of Honduras moved to the mainland to trade with the Mosquito Coast native Americans for silk-grass, a thick-leaved bromeliad used to make rope. A Captain Elfrith dealt with pumpkins, potatoes, and other crops brought from the island at two trading stands located at Upper and Lower Stanns Creek. The town gradually developed into Belize's second largest city. Most of the town's inhabitants are Black Caribs descended from those that

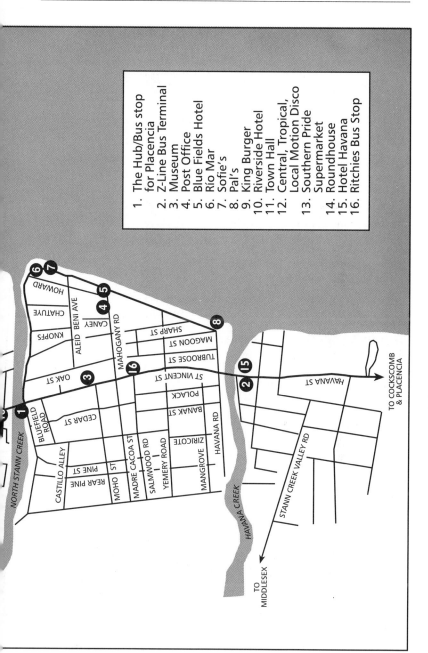

1. The Hub/Bus stop for Placencia
2. Z-Line Bus Terminal
3. Museum
4. Post Office
5. Blue Fields Hotel
6. Río Mar
7. Sofie's
8. Pal's
9. King Burger
10. Riverside Hotel
11. Town Hall
12. Central, Tropical, Local Motion Disco
13. Southern Pride Supermarket
14. Roundhouse
15. Hotel Havana
16. Ritchies Bus Stop

arrived in 1823. St. Vincent, the main street, is named after their ancestral abode, and Dangriga – its new name dating from the 1980s – means "standing water" or "clear water" in Garifuna. These were leader Elijo Beni's first words upon his arrival. The town was almost completely destroyed by Hurricane Hattie in 1961.

Orientation

To the north of town is the Pelican and the airstrip. North Stann Creek divides the town in half, with a ribbon of wooden houses lining its banks. Nearly all of the hotels are within a 10-minute walk of the footbridge.

Transport

GETTING HERE: This is one of the most beautiful bus rides in Belize, despite the dusty, pot-holed road. En route from Belmopan you pass rising hills, cohune palms, citrus groves, and fruit-laden trucks. Along the way you pass villages with names like Middlesex and Steadfast, cross rust-red bridges, and pass through some very green territory.

After Middlesex, the Hummingbird Highway continues as Stann Creek Valley Rd. Approximately seven miles before town, the Dangriga turnoff is marked by a decrepit bus stand, and an asphalt road leads on into town.

If you're planning on driving from Belize City, it's best to take a four-wheel-drive vehicle; remember to fill up your gas tank before departing. Taking the dusty New Road will save you about an hour. The Z-Bus departs from Belize City's Pound Yard Bridge; and the James Bus also runs.

Upon arriving, you're likely to be accosted by a group of jobless touts who'll perform tricks such as opening cab doors for you and attempting to lead you to a hotel. Be cordial, but otherwise ignore them, and don't be concerned if they curse you out. Don't, under any circumstances, give them money. You won't have any problem finding a hotel on your own. There are many hotels in Dangriga, given the number of visitors the town attracts, and more are on the way.

FROM DANGRIGA: Z-Line (☎ 05-22160) departs for Belize City at 5, 6, 8, 10 AM and at 1:30 and 4:30 PM with additional departures on Fri. and Sat. at 7:30 PM. The fare is BZ$6 to Belmopan and BZ$10 to Belize City; it takes four hours unless the bus goes by the New Road, which several do every day.

To the south, Z-line buses run to Punta Gorda at noon, 4, and 7 (with additional trips at 10 on Sat. and Mon.) and to Independence (BZ$9) at 2. Buses to Placencia depart at 12:15 and 4:30. Ritchies Bus Service also runs to Placencia. You should note that pilferage has been a problem along the PG route; keep an eye on your baggage.

All buses to the south stop at the entrance roads to Hopkins and Sittee River, in Independence, and in the main part of Maya Center. Buses also run directly to Hopkins.

by boat: Dangriga is a departure point for trips to Tobacco Caye. (BZ$25 pp, OW) and Bird Caye. Boats generally leave from 7-9 AM. Ask around about weekly boats to Honduras.

by air: Both Tropic Air (☎ 02-45671, 026-2012, 800-422-3435; www.belize.net; e-mail tropic@btl. net) and Maya Island Air (☎ 02-

31348/31362/31403; e-mail ma-yair@btl.net) fly to Belize City, Placencia, and Punta Gorda.

Sights

Truth be told, Dangriga does not host any awe-inspiring places to visit, but there are a few places of minor interest. Inaugurated in 1991 by owner and founder Janice Lambert, **Melda's Historical Museum**, at 21 St. Vincent St. across from Belize Bank, is the only place where you can get an overview of Garinagu culture. Inside, you'll find a collection of cultural items ranging from *egei* and *matate* grinders to mahogany bowls and plates to *makaras* (rattles). It's open daily except Thursday and Sunday; admission is charged.

You might wonder about the ostentatious house just down the river from the Riverside Hotel. It's the residence of a Zabaneh; his mother owns the Riverside, and his brother owns the Blue Marlin Lodge. The most peculiar sight is the "outhouses by the sea" complex – a dock with a shack at the end. The huge dock at the southern end of town is where the citrus concentrate is loaded.

Williams Beach is two miles south of town. To reach it, stay on the coastal road and keep an eye out for the big pier. A BZ$1 admission charge allows you to use the facilities including a changing room and artificial sand beach. Giant pigs wander about on the grass nearby. The water is a bit muddy. It's possible to camp here, but the sand flies are really bad.

Cassava bread is manufactured on **Sabal's Estate** at Four Miles. Making *ruguma*, the bread, is a two-day process. After processing and grinding the cassava root, it is baked on huge griddles.

At Davis Falls Reserve, about 12 mi. from the village of Alta Vista, are magnificent **Davis Falls**. You must hike along and through the Big Eddie River from the settlement of Cow Creek. A guide is mandatory, and it should be reserved for the physically fit.

Artists & Craftspeople

One place to stop by is the studio of internationally famed Garifuna artist **Benjamin Nicholas** (☎ 05-22785) at 25 Howard St. His oil paintings depict events in Garifuna history as well as lifestyle and culture. In Benjamin's words, he paints to preserve Garifuna culture for posterity. Very friendly and sagacious Benjamin is never at a loss for words. A sign in his studio reads: "HAVE YOUR CULTURE. RECOVER IT WHERE LOST. ENRICH IT WHERE POSSIBLE. ACQUIRE AS MUCH FOREIGN TECHNOLOGY AS YOU CAN WITHOUT IDENTIFYING WITH THE CULTURE FROM WHICH IT STEMS. THE REDISCOVERED TRUTH: LIFE IS A LIFE LONG LEARNING PROCESS."

Drum maker **Austin Rodriguez** makes drums from cedar, mayflower, and mahogany. Curing deer and cow hides in the sun with lime and salt, he then uses "tagithe" vine to attach the skin. Drums may be made to order, and his most popular ones are African rather than Garifuna in design. Austin also builds dories, makes round boards for kneading bread, and carves matas, vessels for pounding plantains into *hudut* (plantain mash). Women often bake cassava bread in the backyard. His house is at 32 Tubroose St. If possible, stop by and make an appointment first, because he may not be able to stop work to meet you.

Marcie Sabral makes hand-crafted cotton Garinagu dolls, as well as innovative patchwork quilts. She initially learned these in a class and has perfected the technique on her own. Her cute dolls carry cassava graters and other accessories and are dressed in local style. People come from all over the world to visit her, and her dolls are also sold at the Pelican and other places. Marcie's dreadlocked husband can tell you all about his hunting and farming activities. She's at 55 Citron St. (05-22651); head up the staircase on the right side of the house that has a second-story door with no stairway.

THE TEMPLE: Garifuna religion, the *dugu*, is an important cultural complement to Catholicism. As the Garinagu are a bit secretive about their religion, it's best to visit this religious edifice with a local. To get here turn right by the Housewive's Market. Inside this unprepossessing structure – a concrete, wood, and corrugated iron-roofed building with sand-covered floor – you might see kerchiefed local women chanting *abaímahani* (songs of remembrance) as part of the dugu. A black-and-yellow flag with "Dangriga" cut in black cloth letters is on a pole next to a portrait of Jesus, flanked by pictures of healing ceremonies. Multicolored nylon net hammocks hang on either side.

Accommodations

EXPENSIVE: On the sea front with a dock, 20-room **Pelican Beach Resort** (☎ 05-22044, fax 05-22570; PO Box 14, Dangriga; e-mail pelicanbeach@alt.net; www.belize.net) is close to the airstrip and about a half-hour walk from the main part of town. Despite the name, there is not much of a beach.

One of the few hotels in the nation to have bathtubs in its rooms, the Pelican's compact yet comfortable rooms feature hot water, a desk, and a fan. Brown, wooden slat-style arm chairs face the ocean and benefit from the cool breeze. In addition, there's the town's classiest restaurant, a gift shop, and a display of early paintings by Garifuna artist Benjamin Nicholas. They also offer boat trips to Gales Point and the Manatee Hole and bird sanctuary. Rooms start from around BZ$90 s and BZ$120 d (plus tax) with discounts off-season; children under 12 are free. A number of packages, some combining stays on the reef with a night in the hotel, are also available. You can also stay at their complex on remote South Water Caye, which has simple facilities and similar rates (see page 287).

MODERATE: The 10-room **Bluefields Hotel** (☎ 800-798-1558; 05-22165, fax 05-22296; PO Box 21, Dangriga), 15 Mahogany St., provides comfortable rooms with private bath and hot water, a/c, cable TV, and carpeting. (It was formerly called the Bonefish). Any of a number of tours can be arranged. If you want to stay in the heart of town and have the bucks to burn, this is the place to stay. Rates are around BZ$90 s, BZ$120 d for "deluxe" rooms, and BZ$70 s, BZ$90 d for "semi-deluxe" rooms. A good restaurant is on the premises.

On Ecumenical Drive in Dangriga, the eight-unit **Jungle Huts Motel** (☎ 05-23166/22142, fax 05-23038; PO Box 10, Dangriga) has inexpensive to moderately priced (around BZ$90-100) corrugated tin and thatched-roof cabins with a/c and fans.

BUDGET: Conveniently located right beside the bridge, the 16-room **Riverside Hotel** (☎ 05-2168/2163; PO Box 21, Dangriga) is at 5 Commerce St. Rooms are priced at BZ$21 s and BZ$22 d. It's very clean and good value; baths are shared, and there's a central sitting room. In the US, ☎ 800-256-REEF.

On the other side and slightly superior is the **Hub Guest House** (☎ 05-22397; PO Box 56), 573 South Riverside. Just down the main street a bit to the north, the **Tropical Hotel** (☎ 05-22002), 115 Commerce St., and the **Chameleon**, 119 Commerce St., are less expensive, running about BZ$12. The **Catalina** (☎ 05-22390), 37 Cedar St., charges only BZ$7.50 s.

Located at 977 Waight St. (Southern Foreshore), the nine-room **Rio Mar Hotel** (☎ 05-22201, PO Box 2, Dangriga) has rooms for BZ$35 s, BZ$45 d and on up; rooms have TV. Featuring a balcony with views, nearby 10-room **Soffie's**, 970 Chatuye St., is run by the ebullient returnee from the States of the same name; she charges BZ$50 s or d with TV.

Nine-room **Pal's Guest House** (☎ 05-22095) is at 868 Magoon St; take a left before the bridge. Rooms rent for BZ$40 s and BZ$60 d. Less expensive rooms with shared bath are also available.

Built in 1994, the **Havana Hotel** (☎ 05-22665/22375) is at 490 Ha-

Garifuna Settlement Day

A public holiday in Belize, Garifuna Settlement Day commemorates the arrival of the Garinagu in 1823 from the city of Trujillo in Honduras and reenacts the event. Although the event is celebrated in various locales in Belize, the largest gathering is in Dangriga.

A week before the date, drums pound late into the night, and Garinagu from all over the world descend on Dangriga. In the days leading up to the celebration, a new Miss Garifuna is selected, exhibits are held, and a street parade heads to the grave of community forefather Thomas Vincent Ramos.

Men, women, and children arrive in canoes from out at sea; they sing and chant to the accompaniment of traditional drums. They bring along plantains, bananas, roasted sweet potatos, cassava bread, and seeds for future crops. Upon arrival they request permission from the authorities to allow them to settle and then march jubilantly to a church to give exultant thanks. A Garifuna-style Mass follows with traditional chants and rituals. Many locals attending are dressed in traditional garb.

The events then proceed as follows: Miss Garifuna is officially crowned, and an elder delivers an address to the Belizean Government on behalf of the Garifuna people. It generally centers on an issue of central importance to the Garinagu. A government official responds. There are also cultural presentations. A large parade follows, with a semi-trailer flatbed truck carrying a reggae band. The parade ends at a party site with booths and punta dancing galore.

vana St. Run by a friendly school-teacher, its attractive rooms come with radio and are priced at BZ$33 s and BZ$40 d plus tax. If you're staying in town for a while, furnished houses are available for rent inexpensively. **note:** In the cheapest hotels, be wary of theft.

Food

Just next to the Riverside on Commerce St., **King Burger Restaurant** (formerly "Burger King") is an ordinary Belizean diner offering standard fare, including daily specials.

On Commerce St. near the police station, **Ritchies** is a popular local breakfast and dining spot; breakfasts here feature dishes such as fry jacks and johnnycakes. Computer printout posters extolling God are on the wall, and a 3-D red and gold sign on the cash register reads, "My boss is a Jewish carpenter."

Another popular local restaurant is the **Sea Flame**, 42 Commerce St. Also try **Sophie's**, 970 Chatuye St., and **The Hub** near the bridge and bus terminal. The **Bluefields Hotel**, 15 Mahogany Rd., offers the town's most elegant dining. Also try unmarked **Marlene**'s on Ramos Rd. The **Starlight** and the **Sunrise** are two of the town's Chinese restaurants. There's also a small fish market down by the bridge and along the coast near the Central Fishermen's Co-operative. A **vegetable market** operates here on Thursday and Friday.

Though hard to find unless you dine in a home, local dishes include cassava bread, *sere* (fish cooked with coconut milk), *hudut* (mashed plantains), and *fu fu*. If you attend a ceremonial occasion you may find locals drinking *gafé*, a black, heavily sweetened coffee-like drink made with ground roasted corn or rice.

Entertainment

The happening place is the **Local Motion Disco**. **The Road House** and **The Road House**, both up the beach near the Pelican, have live music on weekends. They share the same name because the original moved and built its own structure; the owner of the first decided that he owned the name, and thus the confusion. One of the two is also known as The Blue Horizon. Otherwise, at night all is quiet save for the whir of bicycle wheels and the thud of reggae. The cool night breeze and the overhead canopy of stars shape the ambience.

Shopping

PJ's Gift Shop, on St. Vincent St. across from Belize Bank, has a variety of local souvenirs including cassettes. **Omar Souvenir and Gift Shop** is at 28 St. Vincent St. **Wong's Store** below the Local Motion Disco sells cassettes. The Pelican also has a small gift shop, which should be stocking this book.

the drums: Both in the stores and on the streets you'll inevitably see two-headed Garifuna drums. They are constructed of hardwoods such as mahogany or mayflower, and the heads are made from peccary, deer, or sheepskin. The thin metal wires or strings strung across the heads serve as snares. Always played by hand, they measure up to three feet across. They're accompanied by *sisira* (gourd shakers).

Services

There's a new **BTL** office in town; it's across from the supermarket and near the police station A **BTIA tourist infomation office** operates inside PJ's Gifts on St. Vincent St. across from Belize Bank. Inside the store there are tapes of Garifuna music along with local handicrafts. The **PO** is on Caney St. The **Z-Line office** is inside the new Z-Line bus terminal to the S of town.

TOURS: The Pelican offers trips to Gales Point, the Citrus Factory, Cockscomb, Hopkins; they can also arrange transport to the islands. **Rosado's Tours** (☎ 05-22119; 22020, 35 Lemon St.), arranges boat charters, car and van tours, fishing, snorkeling and scuba trips. **Tino's Taxi** (☎ 05-22438), 127 Commerce St., provides taxi service, as does **Rodney** (☎ 05-22294), near the airstrip, **Neal** (☎ 05-23309), and **Nash** (☎ 05-23283). **Lester Eiley** (☎ 05-22113), a tour guide who provides boat charters for fishing and scuba, is at 25 Oak St.

For fishing and charters to off-shore cayes, contact Captain Buck or Nolan Jackson Jr. at **Ship Mates** (☎ 05-22171). Passage to Tobacco Caye is BZ$25 pp, OW. Boats generally leave from 7-9 AM. **note:** If going through a third party, be sure to clarify prices with the boat captain *before departure* in order to avoid misunderstandings.

Festivals & Events

Dangriga is one of the best places to experience Garifuna culture, but you must plan on staying around for a while. The town is particularly noted for the **Waribaggabagga dancers**, who sometimes perform at the Pelican, and the Turtle Shell Band, who use turtle shells, guitar, and keyboards. Andy Palacio is the most famous of the town's punta

artists. Island Expeditions stages Garifuna Culture nights at the Eden Rose Bar every Saturday night during peak season and sometimes on Monday as well. Attendance is free to all comers.

The town's major event (and one of the nation's) is **Garifuna Settlement Day** (Nov. 19; see page 279). Yankunu (John Canoe) dancers – a dying tradition – still revel in the streets around Christmas, being traditionally greeted with money, candy, or rum. Conch shells are sounded on **Christmas eve** at midnight. Held on the ninth night after someone dies, a **Nine Night** is an all-night revel; if you think you know how to party, you'll be surprised. One ceremony rarely witnessed by outsiders is the **dugu**, a week-long healing ritual in which a female shaman goes into a trance and talks to the dead. Drumming, dancing, and sacrifice of pigs accompany the ritual (see *Religion* in the *Introduction*).

Vicinity of Dangriga

Often neglected by visitors, the area from Dangriga to the south has much to offer. If you have a vehicle (or go on a tour), you can visit Cockscomb Wildlife Sanctuary (p.), Hopkins (p.), and other attractions. Tours of **Melinda's Farm** (☎ 08-22370) can also be arranged; they make the famous Marie Sharp's Hot Sauce as well as other jams and chutneys.

Some of the least appreciated attractions of this area are its offshore cayes. Here you can still find pelicans, herons, egrets, warblers, and other birds everywhere, as well as opossums, deer and armadillos on

Vicinity of Dangriga

Caribbean Sea

Gales Point

The Shores (lodge)

Mullins River

new road to West Highway

- - - - - Seasonal Roads

To Belmopan

Middlesex

Melinda Forest Reserve

Melinda Forest Station

Hummingbird Highway

Dangriga

N

Silk Grass

Hopkins

Jaguar Reef Resort

Cockscomb Basin Wildlife Sanctuary (Jaguar Sanctuary)

Maya Center

Sittee River (hotel)

Sugar Mill Ruins

Sittee Point

Southern Highway

To Punta Gorda

5 MILES
8 KM

the larger islands. Fishermen live on both Ranguana Caye (see "Vicinity of Placencia") and Laughing Bird Cay (which has now been declared a National Park). Desolate Slasher Sand Bore is bordered by dead coral, which drops off to a lagoon filled with barracuda and other fish.

Gales Point Manatee

Originally founded by logwood cutters, this fishing village of 300 people is 15 miles north of Dangriga. The village is set on an incredibly narrow spit: At places there is room for *only* the road and not much else. A blessed breeze blows across from one side of the spit to the other much of the time.

Gales Point is very much the place time forgot, the classic Caribbean village of yore with picture-postcard homes and a slow-going ambience. If you are heading south from the seeming enclave of Manatee Lodge, you first pass by the police station with its exterior staircase. It has been condemned. Next up is the post office, which is in a local woman's home. She may emerge from her doorway with remnants of freshly kneaded dough still on her hands.

The Belizean government designated some 115,000 acres as the **Manatee Special Development Area** – which includes the Northern and Southern Lagoons, pine ridge, mangroves, as well as 22 miles of beachfront. In addition to being the nation's primary nesting beach for the hawksbill turtle, the area is the home of Central America's largest population of Caribbean manatees.

Formed in 1992, the **Gales Point Progressive Cooperative (GPPC)** is working for small-scale development. The GPPC has formed the Manatee Farmer's Association (a group of cooperating small farmers), the Manatee Tour Operators Association (boat operators and tour guides), and the Gales Point Bed & Breakfast Association. Products produced locally include wines and jams as well as cohune fly brushes and "tie tie" baskets.

GETTING HERE: Dories no longer depart from Belize City on a regular basis. Expect to pay BZ$250 for a charter (see next paragraph). If you're coming by car, you can either approach via Dangriga or turn down Manatee Road (New Road) at La Democracia (Mile 31, where the Midway Inn is situated) on the Western Highway – a distance of 25 miles in all. It may be possible to hitch a ride. Expect to deal with dust until such time as the road is surfaced, a day thousands of Belizeans in the area are wishing and praying for.

FROM GALES POINT: Dories no longer run on a regular basis to Belize City. A charter to Belize City is BZ$250/dory. A 15-mile dirt road leads to the Hummingbird Highway, but there's no regular transportation. A charter could meet you from Dangriga by arrangement, but it would be quite expensive. If heading to Belize City, take Manatee Road 25 miles to La Democracia (Mile 31) on the Western Highway.

THE CANAL TRIP: One of the most wonderfully relaxing trips in the country is the river trip down the canals and through the lagoon to Gales Point. Although Manatee Lodge also delivers its guests this way, Shores may be doing the charter because they presently have a bigger boat. The canal was constructed by the British in 1928 in order to expedite the transport of logs.

Your charter boat will depart from the Texaco Station at the Pay N Save supermarket near the Civic Center (a five min. ride from the airport). Be sure to have your film, water, sunscreen, and binoculars handy. As you begin cruising down the Burdon Canal, rusting refrigerators set by the sides of houses (as well as other detritus) quickly give way to idyllic mangrove-lined stretches. You pass under the bridge on the Western Hwy., and then continue on down and through to the Jones Lagoon, then on down Boom Creek (so named because of the mahoe trees once sent floating down its waters). You will note coconut trees afflicted with the plague of lethal yellowing, ripe banana plants, and blue egrets as well as other aquatic denizens. The vast open expanse of the Northern Lagoon is next.

Then you pass by the roseate spoonbills nesting on Sand Caye. By 5-5:30 PM, the island is covered. Heading straight on, you will arrive at Gales Point. If you are headed for Shores, you must go E through the Manatee Cut and then along the coast – a dramatic ride, which can be thrilling.

ACCOMMODATIONS: Some lodging is provided through the **Gales Point Bed & Breakfast Association.** There are currently eight B & Bs (accommodating a total of 20 guests) and a seven-room, two-story hotel on the waterfront is under construction (and may someday be completed). Five percent of total revenues from the B & Bs is re-

mitted to the GPPC, and profits from the hotel will be used to support the management of protected areas. Some rooms have indoor plumbing. Rates are BZ$20 s, BZ$25 d, BZ$20 per cabaña, and BZ$5 per tent for camping (BZ$30 pw). Weekly rates for rooms are available, as are long-term rates for researchers and volunteers. Meals (served in local homes) are BZ$7 breakfast, BZ$8 lunch, and BZ$10 dinner. Interested parties should contact Ione Samuels (at the general store right at the entrance to town) before or upon arrival. No reservations are required, and business is slow so they could use some help! Contact ☎ 02-78339 or the Gales Point Community Phone, ☎ 05-22087; ask for Ione Samuels.

Another alternative for the world traveling backpacker set is **Gentle's Cool Spot** (☎ 02-12031), a pavilion restaurant that rents spartan rooms for BZ$20 pd and serves food for reasonable prices. It is *the* hangout!

Wishtree Campsite and Bed & Breakfast is run by Doc and Yvette Critten. They offer camping (BZ$5 pp, pn), tent rental (BZ$10 pn), and a partitioned section of their small house and meals at B&B prices. They also rent **kayaks** for BZ$20 (one), BZ$25 (two).

An even less expensive alternative for the backpacker set is **Metho's Coconut Campground,** which offers camping (BZ$5 pp, pn), and inexpensive rooms. Veggie meals are BZ$5. Metho builds drums and teaches drum-making and drumming.

Set on the peninsula's tip, **Manatee Lodge** (☎ 08-23320, fax 08-23334; PO Box 170, Belmopan) has eight attractive and large rooms; canoe use is included in the rates.

The grounds are reminiscent of a British Caribbean outpost with green lawns and attractive white colonial-style buildings. It's a relaxing oasis, and a great place to hang out! Rates (around BZ$160 s and BZ$210 d plus 17% tax and service) include the use of a canoe, and a number of excursions are possible. Tasty, well-prepared food is served in the restaurant, which is popular with tour groups. (Be sure to see the manatee and crocodile skulls). The management also runs Hidden Valley Inn in the Mountain Pine Ridge, and packages are available that combine the two. In the US, ☎ 800-334-7942 or 904-222-2333, fax 904-222-1992, or write 1220 E Park Ave., Ste. 12, Tallahassee, FL 32301.

FOOD: Meals are provided by villagers and are priced at BZ$5 for breakfast, BZ$8 for lunch, and BZ$14 for dinner. Manatee Lodge also serves meals. There's only one small general store in the village, so you should bring everything you might need.

TOURS & EXCURSIONS: If you have your own vehicle, you can use the town as a base to visit a number of places. Bird Caye (see "by boat," page 276) in the lagoon hosts nesting herons, egrets, wood ibis, and roseate spoonbills. The mangrove-lined Northern and Southern Lagoons are rich in birds and other wildlife, including manatees. Hear the roar of bulls during mating season. For information on trips contact Kevin Andrewin. Dories hold six to eight people. Trips (organized by the B&B Association) include the Manatee Watch (BZ$60/dory), Seashore (BZ$60/dory), Cornhouse Creek (BZ$75/dory), Ben Loman (Lomond) Cave (BZ$100/dory),

Bird Caye (BZ$150/dory), and a Night Trip (BZ$100/dory). A walking excursion to Darby Pot Cave costs BZ$40 per guide. Manatee Lodge and Shores also have a number of trips.

☞ *Traveler's Tip*

Miss Iris (who lives in a brown house with cashew trees in front) makes tie tie baskets. Mrs. Samuels reportedly sells some of the best local wines. Soldier Creek, six mi. distant on the road, has relaxing swimming holes with large rocks.

Vicinity of Gales Point

Set on the Caribbean seaside across a cut from Gales Point, **"The Shores"** tel./fax 501-21-2023; www.belize.net; e-mail shores@ btl.net) is a very special place geared toward travelers who are true adventurers. It is the product of one man's vision, intrepid ex-construction contractor David Morris, who brought all of the materials in by boat! Designed to harmonize with the surrounding pristine environment, its simple yet cozy cabanas on stilts command ocean views. Outside, sandy beach lines the coast as far as the eye can see. The totally private beach stretches for several miles. There's very limited hiking in the interior. Birdwatching is good.

The attractively furnished main pavilion is eminently comfortable. There's generally good music playing, and delicious meals are served here. Food is Belizean-style, yet much more innovative and tasty than what you will get in the average restaurant. Vegetarians will be

Cayes near Dangriga

Southern Long Caye

Mosquito Caye

Sandfly Cayes

Columbus Caye

Dangriga

Columbus Reef

Man O'War Bird Sanctuary

Coco Plum Caye

Tobacco Caye

Man O'War Caye

Hopkins

Tobacco Range

Tobacco Reef

Sittee Point

South Water Caye

Stewart Caye

Carrie Bow Caye

Bread & Butter Caye

Wee Wee Caye

5 MILES

catered to, and fish is generally available. The resort is generator-run, and your room is supplied with a kerosene lamp for romantic after-hours frolicking.

David is an avid and highly enthusiastic diver, and diving is one of the resort's features. He offers instruction and will take you out to a remote cay for a picnic lunch and snorkeling followed by more diving.

Rates includes accommodations with three meals and tax. Gratuity (10%) is additional. Rates are around BZ$180 s, BZ$240 d. Children under 12 are charged BZ$70 each. Transfer by boat (imperative as there is no road) is extra.

Tobacco Caye

First settled by English Puritans who introduced tobacco as a crop around 1640, Tobacco Caye lies just north of South Water Caye and opposite Dangriga, from which you can reach it via a 12-mile, hour-long boat ride. One of the most attractive cayes, this five-acre island has a small population and a number of stately palms. Earthwatch volunteers have participated in studies here of nocturnal predators such as moray eels. Sadly, it has become increasingly crowded, and there is a dwelling now on practically every bit of land!

GETTING HERE: Passage to To-bacco Caye is BZ$25 pp, OW. Boats generally leave from 7-9 AM. Otherwise, you'll need a charter. This would be an excellent place to base yourself if you're a kayaker doing day trips. There are no phones, little fresh water is available, electricity comes from generators, and the culinary mainstays are rice and beans, coconuts, and seafood. The reef is 50 feet offshore.

ACCOMMODATIONS: Moderately priced **Island Camps** (☎ 02-72109/05-222109; Box 174, Dangriga) has 10 units. It's been acclaimed by travelers as the best deal in terms of price and quality: around BZ$45 pp for food and lodging. Six-room **Reef End Lodge** ☎ 05-22171; PO Box 10, Dangriga) charges around BZ$80 s and BZ$130 d with meals; better rooms are BZ$150 d. Rates include use of snorkels, fins, and canoes.

Offering attractive Caribbean-style cabanas on stilts, six-unit **Ocean's Edge Fishing Lodge** (☎ 05-22419) charges BZ$130 s and BZ$200 d plus tax, including three meals; fishing is BZ$250 for two and diving is BZ$70 pp, per dive. In the US, ☎ 800-967-8184 or 713-894-0548. The seven-room budget-priced **Fairweather & Noble Rose** (☎ 02-72866; PO Box 240, Belize City) offers meal plans with its lodging.

SNORKELING: According to Kirk Barrett, the best snorkeling here is found outside the reef wall. In *Belize by Kayak* he writes, "For incredible snorkeling, wade through the shallows to the reef wall behind the island (to the east). Walk north up the reef wall around 300 to 500 yards, then carefully dive in on the outer side of the wall. There are mountains and ravines of coral out here and plenty of fish life.... Be careful when going to the outer side of the reef wall. Only attempt this on a calm or low wind day.

Tobacco Range, a group of man-grove islands with sandfleas and a few inhabitants, and Man-O-War Caye (Bird Caye), a nesting island for boobies and other birds, are nearby." Snorkeling is even better way offshore where the water is clearer; you will pay BZ$10 pp to go out to a spot.

South Water Caye

This small, attractive island is part of the **South Water Marine Reserve,** which was declared in Aug. 1996.

ACCOMMODATIONS: Pelican Beach Resort (☎ 05-22044, fax 05-22570; PO Box 14, Dangriga) owns part of this island and has modest accommodations in stilt-style houses.

Holding up to six, **The Osprey's Nest and The Frangipani House** rent for BZ$190 per day; meals (if desired) are BZ$60 pd. Sleeping up to 22 and designed for school groups, **The Pelican's University** charges BZ$110 pp, pd for room and board; the boat is BZ$230 each way. The fence on the property is the result of a a war between the Bowman family and Fred Dodd, who owns the Leslie Cottages.

The 14-room **Blue Marlin Lodge** (☎ 05-22243, fax 05-22296; Box 21, Dangriga; www.belize.net; e-mail marlin@btl.net) is an expensive diving resort. In the US, call ☎ 800-798-1558 or 218-847-4441. All-inclusive all-year diving packages cost around US$1,195 pp, d, and fishing packages are around US$1,650 pp, d; both are for eight days and seven nights. Five-day, four-night and "vacation" packages are also available. Service charges, room tax, and bar tabs are extra. For information about the five **Leslie Cottages** (☎ 05-22004), in the US ☎ 800-548-5843 or 508-655-1461.

Carrie Bow Caye

The Smithsonian rents this small gem of an island from the Bowman family and operates a research station here. Researchers arrive here for brief periods, and the caye may be visited by appointment. The reef to the east of the island has good snorkeling.

Possum Point Biological Station and Sittee River

Near the small village of Sittee River about six miles before Maya Center, Possum Point ecological field center is operated by Paul and Mary Shave. Located in a lowland tropical forest, the attractive facility caters to biology students and natural history groups. Courses in tropical field ecology are offered here, and the marine lab on **Wee Wee Caye**, nine miles east offshore, teaches coral reef biology.

Sittee River is a remarkable place. Although you can tour the tiny island in five minutes, it's truly a living natural history museum – offering an up-close look at a mangrove ecosytem. Understanding what's going on here takes time. Aside from the narrow gangplank leading to the toilet and the en-

trance dock, the mangroves remain as they always have. Although the island is named after the leaf cutter ants, more remarkable inhabitants are the wowlas (boa constrictors), which you can spot hanging in the trees – sometimes they don't change position for days on end.

The island has been leased from the government, and everything has been built on a shoestring.

ACCOMMODATIONS: The Shaves offer reasonably priced packages, which include stays at Possum Point and Wee Wee, and simple but hearty and delicious cuisine. They also offer transport to and from the reef for snorkeling and between the stations on their fleet of wowla boats, 25-foot fiberglass dories equipped with 55-hp outboards. You need to bring all equipment, including your own sheets. Accommodation is simple yet comfortable, and the dining room-study area features Mennonite furniture and hammocks for lounging about. The building on the island that appears to be a Shinto shrine is, in reality, a generator, and electricity is available during the dinner hours – after that, light is supplied by kerosene lamps. There are a few inconveniences that come with the territory. Sandflies can be absolutely ferocious. At night you must walk the gangplank – past mangroves blanching white as your lantern hits them – heading toward the loo, which has a hole so large it might bring back childhood fears of falling in! At night there's not much to do save sit out on the pier and watch the stars. Accommodations (up to 30 people) are similar at Possum Point; it's a paradise for ornithologists, herpetologists, entomologists, botanists and all-around nature lovers. Most of the 44-acre site has been left in its natural state and there's over a mile of trails. Excursions are available. Paul and Mary also run the Sittee River Scenic Park (Bocatura Bank) for tent campers; efficiency cottages are available for rental. Write Paul and Mary Shave, Sittee River S/C, Belize, Central America; community ☎ 05-22888, fax 05-22038.

Another popular place to stay, recommended by travelers, is the **Toucan Sittee Lodge** (no phone; around BZ$75 d). There is also the **Sittee River Lodge** (☎ 05-22888, 212-659-3082) at 99 Freetown Rd, which is an attractive eight-rm lodge right on the river. Rates are BZ$100 s, BZ$160 d; meal plans are available, as are numerous excursions ranging from deserted beach camping to river fishing to waterskiing.

Lillpat (☎ 805-963-2501, fax 805-966-0878; e-mail lillpat@aol.com; www.belize.net) is a fishing resort designed so that fishermen can bring their wives along. Shopping, canoeing, and other trips are offered. Rooms are a/c; and there is a pool and restaurant. In the US write Box 90259, Santa Barbara, CA 93190.

Glover's Atoll Guest House is a set of rundown houses on stilts; they have dorm beds. It is connected with the Lomont operation on Glover's Atoll, thus the name! Also here is the budget-priced four-unit **Sittee Fish Camp** (Box 1820, Belize City) and six-room **Prospect Guest House** (☎ 05-23389/22006).

SHOPPING: There's a small general store in the village with a limited selection of goods.

SIGHTS: The river is a great place to kayak or to canoe. It's a four-mile walk to Hopkins along a dirt road, and a bus may be running.

Set to the southeast of Hopkins, mangrove-clad **Sittee Point** has a light tower and is at the mouth of the Sittee River.

Three miles from the junction with the Southern Highway is the **Sittee Sugar Mill,** the most interesting place to visit in the area. Operated by locomotive steam engines, the Regalia Estate and Serpon Estate mills were imported from England and Scotland. One engine has been identified as having been made in Richmond, VA and is the only known remaining one of its kind. The mills opened in 1863, and the Serpon Estate was operated by a Mr. Thomas Bowman, an ancestor of the Bowmans who today run the Pelican Beach. The engines were hauled in by mules.

The mill was slated for bulldozing in 1989 and was saved only through an 11th-hour appeal. Although the site has been cleared (through the efforts of a student team from Trent College in 1992), the mill still retains much of its foliage. Some parts even have trees growing through them. There is Visitor's Center of sorts. Bring water and slather on *plenty* of mosquito repellent.

Hopkins

This small village, home to some 1,000 Garifuna fishermen and their families, stretches two miles along a curving bay. The town was founded in the aftermath of an unnamed 1941 hurricane. It is named for the late Roman Catholic bishop, Frederick Charles Hopkins. The village was leveled by Hurricane Hattie in 1961.

The Jaguar Reef Lodge

Surprisingly located out in the boonies near Hopkins, **Jaguar Reef Lodge** (☎/fax 092-3452; e-mail jagreef@btl.net) is juxtapositioned on the coast between the barrier reef and the Cockscomb Jaguar Reserve. This well designed luxury resort offers 14 handsomely appointed rooms divided among seven cottages. the units are joined to the main pavilion by an attractive walkway. Some percentage of profits are donated to environmental organizations. Use of sea kayaks and mountain bikes are included in the rates. Rates are BZ$200 s, BZ$240 d, and BZ$260 t. Children under 12 are free. Meals are BZ$14 breakfast, BZ$22 lunch, and BZ$38 dinner. Although well prepared and served in an attractive atmosphere – either in the dining room or on the patio, fans of spicy food will be disappointed! A variety of day trips are organized including ones to Cockscomb a river and reef trip, a trip to the Mayflower archaeological dig, and a hike to Antelope or Hummingbird Falls. Efficient and personable manager Bradley will come by your table at dinner and run down the list of tours for the following day. **note:** Jungle Sea Lodge, a new facility to be geared toward the "family soft adventure market" is in the planning stages and is nearby. The management also operates the Belize Development Company, which attempts to sell land tracts to retirees.

Today, it remains a quiet fishing village that is gradaully becoming geared toward tourism. It has one of the nation's best stretches of beach. Without much in the way of resort-style facilities and amenities, it's a perfect get-away spot – no yuppies here!

GETTING HERE: Head for Dangriga first and check there (not with the touts!) for current information. Buses (one hr.) are now available. Ritchies runs at 11:30 and 4:30 and Z-line is at 11:30 and 12:15 on Fri., Sat., and Mon. By boat (20 min.) is preferable but more difficult; ask around at the dock. Final alternatives are to take the bus to the junction and walk in, take a taxi (expensive) from Dangriga, or walk from Sittee River.

FROM HOPKINS: You can walk to Sittee River (around four miles) via a dirt road in the dry season. Check

locally for transport times back to Dangriga.

ACCOMMODATIONS & FOOD: Run by the only women's cooperative in Belize, six-room, thatched-roof **Sandy Beach Lodge** (☎ 05-37006) is at the southern end by the beach. It was established in 1986. The lodge consists of two attractive thatched-roof cabins. Charges are BZ$18 s (shared bath) and BZ$35 d. Meals are BZ$7 breakfast, BZ$7 lunch, and BZ$10 dinner. Group rates are available, as are two large cabins with cooking facilities.

Popular with kayakers, **Jungle Jeanie**'s (e-mail junglej@btl.net) is a small lodge with two beachfront cabanas for BZ$25 s, BZ$30 d, BZ$45 t; there's an outhouse and outdoor shower. Breakfast (for guests) is BZ$5; coffee is real. Kayaks and windsurfers are available, and hiking, snorkeling, and diving may be arranged. Jeanie is here part of the year; she runs a chain of hospitality schools the rest of the time.

Ransom's Seaside Garden Cabaña (☎ 05-22889, fax 05-22038) is a small "resort" run by an American who lives here with his mother. He charges BZ$200 pp, pw for a two-room unit with cable TV, radio, library, and full kitchen and bath. You can just hang out on the hammocks, take a spin on a bike or paddle a kayak: use of both is included. Laundry and maid service is daily except Sun.

A small set of cottages, **Hopkins Paradise** (☎ 05-37013; Box 121, Dangriga), charges BZ$90 pn or BZ$560 pw. Rooms have refrigerator, coffee maker, and fan. Fishing, bicycle rentals, and trips to the reef (20 min. by boat) are available. It's generally shut up off-season when the owners head to Alaska.

Retired 60-something midwife **Mama Nuñez** offers basic rooms in one of her huts or in her house; she'll also cook for you, and you may camp here for a fee. She's around 200 yards north of the Sandy Beach Lodge; ask a local. **Sybill**, a Swiss expatriate, runs a thatched-roof restaurant that sometimes has music at night. At the junction of the road leading to the Southern Highway, **Hopkins Paradise** is a collection of cabins.

Swinging Armadillos (☎ 05-37016) is a unique restaurant-bar that rents out rooms for BZ$40-50 pn. Lounge in the hammocks.

Other places to eat include **Innies Restaurant** (☎ 05-37026), a local place out on the main road; and **Iris** (across from Caribbean View).

ENTERTAINMENT: As one might expect in a small village, there is not a whole lot to do at night. Bars include the **Laru Béyu** ("Seaside Bar") and the **Watering Hole**.

SERVICES: Fresh veggies can be scarce; however, a truck arrives every Fri. at around noon and sounds its horn. Stores include **C&C Meat/Fish Products, Ventura Grocery,** and the **Nuñez** store. Contrary to what you might read in some outdated guide, there is now telephone service and electricity. As there's no sewage system, take care with the water. Jungle Jeanie's has **e-mail** and **fax** services. Guide **Florencio Bol** (☎ 05-22083) resides in Silk Grass.

Collett Taxi (☎ 05-22033) can take you from place to place. Hopkins Harbor Development (☎ 05-37001) has **cars and trucks for rent.**

The **community telephone** is 05-22033. **Hopkins Assistance** is run by Marsha (☎ 05-37014, fax 37011; marsha@btl.net).

Cockscomb Basin Wildlife Preserve

Cockscomb Jaguar Reserve

Located off the Southern Highway to the south of Dangriga, this is both the first and only jaguar reserve in the world. A tropical moist forest with 180 inches annual rainfall, the reserve covers 99,000 acres. A small Classic Period Maya ceremonial center, the ruins of Chucil Balam lie secreted in the forest. There are abandoned logging camps with such

Cockscomb Basin Wildlife Reserve

Trail Distances	
Antelop Trail	2.2mi.
Ben's Bluff	0.9mi.
BYCC Express	0.1mi.
Currasow Trail	0.4mi.
Gibnut Loop	0.8mi.
River Path	0.3mi.
Rubber Tree Trail	0.2mi.
Tinnamou	0.7mi.
Victoria Peak Trail	0.8mi.
Wari Trail	0.9mi.
Waterfall	0.9mi.

To Maya Center
Crashed Plane
Ben's Bluff
Waterfall
Tinnamou
Currasow Trail
Rubber Tree Trail
Gibnut Loop
CAMP SITE
P
Antelop Trail
Victoria Peak Trail
River Overlook
BYCC Express
Wari Trail
South Stann Creek River
To Victoria Peak
N

descriptive names as *Sale si se puede* ("leave if you can") and "Go to Hell Camp."

Flora & Fauna

Once considered to be just a moving object for hunters to shoot, some 50 of the nation's 500 jaguars are now protected here. Other cats include jaguarundis, pumas, ocelots, and margays. There are also tapirs, kinkajous, pacas, brocket deer, iguanas, tommy-goffs (fer-de-lances) and boas.

The 290 bird species recorded include toucans, curassows, scarlet macaws, Agami herons, and king vultures. (A flock of scarlet macaws was sighted here in 1996). The red-eyed tree frog also dwells within the reserve. Many of the larger trees were felled by Hurricane Hattie, and the canopy height now ranges from 50 to 150 feet.

Climate

A distinct dry season runs from February through May. Between 10 and 180 inches of rain falls during the wet season from June through January.

History

The surrounding forest reserve was set up in 1984; the wildlife sanctuary in its interior was established two years later. In 1984 the New York Zoological Society sponsored a two-year field study of jaguar ecology in the Cockscomb Basin. Conducting the study was Dr. Alan Rabinowitz, who lived among the Maya, radio tracking jaguars for over two years. Rabinowitz recommended that a sanctuary be established in the area, and he received backing from the Belize Audubon Society. The World Wildlife Fund US also promised financial assistance.

In 1986 the government declared 3,000 acres of the 108,000-acre forest to be a sanctuary. The community of Maya who lived within the reserve's confines were relocated in 1986 (without compensation) to the village of Maya Center five miles away, and newly appointed sanctuary manager Ernesto Sacqui was sent to the US for training. In 1990, after assurance of further backing had been received from the World Wildlife Fund US, the reserve was expanded to 108,000 acres. A new chapter in the reserve's history came with the introduction of a troop of 14 howler monkeys from the Community Baboon Sanctuary; further translocations are planned.

Transport

GETTING HERE: Cockscomb is for people who don't mind roughing it a bit, not for those who require every comfort supplied. This isn't a game park you can drive through; it requires both time and effort to see the wildlife here. A permit (obtainable from the site headquarters, the Belize Audubon Society in Belize City, or the Pelican Beach Resort in Dangriga) is required.

If you don't have your own vehicle, you can take any Placencia or Punta Gorda bus and get off at Maya Center; the entrance to the reserve will be on your left just before the bridge at the beginning of the village. (Another alternative is to take a tour from Placencia or Dangriga.)

Before entering the reserve, sign in at the craft center, a cooperative run by village women. The center features stone carvings, beadwork, and basketry. You must walk or drive the six miles from Maya Center on the main Southern Highway. It's a stiff uphill hike, but it's worth it. On your way up, note the home with mahogany doors near the crafts center. Ostentatious by local standards, it's the home of the local Baptist preacher.

Accommodations

Within the reserve, it costs BZ$15 to berth in a bunk or BZ$3 to camp. Berths can accommodate up to 20; gas stoves and all utensils are supplied. New and more deluxe accommodations are available for BZ$30 pp. You should bring all food as the store at the base has only limited supplies. If you don't want to stay here, the nearest accommodations are in Sittee River and Hopkins, but to really see anything you need to spend time around the reserve – especially at dawn and dusk. Be sure to visit the new Visitor's Center. Its displays are the work of Peace Corps volunteer Bonnie Gestring.

Hiking

Director Ernesto Sacqui will be happy to answer all of your questions. There are a continually expanding variety of trails. It's best to get an early start at dawn to maximize your chances of seeing wildlife. The **River Path Trail** and the **Currasow Trail** connect via the **Rubber Tree Trail**. You can swim in the river, but exercise caution. Watch for howler monkeys.

The **Antelop Trail** connects with the **Gibnut Loop Trail**, which connects the **Victoria Peak Trail** and the **Tinamou Trail**. Named after a species of bird, this trail is beautiful, good for seeing wildlife owing to the propensity of wild fruit in the area, but it can be muddy and slippery. An airplane suspended in a tree is near the trail's east end. It's been there since 1983, when it missed the runway (now reclaimed by the jungle). **Ben's Bluff Trail** leads from the riverside and a swimming hole to a ridgetop, commanding a view of the entire Cockscomb Basin. Allow half a day for this venture and keep in mind that it's quite steep in places.

Other trails lead as far afield as 3,543-foot **Victoria Peak**, a three-day hike. Guides can be hired at BZ$25 apiece but, as a minimum of two are required, it's better to go in a group to hold down costs. There are no shelters, but your guides will make a hut. A permit must be obtained in advance from the Forestry Dept. in Belmopan; you must state the number of persons in your party, as well as the exact dates of your visit. It's a rugged but spectacular trip. **note:** The British volunteer group Raleigh International has reportedly improved the trail.

The Maya site of **Maintzunun** ("Small Hummingbird") lies about 10 miles north of Cockscomb.

Placencia Village

Set approximately 100 miles south of Belize City, skinny 16-mile-long Placencia Peninsula points south from the mainland, edged by a white sandy beach stretching from Riversdale to Placencia Village. At its southern tip lies the relaxed, attractive fishing village of the same name. Up until recently, the only way to get to Placencia was by boat, which has fortuitously enabled the area to maintain its charm.

Placencia's main drag is an often-crowded sidewalk, and goods are transported around by wheelbarrow. The village's history dates back to the infamous Portuguese pirate Cabral, who settled the peninsula along with his buccaneer chums. Many of the residents are fair-skinned descendants of English and Portuguese settlers. There have been a number of Spanish galleons wrecked offshore, and Spanish "pieces of eight" are found on the beach from time to time. And then there are the stories about the bales of cocaine that have floated out to the cayes (and, reportedly, even village beaches) in the past few years. Dubbed "sea lotto" by the locals, some 55 bales (24 kg) washed up as recently as Feb. 1997; a previous flotilla came in Nov. 1996.

These days, Placencia is on its way to rivaling San Pedro (Ambergris Caye) as a major tourist destination, and resorts are springing up all along the beach past Seine Bight. Modern construction in the village is beginning to threaten its traditional atmosphere. The new airstrip, which permits flights to land near the village, rather than across the water in Big Creek, also encourages more visitors. More and more Europeans are coming here. Fortunately, there is still no Club Med or Holiday Inn, and there are none planned. There is, however, a reliable supply of electricity as well as piped-in water; both are recent. The biggest threat here is that all of the village's charm will evaporate in the face of renovation and fences (a recent introduction).

Transport

GETTING HERE: Tropic Air (☎ 02-45671, 026-2012, 800-422-3435; www.belize.net; e-mail tropic@btl.net) and **Maya Island Air** (☎ 02-72312) fly to Placencia from both the domestic airport (BZ$93) and from Belize International (BZ$110). With Tropic you can connect to flights from Corozal, or San Pedro, and they also fly from Punta Gorda. From the airstrip, you can walk easily to Kitty's Place and other neighboring resorts, but it's about 1½ miles into town – a taxi ride of BZ$10 or BZ$7 pp for two or more. (This ride is the only one that is set).

If walking, be sure you take the right direction or you'll end up in Seine Bight (about a mile). Buses to Independence leave from Dangriga, and a direct bus runs at 2 or 2:30 from Dangriga daily. You arrive on the Independence side, and must cross by boat – BZ$20 to cross – so it's preferable to take the direct bus to Placencia. While the road trip is quite beautiful, it's also long, and the road is not in great shape, to say the least. If you're driving, watch carefully so that you don't miss the turnoff.

☞ **Traveler's Tip**
For an educational detour (if you have your own vehicle), take the turnoff and go straight through the banana plantations rather than heading straight to Placencia. You'll see the workers' lodging and banana processing. The road reconnects with the main drag to Placencia; turn L.

GETTING AROUND: In the village, it's easy. You walk. You can ride bikes (remember, roads are dusty), but there is no car rental, and taxi rates are fixed only to the airport (and are quite high for the distances covered). The village is small, but

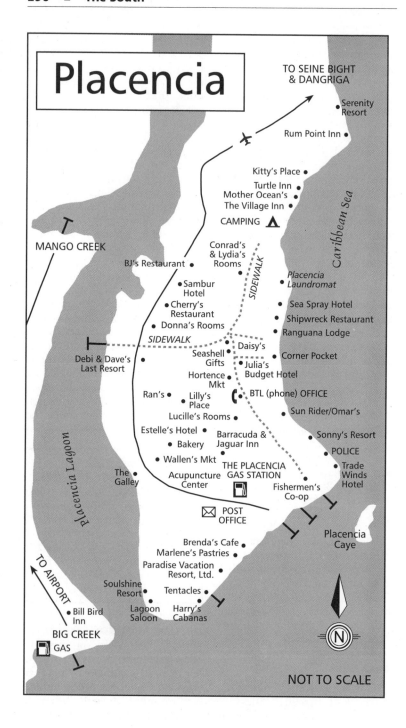

Placencia

TO SEINE BIGHT & DANGRIGA

• Serenity Resort

Rum Point Inn •

Kitty's Place •

Turtle Inn •

Mother Ocean's •

The Village Inn •

CAMPING ⛺

Caribbean Sea

MANGO CREEK

Conrad's & Lydia's Rooms

BJ's Restaurant •

SIDEWALK

Placencia Laundromat

• Sambur Hotel

• Cherry's Restaurant

• Donna's Rooms

SIDEWALK

Sea Spray Hotel

Shipwreck Restaurant

Ranguana Lodge

Daisy's

Debi & Dave's Last Resort

Seashell Gifts

Corner Pocket

Julia's Budget Hotel

Hortence Mkt

Ran's •

Lilly's Place

BTL (phone) OFFICE

Placencia Lagoon

Lucille's Rooms

Sun Rider/Omar's

Estelle's Hotel •

Barracuda & Jaguar Inn

• Bakery

Sonny's Resort

• Wallen's Mkt

POLICE

The Galley

Acupuncture Center

THE PLACENCIA GAS STATION ⛽

Trade Winds Hotel

Fishermen's Co-op

POST OFFICE ✉

Placencia Caye

Brenda's Cafe •

Marlene's Pastries •

Paradise Vacation Resort, Ltd.

Soulshine Resort •

Tentacles •

TO AIRPORT

Lagoon Saloon

Harry's Cabanas

• Bill Bird Inn

BIG CREEK

⛽ GAS

N

NOT TO SCALE

confusing if you arrive at night. The sidewalk – rather crowded at times – varies from a foot to three feet in width and it runs from the edge of town down to the dock area. From there a path leads off to the right, passing a few restaurants, including Brenda's. The dusty clay main road more or less parallels the sidewalk, but it leads up past the outlying resorts to Seine Bight and beyond. From the village, you'll come first to the Village Inn, then Turtle Inn, Kitty's Place, Rum Point Inn, Serenity Resort, Seine Bight (Nautical Inn and others), and then the Green Parrot and Singing Sands.

FROM PLACENCIA: To Belize City, it costs BZ$19 (BZ$6 only to Dangriga) with Z-Line. Buses depart at 5, 9, and noon, with an additional departure at 3:30 on Sat. and Mon. Ritchies (BZ$17) also runs. To get to Punta Gorda you must either fly with Tropic or Maya, return to Dangriga, or get a dory (motorized canoe) to Mango Creek (Independence).

☞ *Traveler's Tip*

The Hokey Pokey (☎ 06-22376) runs at around 10 AM over to Mango Creek. For BZ$10, it is the cheapest way to get across the channel. It returns at 2. And, unfortunately, it does live up to its name.

Accommodations

INEXPENSIVE/MODERATE: One of the nicer places is five-room **Ranguana Lodge** (☎/fax 06-23112), which has a sister operation on the caye of the same name.

Each wood-paneled unit has a double and single bed, as well as a refrigerator. Expect to spend around BZ$150 total. **Westwind** rents attractive rooms by the beach for around BZ$90 d.

First opened in Feb. 1975, **Coconut Cottage** (☎/fax 06-23234) is run by friendly Kay Westby. Each cottage has two beds (a double and single), refrigerator, coffee maker, and hammocks on the porch. You can be met at the Belize International Airport. Rates are around BZ$100 plus tax.

The 12-room **Sonny's Resort** (☎ 06-23103/44975, fax 02-32819) charges BZ$66 s and BZ$88 d; its cabins are more expensive (around BZ$120) but have cable TV.

Tradewinds Cabanas (☎ 06-23101/23109) offers rooms for approximately BZ$130/night.

Set right on the end of the peninsula, the eight-room **Paradise Vacation Resort** (☎ 06-23260, 23179) has simple rooms renting for BZ$26.50 with shared bath to BZ$37.50 and BZ$47.50 for rooms with private baths.

The **D&L Resort** (☎ 23243) charges around BZ$40 s and BZ$50 d; it has four double rooms, with one shared bath and one apartment with two bedrooms, kitchen, and bath. Set on the peninsula's tip, **Harry's Cabanas** (☎ 06-23155) rent for BZ$110; they hold three each, and one of them has a kitchen.

Off the main road, **The Barracuda and Jaguar Inn** (☎ 06-23330, fax 06-23250) has a restaurant. Its comfortable units have refrigerators, coffee makers, and balconies. Rates are BZ$70 d, plus tax.

Right across the channel and near the Lagoon Saloon, **Soulshine Resort** (☎ 06-23347, 800-890-

1-500-863-5580

6082; e-mail soulshine@btl.net; www.soulshine.com) is not exactly on its own "private island" as its promotions claim, but still is something close. They are on a spit of reclaimed land bordering a mangrove cay purchased from an entrepreneur. The owners came upon the unusual name while on their first trip to Belize when the Allman Brothers song of the same name came on the sound system at Rum Point Inn. They decided that "if we ever had a resort, we'd call it Soulshine."

The resort is separated from the mainland by a narrow canal. In order to get to the resort, you have to ring a bell, blow on your whistle, shout, or otherwise arrange for a boat to come across and get you. If this all sounds troublesome, it's not and is well worth the effort.

Soulshine is a peaceful oasis within walking distance from the village. It is the only property in Placencia with a pool. A boardwalk leads to thatched-roof cabanas installed by Maya from the Toledo District. Rooms have two bedrooms and a ceiling fan. Room rates are BZ$270 s, BZ$300 d; tax and 10% service are added. There's a lounge area with a VCR and tape and book library as well as an outdoor lounge area near the pool. Meals are well prepared and quite tasteful. Dishes derive from European, US, Mexican, and Belizean specialties. Service is impeccable, and you are served at your own table. Breakfast and dinner are included in the rates. (Vegetarians will be catered to). The resort is nonsmoking (permitted outside of buildings only), which should come as a solace to many.

Soulshine offers a number of tours (including a Monkey River trip) and can hook you up with a fishing guide and a boat. A variety of packages are offered. In the US write Box 84, Ivoryton, CT 06442.

Right on the same "islet" will be Dave Dial's **The Tourist Trap** (☎ 06-23200/23291; pager 01-78215; e-mail placindltd@btl. net). Dave is planning an ambitious project in which visitors will be able to take tours, eat, and stay for BZ$70 pp, pn. What form this will take and when it will be available is still in the air. It is, however, a beautiful building.

RENTALS: Run by the local acupuncturist, **Ted's Rentals** (☎ 06-23172), near the bakery, has short- or long-term house rentals; houses go for BZ$500 and BZ$650 a month. Near the ball field and off the main road towards the end of town, **Patty's Place** (☎ 06-23121) has a fully-furnished house for rent, as well as four rooms with shared bath; short- or long-term rentals are available. Run by Egbert Cabral, **Carol's Cabins** are good value for the longer term.

To rent a fully-equipped beach house with hot water call **Lydia** (☎ 06-23117) locally or **Lou** (☎ 02-45732) in Belize City.

BUDGET: As it grows more and more popular, Placencia, like Caye Caulker, becomes increasingly expensive and low-priced rooms can be scarce. Count on a minimum of BZ$10 pp, but be prepared to pay twice that. Most of the hotels are run by relatives of either the Leslie or the Eiley families. Arriving here at night poses a problem: it's a bit bewildering to find your way around. Many of the cheapest places are not signed. It can be noisy here (clucking chickens and so on), so it's not a bad idea to bring along a pair of earplugs.

Julia's Budget Lodge (around BZ$16 s and BZ$26 d) is one alternative. At the top of the budget range in terms of price, six-room **Seaspray Hotel** (☎ 06-23148) is across from Jene's and by the water. It charges BZ$21.20 s and BZ$31.80 d.

Conrad's and Lydia's (☎ 06-23117) is farther up the sidewalk to the left. It charges BZ$15 s, BZ$25; breakfast (BZ$6) is available.

Paradise Vacation Hotel is at the pier end of town: when you arrive at the end of the road turn right and follow the path for about 10 minutes.

At the same location as Omar's, **Sun Rider Guest House** (☎ 06-23236) has three rooms for BZ$32 s and BZ$42 d. **Lucille's**, near Sun Rider, charges BZ$10 s and BZ$20 d. Gail's Rooms rent for around BZ$15.

If you are just a wee bit upscale from low-budget, then you can check out **Deb and Dave's Last Resort** (☎/fax 06-23207). Run by internationally renowned naturalist guide Dave Vernon and his wife Debbie, the hotel boasts four modest rooms with shared hot-water bath. Rates are around BZ$30 s and BZ$40 d including tax. They're right off the main road (not the sidewalk) as you enter the village.

Also in this range is **Estelle's** (☎ 06-23300/23301, fax 06-23196), which charges around BZ$40 s, BZ$50 d, and BZ$5 for additional people. (She also has a furnished apartment available for rent). Ebullient Shelly is a refugee from the jungles of LA; it took a sojourn in South Central ("where I learned to defend myself") to make Placencia's charms shine through

to her. Now she works in the phone company office and is back to stay.

CAMPING: At the northern end, unmarked **Mr. Clive's** has inexpensive camping (BZ$2 pp) and is frequented by kayakers. He'll also watch your vehicle while you're out kayaking for a small fee. He's available from 7 AM to 5 PM, and doesn't like to be disturbed other times. There's a toilet here but no shower. Don't leave valuables in your tent.

> 🕭 **Warning!**
> Unless you are going to be in or near town, you will either have to pay hefty taxi fees or have your own wheels. Thus, if spending time in the village is a priority, you should stay no farther away than the airstrip (such as Kitty's Place). Otherwise, coming into town for dinner, for example, will cost you mucho moola!

OUTLYING AREAS: Once you get out of the village, prices climb and, short of a walk or drive, you're confined to eating at your hotel. All those listed have excursions (fishing, snorkeling, hiking, etc.) available for their guests.

Run by a Cuban family, the **Village Inn** (06-23217, fax 06-23267) is inexpensively priced. In the US, ☎ 305-887-6453. Simple but attractive rooms with shared bath rent for BZ$50, and a cabin trailer with kitchen rents for BZ$130. Food is served.

Expensive **Mother Ocean Tropic Hotel and Environmental Research Station** (☎ 06-23233, fax 06-23224; PO Box 007, Placencia) is a half-mile north of the village. It features six cabins with queen-sized beds, has a restaurant and bar, and is set on a long stretch of beach. **note:** It was formerly known as The Cove Resort.

Located a mile north of Placencia and run by US expatriates, **Turtle Inn** (☎ 06-22069) holds up to 20 in six thatched cottages. Numerous trips and excursions are offered – diving, jungle camping, and river voyages. It's popular with student groups, and group rates are available. An unusual feature of the lodge is that all electricity is solar-generated. Bed and breakfast is around BZ$105 s and BZ$170 d, plus tax. (A reader reports some street noise). In the US, ☎ 303-444-2555, or contact Dr. Lois Kruschwitz, 2190 Bluebell, Boulder, CO 80302.

Kitty's Place (☎ 062-3227, fax 062-3226; PO Box 528, Belize City; e-mail kittys@btl.net; www.belize.net), 1½ miles north of the village, is one of the area's oldest resorts. It is an intimate and well-run resort with a variety of uniquely designed hardwood rooms set in small, Caribbean-style houses. One house typically has a total of two to four rooms and is two stories. Rooms have special amenities, such as bedside reading lamps, coffee makers, and hammocks. Each unit is airy and has an overhead fan. Kitty runs a full-service dive ship, rents bicycles, and offers sport fishing and snorkeling trips to the cayes, as well as other excursions. Her attractive restaurant, set upstairs from the office and extending onto a veranda, is well-run and popular. Breakfast is BZ$15 and dinner is BZ$33-44. Prices run from BZ$60 s and BZ$80 d for a room in The Belizean to BZ$180 s and BZ$210 d for a fully-furnished

studio apartment, which sleeps three. Kitty has a variety of tours, some of which are specially designed by her.

Rum Point Inn (☎ 06-22339, fax 06-23240; e-mail toucantrix@netcom.com or rupel@btl.net) is just up the coast. It offers eight dome-shaped ferroconcrete cabanas with fans. Also on the property are a bar, library, restaurant, beach, and sunfish. Dive packages are available. The owners, the Beviers, are Mayaphiles. The beach has seagrass so is less than fantastic for swimming. In the US, ☎ 800-747-1381 or 504-465-0769; fax 504-464-0325.

Consisting of 24 closely spaced but attractive and sunny cabanas with fans, **Serenity Resort** (☎ 06-23232/23231) has one of Placencia's best restaurants, plus a 32-foot glass bottom boat, and can arrange fishing and various excursions. Call ☎ 800-331-3797 to receive a brochure. High season rates run around BZ$350 s, BZ$448 d, and BZ$600 t; 17% tax and service charge is added, and rates include meals. A more expensive duplex unit is available. Breakfast and lunch are BZ$15 and dinner is BZ$30.

STILL FARTHER OUT: Next up is the small Garifuna village of Seine Bight (see description on p.), which now has hotels as well.

Just before the village is **Robert's Grove** (☎ 06-27655, fax 06-23567) with two elegant cabanas. Referred to as the "Taj Mahal" of Placencia, some say it's "like staying at the Plaza."

The **Seine Bight Hotel** (☎ 06-23526/23536/22491, fax 06-23537) has four cabanas (from BZ$140 on up) Their restaurant has European dishes and is quite

Ring Ting

Should you have a chance, be sure to check out the Ring Ting, a classic local game held every Sun. around 3 PM at the Dockside Bar. A line is suspended from a beam and a ring tied to it. The object is to swing the ring onto the nail at the other end of the bar some 20 ft. away. The winner gets BZ$25, and the second-place competitor receives a bottle of rum.

The game's object is to harass the players when it's their turn. Every six months there is a "World Series." All of the winners compete along with the second-place competitors, and the champion receives BZ$100.

Players compete for five rounds and then take a "piss break" before heading into another five. Traditionally, all of the men would urinate off the dock. A sure sign that modernity and puritanism is creeping in is indicated by the fact that the locals now avail themselves of the restroom!

popular with visitors to other hotels. Dishes range from lasagna to lobster; 16 entrées are offered nightly.

The Nautical Inn (☎ 06-23595, fax 06-23594, 800-688-0377; e-mail nautical@btl.net) is on the other side of Seine Bight village; it is one of the newest resorts. The attractive and comfortable units were imported prefabricated from Arizona, which cut down on construction time. Rooms have a/c and phones. Facilities include restaurant, bar, volleyball, canoes, bicycles, beauty salon, gift shop, massage, and a Hobie Cat. Fishing, snorkeling, and scuba are available. Owner Ben Ruoti has invented a new sport: coconut bowling. Carved mahogany pins are lined up at the end of a concrete runway, and coconuts are rolled to knock them down! A buffet BBQ (complete with local dance and drumming) is held every Wed. to coincide with the arrival of the small adventure cruise ship. Visitors are welcome, but reservations are required. Room rates are BZ$198 s and BZ$218 d, plus tax; no service charge. Packages and tours are available.

Hospitable **Blue Crab Resort** (☎ 06-23544., fax 06-23543; e-mail kerry@btl.net; www.belize.net) is on the beach past Seine Bight. Rates for the cabanas are BZ$100 s, BZ$150 d; tax is included and food is BZ$50 pp, pd additional. One of the owners has lived in Taiwan so Chinese food is a specialty, and vegetarians can be catered to. Excursions can be arranged. In the US, ☎ 800-359-1254. It consists of two small cabanas on stilts set side by side on the beach as well as some newer units. The cabanas are not underpriced for what they are, but the exclusivity and isolation are pluses. Two basic rooms are around BZ$50 d; campers pay BZ$14 pp; and several a/c luxury rooms have been built as well.

At Maya Beach seven miles north of Placencia, the **Singing Sands Inn** (☎/fax 06-22243; www.belize.net; e-mail ssi@btl.net) has six attractive thatched cabanas set in a row. Renting for BZ$160 s and BZ$180 d (plus 17% tax and service), they each have hot water, fans and lights. There's a restaurant and bar, and bicycling, canoes, and windsurfers are avail-

Placencia Tourist Guide Association Members

Name	Telephone	Specialties
Black Star Tours	06-23123	Fishing, snorkeling, scuba, and tours
Conrad's Guide Service	06-23117	Scuba, snorkeling, excursions
Joy Tours	06-23135	Sport fishing, snorkeling, excursions
Kevin's Guiding	06-23178	Scuba, fishing, snorkeling, kayaking, camping, excusions
Nature Guide	06-23206	Scuba, sport fishing, snorkeling, camping, excursions
Nite Moves Guiding	06-23117	Scuba, snorkeling, sport fishing, excursions
Ocean Motion	06-23162	Scuba, snorkeling, fishing, camping
Placencia Tours	06-23186	Land excursions
Sea Horse Guides (Brian Young)	06-23166 / 510-452-177 Fax 06-23166	Fishing, snorkeling, water skiing, excursions, manatee tours
Southern Tour	06-23166	Fly and sport fishing, scuba, camping, snorkeling, and sailing
Tracy Guiding	06-23134	Sport fishing, snorkeling, excursions
Ran Villanueva	06-22027	Fly fishing, snorkeling
David Westby	06-23138	Fly fishing
Whiprey Caye Guiding	06-23130 / 214-617-2210	Fly fishing, snorkeling, scuba

able. Diving is one of the resort's specialties, and the full-service dive shop offers certification.

Nearby, **The Green Parrot** (☎/fax 62-2488; e-mail greenparot@btl.net) offers beach houses, each of which features a large deck with a sea view; they can accommodate up to four. Rates are around BZ$190 plus 17% tax and gratuities. Sea kayaks, bicycles, Hobie Cats, windsurfers, and snorkeling gear are available for rent. It has a restaurant.

Food

Food prices here have gone up, and you can actually eat more cheaply at budget places on touristy San Pedro than in the village. Expect to spend around US$10 for a meal with a drink; cheaper if you substitute fowl for fish.

One of the best places to eat is **Omar's Fast Food,** which serves vegetable, seafood, and meat burritos (with handmade tortillas), juices, as well as other dishes; it's way above McDonald's in quality.

The **Driftwood Cafe** (open 7AM-11PM) has moderate prices. The **Shipwreck Restaurant** serves lobster (BZ$23) and shrimp (BZ $20) dishes as well as piña coladas.

BJ's has reasonably priced meals, including breakfast. Run by a large, good-natured lady of the same name, **Brenda's** offers breakfasts (BZ$6-8), lunches, and set dinners (BZ$15 including drink and dessert). She's off the path to the right, heading straight on from the pier.

Legendary expat **Buddha Bill** sells burritos from his stand near the fish cooperative in the morning hours. It may be the only place in the world where you can buy a lottery ticket and a burrito together!

more expensive: Back on the sidewalk and almost to the pier, pricey **Sonny's** is often packed. Attractive and atmospheric but expensive, **Tentacles** overlooks the water; it serves Belizean and Italian dishes.

Located to the right as you head down the road toward the edge of town, **The Galley** has slow service and entrées for around BZ$14. It has an attractive atmosphere, and many locals in the tourist industry come here to drink. You may get an earful about Mutabaruka or any number of other subjects from one of the imbibing guides.

Next to the Acupuncture Center is **La Petite Maison** (☎ 06-23172), which offers French cuisine at the prix fixe of BZ$44 for five courses. Set on the elevated terrace of a home, you dine by candlelight, serenaded by dinner jazz, the tinkling of the seashell and coral strings, and the occasional call of some creature of the night. You are in the company of a retired French chef and his wife, and you know what that means: no grumbling about wine sauces and butter. Sit back, enjoy and worry about purging the cholesterol tomorrow!

☞ *Traveler's Tip*
La Petite Maison is a great place for a splurge, whether you are a budget traveler or more prosperous. It offers good food and personalized service in a romantic, intimate environment.

What started as a lark has become a serious business, and a tasty one indeed. French bread takes the form of thin and crispy home-baked baguettes, followed by an appetizer, salad, entrée, dessert,

and coffee. One sample entrée is fi-
let of snapper meunière. Wine is
available (BZ$8.50 a glass, BZ$40 a
bottle and up). You must make reservations, and only six can dine at
one time.

Out of town near the airport,
Kitty's also has a good and attrac-
tive restaurant. Dinner averages
BZ$30; a set breakfast is BZ$15.
Serenity also has good food. In
Seine Bight, the place to go is the
Seine Bight Hotel.

**FOOD SHOPPING AND BAKED
GOODS:** Bread at **John the Baker
Man** (the local bakery) sells for a
very pricey BZ$3 per loaf. Nearby,
Ms. Nora bakes delicious loaves of
coco bread (BZ$1), which are usu-
ally available in late afternoon.
Crissy's Pastries nearby has cakes,
pies, cookies, *panades*, *sabutes*,
and *tostadas*. **Gloria** is behind the
bakery; her daughter **Mistie** makes
pies and *garnaches* and will cook
for you upon demand.

Off the sidewalk, **Daisy**'s serves
good cakes, ice cream, and other delights; it also serves meals. In front
of Jaime's and near the beach, **Kay**'s
has homemade jams, yogurt, granola, and orange juice, as well as
other items. The **fishing cooperative** next to the pier sells fish
cheaply (when it has them).

Wallen's Market is on the Main
Rd. It has a very limited (and quite
expensive) selection of fresh produce, so try to buy what you may
need before arrival. (Food is costly,
as everything has to be brought in).
It now has competition in the form
of **Olga's**. A vegetable truck arrives
on Tues. and Sat.

SOUVENIRS: There are a few
shops around. Near Wallen's Market, the **Orange Peel Shop** sells
gifts, T-shirts, and other artwork.

Entertainment

Although the power situation has
improved and there is electricity
now right up to Seine Bight, occasional blackouts do occur, so
carry a flashlight if going out at
night. The hottest hangout is
Lorraine's, which has good music; it's diagonally across from
Sunrise. Another choice is the
Dockside Bar at the end of the
peninsula. A popular daytime bar
is the **Lagoon Saloon** (☎ 06-
23289) whose owners, Bonnie
and Mike, can catch you up on
the latest gossip, feed you lunch,
and even sell you real estate. Its
motto is "a nice place if you can
find it," and it features "cheap
drinks and bad jokes." It is assur-
edly the only place that plays the
Chipmunks singing *Achy Breaky
Heart.*

Services

The market will change traveler's
checks at around US$1=BZ95¢.
Hotels will also change money. To
use a Visa card, you must take a
boat over to Big Creek, where a
bank opens on Fri. The mail service
has improved. There's now a real
PO (open Mon. to Fri., 9-11, 3-5),
and it's much more likely that your
letter will actually arrive instead of
getting lost in the shuffle. There's
also a BTL office (open weekdays
from 8-noon and 1-4, Saturday
from 8-noon) with four **phones** inside. Both are just to the right of the
fish cooperative at the end of the
peninsula.

By way of anecdote, the local **cable network** is run by Sonny (of
Sonny's Resort); it is known locally

as "SonnyVision" because when Sonny goes to sleep, so does the network.

Below the rectory is the **library**, run by masseuse Patricia (☎ 06-23271); it's open Monday and Wednesday from 7-8 PM, Tues. 4:30-5:30, and Sat. from 10-noon. A BZ$3 deposit is required. **Patricia** (☎ 06-23271) can also give you a massage; word has it that she is good. She'll love you to death if you bring her some books.

Conveniently located near the airstrip, **Kitty's** will make reservations for Tropic and Maya; many other hotels will as well. Have your clothes washed at the **Placencia Laundromat** (☎ 06-23123). **Ted Berlin** (☎ 06-23172) is the village's acupuncturist (☎ 02-22305). **Deb and Dave's Last Resort** (☎/fax 06-23207) rents mountain bikes.

Tours

Prices are not low for trips – especially for fishing. Dave Dial's **Placencia Tours** (☎ 06-23200/23291; pager: 0178215; e-mail placindltd@btl.net) will take you on the Monkey River as well as to other destinations. **MacDougall's Travel** (☎ 06-23144, fax 06-23186) will make fishing and other tour arrangements; ☎ 916-741-8027 in the US. **PI Tours** (☎ 06-23156/23209) has a variety of excursions, including camping, fly fishing, snorkeling, and scuba. **Ocean Motion** (☎ 06-23162) offers scuba, snorkeling, fishing, and camping.

Nature Guide (☎ 06-23206) features scuba, sport fishing, snorkeling, camping, excursions. **Kevin's Guiding** (☎ 06-23178) offers scuba, fishing, snorkeling, kayaking, camping, and excursions. **Joy Tours** (☎ 06-23135) has sport fishing, snorkeling, and excursions. **Nite Moves Guiding** (☎ 06-23117) offers scuba, snorkeling, sport fishing, and excursions. **Conrad's Guide Service** uses the same phone number and provides similar services.

Ran Villanueva (☎ 06-22027) has fly and other types of fishing and snorkeling. **Mystic Divers Diveshop** (☎ 06-23182) features scuba, snorkeling, fishing, and excursions. **Kingfisher Adventures** leads fly fishing and snorkeling trips to Laughing Bird Caye and to the barrier reef. In the US, ☎ 800-403-9955 or fax 919-848-3624. **Glen Eiley** (☎ 06-23182) conducts fishing and caye trips in a 25-foot skiff. **Bruce Westby** (☎ 06-23370) has been recommended by local lodges for fishing. (Sadly, Joel Westby has passed away.) **Belize Ecoadventures** (☎/fax 6-23250) arranges tours and hotels. In the US, ☎ 604-984-8182 or fax 604-984-8727. **Sea Horse Guides** (☎/fax 06-23166) leads fishing, snorkeling, and other trips. In the US, ☎ 510-452-1771. **Southern Tour** (☎ 06-23166) has fly and sport fishing, scuba, camping, snorkeling, and sailing. **Black Star Tours** (☎ 06-23123) arranges fishing, snorkeling, scuba, and tours. Most of the outlying resorts have excursions. **Kitty's Place** (☎ 062-3227, fax 062-3226; Box 528, Belize City) rents bicycles, and offers sport fishing and snorkeling trips to the cayes (Silk and others) and the barrier reef. **Calbert Gardener** (☎ 06-23487) will take you out on his boat the *Nite Wind*.

Diving

All of the resorts can arrange diving. **Placencia Dive Shop** (☎ 06-23227, fax 06-23226) is at Kitty's

Place. A two-tank dive is BZ$130 pp to the inner cayes and BZ$150 to the barrier reef. **Rum Point Inn** (☎ 06-23239) has a dive shop. **Seahorse Guides** (see above) also offers diving and certification. The **Paradise Vacation Hotel** (☎ 06-23179) has a 33-foot Bertram a/c twin diesel boat for fishing, diving, and caye excursion charters; it will hold up to six. In the US, ☎ 409-245-9203 or fax 409-245-1803.

> ☞ **Traveler's Tip**
>
> *Any hotel can arrange fly-fishing, diving, and tours for you. So don't pick where you will stay based on whether they advertise this feature or not.*

Vicinity of Placencia

Although the village is a great place to relax, the surrounding area is rich in attractions. You may want to visit Cockscomb or take a trip up the Monkey River. Heading out to the cayes, you'll see beautiful islands off in the distance, may spot dolphins running with your craft, catch sight of a sting ray, or visit an island whose shores are piled high with conch shells.

Cayes Near Placencia

Lying a few hundred yards from the coast, **Placencia Caye** is an all-mangrove caye. The horrendous cut through the center was engineered by the US owner in coalition with his Belizean partner; the intention is to sell moorings to well-heeled yachties for a rumored

BZ$100,000 a pop. So far, thankfully, there have been no takers.

Morris Caye is controlled by enterprising Doug (☎ 06-23152/23223) who will take you out there and let you camp; he also runs day trips. Reportedly, it's much like visiting French Louis but more personalized.

On the island of the same name, the four-unit **Wippari Caye Lodge** (☎ 06-23130) offers moderate-to-expensive accommodation from about BZ$40. Inquire at Tentacles.

Laughing Bird Caye National Park is one of the nation's most beautiful small islands. It's a popular snorkeling and kayaking spot. The best snorkeling is on the east side of the island and off the southern end. It's named after the laughing gulls, though they no longer live here. The stream of visitors has driven them off.

Northeast of Placencia, **Rendezvous Caye** is rumored to be owned by a legendary British rock star.

Well offshore near the barrier reef, the **Silk Cayes (Queen Cayes)**, three small islands with three palms, are some of the most beautiful spots for kayaking and snorkeling; outfitters usually camp on Middle Queen Caye, the largest of the three.

To the west of the Queen Cayes, **Hatchet Caye** is the island where an American was caught dynamiting coral heads in order to allow access for a larger boat. Lying to the southwest of Hatchet Caye, **Little Water Cay** is a privately owned island that operated the Little Water Caye Resort as a nudist colony until the authorities found out.

Ranguana Caye

This small sand palm caye has the **Ranguana Lodge and Reef Resort**.

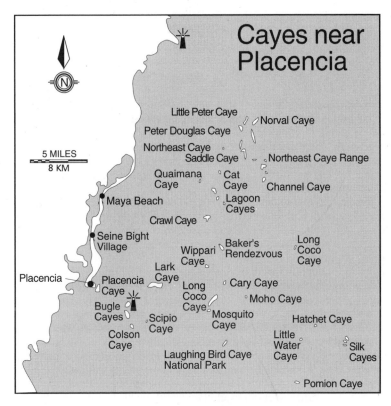

Cayes near Placencia

Little Peter Caye
Norval Caye
Peter Douglas Caye
Northeast Caye
Saddle Caye
Northeast Caye Range
Quaimana Caye
Cat Caye
Channel Caye
Maya Beach
Lagoon Cayes
Crawl Caye
Seine Bight Village
Baker's Rendezvous
Long Coco Caye
Wippari Caye
Lark Caye
Placencia
Placencia Caye
Long Coco Caye
Cary Caye
Bugle Cayes
Moho Caye
Scipio Caye
Mosquito Caye
Hatchet Caye
Colson Caye
Little Water Caye
Silk Cayes
Laughing Bird Caye National Park
Pomion Caye

Attractive cabins rent for around BZ$100 pd. Camping is BZ$20 pp pd, and it costs BZ$320 to charter a boat out here.

Reef-Link Kayaking (☎ 515-279-6699; ask for Sonna Newton) is a kayak rental agency located here; guides are also available. Various kayaking routes can be taken using Ranguana as a base. Write c/o S. Newton, 3806 Cottage Grove, Des Moines, IA 50311. Be sure to obtain a copy of *Belize By Kayak* (from the same source) in preparation for your trip. Bonefish and jack fishing is good, and the best snorkeling is found on the island side of the barrier reef a mile or so southeast of the caye.

French Louis Caye

Rented from the Belizean government by Ran of Kitty's Place, this tiny mangrove island set eight miles offshore was once used as a fishing camp. Its mangrove roots shelter and nurse sealife ranging from anemones to starfish. The island comes fully equipped with hammocks, sea kayaks, a two-story wooden house, campsites, outhouses, and an authentic old salt who serves as caretaker/chef.

Rates are BZ$120 pp, pn with transport, meals, snorkeling gear, sea kayak. A day trip here is BZ$90 pp, which gives you basically the same deal, except that you snorkel at Laughing Bird Caye National Park first and then stop for a simple

Joncunu

Variations of Joncunu, Jonkanoo, or John Canoe are performed around Christmas and New Year's in an increasingly dwindling number of Caribbean islands. Where they do still take place, the streets vibrate with the sound of drums and the syncopated, rattling steps of the colorfully attired Joncunu dancers.

No one is quite sure exactly what this dancing procession is about, or where and how it originated. Its name (meaning "deadly sorcerer" or "sorcerer man") probably comes from the Ewe tongue. Most likely it originated in the secret societies of E. Africa and became linked to Christmas, the only major holiday permitted to slaves. In 1841 riots erupted in Jamaica after Kingston's mayor banned the parade.

Traditionally it includes a cast of colorful characters dressed in flashy rags. Featured may be a cow or horse's head, a king and veiled queen, a devil, and a few Indians. This strangely enchanting amalgam of motley characters wends its way down the road to the polyrhythmic accompaniment of drums and cane flutes.

And, although not often practiced these days, Belize has this tradition too. What makes Belize distinct is that here it is the Garinagu who have adopted the dance, which they call the *wanaragua*. It is likely that this form dates from the Garinagu's days on St Vincent. The British would come in around Christmas time seeking slaves, mainly men. Males would elude capture by wearing a mask so that they might resemble a Caucasian and would cover their arms and legs in plantain leaves so as to look more like women. The dance may be seen as a form of resistance to slavery, a mocking of the British and other slave owners living among and near the exiled Garinagu in Belize, Honduras and Guatemala.

In Punta Gorda, Philip Nicholas has formed the Subas City – a dancing, singing and drumming troupe comprising some 30 boys and girls who range in age from five to 10 years. The group formed as Mr Nicholas went around to local schools giving demonstrations, and some of the children expressed an interest in studying the Garifuna music and dance.

Boys dress in pink wire masks (*igibu*), plantain leaves (*imasoso*) and knee bracelets that substitute soft drink bottle caps in lieu of the traditional but scarce cowrie shells (*irawey*). Other dances performed include the *hunguhungu*, the *paranda*, the *sambai*, the even the world famous *punta*.

In the *chumba*, they mimic daily activities ranging from hanging out clothes to preparing cassava to beating plantains. The young girls relish the sensuous *gunjei*, representative of the days when young women paraded before the chief, hoping he might pick one of them to be his consort.

Philip Nicholas' dream is to set up a formal drumming and dancing school to teach Garinagu arts. "The Garifuna culture is not being promoted, which is what I am trying to do," he says. "Even in Dangriga it's kind of dying out, because people are into too many combos and punta rock. I want kids to dance the Garifuna dances as well as the Creole dances." For more information (or to give a donation for costumes) call Philip, ☎ 07-22333.

but hearty lunch here before heading back via Man 'O War Caye – a seven-hour excursion in all.

Independence

The village of Independence consists of a few houses on a bank opposite Placencia. Although it may be separately marked on maps, it is the same place as Mango Creek. A banana port has been built here by the Zabaneh family; it has been supplemented by a stadium and supermarket!

The town experienced a brief boom in 1962 when the Hercules Powder Co. of Delaware installed a US$5 million plant to extract the remaining resin in pine stumps left after logging. Although there was believed to be enough raw material to last a decade, the plant closed down after only three years and was moved to Nicaragua, leaving 200 households without employment. (Stumps are still harvested however). Although the official reason given was that the price of resins in the US had fallen to the point where the plant was no longer profitable, in fact the number of stumps had been miscounted. The experience provided the internal government of the time with an example of the way in which foreign investment can be a two-edged sword, causing misery as well as creating opportunities.

GETTING THERE: A mail boat runs from Placencia here on Monday, Wednesday, and Friday.

ACCOMMODATIONS: Stay at moderate 16-room **Hello Hotel** (☎ 06-2201) or at **Ursella's Guest House,** #227 Gran Rain St., which offers six inexpensive rooms.

At the corner of Fadden and Seagull in Mango Creek Village (Independence), two-unit **La Quinta Cabanas** (☎ 06-22093) are inexpensive. Anther alternative in Independence is the budget-priced seven-room **Little Jungle Lodge** (☎ 06-22225). The best place to eat (BZ$5 a meal) is **Miss Ella Forman's** house, a cute little white home behind the restaurant with the Fanta sign. You may also stay at the hotel above **People's Restaurant. note:** The a/c 12-room Bill Bird Lodge (formerly the Toucan) managed to burn down and is no more.

Outside of the village in Bakding, the **Amazing Grace Resort** (☎ 06-22436, fax 06-22085) offers cottages (BZ$60 s, BZ$85 d with breakfast) as well as spots for campers and RV owners (BZ$10 pp, pn). They are set near the Injun Creek Lagoon. Tours are arranged.

The **Placencia Lagoon Resort** (☎ 06-22363, fax 06-22482; www.wrldlink.com/plr/Jpegs/about .html) is run by Roland Exum, who offers seven thatched beachfront cabanas that provide "all the comforts of home." They offer river trips swimming, boating, diving, snorkeling, fishing, jungle tours, hiking trails, beach volleyball, a golf driving range, conference/banquet room, and room service. There is live entertainment on weekends, and they have a restaurant, the Malacate Beach Supper Club. Rates are around BZ$130 s, BZ$180 d, BZ$240 t (pp, pn), plus tax and a BZ$10 service charge. All-inclusive special package rates are also available.

Fajina Crafts Center

The **Fajina Crafts Center** (☎ 07-22470; Box 109, Punta Gorda) is next to the Customs Office by the pier. Its name is Mopan and Kekchi for "coming together for the good of the community." Unique in Toledo and opened in 1995, it is the outlet for some 24 Maya women's groups with a combined membership of some 240 talented craftswomen. It was created with the help of Dem Dats Doin, two Peace Corps workers, and a Voice of America employee.

Fajina offers goods from the outback that you would have to go a long way to find. Some special items include cuxtals (brightly colored shoulder bags), Mopan cross-stitch embroidery, codex pages (paper fashioned from the bark of the wild fig, coated with lime plaster, and decorated with glyphs), and slate carvings.

Seine Bight

Three miles north of Placencia, this somnolent but hospitable Garifuna village makes an interesting destination to bike, hitch, or walk to. It's a pleasant walk along the coast, but you bear witness to the debris of our Great Western Civilization, which washes up on the shore. Legend has it that Seine Bight was founded by pirates in 1629; its name was most likely given by immigrant French fishermen arriving after they were expelled from Canada when Britain took control.

PRACTICALITIES: Development has come here only very recently; electricity has only been available since April 1994. The bar, **Wesebahari** (Garinagu for "Feel Good"), has a giant lobster-shaped bamboo root. "Don't ask for Mr. Credit. He is dead" is chalked on the wall to the rear of the bar's counter.

Run by Dewey Nuñez, the **Kulcha Shack** has rooms with shared baths for around BZ$30. He also serves food and provides live entertainment some evenings. In the village center, compact **Auntie Chigi's Place** (☎ 06-22015, 08-22491) charges BZ$80 for one or two people in each of two small, two-bedded rooms with a shared kitchen. It's a good value relative to what you get elsewhere, and it's run by local Edna Martinez. **note:** The Nautical Inn and other accommodations are reviewed in the Placencia *Accommodations* section.

Monkey River Town

This small Creole village (pop. 200) sits at the mouth of the **Monkey River.** Until the early 1960s, Monkey River was a settlement of some 3,000. Then, in the aftermath of the Sigatoka virus (which devastated the banana crop), most of the villagers moved to Independence (and the new banana plantations), taking their houses with them. Today, Monkey River remains a small, somnolent dot on the map. There's a school, colorful architecture, an church or two, and a pet peccary. You'll likely visit Monkey River as part of a trip upriver from Placencia.

Ena's Hotel is the town's only lodging, and there's a grocery shop run by Miss Merna. **Alice's Restaurant** is the sole culinary bistro.

Vicinity of
Placencia

- - - - Seasonal Roads

Cockscomb Basin
Wildlife Sanctuary
(Jaguar Sanctuary)

N

To
Dangriga

Maya
Center

Riverside

Alabama

Georgetown

Maya
Beach

Seine Bight
Village

Mango
Creek

Independence

Southern
Highway

Big
Creek

Placencia

Monkey
River

Palmetto
Cay

Rocky Point
South

Monkey River
Town

5 MILES

Contrary to the song, you can't get anything you want: there is but one entrée on the menu each day. Vegetarians will not be catered to. The beans may well be cooked with pork fat, so plan accordingly. Meals are BZ$10; BZ$2 for soft drinks. Vegetarians should note the fact that the stewed beans are cooked with pork fat. An American has opened **Mike's Tropical Paradise,** a bar up along the coast.

kayaking upriver: This is a pristine rainforest environment. As you cruise by, iguanas dive into the water, landing with a splash, troops of howler monkeys cavort through the trees, and birds flit from tree to tree. In his *Belize by Kayak,* Kirk Barrett tells of spotting a jaguar on a sandbank as he navigated a bend in this river. After 10-12 miles you come to a fork: Bladen Branch is to the left and the Swasey Branch is to the right; both eventually intersect with bridges along the Southern Hwy. Four new archaeological sites were discovered here in 1993; two had been looted prior to their discovery. The largest is on an island in the Monkey River; it is in the form of a C-shaped plaza surrounding a pyramid.

Monkey River Expeditions (☎ 206-660-7777, fax 206-938-0978; 1731 44th Av. SW, Ste. 100, Seattle, WA 98116; e-mail mre@halcyon.com) is based in Placencia and in Seattle. Their eight-day trips (around US$1,400) include a stay with a Maya family, visits to ruins in Toledo, three days kayaking the Monkey, and visits to a caye and to Placencia.

The Monkey River Trip

Belize has a number of diverse river trips. You may visit the ruins at La-manai, canoe down the Macal river, and ply the canals and lagoons from Belize City to Gales Point. But your best chance to see wildlife in a pristine environment (short of creating your own chartered trip) is undoubtedly the boat trip up the Monkey River, a tour scheduled by many agencies and lodges in Placencia. Depending upon the season, you may only be able to head a few miles upriver. But that few miles is quite an experience indeed!

A number of operators offer the trip from Placencia. Soulshine and Kitty's are two that run their own trips. Dave Dial's **Placencia Tours** (☎ 06-23200/23291, pager 01-78215) was the first to use local guides and boatmen, and these have been well trained. If possible, get together a group of friends to go with. That way, smokers can go with smokers, and nonsmokers can enjoy their pristine natural surroundings in peace.

Specifics vary by the trip, but you should leave at around 7:30 AM. Pack an umbrella (Monkey River is known for its rain), plenty of film, binoculars, sunscreen, insect repellent, hiking boots, long pants, and snacks. A thermos of coffee would be the perfect addition! Expect a sometimes bumpy sea ride to the village entrance. En route you pass mangrove cayes and may spy a manatee or two.

The water calms as you come into the village and continue to cruise upstream. You are certain to sight numerous iguanas, a variety of birds, and perhaps even some land mammals. The earlier you get here the better! Commonly sighted birds include kingfishers, oropendolas, egrets, toucans, and blue herons.

You will also stop by a former settlement and have a great tour with a local guide, one of the best introductions to the rainforest you will find anywhere. The strangler fig, the acacia and its ants, and other highlights from the fauna section of this book's introduction will be pointed out. If you are lucky, you will also encounter a troop of howlers. The hike can be as far as you want; most visitors have less stamina than the guides.

Another stop is by a sandbank where you can swim or just stretch your legs. From there you head back to the village for lunch and a stroll before returning to Placencia.

Bladen Branch Nature Reserve

This 97,000-acre reserve created in 1990 encompasses the Maya Mountains, as well as fringing limestone karst foothills pockmarked with caves and sinkholes. The slopes are covered with old-growth broadleaf forests and swiftly flowing streams empty into the Bladen branch of the Monkey River. One Maya ruin, Quebra del Oro (Passageway of Gold), has been discovered, and there may be others. Over 300 animal species include the jaguar, the keel-billed toucan, the river otter, Baird's tapir, and Morelet's crocodile. Proponents of the reserve were the Belize Audubon Society, the World Parks Endowment, and Lighthawk, an organization of volunteer pilots who operate airplanes that assist environmental organizations.

GETTING HERE: You must be a researcher to obtain permission from the Audubon Society, which will help you with transport.

Punta Gorda

Almost 210 miles by road from Belize City, Punta Gorda, popularly known as "PG" (pop. 3,234), is the last sizeable settlement in southern Belize. It was one of the places originally established for the Black Caribs after they fled Honduras in 1823. Today, PG is the capital of the Toledo District. Schools line Front St., and youngsters are imported from surrounding villages on weekdays in season.

PG is always *threatening* to become a major tourist center; it remains off the beaten track and for the resourceful and adventurous. It has the distinction of being omitted from the Fodor's guide to Guatemala and Belize! What makes it fun also makes it trying. The improvement of the highway may serve to open things up, but – for the present – the town remains the gateway to Belize's last true frontier.

Despite its Spanish name, PG contains Garifuna, Creoles, Kekchi, Mopan Maya, Chinese, Lebanese, and East Indians. All of its five streets – Front, Main, Back, West, and Far West – parallel the shoreline. A fishing and farming community (beans, maize, and rice), it receives over 170 inches of rain annually. (Don't be alarmed: most of it falls at night, and it is rare to have a day that is solidly rainy.) Nearby are the ruins of Lubaantun as well as indigenous villages. Trips can be also made to the Sapodilla Cayes.

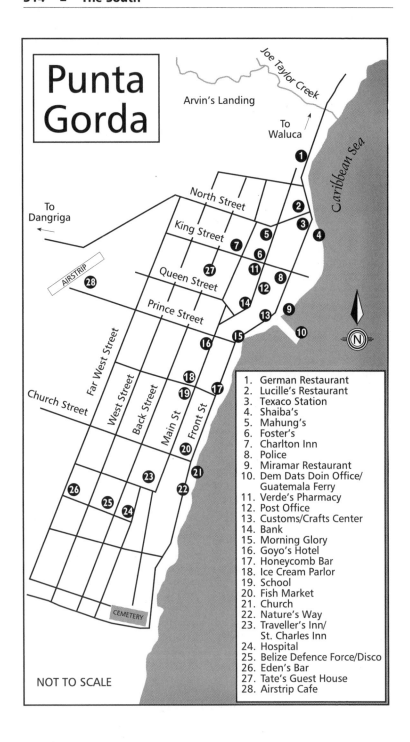

Punta Gorda

1. German Restaurant
2. Lucille's Restaurant
3. Texaco Station
4. Shaiba's
5. Mahung's
6. Foster's
7. Charlton Inn
8. Police
9. Miramar Restaurant
10. Dem Dats Doin Office/
    Guatemala Ferry
11. Verde's Pharmacy
12. Post Office
13. Customs/Crafts Center
14. Bank
15. Morning Glory
16. Goyo's Hotel
17. Honeycomb Bar
18. Ice Cream Parlor
19. School
20. Fish Market
21. Church
22. Nature's Way
23. Traveller's Inn/
    St. Charles Inn
24. Hospital
25. Belize Defence Force/Disco
26. Eden's Bar
27. Tate's Guest House
28. Airstrip Cafe

NOT TO SCALE

Transport

GETTING HERE: The most frequent service is offered by Z-Line (☎ 02-73937), which leaves Belize City at 8, noon, and 3, arriving at 5:45 PM, 9:45 PM, and 12:45 AM. Buses leave Dangriga at noon and 7. James also runs. Allow nine hours or more from Belize City.

ARRIVING BY AIR: Tropic Air (☎ 02-45671, 026-2012, 800-422-3435; www.belize.net; e-mail tropic@cybersim.co) flies from Belize Municipal (BZ$120 OW, BZ$216 RT) and from Belize International (BZ$140 OW, BZ$280 RT), as does Maya Island Air (☎ 02-31348/31362/31403; 800-257-8802; e-mail mayair@btl.net), which flies via Dangriga. If you take Tropic Air's flight, on the way to Punta Gorda you make a last sweep over Belize City and then over the sea before swinging back to the coast, passing marshes, jade green rivers, and pristine rainforest. You will see cohune palms protruding like giant upright feather dusters, small offshore cayes, and citrus farms of staggering proportions. Cut through it all is a road network; the clay color of the strips is clearly visible from the air. As you descend, you spot the former VOA antenna, rainforest-covered Seven Hills, and the former British army base.

FROM PUNTA GORDA: Z-Line buses (☎ 07-22165) depart daily at 9 and noon (arriving at around 2:30 and 10 PM); additional runs are on Fri. and Sun. at 3:30; the fare to Belize City is BZ$22, Independence is BZ$9, and the fare to Belmopan is BZ$19. James buses leave at noon on Tues. and Fri. and at 6 AM on

Thurs., Sat. and Sun. from the terminal opposite the police station. The late departures allow passengers arriving from Guatemala to make connections. All stop in Belmopan, Dangriga, and Mango Creek. They have more leg room than their competitors, and their conductors are trained as tour guides.

The San Antonio bus departs on Mon., Wed., Fri., and Sat. at 12:30 for the 1 hr. 20 min. trip; the San José bus leaves at 12:30 on Wed. and Sat. The San Pedro Columbia bus departs at 1 PM on Mon., Wed., Fri., and Sat. There's also a school bus on school days as well as a freight and passenger truck that leaves the village at 6 AM on Wed. and returns around noon. Buses also run to Silver Creek and Indian Creek. Service to all these locations may have improved by the time you read this; times may have changed as well, so be sure to inquire. Hitchhiking is a viable if slow option. Wait at the bakery along the coast road on the way out of town to the north.

by air: Both **Tropic** (☎ 02-45671, 026-2012, 800-422-3435; www.belize.net; e-mail tropic@btl.net) and **Maya Island Air** (☎ 07-22856; e-mail mayair@btl.net) fly. To reserve and purchase Tropic tickets, contact **Heston Wagner** at his shop next to the St. Charles Inn at 23 King St. **Penell & Sons** at 50 Main St. has Maya and Tropic tickets. Also, both Maya and Tropic have offices at the airstrip.

by boat: The boat for Guatemala leaves on Tues. and Fri. at around 2, and it takes two hours. Fare is about BZ$13. It returns those same days in the morning, arriving around 10. The Tues. boat tends to

Toledo's Logging Controversy

"The logging is a danger not only for the Maya but for the Belizean people as a whole. They (the government who signed the contract) done it themself, it should have been done together with the people. They should have consulted us first. It's total nonsense – not helping nobody!" So relates the Toledo Maya Alcalde Association President, Leonardo Nacal, when asked by the author to comment on the Columbia Reserve logging.

The story of Belize's logging concessions is not atypical. It is the same story from Indonesia to Guyana: the tropical forests are harvested without benefitting the indigenous population, Since 1993, the government has granted at least 17 long-term logging concessions in the Toledo district to foreign-owned companies. These concessions encompass some 224,600 hectares. The most extensive concession was granted to Atlantic Industries, a Malaysian timber company, for around BZ$1.20 per acre! It surrounds 10 Mayan villages that house nearly half of the total Maya population. The Maya were not consulted before the concessions were granted, and the government's actions are believed to be motivated not only by profit but also by the idea of staving off any attempt by the Maya to acquire legal title to their lands. (Belize currently maintains no laws recognizing ancestral land rights.)

Atlantic Industries has built a sawmill right beside the Belize Southern Highway without first obtaining environmental impact assessments required under Belizean law. Maya leaders, who have visited the States in search of support for their cause, are filing a lawsuit in the Belizean supreme court to "defend their land rights and challenge the government's authority to grant logging concessions on their ancestral lands."

Although the government maintains that the logging is being conducted in strict accord with Belizean law and environmental regulations, there have been reports that prohibited species as well as untagged trees in prohibited areas have been cut down; that roads have been bulldozed through interdicted areas; and that logging has proceeded through the rainy season, thus serving to accelerate environmental damage. Of special interest to the loggers are the mahogany trees, which are said to be selectively logged. Estimates are that every mahogany tree harvested requires that 3,000 forested square feet be deforested!

be faster, as there is less demand. The ferry ticket agent (**Indita Maya, ☎** 07-22065) is at 24 Middle St. and sales start at 9:30. Be sure to buy your ticket as soon as you arrive. If you need a Guatemalan visa, you're out of luck. The Immigration office is next to the PO and near the pier. Buy some quetzales from the female moneychanger or from passengers arriving from Gua-temala. Bring food and water for the boat trip, as none is available on board.

Accommodations

Located on the seaside far past the town center, one of the best places to stay is low-budget **Nature's Way Guest House (☎** 07-22119), which charges BZ$16 s and BZ$35 d.

Equipped with bunk beds, many of its attractive rooms face the sea. A large selection of charters is offered. For more information, write PO Box 75, Punta Gorda.

One of the better places to stay smack dab in the middle of town is the expensive 12-room **St. Charles Inn** (☎ 07-22197), 21 King St. The 10-room inexpensively priced **Charlton's Inn** (☎ 07-22197) is at 9 Main St. It has cable TV; rooms have a/c. **Tate's Guest House** (☎ 07-22196), around the corner from the St. Charles, is run by postmaster William Tate. Rooms have a/c and cable TV for BZ$40 d.

The **Punta Caliente Hotel & Restaurant** (☎ 07-22561), 108 José Nuñez St., is clean, very friendly, and has inexpensive rooms.

Just one street over and run by a relative, the **Circle C** (☎ 07-22726), 117 West St., charges BZ$25 d for rooms with shared bath and BZ$35 and BZ$50 for rooms with private bath. The most expensive hotel is **The Travellers' Inn** (☎ 07-22568, fax 05-22814), next to the Punta Caliente. Its attractive a/c rooms have cable TV, and there's a restaurant. Rates are BZ$105 s, BZ$135 d, and BZ150 t, including tax.

Two good values for low-budget travelers are **Mahung's Hotel**, 11 North St. cor. of Main (☎ 07-22044; PO Box 21), and the seven-room **Verdes Guest House** (☎ 07-22069), 22 Main St. at Middle St.

Other hotels include the **Wahima Hotel**, 11 Front St. and the **Isabela Hotel**, also on Front St. You can also camp for a reasonable fee at **Arvin's Landing** just outside of town to the north. **note:** You may check to see if the impressive four-story hotel being built by Larry Smith has been finished. It's on the waterfront and will be known as the **Seafront Inn**. Rates are around BZ$70 s, BZ$110 d.

Food

Reina's is a greasy spoon popular for breakfast. **Bobby's Restaurant**, open only in the evenings, sometimes has conch soup. Serving overpriced Chinese food, the **Mira Mar Restaurant** is at 95 Front St. Also try the **Kowloon**. **Goyo** is near the main plaza, as is the **Palma**, a store featuring snacks such as *garnaches*.

Near the gas station at the beginning of town, **Lucille's Kitchen** has reasonable prices. Lucille herself works on her sewing machine behind the bar when she's not serving. **Shaiba's** is classier but comparatively expensive. **Granny's Kitchen**, across from Shaiba's, serves breakfast as well as rice and bean dishes for BZ$7.50. You can also try the small food stall set right next to Palavi's Hotel, which sells Belizean food as well as flour tortillas every evening. The **Morning Glory Restaurant**, 59 Front St., also provides Belizean meals and opens for breakfast.

For snacks try the **Wahima** and **Punta Gorda Bakery**. Just out of town near the soccer field, the **Roundhouse** is a popular bar and restaurant. A bakery is up the road from the Texaco station along the coast at the town's entrance.

Just down from the Clock Tower, the **Ice Cream Parlor** serves ice cream and sandwiches. **Bar Jax Restaurant** is at the Joe Taylor bridge.

note: Following the death of his wife, Man Man has moved to Puerto Barrios and no longer offers meals out of his home. His departure is a great loss for PG.

Entertainment

Set across from Traveller's Inn, the **Massive Rock Disco** is the most active place in town; video movies are shown in the early evening. **South Side Disco** is the second liveliest place in town. **Bobby**'s sees a lot of action, as does the neighboring **Starlight**. The **Mira Mar** is also a popular spot for imbibing. On the outskirts of town, **Waluco** is a lively bar run by Wil Maheia (pgwil@btl.net). Wil also runs tours and has a party on Sun. evening. A staunch environmentalist, Wil is one of the most interesting locals to talk with.

Services

The government **Tourist Information Center** is on the main street just down from the post office; it shares the space with the reservation service for the Maya Homestay program. **Dem Dats Doin** operates a tourist information office (☎ 07-22470) in the town's center next to the ferry pier. Extremely helpful, they're open daily (except Thurs. and Sun.) from 7:30 AM to 11:30 PM. Ask about "the indigenous experience," as well as their homestays.

Tours

Charter by Land/Sea is at 12 Front St. (☎ 07-22070, PO Box 18). **Indigenous Maya Tours** (☎ 07-22542), 11 Front St., offers a variety of trips. **Jack Nightingale** (Box 11, Punta Gorda) offers sailing trips aboard the *Juanita*; inquire at Arvin's Landing. **Dem Dats Doin** (see above under *Services*) also has a number of tours, as does **Nature's Way Guest House,** which also rents kayaks.

Fish 'n Fun Charters & Tours (☎ 07-22931; #9, Hopeville, Punta Gorda) offers fly fishing, tours, and other services. Prices seem extraordinarily high. A trip to Moho Caye, for example, costs BZ$300 with food; this is for camping.

Boat owners may moor at **Orange Point Marina** (☎ 07-22735), which is to the S of PG. **Memo's Water Taxi** operates from Massive Rock Disco. Meet up with members of the Jacobs Family (☎ 06-22095): Pat, Paul or Jr. and negotiate for trips out to the cayes. Although not cheap, they are more reasonable than some of the others.

adventure tours: Island Expeditions (☎ 800-667-1630 604-325-7952, fax 604-325-7952; 368-916 W Broadway, Vancouver, BC, Canada V5Z 1K7; e-mail island@whistler.net) offers a kayaking trip (US$999) up the Upper Moho, tied in with a stay at Blue Creek.

At Punta Ycacos, **Paradise Christine** (☎ 504-889-1848; gchlup@aol.com) will accommodate you in a tent and run you all over the cayes for BZ$200 pp, pd.

Shopping

One of the best places to shop is in front of Nature's Way Guesthouse, where Maya women come by to sell handicrafts. Little girls will also plaintively implore you to buy baskets as you walk down the street. The **Fajina Crafts Center** is an innovative alternative.

Vicinity of Punta Gorda

Although there isn't much to do in town at present, many places in the surrounding Toledo District have much to offer, and details are found in this section. Because of the paucity of public transport, getting around Toledo can be difficult unless you have your own vehicle. However, people will stop to give you a lift. Toledo continues to grow and diversify. When it is finally constructed, a newly surfaced highway will radically transform this area. Currently, dolomite is being mined in the district, and cacao is being exported by a British firm. Controversy ensued early in 1994 when it was disclosed that Malaysian businessman Ting Jack Heng had been granted a concession to log some 200,000 acres near the Guatemalan border. After protest spearheaded by the Belize Alliance of Conservation Non-Government Organizations (BACONGO), the concession was revoked.

nearby attractions: Operating until 1978, the nearly intact **Saddle Back Sugar Mill** is 1½ miles from town past the airstrip. As it's on private land, permission should be obtained before entry. The remains of **Seven Hills Sugar Mill** can be reached by boat; contact Bobby Polonio at Bobbie's Restaurant for guided tours. The southern end of the barrier reef and the Sapodilla and Ranguana Cayes (see listing under Placencia) can be also reached by boat.

The village of Santa Cruz has a park (the Río Blanco), waterfalls and pools, as well as nearby Uxbenka ruins. It is no longer a participant in the Village Guesthouse Program, but you may be able to stay with a villager.

trekking: One challenging hike is from San Miguel, north of Punta Gorda, through a chicle gathering area to the Valley of Esperanza. It takes one or two days. Contact Alfredo Romero or his uncle in San Miguel for more information. It's also possible to hike from Santa Cruz to Blue Creek; check with the TEA for information.

Village Guesthouse Program

One way to explore the area is with the **Village Guesthouse Program,** designed by the Toledo Ecotourism Association (TEA) Village Guesthouse Ecotrail Program. In 1997, the TEA won the German TODO!96 award for "socially responsible tourism." While the system does not always run smoothly, and you may not always get value for your money in terms of price and quality, it is the only program of its kind in Central America and deserves your support.

Lodges have been built in Laguna, San Pedro Columbia, Santa Cruz, San José, and San Miguel. The basic lodges are generally thatched with cohune palm, and there are eight bunk beds in each; men and women are segregated, and the charge is BZ$18.50 pp pn plus a BZ$10 registration fee. Bathrooms are detached. Meals are served by different Maya families: you will have to walk there from the guesthouse. Breakfast is BZ$6.50, as is dinner; lunch is BZ$8.50. Tours of local attractions are BZ$7 ph. Musical performances are also available. Access to the villages is either by local transportation or by

Capsule Kekchi Vocabulary

Hello.	*Chang ke ru hah wil baal.*
How are you?	*Mah sah hah chol.*
I am fine.	*Mah uh sat.*
What is your name?	*Am hah ka bah.*
My name is...	*Hink a bah hich.*
Thank you.	*To hohk reh.*
Hot.	*Maschihk.*
Rain.	*Haap.*
River.	*Nimah.*
Forest.	*Icheh.*
Hill.	*Zuul.*
Rice.	*Aroz.*
Corn.	*I shim.*
Tortilla.	*Gua.*

charter. Many visitors to Belize maintain that a stay in the village was the highlight of their trip. For information and reservations contact TEA, Box 75, Punta Gorda, or ☎ 07-22119. While in PG, stop by Nature's Way and chat with Chet. Be sure to give him (or mail him) the evaluation program so that the program may be monitored. note: The office for the program is now in the tourist office. However, the representative is not always there, and the office itself is often shut. Hopefully, this situation will have changed by the time of your visit. Otherwise, you might consider going out to a village on your own and asking to stay in a guesthouse.

Sights

Laguna offers a cave with pictographs and another with bats, a swamp with great birding, and hiking. At San Pedro Columbia, you can visit Lubaantun, ride in a canoe, and visit old cacao groves. San Miguel offers visits to caves, hikes to Lubaantun, and river canoeing. The most remote of the Maya villages participating, San José can only be reached by horse or on foot at times; it offers hiking. Other participants include Pueblo Viejo, Santa Elena, San Antonio, and Blue Creek. The Garifuna village of Barranco (see below) also has a guesthouse.

The Indigenous Experience

This innovative project is the brainchild of the Villorias and is an attempt to facilitate contact and cultural exchange between locals and outsiders. For a BZ$10 fee they connect you with a Maya family homestay. You can stay with a family, share a lunch or dinner of pumpkin stew and corn tortillas or a breakfast of eggs and tortillas. As there are no special facilities or tourist amenities offered, nor is there any privacy, it's not for everyone. You'll bathe by moonlight in the cool river, stoop in the out-

Toledo District

- - - - Seasonal Roads

To Dangriga

Nim Li Punit

San Pedro Columbia   Lubaantun

San Miguel

San José   San Antonio

Santa Cruz

Big Falls

Uxbenka   Blue Creek Village

Aguacate   Blue Creek Cave

Laguna

Pusilhá

Machaca Forest Reserve

Toledo

Santa Theresa

San Lucas

Punta Gorda

Gulf of Honduras

Dolores

Barranco

Crique Sarco   Temash River

Sarstoon-Temash Reserve

5 MILES
8 KM

Sarstoon River

GUATEMALA

house and use a corncob to clean yourself (if you wish), watch tortillas being shaped by hand, sleep in a hammock in the same room with the kids, and generally experience life as it's lived by millions all over the world. If you wish, you can have a "hands on experience," such as picking corn in the fields, harvesting coffee and cacao beans, threshing rice stalks, or chopping firewood – all of the innumerable activities that make up a sustainable subsistence lifestyle. But there's one typical "Third World"

experience you won't have – being kept awake all night fending off mosquitoes. There are none.

Rates (all the money provides badly needed income for the family) are BZ$10 for a hammock and BZ$4 for each meal. For more information contact the Villorias at PO Box 73, Punta Gorda and enclose US$3 to help defray duplicating costs. If you're already in PG, visit their offices by the ferry pier (under "services" above). Again, remember to fill out the evaluation forms. If you have complaints and/or suggestions, be sure to let them know.

Forest Home

The remains of this settlement lie to the north of Punta Gorda. Founded in 1867 by defeated Confederate exiles, many of the original settlers at this site, discouraged by the extreme climatic differences and the rigors of existence, quickly returned. Mississippi Methodists bolstered their numbers, and the number of estates operating sugar mills had grown to 12 by 1870. Falling sugar prices sent production into a tailspin in 1890, and the Methodists refused to start producing moonshine, preferring to either dump the molasses or feed it to their cattle instead. The community finally faded in 1910, and only traces remain today.

Nim Li Punit

Lying to the northeast of PG, this Maya site's name (meaning "Big Hat") comes from the carved figure wearing a large headdress on the site's tallest stela. Only partially cleared, this two-plaza ceremonial center features at least 25 stelae, eight of which are carved; one, measuring 31 feet, is the longest found in Belize. Of the several groups of buildings, only the southernmost can be visited. While one structure is 36 feet high, another is only nine feet high, but 215 feet long. The site's center consists of a ceremonial group and two civic and elite groups. Similar architecturally to Lubaantun, the site was discovered by oil workers in 1976. Although initially surveyed by Norman Hammond, in-depth excavation did not begin until Richard Leventhal worked here from 1983-1986. The beginning of the site is marked by a large ceiba tree. There's great birdwatching in the area, particularly from March to July when the fruit trees are producing.

getting here: A half-mile walk from the Southern Highway, Nim Li Punit is 25 minutes north of PG, at Mile 75. The only way to get here is by the bus running to Belize City. There are no facilities. Whitney's store is just below the turnoff for the ruins. A sign on the highway points out the trail; if you're heading south, you'll know you've passed it if you see the Whitney Lumber mill on the east side of the highway. The Maya village of Indian Creek is nearby, and you may see women washing their clothes in the stream flowing along the site's border. They'll see you and be likely to bring out a spread of handicrafts for you to view.

Big Falls

Big Falls is located just to the south of Nim Li Punit at the point where the Southern Highway crosses the Rio Grande. The **Coleman Cafe** serves local fare. There's also a small **hotel** here. The nation's only readily accessible warm medicinal **mineral springs** are on the Alaman Farm nearby. Ask Mr. Alaman at the General Store for permission to camp.

Dem Dats Doin

One of the most unusual places you'll visit anywhere in the world is right here, 1¼ miles down the entrance road to San Pedro Columbia village – just look for the sign. In the course of the past 14 years, Alfredo and Yvonne Villoria have created their own appropriate technology farm that uses sustainable agricultural techniques. Both grew up in Hawaii but first met in LA; while Alfredo is of Filipino stock, Yvonne is German-Hawaiian. Dissatisfied with stifling, routine jobs, they traveled over much of the Caribbean and Mexico, searching for a place to settle. They finally selected Belize because its British-based legal system offered them security. Giving themselves five years to make a go of it, they're still here and doing quite well. With the biogas digester and the photovoltaics on the roof, they've reached 95% energy self-sufficiency. Conscious of the need to change agricultural practices among the Maya, they offer free tours to educators and children, exposing them to appropriate technology techniques.

the farm: For a BZ$10 donation, you'll get a personal tour of this inspirational place. During the course of the visit, Yvonne and Alfredo display flowcharts and illustrations to help you understand what you're seeing. You begin in their house, which, like everything else you'll see, they built by studying books. Supported by rosewood posts, its design is nearly as remarkable as the methane-cooled refrigerator from which they pull the lemonade served to guests. Nearby is a homemade ferroconcrete wash basin, a fuel-conserving Lorena stove, and the insect dryer in which captured bugs are processed for sale. The first stop on this demonstration of a "Self-Sufficient Integrated Farm System" is the pig pen and methane vat. The giant pigs produce excrement, which is fed into the biogas digester, which produces methane sent through a pipe to a "floating drum" storage

container. Filtered, the gas is used for cooking, refrigeration, and lights; the sludge/fertilizer goes to the fruit trees and the garden. The pigs are either slaughtered when still relatively small or, when full-grown, are sold out of the area, so as not to compete with the local market. Nearby are the ferroconcrete reinforced fish ponds. The plan calls for raising tilapia in these to feed the pigs. Since these fish have not yet been granted immigrant visas owing to governmental restrictions, the ponds are filled with ordinary fish for the present.

The more than 70 trees grown on the property include governor's plum, white custard apple, rambutan, acerola (Barbados cherry), macadamia, Ceylon gooseberry, Indian juju, three varieties of star fruit, soursop, Malay apple, anatto, passion fruit, guava, tropical almond, flying potatoes, and frangipani. Plants in the primarily ornamental garden include pineapple, bamboo, torch ginger, and sweet potatoes. The latter are grown in large tires; when it comes time to harvest them, they are flipped over. No chemicals or artificial fertilizers are used; jicama, a tuber that contains a natural insecticide, is ground into a powder and sprinkled on the plants. There's also a small but attractive orchid grove, as well as a plant nursery from which cuttings are sold to locals. Rice hulls from a rice mill a couple of miles away are brought in to use as mulch. The whole tour takes 1½-2 hours. To book, either take a chance and drop in, write them at PO Box 73 in Punta Gorda, or visit them in their office at the ferry pier in PG. The Villorias also run a small and inexpensive bed and breakfast operation, as well as supervising the "Indigenous Experience" (see above).

San Pedro Columbia

This small Kekchi and mestizo village is famous for its Kekchi embroidery. San Pedro must be close to God because there are seven different churches in this village of 150 families. There is a TEA guesthouse outside the village. A good day trip here is to have a local pole you up the Columbia River in a dory. It's quite idyllic, and you can swim at the source.

GETTING HERE: From Punta Gorda, drive west for 1½ miles past the Shell station at the junction with the Southern Highway, then turn right down an unmarked road. San Pedro Columbia is two miles ahead. If you have no car, you must hitch or take a bus (San Antonio bus) along the Southern Highway and get off at the junction for San Pedro Columbia, which will be on your right. You'll know you're entering the village when you cross an iron grating in the road.

Lubaantun

Meaning "Place of the Fallen Stones" – the modern, not the original name – this is the foremost Mayan archaeological site in the nation's south. A major Late Classic ceremonial center, the site sits on a tall ridge near San Pedro, Columbia, which the Maya built up to form a roughly rectangular shape, about 300 yards long by 160 yards wide. Square courts are surrounded by pyramids once topped by thatch buildings. Constructed upon a core of rocks, smaller stones, and layers of earth, the structures were faced with hard crystalline limestone blocks, which resembled marble when viewed from a distance. What makes the site unusual is that there are no stone buildings set on platforms or pyramids, very little stone sculpture, and no stelae. It is thought that decoration was done in wood. From the highest structure you can just barely see the Caribbean more than 19 miles away.

layout: There are 11 major structures grouped around five plazas and three ball courts. Lubaantun differs from other Maya sites in a number of ways. For example, other than ball court markers, there are no stelae or sculpted monuments, and the entire site is essentially one temple complex. Unlike other Maya temples, no mortar is used. Rather than leveling off the site, the Maya systematically shaped and added fill to the slopes, and the tallest structure rises to 40 feet. The site is crumbling badly in the aftermath of too many visitors scampering to the top for a view. There isn't much to see here, but the serenity and ambience – augmented by the whir of cicadas, the crisp crackle of birds and the haunting rattle of a boring woodpecker – is wonderful. Keel-billed toucans and brocket deer frequently visit the ruins late in the afternoon.

The site is open 8-5. The caretaker may or may not be present to collect admission. In terms of ambience, the best times to visit are dawn and dusk. There's nowhere to stay, but it should be no problem to camp. You can stay in San Pedro as part of "the Indigenous Experience" or at the Village Guesthouse, which will afford you a bit more privacy (see above). You can ask the caretaker to ferry you back to San Pedro

The Crystal Skull

Lubaantun's most controversial find is a crystal skull, which was unearthed by Anna Mitchell-Hedges, daughter of expedition leader and Atlantis researcher F.A. Mitchell-Hedges. Coincidentally or not, she found the skull on her 17th birthday! Its origins are uncertain, but all agree it is a remarkable piece of work. A similar skull is found in the Musée de l'Homme in Paris. Today the crystal skull abides with Anna in Ontario, Canada. For a rather zany view of the crystal skull, written by "New Age" folk in Marin County, CA, read *The Message of the Crystal Skull* (see *Booklist*). Note that it has Lubaantun situated incorrectly on its Belize map!

in a dory; tip him a couple of dollars.

Transport

GETTING HERE: Make the first right after the village church, then proceed down the clay and gravel road, turning left when you see the sign – about 20 minutes from the village in all. (The other approach is by boat; you may stop on a trip up to the river's mouth).

History

Lubaantun apparently was occupied only briefly near the end of the Classic Period between 730 and 890 AD. It is believed that cacao was used to trade for the imported objects (jade, obsidian, and lava) found at the site – a thesis supported by the 1970 excavation of a ceramic musician wearing a cacao-pod pendant. The site first came to attention when it was uncovered by members of the Toledo settlement in 1875, and it was first excavated by Thomas Gann in 1903. Harvard University's R. E. Merwin visited the site in 1915. Taking the first photos, he spirited away three carved ball court markers (each depicting two men playing the game) to Harvard's Peabody Museum.

Another of the men who worked here was the famous archaeologist J. Eric S. Thompson in 1926-27 under the sponsorship of the British Museum. As Pusilhá, 30 miles to the southwest, seemed to be more interesting, the British Museum expedition virtually abandoned this site during the late 1920s.

In 1970 a group of Cambridge archaeologists and geologists under the leadership of Norman Hammond continued to excavate here, finding it to be larger than originally thought – surprising in light of the fact that it was used only from approximately AD 700 to 889, or possibly as short a time as AD 730-750. Although the stone was quarried locally, smaller objects such as blades and axes were imported. Some stone carvings have been found on ball court markers and on walls.

Fallen Stones Butterfly Ranch

A roller coaster of a road leads up about a mile from the entrance to the Lubaantun ruins to **Fallen Stones Butterfly Ranch** (☎ 07-22167, in the UK 44 01429 867511; Box 23, Punta Gorda)

Toledo's most remarkable lodge, one notable for its views, wildlife, and overall tasteful ambiance. Falling Stones is all the product of one man's vision and imagination.

the butterfly farm: Outside visitors pay BZ$3 to visit the butterfly farm. Owner Ray Halberd has been intrigued by butterflies since he was eight, but his employment in tropical agriculture kept him busy over the decades and it has only been in recent years that his long-held dream of operating a butterfly farm has come to fruition.

Ray operated a butterfly farm in the Philippines (on the island of Panai in Iloilo City) for 2½ years, until seven gunmen showed up one day with the intention of kidnapping him for ransom. Luckily, he was not on the farm that day. "After that, I wasn't very keen to go back and stay there. The kidnappers were eventually apprehended. One was shot dead while resisting arrest, and the others are languishing in jail."

There are two rooms filled with eight different species of butterflies. As the butterflies have a tiled roof over their heads while Ray himself lives under a thatched roof, his workers consider him to be a bit deranged. The farm's highlight is its blue morphos. They live only about 12 days, but spend their brief time filling the world with color. There will be some 4,000-5,000 blue morpho caterpillars in total when the farm is fully operational. The eggs resemble little drops of water. As it's difficult to tell the eggs from real dew drops in the morning, this is probably a technique used for camouflage purposes. Every butterfly has different colored pupae; some are jade green. You might see a newly hatched one hanging from its pupa. You'll note that the resting blue morphos resemble owl butterflies, except that the eye is not so large. Expertly camouflaged at rest, in flight they turn frighteningly bright. Each of the passion flowers found inside the enclosures caters to a different species. Another enclosure serves as a processing area where the pupae are fed.

When the farm is fully operating, 600 pupae of 35 species will be exported to Europe and the US every week, which should bring in BZ$3,000 gross. However, the process is extremely labor-intensive, and the pupae must be transported by courier, so this cuts down on the profitability. The lodge is intended to help support the butterfly ranch. Ray's intent is to turn the area around the lodge into a breeding ground for butterflies, clearing it for them and enriching the natural vegetation with food and nectar plant sources.

FAUNA: Around the vicinity of the farm you can see magnificent blue morpho butterflies. Lesser-known, but nonetheless spectacular, white morphos can be found some four miles away. There are also three species of owl butterfly, as well as a number of heliconids. All three of Belize's toucan species are here, as are hummingbirds and other flying wonders. You might see an agouti come right up on the property to feast on coconut chunks, and jaguar tracks may be seen on nearby trails. There are also a couple of nests of the stingless Maya bees, which each produce about a pound of honey per year.

PRACTICALITIES: The cabins are a combination of Kekchí and European design elements. You can sit on your porch and view the Columbia and Maya Mountain reserves: only a vast expanse of jungle stands between you and San Ignacio. There are seven rooms in all; some can accommodate up to four. Solar power provides light and operates a fan, and shower water is warmed by individual heaters. Food is highly imaginative and surprisingly well prepared; vegetarians can be catered to. Meals are loosely based on Maya cooking, but an international dish (such as a West African peanut stew) is served for Sunday lunch, which attracts a wide variety of outside visitors as well. Repasts are served in the **Chiclero's Restaurant and Bar** as well as the enclosed **Columbia View Restaurant,** which commands a view of the village of the same name. Room rates are around BZ$130 s, BZ$155 d, BZ$180 t, and BZ$205 quad. Meals cost BZ$12 for breakfast, BZ$16 for lunch, and BZ$30 for dinner. BZ$100 ow is charged for transport to or from PG for one to three persons. For more information, write PO Box 23, Punta Gorda.

Belize Agroforestry Research Center

This remarkable farm is just a short walk from the ruins: take the path left to the river and then along a path and under a barbed wire fence. Pre- and post-Hispanic Maya agricultural techniques are practiced here. Crops grown include corn, bok choy, Chinese cabbage, cabbage, coffee, and cacao. Fruits include pineapple and carambola. In an attempt to revolutionize permaculture in the area, various techniques are under R&D. For example, lucena trees (a type of legume) are planted on slopes, girded, and allowed to die on top. Wingbean, jicama, and flying potato are planted and harvested; their leaves serve as mulch. Eventually, the tree is cut down, and the girdle is used for firewood or left in place as a natural terrace; meanwhile, new sprouts have started under the girdle. Also on the property are beehives and small Maya ruins on hilltops.

HISTORY: The brainchild of environmental activist/attorney Don Wirtshafter and horticulturist Mark Cohen, this innovative project began in the 1980s. Appraising the area in 1980, Don brought back enthusiastic reports, which piqued Mark's enthusiasm. Seeing the potential for a tropical field station here, Cohen began to look for a site. The current property was originally leased from former Peace Corps volunteer Russell Turner who had lived on the parcel before returning to the States. He agreed to lease the land to them in 1988, along with an option to purchase for US$10,000. The Tropical Conservation Foundation was created in order to fund the purchase, and the Belize Agroforestry Research Center was formed as a separate Belizean entity to supervise the property. After finally securing the needed funds in 1990, the Tropical Conservation Foundation became the official titleholder of 147 acres. Despite the name, there is no official government involvement in the project, and there is still little or no involvement on the part of Belizean farmers.

PRACTICALITIES: Anyone with a serious interest in tropical agriculture is welcome to come for a visit or stay for a day or two. A BZ$20 donation per night is requested, along with an additional donation for food. If no one else is around, see Doles, the Belizean caretaker. For more information write the Tropical Conservation Foundation, 14 North Court St., Athens, OH 45701.

San Antonio

There are a few shops here, but not much else. One unusual feature of the town is the stone church and mission house. San Antonio's residents emigrated from San Luis Petén. When the original San Antonians arrived in 1886, they brought with them their patron saint San Luis, the church bells, and images of the saints from their original village. Locals from their original village arrived to reclaim their goods but were rebuffed. Shortly thereafter, the church was struck by lightning and burned to the ground; only the bells survived the fire. Both the school and church were built of hand-quarried stone. Its stained glass windows were a last-minute thought – procured when a member of the Order, walking down a street in St. Louis, Missouri, came upon a church being demolished. He persuaded the demolition company to donate them, collected donations for shipping, and they have been in place ever since.

One of the more amusing incidents in the history of Guatemala's claim to Belize took place in 1962 when Francisco Sagastume, a political opponent of President Ydígoras (who had staged a similarly unsuccessful "liberation mission" to Benque Viejo in 1958), arrived in town. Having already announced

in the border village of Pueblo Viejo that liberation was at hand, and having burned photographs of Queen Elizabeth and the Duke of Edinburgh along with a Union Jack to dramatize the declaration, he encountered hostility from the locals, whose ancestors had fled from Guatemala three generations before. Proceeding to PG, the band was arrested at Stann Creek and sentenced to 10 years hard labor. This was the last Guatemalan attempt at "liberation."

PRACTICALITIES: Stay at low-budget **Bol's Hilltop Hotel**, which has basic but clean rooms with fans. The village pay telephone is at the Bee Cooperative behind Bol's. There's no nightlife to speak of except for a bar or two. The village now has 24-hour electricity.

FESTIVALS AND EVENTS: Sporting a brown masked face and smoking a pipe, a scarecrow-like **Judas** is hung in back of the church on Holy Thursday at around 10 AM and executed by a firing squad on Holy Saturday evening after mass. Costumed young men perform dances at fiestas, like the one that takes place around June 13. A recently revived **deer dance** takes place on September 25. The festival commences with an all-night vigil nine days before, during which the masks and costumes are wreathed in incense and offered food. The story of a hunter and deer told to the accompaniment of marimba music, the deer dance is high melodrama. As part of the celebrations, a pole is greased and a prize (usually money) is set atop it. Three men compete to climb it.

GETTING HERE: Chun's buses run from Punta Gorda's Civic Center daily at 4 PM and return at 5 AM. To get here from Lubaantun, drive to the road leading from Punta Gorda, turn west for about two miles, then turn right at the junction and go two miles.

Uxbenka

A small ceremonial center "discovered" in 1984, Uxbenka is just nine miles east of the Guatemalan border in the foothills of the Toledo District, beyond San Antonio and near Santa Cruz. There are over 20 stelae here, one of which dates back to the Early Classic Period. As is typical in the area, the hills have been terraced and faced so that they resemble large buildings. Its name ("Ancient Place") was given to the site by residents of Santa Cruz. On-site, you'll find two terraces with erosion-erased stelae sheltered under thatched pavilions. All in all, there's not much to see, but the refreshing breeze and views are great.

GETTING HERE: Although some trucks do pass on Saturday, the only assured way of getting here – unless you have your own vehicle or charter – is to make the long, hot four-mile hike along the rock-strewn dirt road. (Watch out for ticks if you sit down!) Turn to the right just before the village to find the entrance road to the site. The caretaker lives at the edge of Santa Cruz and may or may not be at the scene to dispense tickets.

Río Blanco Santa Elena Nature Reserve

Set three miles west of Santa Elena, this 500-acre expanse was declared a reserve in 1993. Santa Cruzeans know it as "Santa Elena Falls" after its waterfall. A proposal to increase the reserve's size to 25,000 acres is under consideration.

Blue Creek Caves

Infrequently visited, this cave and stream combination is out of the way but worth the trip. To get here, return to the junction (marked by Roy's Cool Spot Grocery), and then follow the sign to Aguacate. Blue Creek is five miles farther, past Blue Creek Village. Its entrance is marked by a narrow concrete bridge. Sign the register and follow the trail upstream to an open-sided structure, where there's a swimming spot. From there, take the path along the water. The path follows a creek, which dries up during the rainy season. The trail crosses the creek and then wends through an area with a lot of boulders. After 15 minutes, you must climb up to a canyon that leads to the Hokeb Ha cave entrance.

In 1994, the controversial "Jason Project" was based here and on South Water Caye. Using grants from the US Dept. of Education and large corporations (including at least one defense contractor) who wanted to clean up their image, the project brought a number of "argonauts," US schoolchildren, to Belize to participate in research. Radio reports were beamed to the US. Although the enterprise did help to put Belize on the map, there was little Belizean involvement, and it seemed at times as though Belize was a convenient exotic background with a catchy name instead of a real place with real people and real problems. One lasting legacy of the project is the canopy observation system, which is accessed via a 100-foot tower. There are cabins here that cater to student groups.

Pusilhá

About a mile east of the Guatemalan border, these low-lying ruins, built on a hilltop along the river, can only be reached by boat. There are over 20 carved monuments in the plaza. Some are zoomorphs similar to those found at Quiriguá. They date from the 6th to 8th century AD. There's also a ball court, which is surrounded by walls.

Barranco

Belize's southernmost settlement, this small Garinagu village (☎ 07-22138) of around 200 can only be reached by boat (ask near the market) or by a bad road during the dry season. Its name ("Red Cliffs" in Garifuna) refers to the cliffs on which it sits. Founded in 1862, today the village has a decreasing population. There are no formal accommodations, but it's possible to stay with locals. Arrangements can either be made on your own or through the TEA.

While here, be sure to meet Carlson Tuttle, who is working to revitalize Garinagu culture; he has an excellent library, the **Tuani Garifuna Tuba Liburu,** which contains more than 400 books. He is con-

ducting an oral history project, has contributed a 386 computer to the local school, and is creating Garifuna name maps of Central America and the Caribbean. Contributions may be sent to him in Barranco, Toledo District. Carlson does leave at times to teach traditional craftsmaking in the States in order to survive financially.

Another interesting person to meet is Richard Ebensteiner, whose export herb farm **Sittee River Red Hill Limited** (e-mail info@phyto-therapeutic.com; www.phytothera-peutic.com), is located here. Howler monkeys are found near the village, as are mangroves. The uninhabited Moho River is set between here and PG.

Sarstoon-Temash Nature Reserve

This 80,000-acre tract covers the area surrounding the mouth of the Temash River. It is a haven for waterfowl and can be reached by boat from PG. The Kekchí Maya village of Dolores can be reached by taking a boat upriver to Crique Sarco, then proceeding on foot.

Offshore Cayes

Located near the mouth of the Deep River, **Wild Cane Caye** has mounds and artifacts belonging to the Mayas. Earthwatch has conducted research expeditions here under the direction of Dr. Heather McKillop of Louisiana State University. The **Sapodilla Cayes,** running down to Honduras, are great for snorkeling, as are the **Snake Cayes.** The islands are part of the Sapodilla Cayes Marine Reserve, which was declared in August 1996. Set to the southwest of

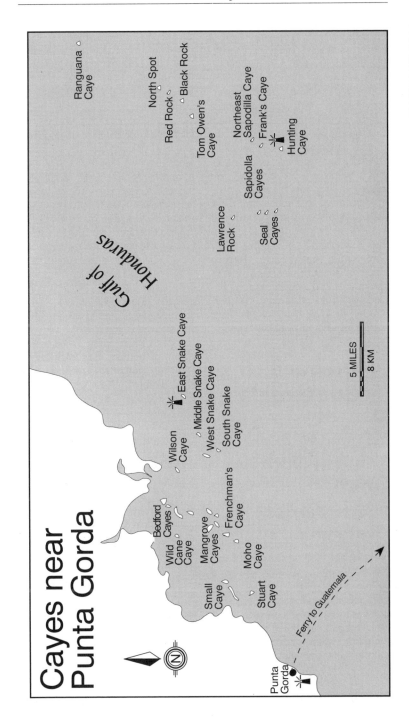

Cayes near
Punta Gorda

*Gulf of
Honduras*

Ranguana
Caye

North Spot

Red Rock

Black Rock

Tom Owen's
Caye

Northeast
Sapodilla Caye

Frank's Caye

Hunting
Caye

Sapidolla
Cayes

Lawrence
Rock

Seal
Cayes

East Snake Caye

Middle Snake Caye

West Snake Caye

South Snake
Caye

Wilson
Caye

Frenchman's
Caye

Bedford
Cayes

Mangrove
Cayes

Wild
Cane
Caye

Moho
Caye

Small
Caye

Stuart
Caye

Punta
Gorda

Ferry to Guatemala

5 MILES

8 KM

Nicholas Caye, **Hunting Caye** is partly used as a base for the Belizean Defense Force. It has the remains of an old ship (as well as an enormous ancient anchor, overgrown by coral) in the depths off a nearby reef to the southeast. There is a lighthouse and a good harbor, as well as Crescent Moon, a lovely beach. If you visit here, be cautious: it is a nesting ground for hawksbill turtles and too much activity could be disruptive to them. **Lime Caye (Low Caye)** is another beautiful island. Tour groups from Livingston visit here. Also known as Sapodilla Caye and South Caye, **Ragged Caye** is the southernmost link in the chain. Although largely denuded by tropical storms, it is a fine snorkeling spot. There is excellent diving around all of these cayes.

Onward to Guatemala

Many travelers arriving in Punta Gorda will be headed toward Guatemala by boat. Two of the best Maya sites (Quiriguá and Copán) are within a few days of PG.

Puerto Barrios, Guatemala

This sleazy port town has little to recommend it, unless you're a sailor on shore leave. Its only attributes are a marvelously sagging cinema building, a lively market, and a fabulous Taj Mahal-style tomb – complete with trumpeting elephants – at the cemetery on the road out of town.

PRACTICALITIES: Probably the best place to stay in terms of con-venience is the **Caribeña** just up the road from the ferry to the left. The dining room of the **El Norte** has the best atmosphere and the hotel itself has a classic Caribbean atmosphere.

GETTING HERE: For information about the ferry see "from Punta Gorda" above. Upon arrival, an immigration official will grab your passports and stuff them into a leather bag. Then, after passing through customs and paying an "inspection fee," you turn left at the corner and enter the Immigration Office. US citizens will generally be asked for US$6 or Q25 for a visitor's card and will be granted a month's stay. The nearest bank still open is the Banco del Café near the market. If you have US dollars, you can change them at the corner near the market. Belizean dollars bring a ridiculous rate so you should change these with the lady moneychanger near PG's pier; she'll also buy your extra quetzales at a fair rate if you return that way. When returning from Guatemala City, hop an express (five hours, US$6) and spend the night here. The ferry runs Tues. and Fri. at around 8. Buy your ticket at the office up the street from the ferry and proceed to Immigration, where you'll be soaked for an exit fee of Q10 for individuals and Q6 apiece for couples. This probably goes directly into the officer's pocket.

Livingston, Guatemala

This predominately Garinagu (Black Carib) village is set across the Bay of Honduras. The ferry no longer stops here so you must either charter a boat in PG or take the ferry from Puerto Barrios, then another (generally crowded) one from there. (The best chance for a direct boat from PG is on Tues. and Fri.) The waterfall, **Las Siete Altares** (The Seven Altars), is a few miles along the beach; visitors have been robbed here, so take nothing of value with you. A popular excursion from here is a boat trip up the Río Dulce to the **Biotopo (Reserve) Chocón-Machacas**. The least expensive transport is with the mail launch, which departs on Tuesday and Friday.

ACCOMMODATIONS & FOOD:
The classiest hotel here is **Tucán Dugú** (☎ 9-481-588), which has rooms for around US$42 s and US$45 d. It offers standard, suite, and bungalow rooms; watersports; a pool, and two restaurants. Other places – all low-budget – include the **Casa Rosada** (☎ 510-525-4470, fax 510-525-5427, in the US), the **Hotel Caribe** (☎ 048-1073), the 13-room classically Caribbean **Río Dulce** (☎ 9-481-059), the German-owned **African Place**, and the **Flamingo.** The **Restaurante El Malecón** is popular. Alternatives include the **Restaurante Margoth,** the **Restaurante Saby,** the **Restaurante Tiburongato, Dante's** (vegetarian dishes and seafood), and eating at some of the hotels.

VICINITY OF PUERTO BARRIOS:
Popular with birders, **Punta de Manabique** is a nature reserve that has seabirds and flamingos. The **Canal de los Ingleses**, a canal dug by the the British, runs through it. Sightseeing boats are generally available on Sat. and Sun.; otherwise, you must charter. Stay at inexpensive **Pirate's Point Lodge** (☎ 2-946-950 in Guatemala City),

which has thatched-roof cabanas at the peninsula's tip. It has a beach and restaurant as well as boat rental.

Quiriguá, Guatemala

Containing the major Quiriguá Classic Maya ruins, Quiriguá National Park is a small expanse of old growth forest surrounded by banana plantations. Studied and excavated since the late 19th century, it has been lovingly restored and, from an artistic standpoint, rivals Copán as the Maya site with the most carvings and reliefs. The earliest structures at the site appear to date from the Late Preclassic (ca. 300 BC-200 AD), but the visible buildings and stelae date from 550-850 AD. Its site plan is similar to Copán. To the south an artificially raised acropolis contains elite administrative and ceremonial structures. The large public plaza to the north holds the remains of public buildings, a ball court, and stelae. This plan contrasts with Tikal's radial format.

Major attractions here are the stelae, which are unmatched in Mayadom. Beginning with **Stela H** (751 AD), each successive stela – erected every five years – was larger and more imposing, until the granddaddy of them all, 35-foot-tall **Stela E,** was erected in 771 AD. The tallest stela known, it weighs some 35 tons. Even more unusual and striking than the stelae, the zoomorphs are scattered over the plaza. The **Great Turtle**, Zoomorph P, is the most famous monument. This enormous boulder has been intricately and delicately carved with stone tools. The massive acropolis at the site is also impressive.

GETTING HERE: Even though it's a hassle to get here, the trip is worth it! Any bus running between Puerto Barrios and Guatemala City will pass by here. Just get out at the junction and transfer to the smaller local bus for a ride through the banana fields, a few miles to the entrance.

PRACTICALITIES: A minimal admission is collected at the entrance, where postcards and other souvenirs are sold. As all but one of the stelae and all of the zoomorphs have been placed in open-faced thatch huts for protection, a flash and/or high ASA film is appropriate for photography. Bring water as well because no facilities are available on-site.

The nearest place to stay is in the budget-priced **Hotel Royal** near the village of Quiriguá. **Hotel y Restaurante Santa Monica** stands next to the Texaco station in Los Amates, and **Hotel Doña Maria** is at Km 181 near Puente Doña María (Doña María Bridge). The first is the cheapest, but the second is most comfortable, and still low-budget at under US$10 d.

Copán, Honduras (Las Ruinas)

With excavated ruins covering some 40 acres and containing an acropolis and five plazas, the ancient Maya city of Copán is located in the southeast Maya lowland zone, on the Río Copán just inside Honduras and near the Guatemala border. The restored structures date from 600-

800 AD, the Late Classic. Evidence unearthed so far suggests that Copán was occupied from Preclassic times on. Although its images are shared by other Maya sites, the presentation is Copán's own, and the site is without a doubt the greatest repository of Maya art. In addition to a large number of extraordinary stelae, there's also the Great Turtle, an enormous and magnificent carved two-headed stone turtle with clawed feet resembling those of a jaguar. Comprising as many as 2,500 glyphs, the Hieroglyphic Stairway is the site's top attraction. Another hallmark is the "Old Man of Copán," a representation of God N depicted at the northeast corner of Temple 11 (The Temple of the Inscriptions).

History

The area surrounding the site is believed to have been inhabited as early as 1000 BC. Although details are sketchy, Copán is thought to have flourished between 250 and 900 AD. The Hieroglyphic Stairway and a number of other imposing structures were completed during the reign of Yax Pac (763-820 AD), and the area is believed to have started its decline thereafter. The last carved date found is 822 AD. By 1200 AD the site had been reclaimed by the forest. The name comes from the indigenous chief of the region, Copán Calel, who used the area as a base against the Spanish aggressors.

The ruins remained neglected until explorers John L. Stephens and Frederick Catherwood arrived in 1841. They employed indigenous workers to hack away at the forest and expose the ruins. Ste-

COPAN

Former bed of Copán River

N

J

TEMPLE 22

HIEROGLYPHIC
STAIRWAY

EAST
COURT

WEST COURT

P Q

ACROPOLIS

CEMETERY
GROUP

200ft.
61 M

BALL
COURT

N

O

L

K

GREAT PLAZA

Entrance

F

D

C

B

E

A

G H

I

Copán's New Museum

The **Copán Museum of Maya Sculpture** contains 3,000 pieces of sculpture, including six building facades. Opened in 1996 and located near the entrance to the ruins, the museum's mission is to play an important role in the investigation and knowledge of the lost Maya culture. The museum's entrance is shaped like a serpent's mouth; each section of the museum is staircase-shaped and is in the form of a tunnel. Each "step" of the staircase is a floor. The exhibits range from religious artifacts to stucco and stone Maya sculptures. One room holds 108 hieroglyphs, the lengthiest intact piece of Maya writing in existence. Another highlight is the replica of the Rosalia Temple. The original was built in 571 AD and is dedicated to the Sun God. It depicts a sacred mountain adorned with large-winged birds and serpents.

---

phens purchased the ruins from their owner for US$50 and for a time actually planned to have them disassembled and shipped to New York. British archaeologist Alfred P. Maudslay arrived to excavate the site in 1885 and successive work has been carried on by Harvard's Peabody Museum, the Carnegie Institution of Washington, DC, and by the Instituto Hondureño de Antropología y Historia. The latest project is to protect the sculptures at the site from destructive humidity and rainfall by moving them to a controlled indoor environment, an expensive proposition.

📖 *Suggested Reading*
Before your trip, read Scribes, Warriors, and Kings: The City of Copán *(1991) by William Fash, Thames and Hudson, NY.*

Transport

GETTING HERE: Entry to Honduras has become something of a cottage industry for both Guatemalan and Honduran customs officials. Buses to the border run from Chiq-

uimula. The border at El Florido is usually open from 7 AM to 6 PM. Change Honduran lempiras with the money changers (US$1= approximately 12 lempiras). You must pay five quetzales to leave Guatemala and a few dollars worth of lempiras to enter Honduras. Let the immigration official know that you will only be visiting Copán (Las Ruinas) and ask for a temporary exit permit. When you return to Guatemala, you should be able to use the same tourist card. Food and drink is available on the Honduran side. From the border, you must take a minibus seven miles to the village of Copán Ruinas.

Sights

TOURING THE RUINS: The entrance to the ruins is a pleasant half-mile walk from the village; your minibus may drop you at the entrance upon request. Don't make the mistake of visiting the site just once. If you're staying in the village, you can easily visit again during the late afternoon hours when there are few visitors. Bring water with you. Food is available at cafeterias, but you might want to pack some snacks. If you take the detour along the way to the left, you'll pass two eroded stelae. As you enter the complex, you'll either need to pay or to show your ticket (which can also be purchased at the museum in the village and is good for all sites). There is one price for Hondurans, another for Central Americans, and a third (highest fee: around US$5) for everyone else. Once inside, there are a few books and T-shirts for sale at the Centro de Visitantes.

Entering the grounds, turn to the left and walk through another gate, where your ticket is checked again. Three scarlet macaws with clipped wings sit on the fence. A variety of caged animals are inside to the left, including a despondent margay and hyper white-faced capuchin monkeys. Farther on, the grounds are essentially tranquil – the peaceful ambience ruffled only by tour guides and workmen doing excavations.

A short walk will bring you to the Principal Group and the **Great Plaza**. Here you'll find the most impressive and delicately carved stelae in the Maya World. Originally all were thought to have been painted, but touches of paint survive only on Stela C. A number of them depict King 18 Rabbit (695-738 AD). In the **Central Plaza**, to the south of the Great Plaza, the ballcourt is Central America's second largest and one of the few that retains its paving; it dates from 775 AD. The bordering rooms were likely to have been used by observers. The magnificent 50-foot-wide, 63-step **Hieroglyphic Stairway** is now shielded from the elements by a tarp. Each block forms part of a sequence of 1,500-2,000 glyphs,

equaling the inscriptions found on 20 stelae combined. Partially because the stairway collapsed in the 19th century and 30 of the risers are not in order, the inscription has still only been decoded in fragments. The Copán Mosaics Project is trying to restore the stairway on paper and decode its meaning. An enormous cache has been discovered below the stairway. The Temple of the Inscriptions nearby is also worth visiting. Set at its base, Stela N has both portraits and glyphs.

The **East Plaza** and **West Plaza** are to its south. The latter's Altar Q has representations of what are thought to be 16 kings of Copán carved along its sides. One of the site's most imposing buildings, Structure 22 on the northern side of the East Plaza, has the most detailed reliefs at its top. Above one of its entrances, each head of the two-headed snake rests atop a figure that is supported by a skull. Carvings of Chaac, the Rain God, are at each corner of the structure. Also notice the carved jaguar heads found at this plaza.

In the immediate surroundings, you might spot a white-faced monkey, deer, and a variety of birds. The *sendero natural* (nature trail) may not have much in the way of wildlife, depending upon your luck. But you can head down straight and reach the river or turn right by some ruins and cross over to complete the circle and return.

About another half-mile down the road and off to the right is **Las Sepulturas**, a site in the process of restoration. The only other important concentration of ruins open to visitors besides those found at the Great Plaza, it was originally connected to the latter by a causeway. The structures here are thought to have housed the elite. It's believed that some 250 people resided here around 800 AD. The best time to visit is early in the morning when you'll have it all to yourself. Except for a few figures, missing their heads, there is little to see here, but the ambience is great.

Back in the village, there's a small museum, the **Museo Regional de Arqueología,** which contains a significant number of artifacts.

OTHER AREA SIGHTS: You can take a minibus (45 min., once or twice daily) to the **Agua Caliente,** set by a river. From the village of Santa Rita (5 mi/9 km from Copán) you can hike to **Cascada El Rubí,** a waterfall situated upriver. **Pená Quemada,** a rainforest reserve, is 12 mi / 20 km away. It has howler monkeys. A guide is mandatory, and admission is charged.

Tours

Contact **M.C. Tours** (☎ 983453) at the Hotel Marina. **Go Native Adventure Tours** may be contacted via the Escuela de Español Ixbalanque (☎ 983432, fax 576215).

Accommodations

If staying at hotels close to the town entrance, expect to be awakened by the sound of early morning buses departing. Copán village is a nice and very friendly place to hang out for a few days. The expensive **Hotel Marina** (☎ 983-070, fax 573-076) is the place to stay if you want comfort. Facilities include a pool, rooms with cable TV, and a restaurant.

Another upscale alternative is the 80-rm. **Hotel Posada Real de Copán** (☎ 983480-97, fax 983498; 800-528-1234), which is a Best Western. It's at Km. 164 on the road between San Pedro Sula and the village, and has a pool and restaurant. Less expensive is the **Hotel Las Jaguares** (☎ 983-451), which has a/c and TV. Next down the list is the 14-rm. **Hotel Maya Copán.**

The hotel prices here are a bit higher than elsewhere in Honduras for the bottom-rung accommodation. Try **Hotel y Restaurant Paty, Hotelino Brisas de Copán, Hotel Las Gemelos,** or **Hotel Honduras.**

outlying: The **Hacienda El Jaral** (☎ 532-070, fax 575-489), offers 16 attractive rooms set in duplex cabins along a hillside. Its lagoon attracts thousands of cattle egrets from Oct. to May. It is near the settlement of Santa Rita (9 km / 5 miles away).

☞ *Traveler's Tip*

*If you would like to settle down for a while and study Spanish, Copán is an ideal place to do it. The **Escuela de Español Ixbalanque** (☎ 983432, fax 576215) provides one-on-one instruction at a very reasonable price. Write them at Escuela de Español Ixbalanque, Copán Ruinas, Honduras.*

Food

Most popular with visitors is the **Restaurante Bar Tunkul,** a budget eatery that offers fare such as burritos and veggie plates. Set across the street, the **Restaurant La Llama del Bosque** serves traditional Honduran food. Pricier is the **Glifos,** which is set inside the Hotel Marina. There are also numerous low-budget dining dives in town;

food is incredibly cheap compared to Belize, so indulge while you can!

Services

The **post office** and **phone company** are near the museum. **Justo a Tiempo** offers laundry service; it is off the square.

El Mundo Maya

One of the most intriguing aspects of Belize to the visitor is the abundant archaeological legacy of the Maya. Even today, some 1,700 years after it is believed to have reached its peak, Maya culture is a very rich and impressive lode. Although pieces are filling in, the puzzle of Maya civilization is far from complete, and much of what is known is mere conjecture based upon fragmentary evidence. As the guessing game continues, perceptions change and mistakes are rectified. The Maya World, its history and culture included, has been cemented together in perpetuity with the European conquerors and colonists whose initial disdain for the Maya turned to wonder as they discovered and explored the ruins. Eventually, they came to regret their initial haste to destroy and denigrate.

The People

GEOGRAPHY: The Maya inhabited some 125,000-225,000 square miles, encompassing the present day boundaries of El Salvador, W. Honduras, Belize, Guatemala, the Mexican states of Tabasco and Chiapas to the west, as well as the entire Yucatán Peninsula. While firm geographical boundaries exist to the north and east, boundaries are more difficult to fix in the southeast and southwest, where they correspond only to zones of cultural transition between Maya and non-Maya. The area has traditionally been subdivided into the lowlands in the north and the highlands in the south. With the exception of Copán, which is located in the eastern portion of the northern highlands, the most famous Maya sites are in the northern lowlands. Maya culture, in turn, is part of Mesoamerica, a larger cultural area extending from northern Mexico as far south as Costa Rica. The Maya both were influenced by and influenced neighboring cultures, such as the Olmec of the Gulf coastal plain, the Zapotec and Mixtec of Oaxaca (west of the Isthmus of Tehuantepec), as well as lesser known societies to the southeast. The borders of the cradle of Maya civilization are delineated by the presence of the sapodilla. This tropical evergreen, famous in the modern era through its sap, which has been used to produce chewing gum, was employed by the Maya for supporting beams and wooden panels. In addition, the sap was used to make the ball for traditional ball games. Mixed with a second regional resin, the tree's sap also supplied a highly prized incense used in Maya religious ceremonies.

HISTORY: Although it is not known what the people actually called themselves, the term "Maya" was applied to the entire civilization. Recent findings indicate that the Maya may have inhabited Belize from as early as 9000 BC, but it is thought that the civilization's influences extend back to the Olmec civilization that flourished on the nearby Gulf of Mexico from 1200-300 BC. The Olmecs were renowned for their carving skill, as well as their calendar and system of hieroglyphics. Maya history is cus-

Selected Web Sites Relating to the Maya

- **www.iglobal.net/pub/ousia/mayanist.html** – A good starting point for information.

- **www.stevensonpress.com** – Mesoamerican Foundation.

- **www.primenet.com/~smudget** – Belizean archaeology.

- **www.netzone.com/~xiolablu** – Caves Branch Belizean archaeology project.

- **www.uacam.mx/campeche/maya/arq_maya.htm** – A Spanish language site focusing on the Maya ruins found in Campeche, Mexico.

- **www.quvision.com/MRP** – Blue Creek Project in Belize.

- **indy4.fdl.cc.mn.us/~isk/maya/maya.html** – Maya pages.

tomarily divided into three periods: Preclassic or Formative (2500 BC-AD 250), Classic or "Golden Age" (AD 250-900), and Postclassic (AD 900-1540). The Preclassic is further subdivided into Early Preclassic (2500-1000 BC), Middle Preclassic (1000-300 BC), Late Preclassic (300 BC-AD 50) and Protoclassic (AD 50-250).

societal decline: No one knows what caused the Maya society to decline. One scenario is that of ecological collapse, brought on by population pressures that had caused over-exploitation of the environment. Other theories hold that the society collapsed because of clashes and fissures within the social structure. Maya expert J. Eric Thompson reasoned that a combination of factors – such as natural disaster and agricultural problems – could have led to disillusionment with the elite, which was followed by a peasant revolt. Others believe that a civil war between population centers led to the civilization's demise, or that the Maya lowlands were invaded from abroad. Yet another theory holds that environmental pressures caused the civilization to splinter and decline. The rainforest may have been over-exploited, there appear to have been water shortages, and the area may have been overpopulated. A final and perhaps the most intriguing theory is that the Maya prognosticated themselves out of existence. Prophecies may have foretold changes at the end of a *katun* (one of the cycles on their calendar), which the fatalistic Maya then brought to fruition, thus bringing about their own downfall. A further refinement of this theory is that the Mayan astronomer-priests may have ordained it. In the 10th century it was announced that the fourth or present world was about to end, giving way to a fifth world without men. This may have brought on an artificial "judgment day," destroying the civilization in the process.

mingling: The story of the ancient Maya definitively concludes with the era of Spanish Conquest, when destruction and mayhem dealt a devastating blow to local culture. Columbus encountered a canoe full of Maya traders in 1502 while exploring the Bay Islands off Honduras, and their decline began then and there. In addition to deaths by war and famine, introduced diseases such as malaria and smallpox took their toll. Ritual and belief were crushed by the repressive church, and the written script disappeared. Traditional crafts such as sculpture, featherwork, lapidary work, painting, and metallurgy were extirpated. The economic system was transformed as well. The best lands were taken over for plantation crops such as coffee and sugarcane, which soon replaced traditional staples, and iron and steel replaced flint and obsidian. Still, a certain amount of ideology and the spoken language survived the transition into this "new world order." For example, the Christian cross was already used by the Maya as their symbol for the "tree of life," the ceiba tree supporting the heavens. So the cross gained ready acceptance when the friars explained that it was the sign of God, who had died on the Tree of Good and Evil and now resides in Heaven. In addition, the Maya already practiced baptism in water, fasting, confirmation, as well as sexual abstinence before rituals, and they were accustomed to dressing their idols and bathing them in incense.

THE MAYA TODAY: As the Chiapas revolt in Dec. 1993 made clear, today's Maya are second-class citizens in an area they once controlled. Condescended to and persecuted, Maya live in Guatemala and Mexico. Human rights violations are numerous. Some 140,000 Guatemalans (largely indigenous) have been killed during the three decades of Guatemala's civil war, and government troops have been known to burn entire villages. In Mexico, 11 Maya were tortured following their arrest in a land dispute in 1990, and a few years ago some 100 Maya were beaten and locked up for 30 hours without medical attention or food. Today, in Chiapas, only around half the population can read (compared with literacy rates of 88% for all of Mexico), 70% lack access to potable water, and infant mortality is 500 for every 1,000 live births – 10 times the national average. For information on Maya in Belize, see the entry under the Introduction.

The Civilization

MAYA CULTURE AND TECHNOLOGY: One major cultural quality was an obsession with the passage of time. Although the Maya did not measure time in smaller increments than European cultures, they invented a sun calendar more accurate than the Gregorian calendar used today, recorded the rotation of Venus, and predicted eclipses of the sun and moon. Conceiving the notion of zero, they were able to calculate numbers to over a million, and in their vigesimal (base 20) numeration system, a system of dots and bars represented numbers from zero to 19. Symbolized as a shell, the Maya zero didn't appear in Europe until the 12th C., and the bar-and-dot notation was superior for mathematical calculations, as compared with the more awkward system of Roman numerals employed in Europe at the same time. The Maya counted by twenties, four hundreds, and eight thousands, and their words for numbers reflect this system of enumeration. Indeed, they were so mathematically focused that little is known about Maya society itself, because most of the glyphs translated thus far relate to calculations of time and astronomical events. In some ways they were far ahead of their time. Modern astronomy has determined that the solar year has 365.2422 days. The Maya calendar has 365.2425 days! One of at least five calendars, the Haab, has 18 20-day months (*uinals*), totaling 360 days. There are then 5-5½ *uayeb*, or unlucky days, left over. The other two calendars are a mysterious one of 260 days – which is interlinked with the other – and the "long count," an extension of the Haab, leading back to a mystical date of 3113 BC. The other two calendars were lunar and Venusian. Their society is believed to have been ruled by a hereditary theocracy. They knew how to build roads and make mortar. They also developed the corbel vault as an arch. Still, despite these advances, they used only the most primitive of agricultural methods, never discovered the wheel, and fashioned Neolithic style tools from polished stone.

WRITING: Maya writing is built on glyphs that are predominately square or oval in shape, and which are generally divided into glyph groups. There are about 800 known glyphs, which are usually referred to by their catalog numbers or by nicknames such as "upended frog."

Maya centers each have their own emblem glyphs that are unique to the site concerned and only found at another when the inscription refers to contact with that center. The writing system is generally agreed to be logosyllabic – a combination of pictographic and ideographic scripts – and is thought to have become more and more phonetic over time.

AGRICULTURE: One of the oldest forms of cultivation was swidden agriculture (more popularly known as slash-and-burn), in which fields were burned and planted with crops ranging from beans, maize, chilis, and squash to manioc and sweet potatoes. After the land is cultivated for several years, it must lie fallow and new tracts have to be cleared. Fertilized by garbage, the household garden provided produce. As any visitor to a contemporary Maya community will soon realize, these practices are still in use today. Methods no longer or rarely found in use today include raised fields and agricultural terracing. Raised fields allowed high-yield use of poorly drained or swampy tracts. With crops raised on intersecting or parallel ridges of fertile, well-drained soil built up from the surrounding swamp, while the low areas between fields provided rich soil as well as drainage. If underwater, fields may have been used to raise fish and other marine life. Many of the raised fields of northern Belize are thought to have been planted with both maize and cacao. Used for ceremonial or burial offerings, maize formed an important decorative and symbolic motif in Maya art and was regarded as the gods' greatest gift to mankind. It was (and still is) planted with a digging stick, which makes a hole into which a seed is dropped. The Maya venerated a maize god and the plant itself, considered an attribute of the earth god. Today's Maya continue to address the plant as "your grace." Another important crop was cacao, which – when roasted, ground, and mixed with maize and water – formed the favorite drink. Prized as an article of trade, cacao also served as a currency.

SEASIDE SETTLEMENTS: Although thoughts of the Maya world bring to mind images of ruined temples in the jungles, settlements on the shore played an important role in the economic structure because of their access to the sea's wealth. In addition to marine life – such as shellfish, fish, manatees, seals, and birds – which provided food, shells were used in toolmaking and jewelry. Stingray spines and shark teeth had their own ritual uses.

The coastal Maya began harvesting salt, an important export, some 2,300 years ago. In addition to its nutritional value, salt was used to preserve meat and fish, for barter, and in a number of ritual and medical procedures. Basalt, jade (jadeite), obsidian, and other resources from the interior were traded for salt, cacao, cotton, feathers, jaguar pelts, and spices.

Maya would travel the coasts in large dugouts, which could hold 40-50 people. They settled Cozumel and Belize cayes, such as Wild Cane, at least 2,000 years ago and are thought to have ventured as far as the Turneffes, 18 miles from the coast. Important Belizean settlements include Cerros (near Sarteneja) and Marco Gonzales (on Ambergris Caye).

Religion

El Mundo Maya

COSMOLOGY: For the Maya, the supernatural permeated every aspect of society, regulating all aspects of daily life up to and including trade and competition. The threat of supernatural retribution kept people in line. Shamans evolved into a priestly class, transforming the society into a theocracy in which priests were rulers and rulers were priests. The world was governed by a cosmological order transcending the distinction between natural and supernatural realms. All objects, animate or inanimate, were infused with an invisible force. Such a power was formless where spirits occupied rocks, trees, or other objects. But in other cases the power was embodied in a zoomorphic or anthropomorphic deity. The universe was viewed as an ordered place in its natural state, and the sun, moon, planets, and stars – each thought to be animate – marked the passage of time. The *kin*, the basic unit of time, is the time it took the sun to rise from the underworld, pass across the sky, and be swallowed by the underworld at sunset.

RITUALS: During the Classic era, the elite practiced ritual bloodletting. Penis piercing and the passing of a cord through the tongue are shown on Maya painted vases, and the ceremonial blood-letting instrument used to cut the penis is also widely depicted. The two types of bloodletting were self-imposed bleeding, and the bloodletting or

MAYA CHRONOLOGY	MAYA EVENTS	WORLD EVENTS
AD 1500 Late Postclassic	Cortez arrives (1519)	Renaissance in Europe (1400+) Ming Dynasty founded (1368) Majapahit Empire (Java) (1292-1398)
AD 1200 Early Postclassic	Marco Gonzalez flourishes (1150-1300)	Kublai Khan attempts invasion of Japan (1274) Crusades in Europe (1096-1271)
AD600 Early Classic	Caracol conquers Tikal (AD 562)	Mohammed born (approx AD 571) End of Roman Empire (AD 476)
AD 250 Late Preclassic	Xunantunich occupied (AD 150)	Yamato Period in Japan (AD 100-600) Silkworm cultivation arrives in China (AD 200)
400 BC Middle Preclassic		Alexandria, Egypt flourishes (300 BC-0 AD) Rice cultivation begins in Japan (300 BC) Mahabarata written (350-300 BC) Parthenon dedicated (438 BC) Gautama Buddha lives (583-463 BC)
800 BC Early Preclassic	Tikal first occupied (750 BC) Altun Ha first occupied (1000 BC)	Moses receives Ten Commandments (1500 BC)
2500 BC		Stonehenge (2000-1500 BC) Sphinx constructed (3000-2500 BC) First year of Jewish Calendar (3760 BC)

sacrifice of a captive. Blood was offered to express piety and call the gods. It is thought that intense pain brought on hallucinatory visions, which have been represented on stelae by a serpent monster rising out of a plate holding blood-soaked ritual tools. Such tools included a rope with thorns that was pulled through the tongue and pieces of paper used to catch blood from penile or ear incisions. It is well known that endorphins, chemicals related to opiates and produced by the brain in response to massive blood loss, can induce hallucinations. Adding to the effect was the use of *balche*, an alcoholic beverage made from fermented honey combined with the *balche* tree bark, and of wild tobacco leaves – much more potent than today's anemic varieties. When these were smoked in gigantic spliffs, they induced a trance-like stupor. Miniature stone figures of mushrooms have also been found, pointing to their ritual use as hallucinogens, and depictions of enemas appear on glazed pots. Bloodletting is considered to have been fundamental to the institution of rulership. The main occasions for bloodletting and sacrifice were ceremonial ones that dealt with the mythology of world order: marriage, the dedication of buildings, planting of crops, birth of children, and burials. Because of its ritual importance, the lancet itself was ordained as a sacred object. Many were ornately carved, but stingray spines were employed as well.

DEITIES AND MYTHS: Creator of the universe as well as god of harvest, sun, earth, and rain, Itzamná is the principal Maya deity. Ix Chel is the goddess of the moon, and Ki-nich Ahau is the lord of the sun. Gods of rain, the Chacs, enjoy continued popularity with today's Maya. The jaguar god of the underworld can be identified by his jaguar ear, a tau (shaped like the Greek letter T) tooth, a cruller (ring-shaped cake) in his forehead, and gathered hair. All told, there may have been thousands of other deities. Ritual acts and their details were governed by the calendar.

HUMAN SACRIFICE: One of several techniques, the most popular method, according to an account by Bishop Landa, was to pull out the victim's heart. Stripped, painted blue, and wearing a peaked headdress, the victim was grabbed by four *chacs* (priests), also painted blue. Then the *nacom* (executioner priest) plunged a flint knife into the victim's ribs just below the left breast. Pulling out the still-beating heart, he handed it to the *chilan* (officiating priest), who smeared its blood on the idol. If the victim had been executed atop a pyramid, the *chacs* threw the corpse down to the base, where low-ranking priests skinned it, putting the hands and feet aside. After removing his ceremonial zoot suit, the *chilan* donned the victim's skin and danced solemnly. If the unfortunate one had been a soldier, his body was sometimes eaten, and his hands and feet were reserved for the *chilan*. Another method of sacrifice was to shoot at the heart with a bow and arrow. Other methods included disembowelment (as portrayed at Tikal) and throwing victims into the Cenote of Sacrifice at Chichen Itza.

THE BALL PARK: One of the features you'll notice at many Maya sites is the ball park. A combination of modern volleyball, basketball, jai alai, and soccer, the game was played by two competing teams of two to 11 members. Weighing an average of about five lbs., the rubber ball could be hit with all body parts, save hands, feet, or calves, and it could be bounced against the court's side wall. Players scored by forcing the ball into the opposing team's end zone or by striking the side markers. Protective clothing fashioned from leather or wicker shielded them from impact.

The Temple Sites

VISITING MAYA RUINS: Unlike Mexico and Guatemala – where manicured Maya ruins have been rebuilt as the archaeologists believe they may have once been rather than necessarily as they actually were – the Belizean ruins have been left intact much as they were found. If something's been broken or fallen over, it's left that way. This has its attractions: the ruins have an aura of authenticity, and the lack of gawking crowds makes it easier to lose yourself in the magic of these places.

ARCHAEOLOGICAL HISTORY: The presence of these ghost cities amidst the hot and humid and nearly impenetrable jungle has long baffled archaeologists. The first explorers deemed it preposterous that the impoverished peasantry residing near the ruins might have any connection with these sophisticated structures. Thus, they invented a mythic race of "Noble Maya," believed to have been descendants of the Lost Tribes of Israel, Greeks, Phoenicians, Vikings, Egyptians, or residents of Atlantis. Published in 1822 in London, the first book about the Maya, *Descriptions of the Ruins of an Ancient City*, was a 1787 report by a Spanish army officer, Captain Antonio del Río who, visiting the large site of Palenque, had taken down all of the partitions and cleared blocked windows and doors. He maintained that the Romans – or perhaps the Phoenicians or Greeks – had arrived and taught the Indians their construction techniques. American John Lloyd Stephens and his English companion, artist Frederick Catherwood, rediscovered Copán in 1839 and purchased the site from a local farmer for US$50. After visiting Palenque to the north a few months later, Stephens hypothesized that the two centers belonged to the same culture. Together they visited over 40 sites. Published in 1841, Stephen's *Incidents of Travel in Central America, Chiapas and Yucatán* caused quite a stir in its time.

In the 1860s an old manuscript, *Account of Things in the Yucatán*, by one Father de Landa, was unearthed in the Royal Library of Madrid. As the first Catholic Bishop of Mérida, the Spanish capital in the Yucatán, Landa had torched irreplaceable sacred painted Maya texts. Ironically, his account – which contained drawings of glyphs used by 16th C. Maya – still stands as one of the basic informational sources relating to the early Maya. The manuscript was found by French Abbé Brasseur de Bourbourg who also discovered a portion of one of the extant pre-Conquest Maya codices. Succumbing to the delusions of the day, Abbé Brasseur came to believe that the civilizations of the Old World and Egypt stemmed from the New World to which they had been brought by colonists from Atlantis. University research boomed during the last two decades of the 19th C. The foremost scholar of the time was Englishman Alfred Maudslay, who spent 13 years studying ruins, producing five volumes in the process. At the same time Austrian-born naturalized American Teobert Maler had arrived in Mexico in 1864 as an Austrian army officer serving with Emperor Maximilian. He carried out work for Harvard's Peabody Museum for two solitary but extremely productive decades. During the same time frame, P. T. Barnum presented to Queen Victoria's dwarf a pair of microcephalic dwarfs claimed to be the last degenerate descendants of a caste of high priests found in a lost Maya city. At the end of the 19th century a major breakthrough came with Dresden librarian Ernst Forstemann's deciphering of the Maya calendar, which permitted scholars to read the calendrical inscriptions. In this century, archaeological excavations have increased the amount of knowledge available, but many secrets remain under the cover of the jungle. During the 1950s, the most prominent archaeologists were Sylvanus Morley and J. Eric Thompson. Many of their suppositions are known to be incorrect today. For example, they maintained that the Maya were a peaceful people, that inscriptions never dealt with historical events, and that Maya city centers were used only for ceremony and never for residence. Undoubtedly, some of today's "truths" will be found to be fallacies as well. Today, there are a number of ar-

chaeologists operating in Belize, and new discoveries are constantly emerging. In addition to the looters and the rainy season, a lack of funding hinders archaeologists. Accordingly, many sites in Belize remain unexplored, and excavations are going forward at a slow pace.

LAYOUT: Most Maya settlements contain a main plaza surrounded by several lesser plazas, each surrounded by temples atop mounds or pyramids and neighboring lesser structures such as sweat baths, ball courts, and palaces. It is believed that the temples were inhabited by priests and nobles, while the plebes lived in surrounding huts. No doubt Maya priests spent many an evening atop a pyramid, conceived as a "link between the earth and the sky," charting the course of the sun, moon, and stars. Typically found in the vicinity of the temple and facing an altar, the stela is a sculptured stone monument, usually an upright monolith. Bearing glyphs and emblem-glyphs, it generally records the lives of a ruler. Stelae were erected at the end of every *katun*, a 20-year interval. At times Mayas demolished their monuments, building new structures on top of the old. According to Maya beliefs, every building has its life span. Once calculated to have reached its end, the building had to be partially destroyed and then rebuilt, a practice that has given many an archaeologist attempting to date a site any number of grey hairs. Offerings (obsidian chips; flint pieces shaped like tridents, half moons, and discs; sea shells; jade fragments; and pearls) were set out under the base of stelae, in temple foundations, and inside buildings under construction. Human remains have been found in the foundations of demolished buildings ready for reconstruction, leading to the supposition that the structures were destroyed upon their deaths. The *sacbe* ("white way") – remnants of long roads found at the sites – must have been used for ceremonial processions. Constructed on the base of large, roughly-shaped stones and topped with gravel or limestone chips, the roadways were pressed by large and heavy stone rollers. Another notable feature of the sites is that there are no defense systems – one of the reasons the Maya were initially supposed to have been a peaceful people.

CONSTRUCTION TECHNIQUES: Amazingly, these cities were constructed without the use of the wheel! Carried on the backs of humans, rubble was dumped and faced with limestone blocks joined together using lime mortar. The landscape was sculptured to suit the builders' needs: hilltops were leveled and, in areas lacking a steady water supply, plazas were cleverly sloped to secure runoff to their reservoirs. The most important structural element is the corbel arch. Also known as the false arch, the corbel is made by building up layers of stone on each side of the room: each layer protrudes further inward until they can be joined at the top with a single stone. Since these arches can support only a short wall, rooms are claustrophobic. The structure contained two or three narrow, dark chambers – each 60 square feet in area. As their function was to support the temple, Maya pyramids were always flat-topped. The temple was decorated with a "roof comb," a masonry backdrop for front-facing mosaic or stucco decorative elements. Most of these gables rise above the midline of a building, but others are supported by the front wall, lending a "flying facade" effect to the building. The best of these are found at Tikal.

Spanish Vocabulary

Days of the Week

domingo	Sunday
lunes	Monday
martes	Tuesday
miercoles	Wednesday
jueves	Thursday
viernes	Friday
sabado	Saturday

Months of the Year

enero	January
febrero	February
marzo	March
abril	April
mayo	May
junio	June
julio	July
agosto	August
septiembre	September
octubre	October
noviembre	November
diciembre	December

Numbers

uno	one
dos	two
tres	three
cuatro	four
cinco	five
seis	six
siete	seven
ocho	eight
nueve	nine
diez	ten
once	eleven
doce	twelve

trece	thirteen
catorce	fourteen
quince	fifteen
dieciséis	sixteen
diecisiete	seventeen
dieciocho	eighteen
diecinueve	nineteen
veinte	twenty
veintiuno	twenty-one
veintidos	twenty-two
treinta	thirty
cuarenta	forty
cincuenta	fifty
sesenta	sixty
setenta	seventy
ochenta	eighty
noventa	ninety
cien	one hundred
ciento uno	one hundred one
doscientos	two hundred
quinientos	five hundred
mil	one thousand
mil uno	one thousand one
dos mil	two thousand
un millón	one million
mil millones	one billion
primero	first
segundo	second
tercero	third
cuarto	fourth
quinto	fifth
sexto	sixth
séptimo	seventh
octavo	eighth
noveno	ninth
décimo	tenth
undécimo	eleventh
duodécimo	twelfth
último	last

Conversation

Spanish	English
¿Como esta usted?	How are you?
Bien, gracias, y usted?	Well, thanks, and you?
Buenas dias.	Good morning.
Buenas tardes.	Good afternoon.
Buenas noches.	Good evening/night.
Hasta la vista.	See you again.
Hasta luego.	So long.
¡Buena suerte!	Good luck!
Adios.	Goodbye.
Mucho gusto de conocerle.	Glad to meet you.
Felicidades.	Congratulations.
Muchas felicidades.	Happy birthday.
Feliz Navidad.	Merry Christmas.
Feliz Año Nuevo.	Happy New Year.
Gracias.	Thank you.
Por favor.	Please.
De nada/con mucho gusto.	You're welcome.
Perdoneme.	Pardon me.
¿Como se llama esto?	What do you call this?
Lo siento.	I'm sorry.
Permitame.	Permit me.
Quisiera...	I would like...
Adelante.	Come in.
Permitame presentarle...	May I introduce...
¿Como se llamo usted?	What is your name?
Me llamo...	My name is...
No se.	I don't know.
Tengo sed.	I am thirsty.
Tengo hambre.	I am hungry.
Soy norteamericano/a	I am an American.
¿Donde puedo encontrar...?	Where can I find...?
¿Que es esto?	What is this?
¿Habla usted ingles?	Do you speak English?
Hablo/entiendo un poco Español	I speak/understand a little Spanish
¿Hay alguien aqui que hable ingles?	Is there anyone here who speaks English?
Le entiendo.	I understand you.
No entiendo.	I don't understand.

Hable mas despacio por favor.	Please speak more slowly.
Repita por favor.	Please repeat.

Telling Time

¿Que hora es?	What time is it?
Son las...	It's...
... cinco.	... five o'clock.
... ocho y diez.	... ten past eight.
... seis y cuarto.	... quarter past six.
... cinco y media.	... half past five.
... siete y menos cinco.	... five of seven.
antes de ayer.	the day before yesterday.
anoche.	yesterday evening.
esta mañana.	this morning.
a mediodia.	at noon.
en la noche.	in the evening.
de noche.	at night.
a medianoche.	at midnight.
mañana en la mañana.	tomorrow morning.
mañana en la noche.	tomorrow evening.
pasado mañana.	the day after tomorrow.

Directions

¿En que direccion queda...?	In which direction is...?
Lleveme a... por favor.	Take me to... please.
Llevame alla ... por favor.	Take me there please.
¿Que lugar es este?	What place is this?
¿Donde queda el pueblo?	Where is the town?
¿Cual es el mejor camino para...?	Which is the best road to...?
De vuelta a la derecha.	Turn to the right.
De vuelta a la isquierda.	Turn to the left.
Siga derecho.	Go this way.
En esta direccion.	In this direction.
¿A que distancia estamos de...?	How far is it to...?
¿Es este el camino a...?	Is this the road to...?
¿Es...	Is it...
... cerca?	... near?
... lejos?	... far?
... norte?	... north?
... sur?	... south?

... este?	... east?
... oeste?	... west?
Indiqueme por favor.	Please point.
Hagame favor de decirme donde esta...	Please direct me to...
... el telephono.	... the telephone.
... el excusado.	... the bathroom.
... el correo.	... the post office.
... el banco.	... the bank.
... la comisaria.	... the police station.

Accommodations

Estoy buscando un hotel.... that's...	I am looking for a hotel
... bueno.	... good.
... barato.	... cheap.
... cercano.	... nearby.
... limpio.	... clean.
¿Dónde hay hotel, pensión, hospedaje?	Where is a hotel, pensión, hospedaje?
Hay habitaciones libres? rooms?	Do you have available
¿Dónde están los baños/servicios?	Where are the bathrooms?
Quisiera un...	I would like a...
... cuarto sencillo.	... single room.
... cuarto con baño.	... room with a bath.
... cuarto doble.	... double room.
Puedo verlo?	May I see it?
Cuanto cuesta?	What's the cost?
Es demasiado caro!	It's too expensive!

Belize Glossary

atolls – Circular or horseshoe-shaped coral reefs with slender, sandy islets formed by wind, storms, and surf.

backra – A "raw back," indicating a white person.

baktuns – Maya unit of measurement comprising 144,000 days or 20 katuns.

bank – Place name indicating the former presence of a log-loading ramp.

boom – Place name indicating where a chain was draped across a river in order to catch falling logs.

bram – Drumming and dancing celebration.

broken ridge – A variety of trees including cohune palms.

bruckdown – Belizean calypso which combines music and words to tell a tale or make fun of a noted personage.

bush – Marijuana.

camioneta – Guatemalan word for bus, generally meaning a light van or truck elsewhere.

cayes – The offshore islands.

chicle – The sap of the sapodilla which was once used as the base for chewing gum.

chiclero – A gatherer of chicle.

chugú – Garinagu ceremony of feeding the dead which is rarely requested by a spirit less than 10 or more than 50 years after death.

cohune ridge – Mixed terrain comprised largely of cohune palms.

dugu – Garinagu feasting of the dead, a complicated and major ceremony. Also the name ascribed to the Garinagu religion in general.

glyph – Name often given to a Maya hieroglyph.

huipil – Maya woman's blouse, generally embroidered.

jumpup – Local dance.

katun – Maya unit of measurement denoting 7,200 days or 20 *tuns*.

kin – Unit of measurement for the Maya day.

landing – High place above flood waters where loggers could land to do their work.

line – Road.

lintel – Beam used to span an opening.

logwood – The first major export of the area, logwood was used to make dyes. The tree lost its attraction with the development of synthetic dyes extracted from coal tar.

Mesoamerica – Area from the Valley of Mexico to Honduras in which civilizations flourished.

milpa – A Maya agricultural plot, it is first burned over, then maize is planted by poking holes through the ashes with a stick. After a few seasons, the plot is abandoned.

palace – Maya temple structure which is more loosely constructed than a pyramid

pen – Place name indicating a cattle farm or enclosure.

pyramid – Pyramid-shaped Maya temple consisting of a large platform of stones faced with finished limestone blocks and capped by a temple.

range – The marshy islands that are mainly semi-submerged mangrove swamps.

roof comb – A Maya temple roof structure resembling the comb of a cock.

spur and groove – Reef topography in which coral ridges divide deep trenches which have sandy floors. Tunnels and overhangs are common, allowing a wide diversity of inhabitants in a small area.

stela – Sculptured stone monument, usually an upright monolith found at Maya temples. Bearing glyphs and emblem-glyphs, these generally record the lives of their rulers.

tea – A meal.

unial – Maya unit of measure denoting 20 days.

walk – Place name indicating a farm.

Booklist

Travel and Description

Association for Belize Archaeology. *Warlords and Maize Men: A Guide to the Maya Sites of Belize*. Belize: Cubola Productions, 1992, Second Edition.

Barrett, Kirk. *Belize by Kayak: A Guide for Sea Kayaking in Belize*. Des Moines, IA: Reef-Link, 1994. This is an outstanding guide for kayakers and well worth the investment. To order call 515-279-6699 (ask for Sonna Newton with Reef-Link) or write 3806 Cottage Grove, Des Moines, IA 50311.

Cubola. *Atlas of Belize*. Benque Viejo, Belize: Cubola Productions, 1991, 16th Revised Edition.

Godfrey, Glenn D. *Ambergris Caye: Paradise with a Past*. Benque Viejo, Belize: Cubola Productions, 1989.

Hunter, Bruce. *A Guide to Ancient Mayan Ruins*. University of Oklahoma Press, Includes descriptions of sites in Belize.

Stephens, John L. *Incidents of Travel in Central America. Chiapas, and Yucatán, Vols. 1 & 2* . NY: Dover Pub., Inc., 1969.

Straughan, Robert P. *Adventure in Belize*. New Jersey: A.S. Barnes, 1975. Written with a childlike simplicity, this book covers an extensive amount of territory.

Vermeer, Donald E. *The Cays of British Honduras*. Berkeley, CA: Department of Geography, University of California, 1959. The first comprehensive description of the area's small islands and reefs.

Flora and Fauna

Ames, Oakes and Donovan Stewart Correll. *Orchids of Guatemala and Belize*. New York: Dover Publications, Inc., 1985. This 779-page, highly technical tome, repackaged from the original, is for the orchid fanatic. A small section on orchids found only in Belize is included.

Anderson, Sydney. *Simon & Schuster's Guide to Mammals*. NY: Fireside, 1983.

Chaplin, C. C. G. *Fishwatcher's Guide to West Atlantic Coral Reefs*. Valley Forge, PA: Harrowood Books.

Emmons, Louse H. *Neotropical Rainforest Mammals*. Chicago, University of Chicago Press, 1990. This exceptional color-plate-illustrated field guide is the finest of its kind. A must for zoologists and serious laymen alike, it contains maps showing the range of species, detailed descriptions and natural histories of the animals concerned, and references to scientific literature.

Forsyth, Adrian. *Journey through a Tropical Jungle*. Toronto: Greey de Pencier Books, 1988.

Forsyth, Adrian and Kenneth Miyata. *Tropical Nature*. New York: Scribner's, 1987. This is a fascinating and fine introduction to the tropical rainforest and its complex ecosytems.

Forsyth, Adrian. *Portraits of the Rainforest*. NJ: Camden House, 1990.

Head, Suzanne and Robert Heinzman, eds. *Lessons of the Rainforest*. San Francisco: Sierra Club Books, 1990. This collection of essays covers everything from activism (by Randy Hayes, founder of Rainforest Action Network) to the canopy (by Donald R. Perry) to extinction (by Anne H. and Paul Ehrlich).

Jacobs, Marius. *The Tropical Rain Forest: A First Encounter*. New York: Berlin Heidelberg, 1988. Calculated to appeal both to laymen and scientists, this comprehensive and technical book was originally written in Dutch. It includes a chapter on Tropical America written by R. A. A. Oldeman.

Janzen, Daniel H., ed. *Costa Rica National History*. Chicago: University of Chicago Press, 1983. Although this superb volume is an excellent introduction to Costa Rican species, many are also found in Belize.

Kricher, John C. *A Neotropical Companion: An Introduction to the Animals, Plants, and Ecosystems of New World Tropics*. Principally researched in Central America. Princeton, NJ: Princeton U. Press.

Moser, Don. *Central American Jungles*. Amsterdam: Time-Life Books, 1975. Includes information about Belize, howler and spider monkeys, etc.

Peterson, Roger Tory and Edward L. Chalif. *Field Guide to the Birds of Mexico*. NY: Houghton-Mifflin, 1973.

Rabinowitz, Alan. *Jaguar*. NY: Morrow, 1986. Authored by one of the moving forces behind the establishment of the Jaguar Reserve.

Richards, P. W. *The Tropical Rain Forest: An Ecological Study*. Cambridge, England: University Press, 1981. First published in 1952, this is an in-depth technical account which is geared more towards biologists than laymen.

Ridgely, Robert S. *A Guide to the Birds of Panama*. NJ: Princeton University Press, 1989.

Rutzler, Klaus and Ian G. Macintyre. *The Atlantic Barrier Reef Ecosystem at Carrie Bow Bay, Belize*. Smithsonian Contributions to the Marine Sciences, No. 12. Washington, DC: Smithsonian Institution Press.

Sanderson, Ivan T. *Living Treasure*. New York: Viking Press, 1941. A handsomely illustrated account of the adventures of a naturalist couple.

Sheppard, Charles R. C. *A Natural History of the Coral Reef*. Poole, Dorset: Blandford Press, 1983. If your curiosity about the reefs has been piqued by your visit, this is a fine book to read.

Smithe, Frank B. *The Birds of Tikal*. Garden City, NY: Natural History Press, 1966. May be available in Guatemala.

Stanley, Paul C. and Samuel J. Record. *The Forests and Fauna of British Honduras*. Chicago: Field Museum of Natural History, 1936. A dry but thorough account.

Stephens, Katie. *Jungle Walk*. A self-published guide to the nation's wildlife. While far from comprehensive, it is well researched and well written.

Terborgh, John. *Diversity and the Tropical Rainforest*. NY: Scientific American Library, 1992

Tomlinson, PB. *The Botany of Mangroves*. NY: Cambridge University Press, 1985.

Wilson, Edward O. *The Diversity of Life*. Cambridge, MA: Belknap Press, 1992. A superb account of the history of extinction, the world's biodiversity and the imminent dangers to its species.

History

Dobson, Narda. *A History of Belize*. London: Longman, 1973.

Foster, Byron. *The Baymen's Legacy: A History of Belize City*. Benque Viejo, Belize: Cubola Productions, 1987.

Guderjan, Thomas H. *Ancient Maya Traders of Ambergris Caye*. Benque Viejo, Belize: Cubola Productions, 1993.

Hovey, Graham and Gene Brown, eds. *Central America and the Caribbean*. New York: Arno Press, 1980. This volume of clippings from *The New York Times*, one of a series in its Great Contemporary Issues books, graphically displays American activities and attitudes toward the area. A goldmine of information.

Koop, Gerhard S. *Pioneer Years in Belize*. Spanish Lookout: G. S. Koop, 1991. Tells the tales of the Spanish Lookout Mennonite Community.

Mannix, Daniel P. and Malcolm Cooley. *Black Cargoes*. New York: Viking Press, 1982. Details the saga of the slave trade.

Thompson, J. Eric. *The Maya of Belize: Historical Chapters since Columbus*. Benque Viejo, Belize: Cubola Productions, 1988.

Politics and Economics

Barry, Tom. *Belize: A Country Guide*. Albuquerque, New Mexico: The Inter-Hemispheric Resource Center, 1989. One in a series, this superb book surveys the political and economic situation, taking in the military, environmental and social issues, and foreign influences.

Barry, Tom. *Inside Belize*. Albuquerque, New Mexico: The Inter-Hemispheric Resource Center, 1989. This extremely well written book details topics ranging from foreign policy to conservation and the environment. Also included are chapters on human rights, the Belize Defense Force, feminism and women's status, agriculture, and foreign influences. A must for anyone wanting an in-depth knowledge of Belize.

Booklist

Barry, Tom. *The Central America Fact Book*. New York: Grove Press, 1986. A guide to the economic and political situation in each of the region's nations together with a list of transnationals active in the region.

Bolland, O. Nigel. *Belize: A New Nation in Central America*. Boulder: Westview Press, 1986. A succinct and superb political, economic, and cultural overview.

Bolland, O. Nigel. *Colonialism and Resistance in Belize*. Benque Viejo, Belize: Cubola Productions, 1988. A collection of essays written over a 16-year period.

Bolland, O. Nigel. *The Formation of a Colonial Society: Belize, from Conquest to Crown Colony*. Baltimore: Johns Hopkins University Press, 1977. Details the social and economic conditions prevailing in the 18th and 19th C.

Carmack, Robert M., ed. *Harvest of Violence: The Maya Indians and the Guatemalan Crisis*. Norman, OK: U of OK Press, 1988. A superb and very frightening account of repression in Guatemala. Must reading for anyone visiting neighboring Guatemala who wishes to learn about the true situation.

Foster, Byron. *The Baymen's Legacy: A History of Belize City*. Benque Viejo, Belize: Cubola Productions, 1992.

Grant, C. H. *The Making of Modern Belize: Politics, Society, and British Colonialism in Central America*. Cambridge, Cambridge University Press, 1976. Focuses on the years 1950-1974.

Lewis, Gordon K. *The Growth of the Modern West Indies*. London: MacGibbon & Kee, 1968. Includes a chapter on Belize.

Shoman, Assad. *Party Politics in Belize*. Benque Viejo, Belize: Cubola Productions, 1989, Second Edition.

Thompson, Eric S. *The Maya of Belize – Historical Chapters Since Columbus*. Benque Viejo, Belize: Cubola Productions.

Sociology and Anthropology

Ashcraft, Norman. *Colonialism and Underdevelopment: Processes of Political and Economic Change in British Honduras*. New York: Teachers College Press, 1973. An anthropological study of small farming and urban markets researched between 1965-67.

Foster, Byron Heart Drum: *Spirit Possession in the Garifuna Community of Belize*. Benque Viejo, Belize: Cubola Productions, 1986.

Ivanoff, Pierre. *Monuments of Civilization, Maya*. London: Cassell, 1975. Although no information on Belizean sites is included in this book, there is an excellent section on Tikal.

Kerns, Virginia. *Women and the Ancestors: Black Carib Kinship and Ritual*. Urbana: University of Illinois Press, 1983. Studies the ancestral rituals and kinship among the Garifuna. A fascinating account.

Sutherland, Anne. *Caye Caulker: Economic Success in a Belizean Fishing Village*. Boulder, CO: Westview Press, 1986. An absorbing account of the island's socio-economic life.

Taylor, Douglas M. *The Black Carib of British Honduras*. New York: Wenner-Gren Foundation, 1951.

Art, Architecture, and Archaeology

Maya: Treasures of an Ancient Civilization. NY: Abrams, 1985.

Association for Belizean Archaeology. *Warlords and Maize Men: A Guide to the Maya Sites of Belize*. Benque Viejo, Belize: Cubola Productions, 1989.

Bryant, Alice and Phyllis Galde. *The Message of the Crystal Skull: From Atlantis to the New Age*. Marin County, CA: St. Paul Lwellyn. If you've heard about the crystal skull at Lubaantun and wondered about it, this book is a fountain of New Age-style misinformation – right down to the misplacement of the site on the map of Belize!

Buhler, Richard, ed. *Recent Archaeology in Belize*. Belize City: BISRA, 1976.

Coe, William R. *Tikal, A Handbook of the Ancient Maya Ruins*. Philadelphia: University of PA Museum, 1988.

Ferguson, William M. and John Q. Royce. *Maya Ruins in Central America in Color*. Albuquerque: University of New Mexico Press, 1984. Covering Tikal, Copán, and Quiriguá, this is a beautiful and informative book.

Hammond, Norman. *Lubaantun: A Classic Mayan Realm*. Cambridge, MA: Peabody Museum, 1975. A highly technical and extremely detailed account.

Morley, Sylvanus and George W. Brainerd. *The Ancient Maya*. Stanford, CA: Stanford U Press, 1983. Fourth Edition. Undoubtedly, the most thorough account, revised posthumously to keep it up to date.

Schele, Linda and Mary Anne Miller. *The Blood of Kings*. NY: Braziller, 1986.

Schele, Linda and David Freidel. *A Forest of Kings*. NY: William Morrow, 1990.

Sidrys, Raymond V. *Archaeological Excavations in Northern Belize, Central America*. Los Angeles: University of CA, Institute of Archaeology, 1983.

Thompson, J. Eric S. *Maya History and Religion*. Norman: University of OK Press, 1970.

Thompson, J. Eric S. *The Rise and Fall of Mayan Civilization*. Norman: University of OK Press, 1954.

Booklist

Language and Literature

Edgell, Zee. *Beka Lamb*. London: Heinemann, 1982. This pioneering novel describes Belizean life – including the relationship between church and school – during the 1950s.

Edgell, Zee. *In Times Like These*. London: Heinemann, 1992. Edgell's latest.

Ellis, Zoila. *On Heroes, Lizards and Passion*. Benque Viejo, Belize: Cubola Productions, 1990, Second Edition. Seven short stories about Belizean life.

Godfrey, Glenn D. *The Sinner's Bossanova*. Spanning post-WWII Belize City life into the 1970s. Benque Viejo, Belize: Cubola Productions, 1987.

Hernandez, Felicia. *Those Ridiculous Years*. Belize: Cubola Productions. An account of childhood in Dangriga during the 1960s.

Musa, Yasser, Kiren Shoman, Simone Waight. *Shots from the Heart: Three Young Belizean Poets*. Benque Viejo, Belize: Cubola Productions, 1991.

Ramirez, Luke. *The Poems I Write*. Belize City: Belize Advert Productions, 1990. An impressive first volume from the nation's preeminent Garifuna poet.

Ruiz Puga, David. *Old Benque: Erasa una vez en Benque Viejo*. Benque Viejo, Belize: Cubola Productions, 1990. A collection of four short stories written in Spanish which deal with fictionalized accounts of supernatural events.

Warde, Shirley A., ed. *"We jus catch um."* Goshen: Pinchpenny Press, 1974. Transcriptions of eight folk tales.

Young, Colville. *Pataki Full*. Benque Viejo, Belize: Cubola Productions, 1991. Short stories commenting on Belizean morality.

Index